GARRICK

by the same author

———

TUNBRIDGE WELLS

with Sir Osbert Sitwell
BRIGHTON

Garrick

BY MARGARET BARTON

The Macmillan Company · 1949

NEW YORK

PREFACE

THIS book does not attempt to give all the facts known, and apocryphal stories told, about David Garrick. As an actor, he played over ninety rôles; as an author, he wrote eighty prologues and epilogues and thirty-five plays, including interludes and adaptations, as well as innumerable verses and songs; as a letter writer, he was tireless; as a theatrical manager, he watched over the fortunes of Drury Lane for twenty-nine seasons; as a member of London society, he knew, or had met, almost everyone of any interest or importance in every class of life, while the friendships he made in Paris during two visits have provided the subject of a long and interesting book. To describe in detail every aspect of his life would take several volumes and would be intolerable to the general reader, for whom this comparatively brief survey is intended. The student must continue to rely on *David Garrick* by Joseph Knight, *David Garrick and his French Friends* by F. A. Hedgcock, *Garrick and his Circle* by Mrs. C. Parsons, and the works listed in my bibliography.

My thanks are due to Mr. C. K. Adams of the National Portrait Gallery and Mr. Croft Murray of the British Museum for their advice in the choosing of illustrations; to Mrs. Enthoven and her assistants of the Victoria and Albert Museum, whose friendly interest and attentiveness enabled me to make the best use of her collection; and to the Keeper of the Records at Stratford-upon-Avon for giving me access to the manuscripts in his care. Finally, I should like to express my gratitude to Miss K. M. Wright, who helped me in many ways, but more especially with the Index.

39315

A CHRONOLOGICAL GUIDE

1717   *Born in the Angel Inn, at Hereford, February 19th*
      [Old Style 1716]
1736   *Attends Johnson's Private Academy outside Lichfield*
1737   *Comes to London with Johnson*
1738   *Sets up as Vintner with Peter Garrick*
1741   *Appears as Richard III at Goodman's Fields Theatre*
1742   *Acts in Dublin during the Summer Season*
      Dissolves Partnership with Peter Garrick
      Acts at Drury Lane under Fleetwood's Management
      In Love with Peg Woffington
1743   *Incites Actors to Strike*
1745   *Breaks with Peg Woffington*
      Acts in Dublin throughout Winter Season
1746   *Acts at Covent Garden under Rich's Management*
1747   *Becomes Co-manager with Lacy of Drury Lane Theatre*
1749   *Marries Eva Maria Veigel*
1751   *First Visit to Paris*
1754   *Buys Hampton House*
1755   *The Chinese Festival Riots*
1763–5   *Travels in France and Italy*
1769   *The Shakespeare Jubilee*
1772   *Moves from Southampton Street to Adelphi Terrace*
1776   *Retires from Stage*
1779   *Dies in London on January 20th*

CONTENTS

PREFACE   *page*   v

A CHRONOLOGICAL GUIDE   vi

I.   LICHFIELD   1

II. DURHAM YARD   14

III. GOODMAN'S FIELDS   31

IV. PEG WOFFINGTON   48

V.   THE SALARIED ACTOR   71

VI. THE MANAGER   80

VII. MARRIAGE   93

VIII. PANTOMIME   107

IX. PROSPERITY   119

X.   BALLET   128

XI. AWAY FROM THE THEATRE   144

XII. QUARRELS   152

XIII. TRAVELS IN FRANCE AND ITALY   169

XIV. BACK TO THE STAGE   181

XV. A COLDNESS WITH JOHNSON   189

XVI. THE SHAKESPEARE JUBILEE   202

XVII. THE OLD AND THE NEW   215

XVIII. FAREWELL PERFORMANCES   235

XIX. IN RETIREMENT   254

XX. POETS' CORNER   275

APPENDICES   286

BIBLIOGRAPHY   297

INDEX   301

ILLUSTRATIONS

1. DAVID GARRICK IN 1764   *facing page*   24
   By kind permission of the Ashmolean Museum

2. COVENT GARDEN PIAZZA IN 1768   41

3. PEG WOFFINGTON   56

4. DAVID GARRICK AS RICHARD III   73

5. MRS. CIBBER *By kind permission of the Garrick Club*   88

6. GARRICK AND MRS. PRITCHARD AS MACBETH AND LADY MACBETH *By kind permission of the Garrick Club*   105

7. GARRICK AS KING LEAR   136

8. GARRICK AND MRS. GARRICK ENTERTAINING FRIENDS AT HAMPTON *By kind permission of the Earl of Durham*   153

9. HAMPTON HOUSE   168

10. GARRICK RECITING THE ODE AT THE SHAKESPEARE JUBILEE   185

11. GARRICK AND MRS. GARRICK IN 1773   200
    By kind permission of Major A. W. Foster

12. GARRICK AS DON JOHN IN *The Chances*   217

13. ADELPHI TERRACE   232

14. FROM THE GARRICKS' CHINESE BEDROOM IN HAMPTON HOUSE   249

15. DRURY LANE IN 1775   264

16. DRURY LANE IN 1776   281

PLAYBILL   *page* 227

A LETTER FROM GARRICK TO HIS BROTHER PETER, ANNOUNCING HIS DECISION TO GO ON THE STAGE   287

CHAPTER I

LICHFIELD

1717 — 1737

ONE afternoon in 1727 a small figure in a military coat, drumming what he hoped would be recognized as the Grenadier's March, strutted up and down an improvised stage. Presently, with the ease of a veteran, he opened the play by addressing the mob—a handful of round-faced children—punctuating his speeches with gestures and grimaces copied from the strolling players he had seen that summer. In self-assurance the young amateur had nothing to learn, and the zest with which he entered into the play's robust humour was long remembered by the listening grown-ups.

They were sitting in Gilbert Walmesley's house in the Close of Lichfield Cathedral, and the ten-year-old boy was one of the swarm of children Captain and Mrs. Garrick were struggling to bring up in gentility on their meagre income. This was Davy's great day, the day he had been longing for ever since Mr. Walmesley had promised him that he could give an entertainment in the drawing-room of the Bishop's Palace. He had long set his heart on getting up a performance of Farquhar's *Recruiting Officer,* a play that had already enjoyed over twenty years' popularity, and one that he felt particularly well qualified to produce. As an officer's son living in a garrison town, he felt sure that he knew all about life in the army, and especially about recruiting, for his father, as a lieutenant of dragoons, had himself enrolled many men. It was, indeed, during one of his father's recruiting campaigns in the west counties, when Mrs. Garrick had left her two elder children at home with their grandmother at Lichfield and had followed her husband to Hereford, that Davy was born and subsequently christened.

1

The first problem was the cast, and this he chose almost entirely from his friends at the Grammar School, for he could count on little help from his own family. Peter, seven years older than himself, was at sea, his eldest sister, Lenny, could manage nothing more ambitious than a chambermaid's part, while Jenny, William, George, and Merriall were too small to be of any use at all. For a prologue he had hopefully aproached Samuel Johnson, the bookseller's son. Davy had often seen this clever, ugly young man at Mr. Walmesley's house, arguing with his host in broad Staffordshire accents. It was two years since Johnson had left the Grammar School, and now he was living at home learning his father's trade and reading voraciously. Surely he could find time, sitting in old Michael Johnson's shop in the market-place and waiting for customers, to think out a prologue for the play? But immersed in day-dreams, half-crazed by the nervous depressions of adolescence, he failed his young friend, and Davy had to content himself with the prologue already in print.

The Bishop's Palace was a misleading name for a comfortable grey stone mansion. By no stretch of imagination could it be described as a palace, and, although it had been built for the bishop of the diocese forty years before, it had never been lived in by anyone of higher rank than the Registrar of the Ecclesiastical Court, the office now held by Mr. Walmesley. Its gates opened on to a walk, bordered on the north side by lime trees, which encircled the beautiful fourteenth-century cathedral. Gilbert Walmesley, a man whose quick temper hid a kind and generous nature, kept open house, and all that was most agreeable in the social life of Lichfield took place within the walls of the Bishop's Palace.

The Garricks lived in a more humble style just outside the Close, in a house that had once belonged to Mrs. Garrick's father, a lay-singer in the cathedral choir. It had been their home ever since their marriage. When he met and fell in love with Arabella Clough, Peter Garrick had nothing but his ensign's pay, and, as the son of an impoverished French refugee, had little hope of seeing better days. For Peter Garrick had been born at Bordeaux of Huguenot parents, who on the revocation of the Edict of Nantes escaped to England, leaving their infant son in the care of his nurse. Eighteen months later she arrived safely in London with the baby in her arms, and the family was reunited. By the time Peter had grown up his parents had anglicized their name,[1] and considered themselves sufficiently English to buy a commission for their elder son in an army that would probably be sent to fight their former compatriots. Thus the young officer, with an ever-increasing family and no private means, found it difficult to make two ends meet, and was obliged to go on half-pay rather than incur heavy travelling and living expenses. Nevertheless, they managed to enjoy themselves surprisingly. Mrs. Garrick, with an easy warmth of manner inherited from her Irish mother, and Peter Garrick, small and dark, typically French both in appearance and in his vivacious way of talking, made an attractive pair and found a welcome wherever they went. No one in Lichfield was rich, or lived other than simply, and their lack of means mattered little in a community remote from the conventions of London society.

Not long after the performance of the play a letter came from Lisbon, where Captain Garrick's younger brother, David, had established himself in the wine trade. Knowing how pinched they were for money, David Garrick suggested that his nephew and namesake should join him in Lisbon and be trained by him in the routine of his business. A father of four sons could not afford to refuse a promising opening. His brother would, of course, make the boy his heir, and one son at least would be well provided for. So away Davy sailed to Lisbon with all his small possessions. The experiment began well. To the colony of English merchants, the arrival of this droll little boy was a godsend. They could not make enough of him. He would stand on the dinner table, reciting scenes from his favourite plays, and keep them amused for hours. But in the counting-house his gifts were less apparent, and his gaiety jarred on his uncle. He could not see the importance of adding up figures correctly. It was hopeless. Within a few months he was back at school in Lichfield.

Davy learnt very little at the Grammar School—in itself a remarkable feat, for the Reverend John Hunter flogged an astonishing number of boys to distinction. The names of his pupils make an imposing list, and include no less than seven Judges of the High Court, as well as several eminent divines. Yet not one of his pupils, having experienced his brutality, cared in later life to send his own son to the same school. Stiff and pompous in his cassock and full-

1 Probably "Garrigues".

3

bottomed wig, Dr. Hunter glowered down on the boys and waited for the first slip. Then out came his birch. 'This I do to save you from the gallows,' he would gasp as he flogged a boy for not knowing the Latin for 'candlestick'. By such means he roused Samuel Johnson from his lethargy and stimulated him into making the best use of his brains. But Davy, coming a few years later, discovered a chink in his master's armour, and took full advantage of his weakness to escape punishment. Hunter had a passion for shooting, and whenever Davy saw trouble brewing he would change the subject by telling him the whereabouts of a covey of partridges. This crusty old schoolmaster's love of sport can be explained by the curious circumstances of his upbringing. He was a foundling, and had been discovered newly born in a field by some fox-hunters. One of the sportsmen, a Warwickshire squire, adopted him, gave him the name of Hunter, and while allowing him to follow his natural bent as a scholar infected him with his own enthusiasm for blood sports.

As the little Garricks grew up the household bills expanded with them, and their harassed parents found themselves more and more hopelessly behindhand in settling their debts. With six active young people to clothe and to feed, a Captain's half-pay soon disappeared; yet would he be any better off on full pay with all the expenses of regimental life to defray? It was difficult for him to decide. But in 1731 his old regiment embarked for Gibraltar, where the garrison was to be strengthened and where living was cheap and agreeable. The matter took on a different aspect, and the Captain began to long for a more active existence. A month or so later one of his brother officers wrote to him and suggested an exchange. The Captain jumped at the offer, and by July he was back on full pay. Mrs. Garrick never questioned the wisdom of her husband's decision, but she grieved most bitterly over their first separation. She travelled with him to London, and the distress of saying goodbye affected her so keenly that her kind friends, the Bronkers, would not hear of her returning to Lichfield until she felt a little calmer. The first sight of her family, six weeks later, gave her a shock that jolted her out of her apathy. Could these ragged urchins really be her own children? She was horrified to see how neglected they looked. 'In our accoutrements,' wrote Davy to his father, 'we was rather like so many beggars than Gentlemen soldiers. With much ado at last she equipt us out a little better and now with a great deal of mending and patching we are in Statu quo.'

The sixteen-year-old Davy had now to take his father's place, and it was his duty to report regularly on their doings. Captain Garrick's family missed him terribly, and no sooner had he arrived at Gibraltar than they began to pester their influential friends to procure leave for him.

'It is not to be exprest,' wrote Davy, 'the Joy that the family was in at the Receipt of Dear Pappa's Letter which we Receiv'd the 7th of this Month. My poor Mamma was in very good spirits two or three Days after she receiv'd your Letter but now begins to grow moloncholly [sic] again, and has little ugly fainting fits. She is in great hopes of the Transports going for you every Day, for we Please ourselves with the hopes of your spending this Summer with the Family. My Mamma rec'd the thirty Pounds you was so good to send her, she has Paid ten Pounds to Mr. Rider for one Year's Rent and ten Pounds to the Baker, and if you can spare a little more as you tell her you will, she is in hope of paying all the Debts that you may have nothing to fret you when you come Home.'

But five years were to pass before their affectionate schemings bore any fruit, and for Mrs. Garrick, who fretted herself into a state of chronic ill-health, the time dragged interminably. After twenty-five years of married life, she longed for him as passionately as though they had been parted on their honeymoon. 'I must tell my Dear Life and Soul', she wrote to him, 'that I am not able to live easy longer without him for I grow very jealous—but in the midst of all this I do not blame my dear. I have very sad dreams for you. But I have the pleasure when I am up to think were I with you how tender my Dear Soul would be to me, nay was when I was with you last. O that I had you in my arms I would tell my Dear life how much I am his.'

Davy frequently had to send worrying news to his father but, although the contents of his letters were sometimes sad, he could never remain serious for long at a time. His mother, whom he sincerely loved, was ill and low-spirited. He noticed how deeply she sighed whenever she passed his father's picture. In her illnesses she was attended either by Dr. Hector, the doctor who brought Samuel Johnson into the world, or young Dr. James, one of Johnson's schoolfellows now on the threshold of a brilliant career. Both men were family friends and, as Davy assured his father, diligent in their attentions to her. And then there was Davy's old Irish grandmother, who complained a good deal of her ailments and used to speculate gloomily on her chances of being alive when his father returned. By the time the family scribe came to Mrs. Lowndes, whoever she may have been, his pen could no longer pretend sympathy. 'She is almost constantly rowling [*sic*] about the flower [*sic*] with the cholik,' he tells his father with evident relish, 'or has her head tyed about with a napkin—for the headack [*sic*]—like one that is a victim for a sacrifice.' Now and then he suggests that they could do with more money. His sisters, Jenny and Lenny, 'are in great want for some lace for their heads, for they have nothing else but plain headcloths which hardly distinguishes them from the vulgar madams'. Or he would throw out a hint for himself. 'I am quite turn'd philosopher,' he begins disarmingly. 'You may perhaps think me vain, but to shew you I am not, I would gladly get shut of my characteristic of a philosopher—viz. a ragged pr of Breeches. Now the only way you have to cure your son of his philosophic qualifications is to send something for a waistcoat and pr of Breeches to hide his nakedness.' And he adds significantly that velvet is cheap at Gibraltar.

Never having known anything but poverty, Davy took the family embarrassments light-heartedly. He longed to disport himself in fine clothes as much as any other boy growing into manhood, but after all he missed nothing from the lack of them. The officers in the garrison did not care how shabby he looked so long as he could make them laugh with his odd talent for mimicry. They treated him as one of themselves and, knowing his passion for the stage, used to take him with them on their trips to the London playhouses. He often wished he were really one of them; the prospect of a lifetime spent in entertaining a mess attracted him far more than that held out to him by his father of spending a few dreary years at a university before settling down to the life of a barrister. If only he could get a commission without having to ask his father to pay for it! Several of his friends readily promised him one—if only this or that would happen. When Sir Thomas Aston fell seriously ill, his young soldier brother-in-law, the Hon. Henry Hervey, told Davy that if Sir Thomas were to die, his estate would fall to his sister.

Then Hervey would live as a country gentleman, presumably at his wife's expense, and Davy could have his commission. Davy was overjoyed at the offer, but Sir Thomas inconsiderately recovered. Later on, no fewer than three lieutenant-colonels, according to Davy, consoled him with promises of commissions as soon as they had acquired regiments of their own, while another swore that he had only to take orders to be sure of at least a chaplaincy.

At the Bishop's Palace, Gilbert Walmesley welcomed him almost as a son, and seldom passed a day without seeing him. When Walmesley planned to ride over to dine with the Offleys, he remembered that there were two boys of about Davy's age. So Davy came too and made friends with the young Offleys, 'fine young gentlemen', he wrote his father approvingly. Just as they were getting ready to go, Walmesley slyly put two half-crowns in Davy's hand so that he could tip the servants himself, making him look, he thought, 'very grand'. In his gratitude he suggested that if his father could possibly send Mr. Walmesley a little wine from Gibraltar, he was sure that it would be taken as a particular favour.

Mrs. Garrick noticed Walmesley's partiality for her son with growing satisfaction. A middle-aged bachelor with comfortable means—what might the attachment not lead to? A handsome legacy or a provision for life at the least. But in fact Walmesley was just as ready to befriend any young man in Lichfield who seemed to him to deserve it. Two or three times a week he invited a number of young people, including David Garrick, Samuel Johnson and the newly qualified Dr. James, to dine at the Palace, and would draw out their views on every subject with an indulgence rarely shown them by a man of his age and standing. When Samuel Johnson, dogmatic then as in later life, argued the claims of the Stuarts with an enthusiasm he had caught from Dr. Hunter, Walmesley listened calmly before refuting them. 'He never received my notions with contempt,' recalled his guest many years afterwards. 'He was a Whig with all the virulence and malevolence of his party; yet difference of opinion did not keep us apart. I honoured him and he endured me.'

The seven years' difference in age between Samuel Johnson and David Garrick made intimate friendship between them impossible but, meeting constantly in the houses of common friends, they accepted each other with the good-natured tolerance of two distantly

7

related members of one large family. To Davy, Johnson was a brilliant scholar of whom he stood slightly in awe; while Davy amused Johnson with his light-hearted rattle but bored and irritated him as soon as he started buffooning. One taste at least they shared: they read every play they could lay their hands on, and whenever the strolling players came to Lichfield, two figures, one tall and lanky, and the other small and lithe, could have been seen among the earliest arrivals manœuvring for good places. On one occasion Johnson's determination to keep his seat led to a scene that Davy remembered long after he had forgotten the performance that followed. Johnson had chosen a certain position on the stage and, having placed his chair there, left it for a few moments unguarded. On his return he found a usurper who refused Johnson's politely worded request to give up the seat. Thereupon Johnson, without another word, took up the chair and its occupant and threw them bodily into the pit. It was only by the kindly intervention of Mr. Walmesley that a general riot was averted.

Thus David Garrick and Samuel Johnson shared many memories of a time that Garrick could remember on the whole with pleasure. With his mother's ill-health and their chronic shortage of money his home was not always a cheerful one. Yet the family income, small as it was, arrived regularly, the present seemed reasonably secure, and to a boy healthy in body and mind the future could take care of itself. Johnson's circumstances were very different, and his meetings with Garrick in those early years were to be associated in his mind with the few agreeable experiences during a youth poisoned by a sense of insecurity and frustration. While Davy was coaxing Dr. Hunter into good humour, Johnson was at Oxford, a prey to the melancholia that dogged him throughout life. In his terror of insanity he consulted his godfather, Dr. Swinfen, during a vacation, putting before him a full description of his mental symptoms in his best Latin prose. Dr. Swinfen, struck less by his suffering than by his scholarship, proudly exhibited his godson's paper in Lichfield—a breach of confidence his mortified patient never forgave. But Johnson's troubles had not yet begun. His remittances from Lichfield, never anything but scanty, steadily decreased. His college bills mounted up, his shoes wore until his toes appeared through the leather and he was ashamed to show himself in public. Finally his allowance stopped altogether. His father's business had failed, and in the autumn of 1731 Johnson found himself back in Lichfield without a degree or any idea of how he could earn a living. Before the year had ended, his father was dead, and Johnson had not only his own future to consider but those of his mother and his younger brother, Nathaniel.

By the following year he had somehow straightened out the confusion of his father's affairs and, after a miserable experience as a schoolmaster in Leicestershire, went to live in the neighbouring town of Birmingham; first as the guest of a school friend, and then in lodgings of his own near-by. His young host, the nephew of Dr. Hector of Lichfield, had lately set up in practice as a surgeon and was doing well enough to help his friend through one of the most difficult periods of his life. For how Johnson managed to exist during the ensuing eighteen months unless Hector supported him is not very clear. His known earnings amounted to five guineas, the fee for translating Lobo's *Voyage to Abyssinia,* and even that would never have been accomplished without his friend's assistance. Demoralized by despair, he lay in bed with the heavy book on his lap and dictated the translation to Hector. Once finished, it was Hector who carried the manuscript to the printer and subsequently corrected almost all the proofs.

On happier days the two young men went visiting together, and among the people to whom Hector introduced his friend were a certain Mr. and Mrs. Porter. Now although Johnson did not remember it, he had seen their flaxen-haired daughter before in the house of his old schoolmaster, Dr. Hunter. Porter, oddly enough, was Dr. Hunter's brother-in-law by a second marriage, and his daughter had met Johnson in Lichfield while visiting her aunt, Mrs. Hunter, some two years before. Johnson made no sign of recognition, and Hector never doubted in after years that he had first introduced Johnson to his future stepdaughter. For it was not the good stolid Lucy who attracted the young man, but her red-faced giggling mamma, who after the death of Mr. Porter accepted him as her second husband.

Just what it was this queerly matched couple saw in each other no one can say. At twenty-five, Johnson was so thin that his shabby clothes seemed to hang on a huge animated skeleton; a skeleton, moreover, whose convulsive movements and odd gesticulations surprised people into laughing outright. At a time when wigs were almost universal among the gentry, he wore his own lank hair parted behind like any countryman, and the skin disease that for many years deprived him of the use of one eye had left a terrible scar on his forehead. But as soon as he began to talk his ugliness was forgotten. 'This', said the future Mrs. Johnson after their first meeting, 'is the most sensible man that I ever saw in my life.' And now the grotesqueness of his appearance was to be accentuated by a bride whose peculiarities seemed complementary to his own. Standing together, they might have stepped out of a caricature. Mrs. Johnson was forty-six and very fat, 'with a bosom of more than ordinary protuberance', as David Garrick afterwards recalled for Boswell's benefit, 'and swelled cheeks of a florid red, produced by thick painting and increased by a liberal use of cordials; flaring and fantastic in her dress and affected both in speech and general behaviour'. Pretty dear, thought Johnson, as he peered fondly at her with his one good eye, but no one else who had ever seen her could understand why he admired her.

'Sir,' said Johnson, 'it was a love match on both sides,' and there is not the slightest reason to doubt his word. But it is difficult to see how he could have married her without the eight hundred pounds left her by Mr. Porter. Part of this sum Johnson spent in opening a boarding school or, as he preferred to call it, a private academy. He took a large square house, enclosed by high prison-like walls, a couple of miles or so from his native town, and in due course young gentlemen were invited in the advertisement columns of *The Gentleman's Magazine* to come to Edial, near Lichfield, where they would be 'boarded and taught the Latin and Greek languages by Samuel Johnson'. Walmesley did what he could to provide him with pupils; by his advice Mrs. Garrick sent her two sons, David and George; his friend, Mr. Offley, sent one of those 'fine young gentlemen' whose servants Davy had proudly tipped, and it was hoped that many other parents would follow their example. But the response was most disappointing. A few boys attended daily, but the total number never exceeded eight.

The inducements, indeed, were difficult to see. Without a degree or reputation for scholarship, how could Johnson ever have expected pupils? His impatience and short temper were noticeable even then, and teaching was the last profession in the world he should have chosen. His oddities of manner excited disrespectful laughter, and Davy's mimicry of the awkward gallantries blushingly received by Mrs. Johnson turned them both into objects of ridicule. One by one, the boys used to listen at the keyhole of their master's bed-chamber, and Davy's reproductions of the dialogues he pretended to have overheard became one of his most popular parlour tricks.

Little as David Garrick had learnt at the Grammar School, he learnt even less at Edial. It was impossible to make a classical scholar of him: 'He has not Latin enough,' Johnson said of him in later life. 'He finds out the Latin by the meaning rather than the meaning by the Latin'—an experiment familiar to many of us who have graduated from more expensive establishments than Lichfield Grammar School and Edial Private Academy. He could not interest himself in Terence, Tully, Sallust or Nepos, or in any of the other classical writers whose names figure in Johnson's famous curriculum. When Johnson demanded a Latin exercise Davy showed him instead some scenes for a comedy, hoping that in reminding him of the engrossing problems of play-writing he would forget what it was he had asked for. This play, Davy told Johnson, represented his third attempt as a dramatist.

For Johnson, as Davy knew perfectly well, was also engaged on a play—a tragedy in blank verse based on an episode he had come across in a book lent him by Davy's elder brother, Peter. Knolles's *General Historie of the Turkes* had stirred Johnson's imagination as it was one day to stir that of Byron, and this partic-ular episode had already inspired two unsuccessful tragedies and was now to suggest a third. In fifteenth-century Constantinople, Knolles tells us, Mahomet, Emperor of the Turks, was infatuated with his Grecian slave-mistress, Irene, and the neglect of his duties seemed likely to cost him his throne. Summoning his discontented subjects to the palace, Mahomet invited them to admire Irene in all the radiance of her youth and beauty. Then, in order to demon-strate his mastery over his feelings, and without having given any-one the slightest warning of his intentions, he seized Irene by the hair and struck off her head then and there with his falchion. It is easy to see the fascination of this gruesome story, but considerable modifications were obviously necessary for its presentation on the stage. In Johnson's hands, it became an enfeebled version of

11

Othello—an unconscious plagiarism, for at that time he had not read Shakespeare's play. Johnson's Irene, after a struggle with her conscience as a Christian, is on the point of marrying the Moslem Emperor when he finds out that she is guilty, as he thinks, of treachery. He orders her execution (which is carried out off-stage) and only discovers her innocence when it is too late. Irene's agony of mind is painfully unfolded in page after page of lifeless blank verse, which the author read aloud to Walmesley. The distress of the heroine in the first two acts of the play was appalling, and the climax had yet to come. 'How can you possibly contrive to plunge her into deeper calamity?' objected Walmesley. 'Sir, I can put her into the Spiritual Court,' replied Johnson, alluding slyly to his friend's jurisdiction. Walmesley, however, admired the play immensely and urged Johnson to go on with it.

The year 1736 saw Captain Garrick reunited to his family. He found Davy very little changed, as small and talkative as ever. 'I daresay', was the flippant remark with which he greeted his father, 'I have now a good many brothers and sisters at Gibraltar,' and it was only when he noticed how his mother's eyes filled with tears that he realized the clumsiness of his joke. He was now close on twenty and it was high time to get him started in life. In two years' time Captain Garrick hoped to find the money to send him to the Bar, but meanwhile he needed coaching, for he was still backward in his studies. Johnson's Academy was on the point of closing down, and the family could not run to the expense of a university education. In this dilemma Captain Garrick applied to Walmesley for help, although that gentleman's recent marriage to one of the Miss Astons had shattered Mrs. Garrick's maternal hopes, and made it improbable that he would offer anything more substantial than advice. But the advice, when it came, seemed very much to the point. Walmesley recalled a certain John Colson, his old friend and fellow-townsman, who taught mathematics in Rochester, and he suggested that Davy should be sent to him as a resident pupil. Captain Garrick approved of the scheme, and so Walmesley wrote to Colson cordially recommending 'this very sensible young man of sober and good disposition' for his instruction in 'mathematics, philosophy and humane learning'. In the intervals of study he would find him an agreeable companion, and indeed he felt sure that if Colson were to take him into his family he would share the writer's own affection for the young gentleman. Captain Garrick, he concluded, would pay, if he possibly could, the necessary fees.

Meanwhile Johnson had realized that he would never make a successful schoolmaster, and he decided to leave Mrs. Johnson at Lichfield for the time being and go with his ex-pupil to London. On the 2nd of March 1737 Johnson, aged twenty-seven, and David Garrick, younger by seven and a half years, set out on horseback together. As soon as they were out of sight, Walmesley sat down to compose a second letter to Colson. 'I am extremely obliged to you,' he wrote. 'Had I a son of my own, it would be my ambition, instead of sending him to the university, to dispose of him as this young gentleman is.

'He and another neighbour of mine, one Mr. S. Johnson, set out this morning for London together. Davy Garrick is to be with you early the next week, and Mr. Johnson to try his fate with a tragedy and to get himself employed in some translation either from the Latin or the French. Johnson is a very good scholar and poet, and I have great hopes will turn out a fine tragedy writer. If it should anyways lay in your way, I doubt not but you would be ready to recommend and assist your countryman.'

CHAPTER II

DURHAM YARD

1737 — 1741

Soon after the two young men had arrived in London they discovered that their small stock of money had melted away. They
had no friends from whom to borrow, and there was no alternative
but to apply to a tradesman for a loan. At David Garrick's suggestion, Johnson and he called at a bookseller's shop in the Strand,
and with disarming simplicity told him their plight. They had
started out together from the same town, they said, and had come
to make their way in London. They had spent their ready money
and would be obliged if Mr. Wilcox would lend them five pounds.
Their straightforward manner told in their favour and, on no
better security than their joint note of hand, the bookseller handed
them the money. And now with his purse replenished, Garrick
decided to enter himself forthwith at Lincoln's Inn, and on the 9th
of March 1737 he paid £3 3s. 4d. for that privilege. This done,
the two friends separated: Johnson to offer his services to the booksellers, and Garrick to put himself under the care of Mr. Colson.

But that absent-minded philosopher, absorbed in the mysteries
of higher mathematics, took little interest in a young man intended
for the Bar; as for Johnson, all Colson ever did for him was un-
consciously to provide him with a subject for satire in one of his
essays for *The Rambler*. There he appears, under the name of
Gelidus, as a scholar of 'remote and unnecessary subjects' who neglected his family 'to count the drops of rain, note the changes of
the wind, and calculate the eclipses of the moons of Jupiter'. He
lived entirely in the highest room of the house, according to John-

14

son, aloof from all human emotions, and hardly raised his head from his books when a servant rushed in to tell him that a neighbouring town was on fire. Just what benefit Walmesley expected the young law student to derive from such a tutor it is difficult to see, and, apart from a local tradition of private theatricals, no record of David Garrick's year in Rochester has survived.

Meanwhile much had happened in Lichfield to the families of both young men. Three days after they left there, Johnson's younger brother, Nathaniel, was buried. Johnson never referred to the tragedy in later life, and the sudden death of a hitherto healthy young man of twenty-four remains something of a mystery —particularly as he is known to have been in some sort of trouble at the time. And within a week Captain Garrick too was dead. By the terms of his will, made eight weeks before the historic ride to London, he left his second son, David, the sum of one shilling. His other children received from three hundred to five hundred pounds apiece. There is no need to deduce from this that they had quarrelled; Captain Garrick knew that under the will of his brother, David Garrick, the wine merchant, who had died a fortnight before while on a visit to England, his son would inherit a thousand pounds on reaching the age of twenty-one 'unless he proved disobedient to his father and mother'.[1]

In 1738 Garrick came of age and was free to drop all pretence of studying law—a subject profoundly uncongenial to him—and within certain limits to choose his own career. Those limits were set by his consideration for Mrs. Garrick; as a dutiful son, he did not even put into words his longing to go on the stage; he could not break her heart by suggesting anything so shocking. As it happened, his elder brother, Peter, was in much the same unsettled frame of mind, having left the navy on the strength of his inheritance, and the two young men met in Lichfield to discuss the problem of finding occupation. Trade seemed the obvious solution, and, as members of a family that had its origins in the wine-producing town of Bordeaux, their thoughts naturally turned to the wine trade as a means of making money. The two brothers decided to set up in partnership as vintners; David was to be the

[1] Tom Davies, Garrick's earliest biographer, tells a slightly different story but A. L. Reade in his *Johnsonian Gleanings*, Part VI, 1933, shows that the facts are as above.

London representative of the new firm of Garrick Brothers, while Peter would remain in Lichfield. They rented premises off the Strand, in what was then Durham Yard on the site of the Adelphi arches, and in their vaults they stored port from Lisbon, hock from the Rhine, sweet white wine from the Canaries, and rough red wine that purported to come from France but more often came from Portugal. Garrick began to solicit diligently for custom.

To a young man with social gifts this was by no means a disagreeable occupation; it involved frequenting coffee-houses in the hope of supplying them with wine, and where at the same time he could make acquaintances and persuade them to become his private customers. And when those acquaintances happened to be actors and he could hear all the latest gossip of the theatres—well, the days might have been worse spent. He concentrated on Covent Garden, a neighbourhood as famous then for its coffee-houses as Saint James's Street was for its clubs a little later in the century. It had changed in character since the courtiers of King Charles II had sauntered under Inigo Jones's new arcade and imagined themselves in an Italian piazza; and since *The Spectator's* fine ladies had walked across the square to Saint Paul's Church, followed by black pages carrying their mistresses' prayer books. The centre of the square, which had long served as a market-place for the sale of fruit and vegetables, was steadily increasing in importance as a place of business, and the neighbourhood in consequence was losing its air of gentility. The nobility and gentry naturally preferred to build their London residences farther out of the city; the general move westwards had already begun. By the time Garrick came to London, the houses that had been built for persons of rank had been turned into lodgings for actors and actresses, and cheap taverns, wine cellars and disreputable night houses of every variety sprang up round them—a curious fate for the site of a convent garden.

Thus it was that in the almost entirely masculine crowd that lounged under the Piazza at midday, actors predominated; for no actor of any repute lived far from Covent Garden. In the 1730's the middle classes had not yet risen to the prosperity that gave them the right to take part in a general social life, and each trade and profession had its own residential quarter, seldom venturing

16

far outside it. Merchants lived in the City over their counting-houses, lawyers lived in their Inns of Court or near Westminster Hall, and actors and actresses playing at the two great theatres, Drury Lane and Covent Garden, lodged near by them—sufficiently close together to be mustered for rehearsals by the beat of a drum.

But the coffee-houses under the arcade, misleadingly called the Piazza, still attracted artists and intellectuals from every class of life. By 1739, Button's Coffee-house in Russell Street, the favourite haunt of Addison and Steele, had closed down for ever, but the Bedford Coffee-house on the north-west corner of the Piazza had succeeded to its popularity. Its patrons were drawn from the theatrical world; actors, dramatists, and critics met there to discuss the merits of the previous day's performances, and on their verdict the fate of a new dramatist or a new actor would largely depend.

In these congenial surroundings the young wine merchant appeared to advantage. Although he seldom said anything worth repeating, his conversation sounded amusing at the time; probably because he acted, half-unconsciously, all the while he was talking, changing the expression of his face and varying the tone of his voice, turning before the eyes of his listeners into the person he was describing. He seemed eager to please everyone, and as his humour had none of the ill nature that gave point to most of the other men's anecdotes, he offended no one. His provincial origin passed unnoticed and, indeed, from the wealth of his stories drawn from his brief experiences in Lisbon, one at least of his new friends took him for a much-travelled man. In short, he soon became as welcome both here and behind the scenes of the theatres as he had been in the mess-rooms of Lichfield.

Among his new acquaintances was an actor called Charles Macklin, whose unorthodox views on acting Garrick immediately accepted. The two men had little in common apart from their interest in the stage; nevertheless, they became intimate friends. In a tremendous Irish brogue, which he was doing his best to overcome, Macklin used to lay down the law on what he regarded as the decadence of the tragic stage, and how he would reform it if only he were given an opportunity. He made a good deal of noise and easily lost his temper in an argument, but as he had a powerful physique and knew how to use his fists it was usually

17

thought best to agree with him. His heavy features marked him out as the perfect stage villain; managers, however, disapproved of his tragedy manner and usually cast him for comedy parts, or employed him as a clown in the Harlequinade, for every comedian of his day was a clown under his skin. He had spent many years of his life as a strolling player, and it was only since his trial for murder in 1735 had brought him some useful notoriety that he had ranked among the principal actors at Drury Lane theatre.

Although by no means generally liked, Macklin earned considerable admiration by his courage in the great crisis of his life —particularly from the butchers of Clare Market, a small community who lived among the actors and followed their affairs with interest. As regular playgoers, their support was well worth having when, as not infrequently happened, the audience began to smash everything within reach as a demonstration of its dissatisfaction with an actor's performance. In the quarrel that had ended tragically Macklin had for once been in the right, and no one regretted more than he the horrible accident that cost a fellow-actor his life. While they were tussling over the possession of a wig behind the scenes of Drury Lane, the man's eye-socket was penetrated by the point of Macklin's cane and he died in agony within a few hours. Instead of going into hiding, as advised by his friends, Macklin gave himself up at the Old Bailey, and in the trial that followed the jury acquitted him of murder but found him guilty of manslaughter. It does not appear, however, that he underwent any punishment. On the contrary, the publicity benefited him in his profession.

Macklin had a good deal to say about the acting of his older contemporaries: he complained of the absence of stage discipline, the egotism of the actors in trying to attract attention to themselves by tricks out of keeping with their parts, and at moments when they should have been listening with the audience to some other character in the play; and over and above everything else he detested the worn-out formalism of the tragic stage. The tragedians at that time invested their acting with a solemnity more usually associated with religious worship than the theatre, intended to uplift the audience into a state of aesthetic ecstasy rather than to excite emotion by a realistic portrayal of human suffering. Their

18

conceit was overwhelming: they moved and spoke both on and off the stage with heavy pomposity as though they believed that the nobility of their rôles accurately reflected their own private characters. ' "I have heard the town of Lichfield much commended for its ale," ' quoted one of these tragedians to Garrick in the green-room, but he intoned it with all the solemnity of a tragedy king. The acting of comedy was as broad as that of the modern farce, and, in consequence, comedy and tragedy were two totally different kinds of entertainment. As Shakespeare had somewhat confused them, it was found necessary to omit the comic scenes in his tragedies lest a laugh should rouse the audience from its trance. On tragedy days strips of green baize over the stage floor for the greater comfort of the dead and dying proclaimed the solemnity of the occasion, and when the curtain rose the audience listened with respect rather than with enjoyment, waiting with ill-concealed impatience for the Harlequinade or the short farce that brought the evening's entertainment to an end. In consequence, tragedy ranked higher as a work of art than comedy. Throughout five long acts the unhappy heroine, in the black velvet hooped dress she wore for all situations, periods, and climates, and the hero, dignified by a tall plume of feathers on his powdered periwig, delivered their speeches with a minimum of stereotyped gestures and in a monotonous chant.

This style of acting had been introduced into England after the Restoration in imitation of the French contemporary stage. Thus Racine had taught Mlle Champmeslé to act the parts he had written for her; and under his tuition she delivered her tirades in a cadenced monotone. Formalism of speech and action suited his plays to perfection, for measured beauty of diction was necessary for their successful presentation. It was appropriate, too, to certain English plays: to the heroic couplets of Addison's *Cato,* a calm and dignified poem masquerading as drama, and it made palatable to English taste those dull heroic tragedies of French derivation that the dramatists of the time obstinately insisted on writing. The skill with which this school of actors managed their voices constituted in itself a now forgotten art—one that owed nothing to the meaning of words but consisted only of beautiful sound. When the principal tragedian of the day intoned the following speech from Lee's *Rival Queens,* the audience hushed in rapture:

19

When Glory, like the dazzling Eagle, stood,
Perched on my Beaver, in the Granic Flood,
When Fortune's self, my standard trembling bore,
And the pale Fates stood frighted on the Shore,
When the Immortals on the Billows rode,
And I myself appear'd the leading God.

It probably sounded magnificent when chanted, but read in an ordinary tone of voice it is nonsense.

So long as the English were content to take their culture from France they accepted their stage conventions unquestioningly; but these could not have satisfied Shakespeare's countrymen for ever. Although coffee-house critics complained that Shakespeare's poetry lacked polish, his plays, or rather the adaptations of his plays that went by his name, had never entirely lost their hold over English audiences, and, moreover, much of the contemporary drama was derived directly or indirectly from the Elizabethan. In all these plays, intoning was inherently ridiculous. In 1731 Aaron Hill was already complaining of the actors' 'stage voice, their eternal affectation of forced tone with which they cover and efface the passions they are endeavouring to heighten'. But without it, no actor could hope for an engagement. Macklin's refusal as a young man to declaim in a sing-song manner had resulted in his dismissal from Covent Garden. 'I spoke so familiar,' he recalled in old age, 'and so little in the hoity-toity tone of the tragedy of that day that the manager told me that I had better go back to grass for another year or two.' Reluctantly he took the advice and went back to his life as a strolling player.

Yet during the sixty years or so that the convention lasted many actors had arisen whose genius cannot be doubted; actors whose underlying sincerity gave point to the most mechanical actions and whose voices swayed their audiences. For the art of acting has no fixed standard of value; an actor can only be judged by his ability to transport an audience of his contemporaries into a world of illusion, and it is dangerous to compare the technique and merits of an actor of one period with those of an actor of any other. Each school of acting has its conventions, which are justified so long as they help the less talented of its members to create illusion. Genius can look after itself. But in acting, as in all the

arts, a technique that helps one generation to expression is ap
to paralyse the next, and by the time Garrick came to London
formalism in acting had outlived its usefulness.

The opportunities for acting in London were, for all practical
purposes, monopolized by the companies at Covent Garden and
Drury Lane theatres, and, since they drew on the same stock of
plays, the casting of parts was settled rather on the lines of a
sporting event. Once an actor had proved himself the champion
Othello or Richard III that rôle was his prescribed right, and
the manager of the other house would not venture to put forward
one of his own actors in the same part unless he had some chance
of winning the title from his rival. Thus at Covent Garden, Lacy
Ryan specialized in tragic lovers and fops, and at Drury Lane,
James Quin appropriated noble Romans and jovial drunkards.

Of these two leading actors, Quin was by common consent the
better. His magnificent elocution and dignified movements fitted
him admirably for Cato, Brutus, and Coriolanus, but in more
emotional and romantic parts the monotony of his acting seemed
to justify Macklin and Garrick in their distrust of his technique.
We see him through the youthful eyes of Richard Cumberland
acting Horatio 'in a green velvet coat embroidered down the
seams, an enormous full-bottomed periwig, rolled stockings, and
high-heeled square-toed shoes. With very little variation of cadence,
and in a deep full tone, accompanied by a sawing kind of action,
which had more of the senate than of the stage in it, he rolled out
his heroics, with an air of dignified indifference that seemed to
disdain the plaudits that were bestowed upon him.' But Cumberland, like most of those who have left us their impressions of
Quin, greatly preferred the technique that superseded his, and
consequently it is difficult to arrive at a just estimate of his powers
as a tragedian in the days when all London admired him. In the
few comic rôles he attempted his success has never been disputed.
He belonged to that numerous class of actors who mould their
parts to fit their own personalities rather than the other way
round, and whenever his stage character happened to have qualities
in common with his own, he made a tremendous hit. In private
life he exhibited a gross and rather brutal sensuality, the quality
that distinguished both Falstaff and Henry VIII. With his burly
form and deep voice, Quin's impersonation of those two characters

21

satisfied the imagination of his contemporaries more completely than any other actor succeeded in doing either before or after his time.

Macklin hated Quin with all the intolerance that the innovator in an art habitually displays towards the leading exponent of the orthodox technique. Whenever they were on the stage together, Macklin deliberately clowned during Quin's speeches, with the result that Quin could not make himself heard through the audience's laughter—an instance of the inartistic behaviour that Macklin disapproved of in others. One day he goaded Quin into losing his temper, and they came to blows in the green-room—to the consternation of all the noblemen who, in their embroidered silk coats, large wigs and swords, gave it the appearance of a levee. In their alarm they jumped upon the benches, much too careful of their finery to make any attempt to separate the two actors. By the time Macklin had finished pummeling his enemy's face, Quin's injuries prevented him from articulating distinctly, and he was obliged to throw up his part for the evening. After this they barely spoke to one another, and Quin, not unnaturally, took every opportunity to run down Macklin's acting and say something spiteful about him. When an acquaintance of his remarked that Macklin should make a good actor, having such strong lines in his face, Quin retorted, 'Lines, sir? I see nothing in the fellow's face but a damned deal of cordage,' and this joke, which was a poor one for Quin, went the rounds of the coffee-houses.

It is no wonder that the stage, as Garrick found it, was not considered suitable as a profession for anyone who wished to be described as a gentleman. Cheating, drunkenness and brawling were not unknown among men who claimed that title with assurance; even so, in comparison with their contemporaries, the actors were a very rough and ignorant set of men. 'The stage, like the sea-service,' wrote Colley Cibber, 'refuses no man for his morals that is able-bodied.' Yet Garrick, at the age of twenty-three, took only what was of real value from their companionship and dissociated himself from their vices and follies—a circumstance that may account for some of the malicious stories that they invented about him after he rose to fame. He had nothing in his way of living to conceal when his elder brother, Peter, paid his periodical visits to London; on the contrary, he introduced his new friends to him, and even infected him with a little of his own interest in the stage.

In voice and appearance, the two brothers were extraordinarily alike, typically French in their small light build, swarthy colouring and expressive features. Johnson did not distinguish very much between them; indeed, it is possible that he rather preferred the older and more sedate of the two. That Peter possessed none of his brother's powers of mimicry seemed to Johnson nothing but a blessing, for he never ruined conversation by relapsing into what Johnson called buffoonery. In the early part of 1740 they dined together at the Fountain Tavern, and Johnson paid the ex-naval officer the compliment of reading aloud the whole of his recently completed tragedy, *Irene*. Peter, duly impressed, offered to intercede with Charles Fleetwood, the manager of Drury Lane, whom he had met in David's company, to present it on his stage. Both Peter and David did all they could to further their friend's interests, but although Fleetwood made many vague promises that he had no intention of fulfilling, the manuscript of *Irene* lay idle until David himself was in a position to make use of it.

Johnson was much too poor to frequent the Bedford Coffee-house. He could scarcely pay for the bare necessities of life with the pittance he earned writing for Cave's new periodical, *The Gentleman's Magazine*. If Garrick wanted to see Johnson, he could generally find him at Cave's printing-office in the gateway of St. John's, Clerkenwell, where he concocted those reports of parliamentary debates (making sure that the Whig dogs did not get the best of it), or eating his dinner in a back room on the days when he felt too shabby to be seen in a tavern. Sometimes Garrick persuaded him to spend the evening with him, and then Johnson, stirring his tea contentedly, would discuss literary topics and exercise his amazing gift for producing good verse almost extempore. When he went back to the printing-office, he talked about his friend, David Garrick, and his turn for play-acting until Cave expressed a wish to see him in some comic character. Garrick was only too delighted to comply. The room over the great arch of the gate was converted into a tiny theatre, and, with the help of a few printers to read the other parts, Garrick played the title rôle of Fielding's adaptation of Molière's play *The Mock Doctor*, with an epilogue written for the occasion. In September 1740 the poem appeared in *The Gentleman's Magazine* over the initial G., and for the first time Garrick saw his work in print.

Garrick had not a great many ideas of his own to impart, but those that came to him he had always been able to express with facility. As a schoolboy he had sent his father verses satirizing various people known to them both. Judged as literature, the poems were not very good, but at any rate Captain Garrick enjoyed them enough to keep the letter and bring it back with him from Gibraltar. Or when circumstances called for a love lyric, young Garrick could be relied upon to produce one of slightly above average quality—provided, of course, that he could be sure of a wide circulation.

A few years later Garrick was writing prologues which are among the best of their kind, but in 1740 his more serious thoughts were taken up with the technique of playwriting, particularly with the art of writing dialogue. This he practised until he developed an easy and agreeable style. His mind was constructive rather than inventive, but he knew what the public wanted in the way of plot and character, and he knew where to find them in the words of older dramatists. He could borrow as much as he liked without discredit to himself; what had once been written for the stage was regarded as common property, and free adaptations of old plays were more often seen than new ones. With an almost unerring sense of what would act well, he learnt how to mould his material into an entertainment that moved swiftly and smoothly, and contained all the favourite jokes of the day. In the spring of 1740 he finished his first comic sketch, *Lethe,* which Fleetwood, while still hesitating over Johnson's tragedy of far greater literary pretensions, accepted without any misgivings. The plot of *Lethe* is nearly non-existent, but the fantastic characters of the Beau and the Lady were introduced to exploit the comic powers of Harry Woodward and Kitty Clive. The sketch received its first performance in April and entered on a long popularity. From time to time, he inserted fresh characters—Lord Chalkstone, for instance, was a much later addition. *Lethe* only ceased to amuse audiences when the types it satirized had passed out of contemporary life and were forgotten.

All we know of that evening in April is that the takings went to Garrick's friend, Giffard, the actor. It was his benefit night, when, in addition to his salary, he was entitled to the doorkeeper's

1. DAVID GARRICK IN 1764
from a painting executed in Rome by P. G. Batoni

receipts minus £60 for the use of the theatre. In the intervals of acting at Drury Lane, Giffard managed a theatre of his own at Goodman's Fields, a small unlicensed playhouse in the east end of the city frequented by the merchants and their families. At this point it becomes necessary to explain the relationship of the two patent theatres, Drury Lane and Covent Garden, to the unauthorized places of entertainment, but, as the history of the struggle for a free stage is as dry as all other forms of dead politics, the explanation will be made as brief as possible.

The two patents granted by Charles II to Killigrew and Davenant were represented in 1736 by those held by Fleetwood at Drury Lane and John Rich at Covent Garden. Theatrical performances held elsewhere than in those two theatres were unauthorized by the Crown, but the law provided no punishment for those who took part in them. In consequence, there existed a few irregularly formed companies, who, as a protest against their lack of status, acted satires directed against the government. The chief offender was Henry Fielding, whose satirical farces at the Little Theatre in the Haymarket goaded Sir Robert Walpole into taking indirect action against him. He wrote, or caused to have written, an outrageously libellous sketch, which his agents submitted to Giffard in his capacity as manager of Goodman's Fields Theatre. But Giffard refused to walk into the trap. He knew that its performance on his or any other stage would ruin him, because it would provide the government with an excuse for silencing all the unlicensed theatres by a new Act of Parliament. Hoping to ingratiate himself with Walpole, he turned informer and sent him the manuscript. The result was the same as though it had been acted. In June 1737 the Licensing Bill became law, and henceforth theatrical performances for 'hire, gain or reward' unsanctioned by 'letters patent from the Crown, or licensed by the Lord Chamberlain' were prohibited under penalty of £50. Thus Drury Lane and Covent Garden, protected by their 'letters patent from the Crown', regained their monopoly; the Lord Chamberlain had no intention of granting licences to their rivals, and Goodman's Fields and the Little Theatre were obliged to close down.

For some considerable time Giffard cherished hopes that his services to the government would be rewarded by a licence. In July 1740 David Garrick writes to his brother telling him that

Giffard has procured for them the custom of the Bedford Coffee-house, 'one of the best in London', and in return he feels himself under an obligation to do anything in his power to help Giffard in his theatrical venture. Peter will naturally feel the same. Giffard has received a very hopeful letter from the Lord Chamberlain, and David is sure that if only his friends will back his interest the affair will be satisfactorily settled. Will Peter ask a certain influential acquaintance of his to do what he can? David stresses the value of Giffard's recommendation of their wine, so as to convince Peter that his help will be all in the way of business.

It is an amiable letter, full of family affection and good nature. He expresses his great relief to hear of their mother's health, which had evidently been causing them all grave anxiety. He is keeping a solicitous eye on a young fellow-townsman, who has come to London to study medicine. Peter can tell his uncle that the youth is very well. 'He is a very honest, sober, sensible young fellow,' writes David with all the wisdom of his six or seven years' seniority, 'and I don't doubt but will turn out well. He cannot get into Hospital till Michaelmas and he is therefore advised till then to attend Dr. Nichol's lectures. I will take care of him and preach up Oeconomy and virtue to him; I have already given him a just detestation for the lewd night-walkers and vile polluters of youth. Draper tells me he is an understanding youth and wants nothing but a little polishing of his Dialect, which has much of the Staffordshire twang with it.' David thinks that their friend should certainly allow his nephew to attend the lectures, and sends him a teasingly affectionate message. 'Tell him I say so, and that Damn him I have a small veneration for his rotund Paunch and no despicable opinion of his Brains.' Sobering down, he reverts to his mother's better health, and his hopes for her recovery. But they were not to be fulfilled; she had a relapse and died soon afterwards.

David's scheme to help his friend came to nothing, and Giffard, realizing that the Lord Chamberlain did not mean to give him a licence, determined to manage without one. The vague and careless wording of the Act provided a loophole for escape. He would call the entertainment a concert for which tickets would be issued and sold. In the intervals, a play would be performed free, and the entertainment would be within the literal interpretation of the law. In October 1740 he announced: 'At the *late* Theatre in Ayliffe Street—a Concert of Vocal and Instrumental Musick in 2 Parts—Between the Parts of the Concert will be presented *gratis* a Comedy called the Stratagem—By Persons for their diversion.' For a time the device succeeded, and Giffard gave his usual performances unmolested.

The death of Mrs. Garrick brought David nearer to making his great decision. All that winter the wine business languished while its junior partner haunted the theatres, identifying himself with each one of the actors in turn and studying the details of every branch of the art from tragedy to pantomime. One evening at Goodman's Fields, a sudden sickness attacked Yates while the audience waited to see him as Harlequin. The pantomime opened, and the dumb show went on as merrily as usual; no one but Giffard and Yates knew that Harlequin's mask hid the features of young David Garrick.

Meanwhile Macklin was on the eve of realizing his ambition of demonstrating naturalism on the stage. As Fleetwood's chief adviser and acting manager, he persuaded him to revive Shakespeare's *Merchant of Venice,* which had been superseded for many years by *The Jew of Venice,* Lansdowne's free adaptation of the same play. In this version Shylock appeared as a low comic figure in a play that was treated as a farce. Macklin determined to take everyone by surprise by playing Shylock seriously as a villain, and by representing his conflicting passions realistically.

The 14th of February was the date fixed for the performance, and only Macklin's most intimate friends knew what to expect. At rehearsals he walked through his part without a look or a gesture. On the night he came a little defiantly into the green-room, the natural lines of his face deeply scored in black, a wispy beard on his chin and wearing a red hat and loose black gabardine, the distinctive dress of the Venetian Jews of the sixteenth century. His fellow-actors stared at him with dismay; they were accustomed to see Shylock in the nondescript clothes of a buffoon, and never before had an actor paid any attention to the historical accuracy of his dress. 'Well, sir,' said Macklin, as he recalled his great night, 'hitherto all was right till the last bell rang; then, I confess, my heart began to beat a little. However, I mustered all the courage I could and, recommending my cause to Providence, threw myself boldly on the stage, and was received by one of the loudest thunders of applause I ever before experienced.

'The opening scenes being rather tame and level, I could not expect much applause, but I found myself well listened to. I could hear distinctly in the pit the words, "Very well—very well indeed! This man seems to know what he is about." These encomiums warmed me, but did not overset me. I knew where I should have the pull, which was in the third act, and reserved myself accordingly. At this period I threw out all my fire, and as the contrasted passions of joy for the merchant's losses and grief for the elopement of Jessica, open a fine field for an actor's powers, I had the good fortune to please beyond my warmest expectations. The whole house was in an uproar of applause, and I was obliged to pause between the speeches to give it vent, so as to be heard. When I went behind the scenes after this act, the manager met me and complimented me very highly on my performance, and significantly added, "Macklin, you was right at last." '

It was Macklin's one great triumph, and he lived on it for the rest of his life. No other part ever suited him as well. In general, his theories on acting were far in advance of his performance. He talked about the need for what he called 'grace and dignity' very convincingly, but, according to a fellow-actor, 'to see a man *like Macklin* gravely attempting to wave his neck in all the undulating forms of elegance was laughable in the extreme'. Then again, he advocated a more natural intonation and mode of delivery, but his systematic use of three pauses of carefully graduated duration was in effect no less mechanical in its way than the older style of elocution, and sometimes held up the action of the play. On one occasion he paused so long that the prompter, thinking that his memory must have failed him, gave him his cue. Macklin rushed to the side of the stage and knocked him down. 'The fellow interrupted me in my Grand Pause,' he explained to the audience. But his sour expression, furrowed face, and naturally clumsy movements helped to make an effectively repellent Shylock. Even Quin, as he played Antonio, could find no worse aside than the ambiguous: 'If God Almighty writes a legible hand, that man must be a villain.' King George II, who was no friend to the drama and as a rule cared only for clowns, lay awake all night after seeing Macklin as Shylock.

28

'I wish, your Majesty,' said Sir Robert Walpole the next morning, 'it was possible to find a recipe for frightening the House of Commons.' 'Vat do you tink,' suggested his teutonic Majesty, 'of sending dem to see dat Irishman play Shylock?'

Macklin had made theatrical history. In a single evening he had revived a flagging interest in Shakespeare; he had prepared the audience for Garrick's greater genius in the new naturalistic style, and finally he had given the stage an interpretation of Shylock that held it for over a century—one in which pity played no part.

> *This is the Jew*
> *That Shakespeare drew,*

Pope is said to have ejaculated, and he might have said the same of Edmund Kean's more powerfully played villain over a half a century later. It was not until Sir Henry Irving reflected the liberalism of the nineteenth century by giving a more sympathetic rendering of the part that Shylock was credited with any human feelings at all. And nowhere, by the way, was Irving's interpretation more admired and applauded than in Germany.

In May the London theatres closed down as usual for the rest of the summer, and the actors dispersed. Star actors went to act for a short season in Dublin, the comedians went to clown at fairs, and the rest formed what they called sharing companies for performances in the provinces. In 1741 Giffard took such a company to Ipswich and hired the hall that formed part of the principal inn and served the town as a theatre. Garrick went with him and, under the name of Lyddal, made his first appearance as Aboan, in Southerne's tragedy, *Oroonoko*. It was a small part, but a strongly emotional one with plenty of action, which Garrick needed for the exercise of his particular gifts. It gave him an opportunity, moreover, to stab himself and die on the stage—a performance he always thoroughly enjoyed and at which he excelled. It has been supposed that timidity prompted Garrick to choose the part of Aboan; had he failed, his blackened face would have hidden his discomfiture and his identity. On the contrary, the choice was too daring to be wise; to reconcile high tragedy with a blackened face and a small physique is a feat that has only once been achieved in all the history of the stage,[1] and, considering that he afterwards failed as

29

Othello with years of experience and all Shakespeare's genius behind him, it seems unlikely that he succeeded as a beginner in a less inspired play. However, his performance pleased the provincial audience, and many other parts followed, both tragic and comic. By the end of the summer he had served his apprenticeship, and was ready to try his fortune on the London stage.

[1] Edmund Kean as Othello.

CHAPTER III

GOODMAN'S FIELDS

1741–1742

A FEW months elapsed and two letters addressed to Peter Garrick arrived in Lichfield; one in David's untidy scrawl and the other in the small, neat handwriting of John Swinfen. Peter opened his brother's letter first. It began innocently enough with a reference to a shirt, but its nervous, apologetic tone seemed to herald some disagreeable news. He read on, and his suspicions were confirmed. David had appeared as Richard III on the stage of Giffard's theatre in Goodman's Fields, and on the strength of a few compliments (so it seemed to Peter) he was actually proposing to throw up his business in order to become a professional actor. David wrote as though his incompetence as a salesman excused him for disgracing the family. But how much of the firm's money, speculated Peter with some bitterness, had gone into Giffard's pocket? He showed the letter to his sisters, and they were even more horrified. Their thoughts turned uneasily to their rich relations at Carshalton. Jane Garrick, their father's only sister, had married another Huguenot immigrant, Louis La Condé, who had built up for himself a prosperous business in the country of his adoption. Being childless, Mr. and Mrs. La Condé were regarded with hopeful interest by the young Garricks. How would Uncle La Condé relish having a nephew on the stage? As it happened, that respectable merchant was reading a very similar sort of letter, and was preparing to come down heavily on both of the brothers; on Peter for not having confided in him how badly they had been doing in business, no less than on the culprit himself.

31

Peter turned to the second letter. John Swinfen, the son of Samuel Johnson's godfather, had known the Garricks all his life, and had seen Captain and Mrs. Garrick depriving themselves of necessities in order to give each of their sons the education of a gentleman. Yet here, to Peter's indignation, was John Swinfen pleading on David's behalf! The letters are too interesting not to quote almost in full.

'*October 20.*

'Dear Peter,

'I rec'd my shirt safe and am now to tell you what I suppose you may have heard of before this. But before I let you into the affair, tis proper to premise some things that I may appear less culpable in your opinion than I might otherwise be.

'I have made an Exact Estimate of my Stock of wine, and what money I have out at Interest, and find that since I have been a Wine Merchant I have run out near four hundred pounds. And trade not increasing I was very sensible some way must be thought of to redeem it. My mind (as you must know) has been always inclin'd to the Stage, nay so strongly that all my illness and lowness of Spirits was owing to my want of resolution to tell you my thoughts when here. Finding at last both my Inclination and Interest requir'd some new way of Life, I have chosen the most agreeable to myself and, tho I know you will be much displeas'd at me, yet I hope when you find that I have the genius of an actor without the vices you will think less severely of me and not be asham'd to own me for a Brother.

'I am willing to agree to anything you propose about the wine. I will take a thorough survey of the vaults and, making what you have at Lichfield part of the Stock, will either send you your share or any other way you propose. Last Night I play'd Richard the Third to the surprise of Every Body and as I shall make very near £300 per annum by it, and as it is really what I doat upon, I am resolv'd to pursue it. Pray write me in answer immediately.

'I am, dr. Peter,
Yours
D. GARRICK

'I have a farce (The Lying Valet) coming out at Drury Lane.'

John Swinfen's letter bears the same date. 'I dont doubt', he writes, 'but you will soon hear my good friend, David Garwick [*sic*] perform'd last night at Goodman's Fields theatre, and for fear you should hear any false or malicious Account that may be disagreeable to you, I will give you the truth which much pleased me. I was there and was witness to a most generous applause he gain'd in the character of Richard the Third; for I believe there was not one in the House that was not in raptures. I heard several men of judgment declare it their opinion that nobody ever excelled him in that part, and that they were surprised with so peculiar a genius how it was possible for him to keep off the stage so long. Many of his country friends, who have been most used to theatrical Performances in Town Halls by Strollers, will be apt to imagine the highest pitch a Man can [attain] on the stage is about that exalted degree of Heroism [reached by] the Herberts and the Hallams. And there are many others who, because their fathers were called Gentlemen, will think it a disgrace that the child of an old friend should endeavour to get an honest Livelihood. I think I know you well enough to be convinced that you have not the same sentiments, and I believe there are some others of his friends who will not alter their opinion or regard of him till they find the stage corrupts his Morals and makes him less deserving, which I do not take to be a necessary consequence nor likely to happen to my honest friend, David.'

But Peter could not be flattered or coaxed into approval. Boiling over with fury, he sat down and wrote a letter that distressed David although it did not surprise him. In a correspondence that went on the whole winter, David explains[1] over and over again why he has exchanged the life of a wine merchant for that of an actor, setting out every little circumstance that justifies him in his decision in an eager wish to be forgiven. His financial losses have been entirely due to his own lack of interest in the business; they cannot be attributed to the normal fluctuations of trade; still less to the misuse of the firm's capital. Giffard does not owe him a farthing; it is true that he once lent him £30, but that was paid a long while ago, and Giffard is now repaying whatever service he received at David's hands in kindness and generosity. As for being in debt, Peter can be very easy on that subject. He has not a debt of twenty

[1] See Appendix I.

shillings. But even allowing for some improvement in their sales, their profits could never have supported him and a servant handsomely. Now as an actor he is already receiving six guineas a week and, in addition, has been promised a benefit night which will bring him at least £120. If only Peter would come up to London and see him act, he might look at it in a different light; and he promises him that neither his seat not his lodging will cost him a penny.

Peter accuses him of wishing to injure him in his business, continues David; that is absurd. On the contrary, he will always help him in every way in his power. If Peter is ever in need of money and David has any of his own, Peter can have every penny of it. Meanwhile he offers to buy £200 of the firm's stock of wine out of his salary. He suggests that the stock should be sold in London, and the proceeds divided between them. If Peter is not satisfied with his share, he can have all David's as well. Perhaps it would be wise to appoint their uncle to act as agent in this matter. David has, in fact, been selling rather more wine than usual lately, but his mind is quite turned another way, so he wishes to be released from his partnership as soon as possible.

The compliments that are being showered on him daily almost pass belief. His genius, by the best judges, is thought wonderful, and far from being cold-shouldered by persons of rank, he has received more invitations this winter than ever in his life before. Mr. Pitt, who is reckoned the greatest orator in the House of Commons, is reported to have said he is the best actor the English stage has produced; and on one of Mr. Pitt's visits to Goodman's Fields he sent a message to the green-room to say that he and his friends would be glad of some conversation with the actor. David has supped with the great Mr. Lyttelton, the Prince's[1] favourite, who treated him with marked civility, and assured him that he had only been born to act what Shakespeare had written. He has dined with Lord Halifax and Lord Sandwich—two very ingenious noblemen, he adds with the tone of an experienced man of the world. In short, he believes that nobody as an actor was ever more caressed, and his character as a private man (all this, he writes, is between themselves from one brother to another) makes them more desirous of his company.

[1] Frederick Prince of Wales.

34

It took many months to convince Peter that these extraordinary letters told no more than the truth, but as he discovered that, instead of being disgraced by his relationship to an actor, he had become a person of some importance as the brother of the famous David Garrick, his opposition gradually weakened. And then the day came when the household in Lichfield was glad enough to recognize David as its head; it was he who now took the lead in the family affairs, lent Peter money to be repaid at his own convenience and established his not very bright nineteen-year-old brother, George, in a solicitor's office in London.

On his return from Ipswich in the summer, it is said that Garrick had offered his services in turn to the managers of Drury Lane and Covent Garden, but that they turned him away with contempt as a mere strolling player. If this is true, it is the only discouragement that he was ever called upon to endure in a career that from the outset was almost monotonously successful. Yet he never overcame a nervous distrust of his powers, and a fear of being humiliated in public. Thus it seems much more likely that he deliberately made his first London appearance in an out-of-the-way theatre rather than risk the disapproval of a critical west-end audience— one, moreover, that would certainly recognize him. For he did not venture yet to use his own name, but announced himself with simple dishonesty on the programme as 'A Gentleman, who never appeared on any Stage'. Then again, had he persuaded Fleetwood to give him an engagement at Drury Lane, he would only have been given a small part; whereas under his friend's management at Goodman's Fields he had an opportunity to display his gifts to their fullest advantage. These considerations must have weighed with him.

The choice of Richard III could not have been happier. It was the first idea that occurred to him, and, when he talked it over with Macklin, he pointed out that being short he could easily make himself look like the small hunchback king; he was determined never to choose a character that did not suit his physique. If he were to come forward as a hero, he said, or any part that was generally acted by a tall fellow, he would never be offered a larger salary than forty shillings a week. Here he was alluding half-jokingly to the actors' theory that the managers, being incapable of intelligent discrimination, measured a man's merit by his size.

But there were many better reasons than that for his choice. Colley Cibber's version of Shakespeare's *Richard III* had been immensely popular ever since its first performance in 1700. It was the perfect vehicle for Garrick's tumultuous style of acting; the title rôle might have been especially devised for him, and by great good luck had never been other than atrociously badly played since the far-off days of its creator, Burbage.

This play, written while Shakespeare was still under the influence of Marlowe, is so nearly melodrama that it is difficult to present it to a modern audience satisfactorily. The soliloquies, in which King Richard comes forward and tells us frankly that he is a villain, and intends to behave like one, destroy illusion, and his cynical glee at his own wickedness, which once made him appear all the more repellent, seems almost as though the actor is smiling at the absurdity of his part. But perhaps we are unduly influenced by the recollection of the cheap melodrama Cibber's version of Shakespeare's play helped to inspire, and, if only we could forget those ridiculous nineteenth-century plays with their bold, bad baronets and innocent heroines, the character of Richard III would thrill and repel us as much as ever, and we should be better able to appreciate this work of Shakespeare's youthful genius. Oddly enough, the scene that most convinces us is one that meant nothing to an eighteenth-century audience. When Lady Anne, whose husband Richard has murdered, yields to his love-making, her sudden submission was considered too fantastic to merit serious acting, and no actor troubled himself over that scene. Later on in the play her misfortunes served her right, and no one wasted any pity on her. But since then, the power certain types of murderers have over certain types of perfectly virtuous women has become apparent to the readers of newspapers; and when in the winter of 1937 Mr. Emlyn Williams and Miss Angela Baddeley, fresh from their joint performance in a thriller based on that psychological fact, acted the scene together, Lady Anne's brief infatuation for the triumphant villain seemed entirely plausible.

Until Colley Cibber presented his version of the play in 1700, *Richard III* had not been seen on the stage since before the Civil War; since King Charles I and Queen Henrietta Maria witnessed a performance soon after the birth of their second son in 1633. When the theatres reopened, *Richard III* found no place in their repertories; it was too lavishly provided with ghosts and executions for a three hours' entertainment, and too untidily constructed to achieve the unity laid down by the new canons of taste. To remedy these defects, Cibber cut out the scenes he considered irrelevant to the theme, and gave the whole work a rather different shape by inserting scenes and speeches from those of Shakespeare's other historical plays that deal with the same period. His object was to focus interest on the central figure and make him an even greater villain. It never occurred to him that the scenes be omitted—Clarence's dream and Queen Margaret's curse—were among the most poetic in the play, or that one at least of the speeches inter- polated was totally uncharacteristic of the person to whom it was allotted. Had his activities stopped here, no great harm would have been done. But, while treating Shakespeare with rather greater respect than many of the Restoration dramatists who would calmly rewrite whole scenes, he had the impertinence to tinker with his lines. For instance, when Richard wants to know whether his orders to murder the princes have been carried out, he asks: 'Kind Tyrell, am I happy in thy news?' But Cibber wanted to sound a more sinister note, so he changes it to: 'How are the Brats disposed? Say, am I happy?' And whenever he considered that a speech did not give the actor time to register his emotions, he prolonged it with insipid lines that added nothing to their meaning; those he considered too long and involved, he broke up into dialogue to lighten the effect.

This adulteration of the original is in one sense aesthetically justified by making less obvious the Cibberism of the scenes he invented. The vulgarity of these scenes is amazing. After Richard has married Lady Anne, Cibber interpolates a scene in which he tells her that he wishes to be rid of her and soliloquizes thus:

> *Why don't she die?*
> *She must; My interest will not let her live.*
> *They say that women have but tender hearts,*
> *'Tis a mistake I doubt; I've found 'em tough.*

Cibber's *Richard III* contains approximately two thousand lines; of these over half are Cibber's. Yet when Lyttelton told Garrick that he had been born to act what Shakespeare had written he had only seen him in Cibber's play, and Garrick saw nothing incongruous in the tribute. Like the majority of their contemporaries, they valued Shakespeare's plays primarily for their situations and were incapable of discriminating between the genuine and the spurious Shakespearian verse. 'Off with his head! So much for Buckingham!' cried Garrick with a telling look and gesture, and this line of Cibber's became one of the best known of 'Shakespearian' quotations.

> *Hence babbling dreams; you threaten here in vain.*
> *Conscience avaunt! Richard's himself again.*

Garrick's rendering of these lines evoked thunderous applause, and there may be some people still who assume from their familiarity that Shakespeare wrote them.

On paper it is easy enough to see the absurdity of Cibber's bombast, but as pure entertainment Cibber's version was much more effective than the original, and it was not driven from the stage until the end of last century. From 1821 and onwards, actor-managers tried to induce their audiences to accept the play in its original form, but again and again it was rejected in favour of the old blood and thunder entertainment. In the days of star-acting, it gave the leading tragedian a chance to display every kind of emotion possible for a villain—courage, cowardice, hypocrisy, remorse, rage, cynical amusement, horror, despair, and agony. He could go through every kind of stage business; Cibber's Richard stabs and murders, makes love, fights and dies on the stage. It was rich in telling situations, and no amount of bad acting could wholly spoil the enjoyment of the audience.

Having restored a supremely effective character, Cibber could not bear to let anyone but himself play it; although it must have seemed at that time as though it had been created for Sandford, a naturally hunchbacked actor, who specialized in villains of the deepest dye. Cibber used to say that while he was preparing the part he based his acting on that of Sandford. But his audiences could see no resemblance. In his high weak voice, which swelled occasionally to a drawling tone, he intoned the vigorous speeches, and accompanied them with gestures that were described as the 'distorted heavings of an unjointed caterpillar'. And then he minced across the stage with the daintiness that had made his name as the fashionable fop of Restoration comedy. In their irritation audiences sometimes hissed him off the stage; yet, with the unruffled calm that never failed him throughout a lifetime of well-directed insults, he persisted in acting the part until he retired from the stage in 1733. Since then, it had fallen to Quin, whose singsong elocution was no less monotonous than Cibber's for a voice of deeper and fuller quality, and whose action resembled, it was said, the heaving of ballast into the hold of a ship. Although the part belonged primarily to Quin, Ryan occasionally played it at the rival house, and it was, in fact, his performance that Garrick used to watch while familiarizing himself with the play as a whole. But there is no reason to suppose that Ryan's acting differed in style from that of Quin, or that Garrick's rendering of the part was not entirely his own.

The announcement that 'A Gentleman' would appear on the stage for the first time at Goodman's Fields excited little attention. So many amateurs had exposed themselves to ridicule on those boards that on the afternoon of the 19th of October 1741 the door-keeper took no more than £30; and those who sat waiting for the play to begin expected very little, and had come there only to kill time. But from the moment Garrick came on to the stage a thrill ran through the audience. Before he had uttered a word, Richard's evil passions were legible on every feature of Garrick's expressive face; he identified himself with his part as no actor had done within living memory. Indeed, the vehemence with which he threw himself into his part exhausted him, and by the end of the second act he was inaudible from hoarseness. It was only by sucking an orange, runs the story, given him behind the scenes by a sympathetic printer, that he recovered his voice in time to begin the third act. At first the spectators hesitated, puzzled by the startling departure from the accepted style of acting. He had gone through a number of scenes before they broke into loud and enthusiastic shouts of applause. Here was a Richard who set himself so high a standard that he actually went on acting in between his speeches! 'His voice,' notes a slightly later critic, 'is neither whining, bellowing, nor grumbling, but perfectly easy in its transitions, natural in its cadence and beautiful in its elocution. He is not less happy in his mien and gait in which he is neither strutting nor mincing, neither stiff nor slouching. When three or four are on the stage with him, he is attentive to whatever is spoken, and never drops his character when he has finished a speech by either looking contemptuously on an inferior performer, unnecessary spitting, or suffering his eyes to wander through the whole circle of spectators.'[1]

At the age of twenty-four Garrick had leapt to the top of his profession by the success of a single performance. The tragedy was repeated six or seven times, and every evening a string of coaches stretched the whole way from Temple Bar to Goodman's Fields as the playgoing public hurried eastwards to see the wonderful new actor for themselves. On one of those evenings, Garrick experienced his first taste of stage fright. As he came on, made up as a hunchback, he caught sight of a little figure in black, similarly but genuinely misshapen, seated in a side box near the stage, and scrutinizing him with keen, critical eyes. It was the great Mr. Pope, who had emerged from his retirement at Twickenham to compare the new tragedian with his long-cherished memories of Betterton. The eyes of the two men met, and for a few seconds Garrick could not find his voice. But recovering suddenly, his genius reasserted itself and Richard, as he put it, blazed forth. And then, with a thrill of triumph, he saw the poet's frail hands adding to the applause as he turned to make a remark to Lord Orrery. 'That young man never had his equal,' he was saying, 'and he never will have a rival.'

It could hardly be expected that Quin would enjoy a performance that discredited his own style of acting. 'If the young fellow is right,' he said firmly one evening, after the play was over, 'I and the rest of the players have been all wrong,' But instead of the reassurance he longed for, he heard to his disgust of the crowded houses that had applauded the young fellow every evening. 'Garrick is a new religion,' he went about saying to everyone. 'Whitefield was followed for a time; but they will all come to church again.'

Every actor, no matter how gifted, is limited to a certain range of parts by his physical make-up—his face and build, the quality and volume of his speaking voice and his powers of muscular control. Betterton had to make the best of a clumsy, corpulent body and a pair of beady little eyes lost in a broad, pockmarked face; Kemble's classical profile fitted him admirably for tragedy, but no amount of red paint would ever have hidden the nobility of his nose and brow; and Irving's stiff dragging walk and angular gestures made it difficult for him to simulate youth. Garrick was

[1] Quoted by Fitzgerald in his *Life of David Garrick*.

40

2. COVENT GARDEN PIAZZA IN 1768

from an engraving by E. Rooker from a drawing by P. Sandby
in the Print Room, Victoria and Albert Museum

no exception: his short stature (he was five feet four inches according to his own measurements) proved an irritating handicap. Nevertheless, no other English actor of his standing has been better
equipped for his calling. When he held the stage for a prologue or
a soliloquy, his slight build gave the illusion of average height, and
as soon as the action began, he moved about the stage rapidly and
added so much new and ingenious byplay that the audience forgot
to make comparisons. Without being handsome off the stage, his
large well-marked features and compelling black eyes were ideal
for an actor in the days when facial expressions were eagerly
watched, and had to be visible from a stage lit only by candles. His
voice had a pleasant tone and, except for those few occasions when
he shouted himself hoarse, carried well. Every muscle in his lithe
young body was in perfect control, he could fence and dance with
finished skill, and every gesture and attitude had its own apparently
unstudied grace.

Having scored a tremendous success as a tragedian, Garrick
astounded his admirers by descending, as they thought, to comedy;
they were horrified to see him deliberately sacrifice his newly won
dignity for the sake of raising a laugh. But Garrick had great comic
powers that had to find expression whether it affected his prestige
as a tragedian or not, and after the hunchback king came a coxcomb, a lout, a rascally servant, a romantic young lover, a foolish
old husband, a lying soldier, a conceited poet, an aged madman,
and many more, following in a dazzling display of versatility until
it became an open question whether he excelled in comedy or
tragedy.

With a few inevitable failures, Garrick chose his parts well. He
did not always play the principal rôle; sometimes he took one that
seemed unambitiously small. But it would have the flamboyance
necessary to his particular genius. Above all, he needed action and
rapid changes of mood; repose was foreign to his nature. This is
perhaps why his fine gentlemen were not wholly convincing; he
never learnt to assume their air of easy languor, the hallmark of
what was considered good breeding. As Chamont, however, in
Otway's *Orphan*, which he played on November 6th, a dashing
manner suited the part of a spirited young soldier, while his sudden
transitions from rage to calm gave the actor plenty of scope. In this
popular Restoration tragedy, Monimia contracts a secret marriage

with Castalio, who is forestalled on his wedding night by his brother, Polydore. Garrick played the part of the deceived heroine's brother, and his indignant, 'Gape hell, and swallow me to quick damnation if I forgive your house!' shook the spectators to their very souls. The sight of Monimia's humiliation lacerated their feelings no less for the fact, that on another evening, they might be laughing heartily at much the same sort of situation in a comedy.

On December 2nd Garrick ventured for the first time to use his own name. As Lothario, 'the haughty, gallant, gay Lothario', in Rowe's tragedy, *The Fair Penitent,* he fulfilled the feminine ideal of the handsome betrayer of innocence. Garrick made a delightful stage lover, especially when he was not expected to take the matter too seriously; in short, he made a better Lothario or Don Juan than Romeo. *The Fair Penitent* owed some of its popularity to the setting of the last act with its churchyard atmosphere of awe and gloom—the fashionable aesthetic emotion of the day and the first expression of the new romanticism. 'A room is hung with black,' runs the stage direction. 'On one side Lothario's body on a bier; on the other a table, a skull and other bones, a book and a lamp on it.'

On February 3rd as Bayes in the Duke of Buckingham's *Rehearsal,* Garrick challenged comparison with Cibber on his own ground, for the part of the conceited playwright had been one of his best rôles. Since his retirement it had been played by his son, Theophilus, who had contributed some amusing new byplay, but had spoilt his performance by tiresome grimaces. In this play, the first and perhaps cleverest of all back-stage satires, Bayes, the popular playwright, takes two acquaintances, Johnson and Smith, to watch a rehearsal of his new tragedy. The play within a play burlesques heroic tragedy, and is constantly interrupted by the self-satisfied comments of its author, the blunderings of the bewildered players, and the two onlookers, who, like the players, cannot make head or tail of the plot. The interest centres throughout on Bayes, who disconcerts the players by trying ineffectually to coach them, and puzzles Johnson and Smith still more hopelessly by his explanations of the absurdly tangled plot.

Much of the success of the play depended on the ingenuity of the principal comedian in directing the satire at living persons, and with this end in view tradition permitted a certain amount of

42

gagging. Bayes himself was originally aimed at Dryden and, so long as he lived, the actor playing Bayes tried to look as much like him as possible. By Garrick's time, however, Bayes did not differ in appearance from any other stage fop, and Garrick was free to dress as he liked. He came on as a shabby old-fashioned beau with a small hat perched on the top of an enormous periwig of the style worn by an earlier generation. With red-heeled shoes, scarlet stockings and cut-fingered gloves, he gave the impression of a self-important little bore, delighted with himself and unconscious of ridicule. But the climax of the evening came when, in coaching the players, he burlesqued the contemporary style of acting, mimicking in turn various of the leading actors. The justice of his implied criticism was instantly admitted, and the reputation of his victims suffered a serious decline. So serious, indeed, that they came to him and accused him of deliberately trying to ruin them, and, when he saw how many enemies the imitations were making for him, he gave them up and never resumed them.

Although neither Quin nor Cibber ever suffered in this way at Garrick's hands, their jealousy reached laughable dimensions. Cibber obstinately denied that Garrick's Bayes, though good enough in its way, varied at all from that of his son, Theophilus, and he flinched visibly when others praised Garrick's more serious rôles. At last Mrs. Bracegirdle, a celebrated actress of his own generation who had retired from the stage over thirty years before, said to him with the freedom of an old friend, 'Come, come, Cibber, tell me if there is not something like envy in your character of the young gentleman. The actor who pleases everybody must be a man of merit.' The old man took a pinch of snuff and, after a pause, said frankly, 'Why, 'faith, Bracey, I believe you are right. The young fellow *is* clever.'

Meanwhile Garrick was casting about in his mind for a part that would make a fitting climax to his season in the city and would, moreover, ensure a good engagement for the following winter at one or other of the two patent theatres. He thought of King Lear and consulted Macklin, who after some hesitation encouraged him to attempt it. While he was preparing the part and considering how best to simulate madness, an acquaintance of his, who lived a few doors away from the theatre, obligingly gave him a demonstration of the genuine state. This man was

43

leaning out of his dining-room window holding his two-year-old child in his arms, when she accidentally slipped from his grasp. The little girl's body was dashed to pieces on the flagged area below, and the unfortunate man went out of his senses with shock. He lived on in the same house with two keepers, and Garrick often dropped in to see him on his way to the theatre. He watched him as he dandled an imaginary child out of the very same window, appeared to drop it and then burst into terrible shrieks of anguish. In after years Garrick often gave a realistic imitation of his friend's agony for the after-dinner entertainment of a room full of his admirers. 'Thus it was,' he would say as he brought the demonstration to an end, 'that I learned to imitate madness.'

Yet in spite of his friend's timely though involuntary help, his first rendering of King Lear on the 11th of March 1742 did not wholly satisfy either himself or Macklin. His clothes were appropriate enough, as Macklin told him after the performance, but he did not move like a feeble old man of over eighty; he lacked the dignity of a king, and by misplacing his cadences lost the full effect of certain speeches. Garrick took the criticism very well; he admitted its truth and declared that he would not appear in that part again until he had thoroughly revised it. But he had forgotten that the tragedy was already advertised for the following week, and he was bound to fulfil his obligation to the public. The next time he played rather worse, finding it difficult, he said, to get rid of his old habits in so short a time. Then it was laid aside for some weeks.

In April the tragedy was announced again. Macklin begged hard to be admitted to the final rehearsal, but Garrick firmly refused to let him in. It would be too late to correct mistakes, he said, and the knowledge of them would only add to his nervousness and might spoil his performance on the night. But he need not have had any misgivings; when the time came Macklin had nothing but extravagant praise, and ever afterwards, however bitter his feelings towards Garrick as a private individual, he spoke of that night with rapture. He used to describe how the young actor transformed himself into a little old man with spindle shanks and tottered across the stage, looking about him with the dim eyes of old age; how when he uttered the curse, the audience shrank with horror, and how the pathos of his scene with Cordelia drew tears from the whole house. 'In short,' added Macklin complacently, taking a good deal of the credit to himself for his valuable advice, 'the little dog made it a *chef d'œuvre*, and a *chef d'œuvre* it continued to the end of his life.'

Once more Garrick had won fame as a Shakespearian actor, and once more the part as he played it would probably have been disowned indignantly by Shakespeare. For it was not the *King Lear* we know, but a Restoration version by Nahum Tate with a happy ending, almost entirely rewritten in the worst possible blank verse. In it the King regains his throne and his sanity, the wicked sisters die of poison, and Cordelia and Edgar, who have been in love with each other since the beginning of the play, marry and live happily ever afterwards. The Fool is omitted altogether as incongruous and disturbing to the balance of the play. No adaptation of Shakespeare has been more abused than this one; yet an eighteenth-century audience could never have endured the horror of the original play, the text of which was familiar only to students of literature. Tate's version was as much as they could bear, for we read that Garrick's performance was held up at times by open sobs and weeping. When Johnson read Shakespeare's *King Lear* for the first time, Cordelia's death so shocked him that he could not bring himself to re-read the last scenes until his duty as an editor forced him to study them. Even Lamb, coming many years later, while censuring Tate for tampering with so great a work of art, gave it as his opinion that Shakespeare's *King Lear* could not be represented on a stage. Tate's version reduced the play to the comfortable dimensions of a melodrama, with an entertainment value nearly equal to that of Cibber's *Richard III*. In spite of its weaknesses, it held the stage until Macready restored the play in its original form in 1838. By then, several editions of Shakespeare's works were in circulation, and familiarity with the text of *King Lear* reconciled audiences to the inevitable tragedy of its theme.

The season came to an end in May when all the London theatres put up their shutters for the summer. In seven months Garrick had played over eighteen different characters, a feat that seems astonishing now for a beginner, but one that passed without comment in the days of repertory, when plays were less carefully rehearsed and when actors were accustomed to rely on the inspiration of the moment for their effects. Giffard began by giving him six or seven pounds a week, and the salary appeared so munificent to Garrick that on his first payday he actually refused to take it. In the course of a friendly squabble, the coins fell to the ground, and Giffard's young son settled the dispute by grabbing them and running from the room. Then, as weeks went by, it became increasingly clear that the public came only to see Garrick, for on the nights he did not act the company played to empty houses. Garrick protested no more, and when his friend offered him a half-share of the profits he accepted it quietly. Henceforth, he fully recognized his 'box-office' value.

With all London discussing the merits of the wonderful new actor in the east end, Covent Garden and Drury Lane were poorly attended. Sinking their rivalry in the face of common danger, the two managers exerted their influence with the authorities, and succeeded in forcing Giffard to close down his theatre, while Garrick was engaged for the following season at Drury Lane for the sum of five hundred guineas—a record salary for an actor. As a sort of rehearsal for his first appearance in the west end, Garrick acted three times at Drury Lane during the last weeks of the season. He chose for those nights the rôles he considered his most important achievements—Bayes, King Lear, and Richard III.

The chorus of praise that greeted Garrick's acting becomes monotonous from constant repetition. Of the playgoing public Horace Walpole and Thomas Gray were among the very few who remained scornfully aloof; they failed to perceive in it an expression of the new romanticism, a revolution in taste which they were themselves helping to bring about in other mediums of art. 'Did I tell you about Mr. Garrick that the town are horn mad after?' wrote Gray to a friend. 'There are a dozen dukes of a night at Goodman's Fields sometimes; yet I am stiff in the opposition.' Walpole, equally unsympathetic, refers to 'the young wine merchant turned player at Goodman's Fields.' He saw nothing wonderful in his acting.

Samuel Johnson saw nothing wonderful either. He never had and never would. But then he did not recognize acting as an art at all. An actor, as he once explained, was a fellow who clapped a hump on his back and a lump on his leg and cried, 'I am Richard the Third.' Davy, he would have admitted, did it rather more convincingly than anyone else, but Johnson, as an intellectual, was constantly irritated by mistakes in elocution that passed unnoticed by audiences who were far too much engrossed with the action to consider the exact meaning of a line. 'The players, sir,' said Johnson to Giffard, as they sat with Garrick in a tavern one evening after the performance, 'have got a kind of rant with which they run on, without regard either to accent or emphasis.' The two actors indignantly contradicted him. 'Well now,' continued Johnson, 'I'll give you something to speak, with which you are little acquainted—then we shall see how just my observation is. Let me hear you repeat the ninth commandment, "Thou shalt not bear false witness against thy neighbor".' Each in turn made the same mistake, emphasizing the words 'false witness', instead of 'not', and Johnson scored as usual.

CHAPTER IV

PEG WOFFINGTON

1742 – 1745

G ARRICK had fallen in love. During his last winter as an unsuccessful vintner, while he was haunting the green-rooms stage-
struck and discontented, he had seen the rise of a new actress. She
had come over from Dublin, and her name was Margaret Woffington. She owed her success as much to her warm and generous
personality as to her acting, and a quick temper and sharp tongue
added rather than detracted from her popularity behind the scenes.
In short, apart from a certain crudeness of outlook and conversation, she really did resemble the heroine of Charles Reade's romantic biography. The face in her portraits, like those of many
of that date, has features too large and irregular to appeal to the
modern eye; nevertheless, her contemporaries admired her, and
the young wine merchant was only one among many who fell
head over heels in love with her.

Although she attempted all kinds of parts, she shone most in
comedy; her abounding vitality and outstandingly beautiful figure
marked her out particularly for rôles that involved dressing up as
a boy. Breeches parts, as they were called, originally written for
the boys who took the place of actresses before the Restoration,
had acquired fresh interest since the introduction of women on
the stage. Not only was it amusing to see a woman impersonating
a man, but it provided an excuse for the display of well-shaped
legs—a daring novelty, and the nearest approach to nudity on the
stage an eighteenth-century audience was permitted to enjoy. For
no matter what rôle, whether Egyptian queen or negro slave,

actresses never discarded the contemporary wide skirt. Turbans or a headdress of feathers constituted their only disguise. Peg Woffington as Sylvia, the heroine in *The Recruiting Officer* who masquerades as Jack Wilful, was incomparable; such exuberance had not been seen on the stage since the death of Nell Gwynn.

But a male impersonator with her gifts did not remain content with mere breeches parts. Her next London success was Sir Harry Wildair in Farquhar's *Constant Couple*, a male part throughout, and so long as she lived to play it, no actor, not excluding Garrick himself, could satisfy an audience in that rôle. Only her love-making was considered insipid. 'I have played the part so often,' she once said laughingly, 'that half the house believes me to be a real man.' 'By God, madam, if they do,' retorted Quin, 'the other half knows you to be a woman.'[1] It was an insulting remark, but there is no evidence that she resented it. Peg Woffington had had many lovers, and long since ceased to care who knew it.

She had risen from a Dublin gutter to the top of her profession by her own unaided efforts, and such a feat would have been impossible had she not lived with the same freedom as a man. From the age of two she had contributed to the family earnings. In about 1716 a French tight-rope dancer, a Mme Violante, was performing in Dublin. The high-spot of the evening came when she walked across the rope, a basket tied to each foot and a baby in each basket. Little Peg Woffington peeped out from one of those baskets. At six years old she lost her father, a bricklayer by trade, and her mother found herself in debt with two children to support. Mrs. Woffington took to selling watercress in the streets, carrying Polly, the new baby, in her arms; while Peg, ragged and bare-footed, ran by her side calling their wares in her small harsh voice. Years passed, and Peg grew up into an intelligent, bright-eyed little girl. One day as she was fetching some water from the Liffey for her mother, a foreign lady noticed her and spoke to her. By an odd coincidence it was Mme Violante again, who had come back to Dublin with the idea of forming a company of child actors, whom she intended to call the Lilliputians. This lively urchin seemed promising material, and Mme Violante had no difficulty in enrolling her. Peg showed unmistakable talent, and despite her unmusical voice was chosen to play the part of Macheath in

[1] The remark has also been ascribed to Kitty Clive.

a children's performance of *The Beggar's Opera*. The moment she was tall enough she began playing grown-up parts, and by 1737 she had become one of the leading actresses in Dublin. Three years later, at the age of twenty-six, she decided to try her fortune in London.

As soon as she arrived there, she went straight to see John Rich, the famous Harlequin and manager of Covent Garden theatre. Ever since she could remember, Peg Woffington had heard of the man who had first produced *The Beggar's Opera;* he must be, she thought, the greatest manager in the world. And he thought as much himself, for it was at this stage of his career that he refused to see anyone under the rank of a baronet—or so the story ran. At any rate, he was inaccessible to Peg Woffington, and she had already been refused admittance eighteen times when she forced her way into his room. Then an extraordinary scene met her eyes. There was the great man lying on a sofa, in a startling state of undress, holding the manuscript of a play in one hand and a cup of tea in the other. Around him were seven and twenty cats of all sizes, colours and kinds—tortoiseshell, tabby, black, white, and yellow. Some were frisking over the floor, others lay asleep on the rug; one was licking the buttered toast on his breakfast plate, another was lapping up the cream out of a jug; two cats lay curled up on his knees, one was asleep on his shoulder and another sat demurely on his head. Peg was too much astounded to speak. Rich in his turn was equally confused by her beauty, and lay there staring at her for a long time before he pulled himself together sufficiently to offer her a chair. 'It was a fortunate thing for my wife,' he said long afterwards, 'that I was not of a susceptible temperament.' But before the interview ended, Peg Woffington was engaged for the season.

A year later, having earned her right to a larger salary than Rich was willing to pay her, she transferred herself to Drury Lane. Thus it was that when Garrick appeared there in May 1742 he found himself playing Lear to Peg Woffington's Cordelia. By then his admiration for her was common talk, and when the season came to an end it surprised no one to hear that they had left for Dublin together. They had accepted an engagement to act at the new theatre in Smock Alley for the rest of the summer.

The Dublin of that day was a city of contrasts; of wealth and poverty, of gaiety and misery. Magnificent public buildings and large private mansions stood within a stone's throw of slums so filthy that problems of overcrowding were solved by frequent outbreaks of typhus. 'I never knew before what the beggars in England did with their cast-off clothes,' remarked Samuel Foote after a visit to Dublin. And while ragged scarecrows roamed the streets in hundreds, some of them actually mad with hunger, the Anglo-Irish nobility and gentry vied with each other in the splendour of their establishments. A brilliant social life centred round the Castle, where the Lord Lieutenant held a miniature court and upheld the dignity of the English Crown. Entertainments of every kind flourished and the theatres ranked second only to those of London. There was no dearth of natural talent, for the Irish are born actors, but the theatrical season reached its height in June and July when the stars of the London stage were free to accept summer engagements in Dublin.

The theatre in Smock Alley was ill-placed in a miserable little lane down by the river, yet it was larger and better-built than the so-called Theatre Royal in Aungier Street just behind the Castle. The two theatres competed fiercely against each other, and it was after a brief season of Quin and Mrs. Cibber at Aungier Street that Garrick and Peg Woffington were engaged for Smock Alley as a counter-demonstration of talent.

At twenty-seven, Mrs. Cibber was better known in Dublin as a singer than as an actress. Before her marriage into a theatrical family had turned her thoughts to the stage, both she and her brother, Tom Arne, had supported themselves by their musical gifts—he as the leader of Drury Lane orchestra, and she as an opera singer. Handel had written the contralto airs in *The Messiah* especially for her, and consequently when the great composer accepted an invitation to Dublin in December 1741, to conduct the first performance of his oratorio, Mrs. Cibber came over to take part in it. Her singing lacked musicianship, but she declaimed the long recitatives with an effectiveness she owed to the dramatic training of her father-in-law, Colley Cibber. Handel's music, which in London provided no more than a background for fashionable chatter, found here a deeply appreciative audience. 'Woman, for this be all thy sins forgiven thee,' exclaimed a clergyman from the fullness of his heart as the last strains of Mrs. Cibber's voice died

away. Poor Mrs. Cibber! the only sin she ever committed—of the
kind the clergyman probably had in mind—was to leave Theophilus, a dissipated little cad of a man, for the protection of a Mr.
Sloper, to whom she remained faithful, so far as is known, for the
rest of her life. Yet because she lived with him openly nineteenth-
century writers usually describe her as morally 'frail'.

By the time Garrick and Peg Woffington arrived in Dublin,
Handel had given his last concert, Quin had gone back to England
and Dublin was ready for a new sensation. Peg Woffington's old
friends gave her a warm welcome, and Garrick played many of
his London parts with his usual success. His nickname of Roscius
dates from this summer, and, in commemoration of his visit, the
epidemic that swept through Dublin and cost many hundreds of
its half-starved inhabitants their lives was whimsically called the
Garrick Fever.

At last after an exhausting summer they were free to follow
their own desires for a while. Peg Woffington stayed on in Dublin
to see her old mother and arrange for her clever young sister's
education, while Garrick travelled back to London with Mrs. Cibber and her brother, Tom Arne. When they met again it was at a
house in Bow Street, where Macklin and Peg Woffington had inde-
pendently taken lodgings for the winter. Garrick spent much of
his time with his two Irish friends, and it was assumed that the
three of them were sharing one home between them. But his relationship with Peg Woffington never brought him any real happiness,
for in private life he was the very reverse of the Lothario he could
play convincingly enough on the stage. He had no desire for casual
sexual adventures; he was looking for a woman with whom he
could share the rest of his life, and he could not make up his mind
whether or not he had found her. He was deeply in love with Peg
Woffington and at one moment actually bought the wedding ring.
But would she, he wondered, ever change her way of living for
him or for anyone else? She seemed to be without any moral sense
at all. When Lord Darnley arrived unexpectedly at her lodgings,
and noticed Garrick's scratch wig lying on her dressing-table, the
young nobleman reproached her for having deceived him. With
perfect composure, she assured him that she had been wearing the
wig herself while rehearsing a new breeches part. She scolded him
for having suspected her, and succeeded in extracting an apology.

The next morning she told Macklin and Garrick what had happened, and they all laughed heartily together at her visitor's simplicity in believing her.

Garrick was much too cautious ever to take that wedding ring out of his pocket, but he could not give her up altogether, and he persuaded her to set up house with him in Southampton Street. They agreed to take turns in paying the household bills. It was a fatal experiment. Their ideas of what it was reasonable to spend on food and drink differed hopelessly. Peg Woffington, during her month of housekeeping, entertained on a lavish scale, and not unnaturally felt aggrieved when Garrick in his turn, with two or three times her income, cut down the expenditure to the minimum. Johnson sat with them one evening while Garrick scolded Peg for making the tea too strong; for tea was then an expensive drink. 'Why it is as red as blood!' he exclaimed irritably. Johnson never forgot this incident, but he knew too much of Garrick's early life not to make allowances for what looked like meanness in a man who was earning nearly a thousand a year. 'He had then begun to feel money in his purse,' Johnson used to say as he told the story, 'and he did not know when he should have enough of it.' Moreover, Garrick came from a home where every penny mattered, and economizing had become second nature to him; he had no wish to live other than simply himself, and never could understand the pleasure his stage friends derived from throwing away money unnecessarily.

It was the one unforgivable sin in an actor, especially a successful one, and henceforth his back-stage popularity waned. Macklin began to complain that Garrick did not even pay his share of the day's expenses; that whenever they rode out to Richmond for dinner, Garrick found either that he had changed his breeches that morning,' or would pull out a thirty-six-shilling piece which could not be changed. It is impossible to believe such a story, but it passed from mouth to mouth with many others like it, and whenever anyone wanted to score off him in public, he would allude in some way to Garrick's alleged meanness. For instance, Fielding, after dining at Garrick's lodgings, left the customary tip for the servant wrapped up in paper. It proved to be no more than a penny. When Garrick remonstrated with him the next day for playing such a trick on a servant, Fielding replied that he had

53

given it with the best motives. Had he given the man half a crown, he said, his master would have appropriated it; whereas he now had a *chance* of keeping it for himself.

In his first season as a salaried actor at Drury Lane, Garrick played thirteen characters, three of which were new to London audiences. He had already acted Hamlet in Dublin, and in December he played the part again at Drury Lane. What version he used then in these early years before he revised the play himself is not very clear. It was probably an acting copy of the original, mutilated and slightly corrupt, without being actually rewritten. All we know is that, unlike his predecessors, he left out 'all that would offend a modest ear', and came on without being 'attended by music'. His start of terror on seeing the Ghost became one of his great moments, and attracted more notice than his interpretations of Hamlet's complex character. Fielding immortalized it in *Tom Jones* when he describes the effect of Garrick's acting on the unsophisticated Partridge. When the Ghost makes his entrance, Partridge sees only an absurdly dressed actor, but Garrick's display of terror at the apparition startles the simple-minded countryman out of his senses, and convinces him that the figure is supernatural. He falls into such a violent fit of trembling that his knees knock against each other. Bewildered by Garrick's naturalism, he forgets that he is only watching a play and becomes thoroughly muddled. '*He* the best player!' cries Partridge, with a sneer as his friends praise Garrick. 'Why I could act as well as he myself. I am sure if I had seen a ghost, I should have looked in the very same manner and done just as he did. Indeed, though I was never at a play in London, yet I have seen acting before in the country; and the King for my money; he speaks all his words distinctly, half as loud again as the other. Anybody may see *he* is an actor.'

Until the present century, no artist in any medium could earn higher praise than to be told he was copying nature with the utmost exactness. Yet every artist has always had his own idiom, his own deliberate deviations from truth, which passed undetected until the various mechanical methods of reproduction exposed him. So far as acting is concerned, we have only to see an early film to realize how easily we ourselves have accepted certain conventions which a decade or two later seem ridiculous. Even so, it is difficult to believe that Garrick's acting with its extravagant byplay could

ever have been mistaken for realism; as we see it, the modern
naturalistic technique only dates from the middle of the nineteenth
century, when high tragedy and broad comedy gave way to the
Robertsonian school of drama—the drama that purports to hold
up a mirror to life. And only then did it become desirable. Over-
emphasis was essential in order to evoke the emotional response
demanded by the parts Garrick played, and the subtleties of the
modern stage production would have been lost on a dimly lit
stage. Garrick did not set out to imitate the reactions of the man
in the street. 'If you act only according to your own standard,' he
said, 'or indeed according to the most natural model that exists,
you will never be more than mediocre.' Yet when Johnson complained that Garrick over-acted, we find that only those who had a
personal grievance against Garrick agreed with him. As an intellectual, Johnson received his impressions primarily through the
printed word; neither speech nor music could move him. Moreover, his defective eyesight prevented him from seeing the faces
of the actors clearly. Consequently, when he watched Garrick act,
he noticed what others, more sensitive to his art, failed to perceive.
'The action of all players in tragedy is bad,' he said in later life.
'It should be a man's study to repress those signs of emotion and
passion, as they are called.' Boswell, shocked at the heterodox
opinion, asked him whether he disagreed with Fielding in thinking
Garrick's terror at the sight of the Ghost extraordinarily realistic.
'Would not you, sir, start as Mr. Garrick does if you saw a ghost?' 'I
hope not,' replied Dr. Johnson. 'If I did, I should frighten the
ghost.'

As it happens, we have an exact description written by a contemporary of what it was that Garrick did to express terror, and,
although seriously intended, it reads like burlesque. 'Hamlet appears in black,' wrote Lichtenberg.[1] 'Horatio and Marcellus are
with him, in uniform; they are expecting the Ghost. Hamlet's arms
are folded, and his hat overshadows his eyes: the theatre is darkened.
Suddenly, as Hamlet retires somewhat farther from the front to
the left, turning his back upon the audience, Horatio starts,
exclaiming, 'Look, my lord, it comes!'" pointing to the right, where
the Ghost is seen standing motionless. At these words Garrick

[1] George Lichtenberg, a German professor who visited England in 1770 and
1775.

turns suddenly about, at the same instant starting with trembling knees two or three steps backwards; his hat falls off; his arms, especially the left, are extended straight out, the left hand as high as his head, the right arm is more bent, and the hand lower, the fingers are spread far apart; and the mouth open; thus he stands, one foot far advanced before the other, in a graceful attitude, as if petrified, supported by his friends who fear that he will fall to the ground.'

Garrick always enjoyed showing his public how rapidly and completely he could change his stage character: on one night he would appear as a heroic figure, and on the next a low comedian, parts so contrasting that it was difficult to believe that the same actor could have taken both of them. 'You are in your element when you are begrimed with dirt, or up to your elbow in blood,' remarked Hogarth, after seeing him first as Abel Drugger and then as Richard III. He played Abel Drugger in Ben Jonson's *Alchemist* for the first time in March 1743, and his witty rendering of this small part gave Jonson's satire a new lease of life. As he put on the tousled wig and crumpled smock his whole being merged into the part of the foolish tobacconist, and those who came expecting to see a romantic actor were disillusioned when a dirty little fellow shambled on to the stage. Among them was the legendary young lady who fell in love with him as Chamont, and was immediately cured of her infatuation when she saw him the next night as Drugger. But this story, which may have inspired Robertson's comedy, *David Garrick*, although by no means incredible, savours strongly of the nineteenth century when it first found its way into print. Personal glamour in the modern sense was unknown before stage lighting and make-up were elaborated, and a man who acted by candlelight depended on his merits, not on his sex appeal, for his popularity. Garrick, deservedly more admired for his acting than any Englishman before or since his time, was never pursued by lovesick women.

Much the best of these stories, and one that Johnson liked to tell, is that of the Lichfield grocer, who came up to London with a letter of introduction from Peter Garrick to his brother. He arrived late in the afternoon and, seeing Garrick's name on the bills outside Drury Lane Theatre, went straight in and sat down in the two-shilling gallery. The play for the evening was *The*

3. PEG WOFFINGTON

*from a mezzotint by J. Faber from a painting by E. Haytley
in the Print Room, British Museum*

Alchemist, and the grocer waited in great excitement to see his fellow-townsman who had become a famous actor. But when Abel Drugger came on to the stage, the grocer was puzzled; like Partridge, he confused the actor with his part and could not believe that the mean little man was Garrick, until the comments of those round him convinced him of the truth. In his disgust he went back to Lichfield without bothering to call on the actor at all. As soon as he got home, Peter Garrick naturally wanted to know how Davy had received him and how the tradesman had liked Davy's acting. The man looked embarrassed, and tried to avoid giving a direct answer. Finally, he admitted that he had never delivered the letter. 'Not deliver my letter!' cried the astonished Peter. 'How did that happen?' 'Why, the fact is, my dear friend,' replied the other, 'I saw enough of him on the stage to make that unnecessary. He may be rich, as I daresay any man who lives like him must be; but, by God, though he is your brother, Mr. Garrick, he is one of the shabbiest, meanest, most pitiful hounds I ever saw in the whole course of my life.'

By the terms of his contract, Garrick was entitled to a salary of six hundred guineas and the profits of two evenings' performances. He played to full houses, and all would have been well under any other management. But Fleetwood, after losing most of his inheritance at dice and cards, had bought the Drury Lane patent with what was left of it, and was now gambling with his theatrical assets. He knew nothing whatever about the stage, and relied on Macklin to choose the plays and cast the parts, while he disported himself at White's Chocolate-house, where his distinguished air excited the most gratifying interest even in those to whom he owed considerable sums of money. His powers of fascination were quite extraordinary: when he wanted to borrow money, he looked so embarrassed, so distressed, so boyish, that only those who had seen the performance many times before could refuse him what he asked for. Sick and tired of waiting for his salary to be paid, Garrick called on him early one Sunday morning fully intending to say that he was about to sue him for debt. Never was the manager's company more delightful nor his manners more entrancing than that morning, and Garrick could not bring himself to mention the sordid subject of money at all.

Fleetwood's debts were accumulating. Bailiffs took possession of the theatre, and even the stage properties were sometimes seized for the payment of a debt. It was only by the zeal of his personal servant that Garrick kept the jewelled hat he wore as Richard III. 'You must not take that. It belongs to the King,' and the bailiffs, awed by the man's tone of voice into thinking that he referred to King George II, reluctantly gave it back. In May 1743 Macklin and Garrick decided to organize a strike, and eight of the company followed their lead in staying away from the theatre. At Garrick's invitation they met at his lodgings and signed an agreement to stand by each other until their grievances were settled. Garrick's idea was to put the facts before the Lord Chamberlain, and apply for a licence to act plays in a theatre of their own. He felt confident that the Duke of Grafton would not allow them to be ill-treated. But when the day of the interview came, the Duke received the actors with unexpected coldness. He asked Garrick the amount of his salary, and received the cautious answer of five hundred pounds. His Grace was astonished to hear that a man, merely by acting, could earn as much as that. Why, his own son, he remarked severely, the heir to his title and estates, risked his life for his King and country for less than half that sum. He refused to listen to another word, and from that moment the actors knew that they were beaten.

September found the rebels without work, and in some instances without money to live on. There was nothing for it but to go to Drury Lane and eat humble pie. Fleetwood offered to take back all but one of the actors; some he would re-engage on the same terms; others at half their previous salary. He bore Garrick no ill will; on the contrary, he offered him an extra hundred guineas a year to come back. But in no circumstances whatever would he allow Macklin inside the theatre. He accused him of treachery and ingratitude, and nothing would induce him to have anything more to do with him. Those were his terms; they could take them or leave them. But the actors had agreed to stand by each other, and Macklin had no intention of allowing them to forget it. They met again and again, and could not reach a decision. Garrick did all he could to pacify Fleetwood. He offered to play for a hundred guineas less than his original salary if Fleetwood would reinstate Macklin. The offer was refused. Garrick urged Macklin to take pity on the distresses of their fellow-actors, and to release them from their promises. Fleetwood would recover his temper in time. In the meantime Garrick had persuaded Rich to offer Mrs. Macklin an engagement at three pounds a week, and he would himself add six pounds a week from his own salary until he could effect a reconciliation. If Macklin's friends did not think that enough, he was willing to pay more. Macklin refused to listen. He held Garrick to his word, and reminded him how they had planned, if all else failed, to set off for Ireland and act over there. When rumours of this scheme reached the other actors, they were in despair. They knew that without Garrick their chances of being forgiven were negligible. They wrote a pathetically worded letter to him, begging him not to sacrifice them to a personal quarrel between Macklin and Fleetwood, and reminding him that he was bound in honour to them as much as to Macklin. What was Garrick to do? To stand by the agreement would have been heroic, but it would have meant a serious setback to his career, brought ruin to others, and would not even have benefited Macklin. He wavered, and finally went over to the enemy.

Macklin was furious. With help from his newspaper friends, he wrote a pamphlet describing the quarrel from his point of view, and arranged for its publication on the day of Garrick's reappearance. He filled the gallery and pit with his supporters, and when Garrick came on, cries of 'Off! Off!' greeted him from every part of the house. Rotten eggs and apples drove him to the back of the stage. He bowed very low, and with humble submission expected from an actor, begged for a hearing. But it was useless; he was forced to withdraw.

The rioters did not enjoy their triumph for long. Fleetwood may have known nothing about theatrical management, but this was a situation he could handle. For the following evening, he hired thirty prizefighters, armed them with sticks, and distributed them through the theatre. As the orchestra played the last notes of the overture, the leader of the gang stood up and called for silence. In a voice that reached every corner of the house, he announced that certain persons, he had reason to believe, meant to interrupt the play. He had come to hear it. He had paid money to hear it. Would all those who had come to make a disturbance leave the theatre at once? Boos and hisses disclosed the whereabouts of the Macklinites, and without waiting for a better excuse, the prizefighters fell on them and threw them out into the street.

After that Garrick was left to act in peace. The next day the public read his vindication of himself in the form of a pamphlet written for him by one of his friends on the staff of *The Gentleman's Magazine*. Its moderate tone compared well with the abuse of Macklin's reply which followed a week later. Garrick's 'treachery', his 'mean disposition', the 'vanity and dirtiness of his temper' are only some of the epithets Macklin hurled at him in print, and their extravagance lost him the sympathy of his readers. It was in conversation that Macklin succeeded in getting his own back. His after-dinner stories of Garrick's greed and miserliness delighted all those who resented equally Garrick's large salary and his reluctance to squander it. The legend, once established, swelled to fantastic dimensions, until it is difficult now to decide how much of it was based on fact and how much was invented or inspired by Macklin.

Garrick chose Macbeth for his first new part that season, and when Quin read in the newspapers that the play was to be given 'as written by Shakespeare', he was puzzled. 'What does he mean?' he asked. 'Don't I play Macbeth as written by Shakespeare?' And it came as a surprise to many besides Quin that the *Macbeth* to which they were accustomed was not Shakespeare's but a Restoration version by Sir William Davenant. He had rewritten many of the scenes, and, with some lively singing by three comic Witches and dancing by the Furies, the play was almost as diverting as an opera. Since 1671 this entertainment had given perfect satisfaction, and the newspapers could not see why any change need be made. At this Garrick took fright. The slightest murmur of disapproval was enough to shake his self-confidence. Without waiting to give his experiment a chance to justify itself, he wrote a satirical pamphlet directed against himself, and published it anonymously. Its purpose was to expose the folly of those who did not admire his acting; and he hoped that, by taking the words out of the mouths of his critics, he would silence them and bring about a reaction in his favour. Henceforth he adopted this tortuous device as part of his technique in building up his reputation with the public.

After all this, it is sad to record that when he made his long-promised appearance as Macbeth on the 7th of January 1744, the play was not exactly as written by Shakespeare. He allowed the Witches and Furies to sing and dance as before, and although he kept more or less to the original text, he omitted a few of the scenes, 'judiciously pruned' others, and wherever he considered Shakespeare's meaning obscure added explanatory passages. Worst of all, he wrote a long dying speech for himself so that he could go through all those long-drawn-out agonies his public expected of him. But these were small lapses of taste compared with the outrages perpetrated by Davenant. The essence of the drama remained. Hitherto it had been said that the interest of the play was exhausted after the second act; once the murder was committed, the audience had soon tired of hearing Quin monotonously intone Macbeth's agony of mind. But instead of the pompous villain that had droned through Davenant's version, Garrick gave what was, for his period, a sensitive interpretation of a complex personality. At first, in his effort to show the doubt and remorse that tortured Macbeth, he only succeeded in looking dejected, but after an unknown correspondent pointed out that this gave an impression of cowardice he modified his performance.

As usual, it was where rapid changes of facial expression were needed that he earned most applause. His start on seeing the visionary dagger was accompanied by an extraordinary sense of real seeing in his face, which seemed to whiten and grow haggard as he looked. Nothing like it had been experienced before. Earlier in the season at Covent Garden Quin had made that moment ridiculous by clutching at the air, first with one hand and then with the other, and kicking out his legs convulsively at the same time—like a drowning man struggling to reach the surface. Garrick's sincerity of acting affected even those on the stage with him. When he said to the murderer in the banquet scene, 'There's blood upon thy face,' the actor was so taken aback by the intensity of his look that he put his hand up to his face and cried involuntarily, 'Is there, by God?'

But Macbeth is not a solo part like Richard or Lear. In spite of scoring a personal success, Garrick felt the lack of adequate support from the actress taking the part of Lady Macbeth, and the play did not really grip its audiences that winter as it did four years later when he acted it again with the more competent Mrs. Pritchard. With Mrs. Cibber in retirement and Mrs. Pritchard at

61

Covent Garden, Garrick had to make the best of Mrs. Giffard, an indifferent tragedy actress, but the best that Drury Lane could boast that year. On the comedy side, Peg Woffington was as lively a leading lady as Garrick could wish for, fully equal to Kitty Clive who rivalled her at Covent Garden, but it would have been better for her reputation had she not good-naturedly accepted any part, tragic or comic, large or small, allotted to her. With a voice that earned her the description of the screech owl of tragedy, she should never have been given the part of Ophelia when they came to act *Hamlet*. It must have been a painful performance.

In the autumn of 1744 Garrick's gift for simulating drunkenness found full scope in the part of Sir John Brute in Vanbrugh's *Provok'd Wife,* and it became one of his favourite comedy rôles. At first it seemed likely—particularly to the burly Quin, whose interpretation it challenged—that his physique would handicap him. 'He may possibly act Master Jacky Brute,' said Quin, 'but he cannot possibly be Sir John Brute.' He was wrong, and, although there remained some who preferred Quin's drink-sodden boor, most people preferred Garrick's more subtle rendering of a gentleman coarsened by drink and debauchery.

'In the beginning, he wears his wig straight,' wrote a spectator of much later date, 'and one sees the full, round face. Afterwards, when he comes home quite drunk, his face looks like the moon of a few days before the last quarter, nearly half of it being obscured by the wig. The part which one does see is flushed and greasy, yet it is extremely friendly, and thus makes up for the loss of the other half. . . . He enters his wife's room, and to her anxious inquiry what is the matter with him, replies "As sound as a roach, wife." Yet he does not stir from the doorpost, against which he leans as heavily as if he wanted to rub his back on it. He then becomes in turn brutal, tipsily wise, and again friendly, all to the loud applause of the audience. In the scene where he falls asleep he amazed me. The way in which, with closed eyes, swimming head, and pallid face, he quarrels with his wife, and melting his r's and l's into one—into a sort of dialect of medials—now abuses, now falters out scraps of morality; then the way in which he moves his lips, so that one cannot tell whether he is chewing, or tasting something, or speaking—all this as much exceeded my expectation as anything else I have seen this remarkable man do. I wish you could hear him say "pre-ro-ga-tive" in this part. It is only after two or three efforts that he is able to get as far as the third syllable.'

Peg Woffington played Ophelia again this season—unnecessarily bad casting, as the company had been strengthened by the addition of Mrs. Cibber, who afterwards proved herself one of the best Ophelias the stage has ever seen. With her sweet low voice, her gentle manner, her slender figure and naturally sad face, she suited the part to perfection. It is quite likely, however, that Garrick had never seen her in tragedy; some years had elapsed since she had left the stage to live with Mr. Sloper, and her brief career was remembered more for her quarrel with Kitty Clive over the part of Polly in *The Beggar's Opera* than for her few successes in tragedy. At first, Garrick felt dubious of her powers; her intoning, which she owed to the training of her father-in-law, Colley Cibber, was distasteful to him, and when he agreed to act with her in Shakespeare's *King John* it was because he had no other choice. 'Don't tell me, Mr. Garrick,' Quin said indignantly when Garrick confided his misgivings to him. 'That woman has a heart, and can do anything where passion is required.' And Quin was right; she played the part of Constance with great emotion, and her sing-song elocution was forgiven her for the passionate sincerity with which she portrayed a mother's grief. When she sank on the ground, her hair dishevelled and her eyes wild with distress, a burst of applause came from the audience. Even Garrick was outshone that evening.

King John was never a lucky play for Garrick. When he took the title rôle, he found it almost impossible to enlist sympathy for a coward. John's personality lacked the grandeur expected of a villain, and when the time came for him to die, the audience heartily despised him, and even Garrick's magnificently horrible death agonies excited little pity. When, in subsequent productions, he attempted to play Faulconbridge, his size was hopelessly against him. No matter how spirited his acting, he was too small to give the impression of virility and exuberance. As a play, moreover, *King John* was too loosely constructed for eighteenth-century taste. Its interest does not centre round the fortunes of its hero but shifts from one character to another; Faulconbridge, Arthur and Constance in turn steal the play. For such popularity as it enjoyed, it depended partly on the poignant scenes that lead up to the murder of a lovable child and the frenzied grief of his mother and partly on the relevance of its main theme to contemporary politics.

Colley Cibber was the first to notice the significance of the history of King John's struggle against papal interference at a time when the Protestant throne of England was endangered by the claims of a Roman Catholic Pretender. But Shakespeare, he thought, in rewriting *The Troublesome Reign,* should not have toned down the anti-Catholic bias of the original play, and Cibber set himself the task of reconstructing the tragedy from the same source, helping himself freely to Shakespeare's ideas and expressing them in his own feeble verse. The result was a much more serious mutilation of Shakespeare than his *Richard III,* which at least had the merit of being dramatically effective.

In 1736 he offered his version, which he called *Papal Tyranny in the Reign of King John,* to Fleetwood, as manager of Drury Lane, but as soon as it became known that old Colley had forced his way into tragedy again, his enemies set up such a howl of indignation that, with uncharacteristic timidity, he withdrew the play while still in rehearsal. By this time the merits of Shakespeare's play, which had lain neglected since 1598, were much more generally recognized, and Rich decided to revive it. A few months later it was performed several times at Covent Garden. But Cibber still preferred his own version, and in 1745, on the eve of the rebellion, he brought out the manuscript again. Taking it this time to Rich, he persuaded him to put the play in rehearsal at Covent Garden. Fleetwood, or more probably Garrick in his name, promptly retaliated by announcing Shakespeare's play for the same week, arguing ingeniously that since the *Papal Tyranny* according to its author was not an alteration of *King John,* but a new tragedy on the same theme, there could be nothing malicious in his choice. Thus it was that playgoers had the opportunity of comparing the two versions before rejecting *Papal Tyranny* once for all in favour of Shakespeare's *King John.*

Besides pitting his strength against Shakespeare as a dramatist, Cibber emerged from his retirement to demonstrate the superiority of the old school of acting—and with as little success. He coached the whole company in what an eyewitness describes as 'the good old manner of singing and quavering out their tragic notes', and, despite his great age and the loss of all his teeth, insisted on

64

mumbling through the part of the Papal Legate himself. 'He affected a stately magnificent tread,' says Tom Davis, 'a supercilious aspect with lofty and extravagant action, which he displayed by waving up and down a roll of parchment in his hand.' For all his cardinal's robe and tragedy voice, his performance was only a variant of his old coxcomb part. At Drury Lane the part, to be sure, was not much better played by Macklin (for Macklin, just as Garrick had foreseen, had slipped back into his old place) and perhaps, as Quin said, he really did look like a cardinal who had very recently been the parish clerk. But at least the audience could hear and follow the sense of what he said. Quin's wooden rendering of King John compared badly with that of Garrick, and Theophilus Cibber, as the Dauphin, received all the hisses and catcalls the audience spared his seventy-four-year-old father. In short, Mrs. Pritchard as Constance, who failed 'to tone her words' to Colley Cibber's satisfaction, was the only member of the cast to gain any applause at all.

Garrick's failure as Othello in March 1745 is generally put down to his humiliation at the laugh that greeted his first entry. To the traditional army officer's scarlet tunic and blackened face, he had the unfortunate idea of adding a high oriental turban with an upstanding plume. He must have hoped that the headdress would add some inches to his height. It was just at this time that Hogarth's series of pictures, *The Harlot's Progress,* were at the height of their popularity, and the scene where the heroine upsets the breakfast table just as a little negro page, in a laced coat and an enormous turban, is bringing in the tea kettle, must have been familiar in reproductions to everyone in the house. Garrick, in his make-up as Othello, bore a fatal resemblance to the boy, and when Quin remarked to his neighbour in an all too audible voice, 'Here's Pompey—but where is the tea kettle?' the laugh that echoed through the theatre destroyed Garrick's confidence in that part for ever. So the story runs. But it could not have been the only reason for his failure; the audience always laughed at that point of the play, for every Othello played by a white man with a blackened face looked, and still looks, to some extent incongruous. Quin in the part wore a large powdered bag wig, which with his black face reminded the audience of a magpie. He strutted on with great dignity, wearing a pair of white gloves, which he drew off slowly and ostentatiously in order to reveal to the fascinated audience a pair of coal-black hands.

It is hard enough for any actor to command respect with a blackened face; to Garrick, who depended on facial expression for nearly all his best effects, it was a particularly serious handicap. But had Othello been a white man, it is doubtful whether even then the part would have been within his scope. Versatile as he was, his range in tragedy had its limits. Anger, horror, despair, physical suffering and madness he could simulate with genius, but when the theme turned on jealousy or any other form of sexual emotion, his insincerity betrayed itself in the over-violence of his gestures. On the whole, he chose his parts with great skill. But *Othello*, more or less as written by Shakespeare, was a favourite stock piece in the Drury Lane repertoire, and it may be that it was almost impossible for him to refuse the title rôle. After two performances in 1745, and one more in 1746, he sensed the general disapproval and London never saw him as Othello again.

During his visit to Dublin in 1742, Garrick had made friends with Thomas Sheridan, a young man not long down from Trinity College, whose enthusiasm for the stage equalled his own. Ever since his victories in undergraduate debates, when he had experienced the thrill of swaying the emotions of an audience by his gift for rhetoric, Sheridan had hankered for the applause of a larger world. Correct elocution and a clear understanding of the dramatist's meaning were his only qualifications for the stage career on which he had set his heart. In January 1743, he made his first appearance in the ever-popular part of Richard III on the stage of Smock Alley Theatre. His voice carried badly and his facial expressions were those of an orator rather than a character actor. Yet he declaimed well in the old formal style, and his complacent delight in his own performance communicated itself to the audience. Many other parts followed, both tragic and comic, and, strange to relate, he was accepted at his own valuation.

Garrick showed no sign of jealousy when he heard of Sheridan's success. On the contrary, he invited him over for the summer and suggested that they should act together at Drury Lane the following winter. He even went so far as to offer him the choice of any parts usually played by himself. But Sheridan refused to come; he was afraid, he wrote, that they would clash in their choice of characters, and that for this reason they could not be in the same house. Richard, Hamlet and Lear were his own favourite characters, no less than Garrick's. But he had a scheme to propose—one that he realized might seem at first a little extraordinary: if Garrick would divide his immortality with him, they might like Castor and Pollux appear always in different hemispheres; in plain English, what did he think of dividing the kingdoms between them? Garrick to play one winter in London and another in Dublin. Considering that Sheridan at this time had made only a few appearances in a small Dublin theatre, while Garrick reigned supreme in London with two years' hard work behind him, it is not surprising that Sheridan's ingenuous suggestion fell on deaf ears. But eighteen months later he reconsidered Garrick's offer, and in the autumn of 1744 we find him at Drury Lane, playing many of Garrick's most successful rôles alternately with him.

Peg Woffington left Garrick that winter and went to live with her young sister, Polly, at Teddington. They still met now and then, but her infidelities had nearly exhausted his patience, and now that he had found his ideal stage partner in Mrs. Cibber, he felt less in need of her. Yet her company had not lost all its charm for him, and he was ready enough to visit Sheridan at his lodgings in Kingston for the pleasure of meeting her among the Irish exiles who enjoyed their fellow-countryman's lavish hospitality. When Polly Woffington's future came under discussion, Garrick went to some trouble to discover whether she had any talent for acting; for Peg had always intended her sister for the stage. He rehearsed her in the part of Hermione in *The Distrest Mother,* taking Orestes himself, and, with the help of a few friends, gave a private performance of the play in a neighbouring barn. Polly was enchantingly pretty, even more so than her sister, but her deficiencies as an actress were made glaringly apparent by the performance of a little girl from Dublin. At the age of fourteen[1] George Anne Bellamy was already playing the lead with the elderly Quin at Covent Garden, and Garrick could not help noticing how much more in earnest she was than Polly. After one appearance as Cherry in *The Beaux Stratagem* on her sister's benefit night at the end of the season, Polly gave up all thoughts of the stage, and nothing more

[1] In her autobiography, George Anne Bellamy gives the date of her birth as 1733, but her contemporaries believed her to be two or three years older.

is heard of her until she married Horace Walpole's nephew and blossomed into the delightful Mrs. Cholmondeley, whose confident criticisms on contemporary literature were the amusement of Dr. Johnson and the admiration of her fellow-Blue Stockings.

The final break between Garrick and Peg Woffington came some time that winter. Exactly what they quarrelled about no one can say. He may have tired of sharing her with other men and she, in her turn, may have become jealous of Mrs. Cibber, with whom he much preferred to act. Neither of them ever gave any explanation. Caricatures of the scene, unsympathetic to Garrick, found their way into the print shops and ridiculous stories went the rounds of the coffee-houses. It was rumoured that when they returned their presents Garrick, mean to the last, kept back a valuable pair of diamond buckles and, although Peg Woffington wrote and asked for their return, refused to give them up. Garrick said nothing; he tore up her letters, and so long as he lived no one dared in his presence to make the slightest reference to his association with her.

On the strength of some playfully affectionate letters from Mrs. Cibber to Garrick at the time of the quarrel, it has been assumed that she supplanted Mrs. Woffington in his affections. But no one seriously believed them to be lovers at the time,[1] and the survival of these letters is one of many reasons why they should not be interpreted too literally. They formed part of the large collection discovered by Garrick's executors, and the care with which he preserved only those letters that show him in a favourable light suggests that they were intended as material for a biography. We learn nothing from them of his love-affair with Peg Woffington, and in view of his long and ideally happy married life, it is unlikely that he would have kept Mrs. Cibber's letters had he realized that they

[1] In the interests of historical accuracy, however, the following undated letter from Lord Rochford must be quoted: 'How agreeably you surprise me in telling me we shall see you and Mrs. Cibber together, but how will Woff relish that, or to speak more properly how will you relish it, for I believe the other party can wean herself much easier than you can or I have no skill in woman's flesh; but don't play me and blab now. . . . I have heard you say you have a retentive quality or else I should not venture to speak my mind.' This letter is open to more than one interpretation. Garrick had evidently written to say he and Mrs. Cibber would be seen together. Did he mean on the stage, and did Lord Rochford misunderstand him? Or did he mean in private life? The answer is anyone's guess, for there is nothing more to go on.

compromised him. He probably saw in them only an interesting reminder of their perplexities when Fleetwood finally came to grief and sold the patent of Drury Lane in 1745.

Garrick fell ill in the April of that year, and it took him the rest of the summer to recover his normal health. He went from one watering-place to another, not sorry, perhaps, of an excuse to be away from the theatre at a time of quarrelling and confusion. The patent had passed into the hands of two bankers who then divided it into three shares, offering one to the stage manager of Covent Garden, an Irishman called James Lacy, on condition that he left Rich's employ and took over the management of Drury Lane. If he could not produce the purchase money at once he would be permitted to pay it gradually out of his share of the profits. Lacy accepted these terms and installed himself at Drury Lane. But he could not get the actors to work smoothly under him and as the summer wore on it seemed as though the company would break up in disorder. 'I hear,' wrote Mrs. Cibber to Garrick in July from the country house she shared with Mr. Sloper, 'we are both to be turned out of Drury Lane Playhouse to breathe our faithful souls out where we please. In this melancholy situation, what think you of setting up as a strolling company? Had you given me timely notice of your going to Buxton, I am sure the landlord of the Hall Place would have lent us a barn, and I don't doubt but we could have picked up some odd pence: and when Lacy found we could get our bread without him, it might possibly have altered these terrifying resolutions. But joking apart, I long till you come that we can consult together: don't let the charms of Buxton make you break your word; and since I am to be plundered, you need not grudge the expense you put me to in victuals and drink.' But he did not come, and in the autumn she wrote to him again, still anxious to see him and discuss various schemes that were running through her head. By then the Pretender had landed in Scotland, and the unsettled condition of the country deepened their sense of insecurity. But so far, she told him, the theatres had been as full as ever. Would he join with Quin and herself in getting together a new company? She felt confident that by offering to take no more than their usual salaries, and to give the rest of the profits to the Government, they would, in this time of national stress, be given a licence for fifty or sixty nights at least. When Garrick failed to take any interest in this most impractical scheme, she thought of another. But it was one she could not prudently put down on paper. She had reason to believe that Lacy was ready to dispose of his share of the patent. She wondered whether Garrick would join with her in buying it. But before she had an opportunity to talk it over with him, she heard to her astonishment that he had left the country. He had accepted an offer to act in Dublin for the whole of the winter season.

CHAPTER V

THE SALARIED ACTOR

1745 – 1747

GARRICK was at Bath with Colonel Wyndham when Sheridan's letter arrived. He opened it with mixed feelings, for they had parted coldly. Sheridan wrote without any pretence of cordiality. Garrick, he heard, had expressed a wish to pay a second visit to Ireland, and as he now controlled the Dublin stage, he was in a position to invite Garrick to act under his management. He offered him half of the profits made on all the performances in which Garrick took part. He told him frankly that he must expect nothing from his friendship, for he owed him none, but that he would have every privilege a good actor could reasonably expect. 'This is the oddest epistle I ever read in my life,' remarked Garrick as he handed it to Colonel Wyndham to read. 'It may be an odd one,' replied the other, after looking it through, 'but it is surely an honest one. I should certainly depend upon a man that treated me with that openness and simplicity of heart.' Garrick agreed; and, sending a note to Mrs. Cibber to let her know his decision, set off immediately for Dublin. As soon as he arrived, he went to see Sheridan who repeated his offer of sharing the profits. Garrick would have preferred a sum down, but when he said as much, Sheridan took out his watch and gave him five minutes to make up his mind. Garrick had no alternative but to give in.

In company, Sheridan never appeared to advantage. 'Why, sir, Sherry is dull, naturally dull,' Johnson used to say of him in later life, 'but it must have taken him a great deal of pains to become what we now see him. Such an excess of stupidity, sir, is not in

71

nature.' But Sheridan was no fool, whatever Johnson might say. He took over the two Dublin theatres at a time when lack of discipline had brought them to the verge of ruin, and formed one company which performed sometimes in Aungier Street and sometimes in Smock Alley. Within a few months the reputation of the Dublin stage stood higher than ever before. He insisted on proper rehearsals, conducting them himself, paying meticulous attention to every detail; he raised the actors' salaries and saw to it that they were punctually paid, and as soon as the higher standard of performances brought fuller houses, he laid out money judiciously in scenery and dresses. He had already engaged several actors and actresses of outstanding merit when Garrick arrived in November, and the season opened well with Otway's *Orphan* in which the youthful George Anne Bellamy took the lead with Sheridan as Chamont and Spranger Barry as Castalio.

At this time Barry was a newcomer to the stage, and had never yet appeared out of Dublin. Like Garrick and Sheridan, he had made his name overnight on the strength of a single performance, and it was already obvious that a great career lay ahead of him. As soon as Garrick saw him act, he wrote home to his friends telling them that this young Irishman was the best lover he had ever seen on the stage. Tall and handsome, with a voice that could melt an audience to tears, Barry outshone Garrick as Othello, and Garrick after two more attempts that season surrendered the part to him for ever.

On the whole, the three young actors worked smoothly together; Sheridan, as manager, allowed Garrick to appear alternately with him in the parts that each of them considered particularly his own, and in *Othello* took it in turns to play Iago so that Barry could triumph in the title rôle. The only friction recorded of that season occurred between Garrick and little Miss Bellamy, who flew into a temper at his refusal to play King John to her Constance. He thought that at her age she would do better as Prince Arthur, and Mrs. Furnival, an experienced tragedy actress, seemed to him the obvious choice for Constance. But although she behaved very spitefully Garrick refused to quarrel with her, and when the time came for planning his benefit night, he asked her to play the lead with him as though nothing had happened. He wrote to her in a foolish mood, promising her 'a goody goody epilogue, which with the help

72

4. DAVID GARRICK AS RICHARD III

from an engraving by W. Hogarth and C. Grignion from a painting by W. Hogarth in the Print Room, British Museum

of your eyes will do more mischief than ever the flesh or the devil has done since the world began.' He addressed it facetiously 'To my soul's idol, the beautiful Ophelia.' By an accident, in which George Anne in her memoirs professes to have had no hand, the letter with its strange direction fell into the hands of a journalist, and to Garrick's mortification appeared the next day in the Dublin newspapers.

Garrick had no reason to regret his bargain with Sheridan; he made a large sum of money and found himself with as great a following as before. His only rebuff came from Lord Chesterfield, the new Lord Lieutenant, who deliberately ignored him although they had met often enough in London society, and instead signalled out Sheridan for his favours. It was Sheridan, not Garrick, whom he received affably at the Castle; and on the night of Garrick's benefit, when the two actors ceremoniously lighted him to his box, he spoke very kindly to Sheridan in view of the audience but did not even acknowledge Garrick's bow. It seems unnecessary now to look far for any explanation of his ungraciousness; we know how both Sheridan and Johnson were to suffer from his capriciousness as a patron. But at the time it was suggested that Lord Chesterfield was trying to show the Irish that his sympathies were exclusively for them. Only a few months later Gilbert Walmesley was chatting with him in the Coffee-house at Bath and he greatly pleased Garrick's old friend by saying that while he did not care for Garrick's comedy, he considered him the best tragedian the stage had ever seen. Garrick received a full account of the conversation in Walmesley's next letter, and, feeling mollified, he put the document away carefully among his other tributes.

By the time Garrick arrived home in May, the Rebellion had been crushed, and London was waking up from a nightmare. Drury Lane, deserted by its public, had been on the verge of closing down; for three weeks the manager had been unable to pay any salaries, and Mrs. Cibber resolutely refused to act at all in such miserable circumstances. John Rich at Covent Garden had done a little better, but when confidence suddenly returned at the end of the season, he was quicker than Lacy in taking advantage of the cheerful mood that brought people flocking to places of amusement. It was over a year since London playgoers had seen their favourite actor and, without Garrick, Quin, and Mrs. Cibber, the theatres that winter had not given a single performance of any real merit. Covent Garden had already closed down for the summer when Rich approached Garrick with an offer of half the profits if he would appear in six leading rôles of his own choice. Garrick accepted, and he and Rich made three hundred pounds apiece.

Rich pocketed the money gladly enough, but he would rather have made it in almost any other way. He heartily disliked all straight actors; the better they acted the more he affected to despise them. Like his father, Christopher Rich, before him, he concentrated his attention on the light entertainment that brought the evening to an end, and regarded the full-length play as hardly more than a necessary evil. Authors calling on him for his verdict on their plays would be shown a mountain of obviously unread manuscripts, and invited either to find and take back their own or to accept any other in exchange. The inventor of a new device for his pantomime, on the other hand, could be sure of his closest attention, with the result that in workmanship and design English stage machines were the best in Europe. Thirty years had gone by since he had first presented an entertainment in dumb show, introducing the stock characters from the Italian Comedy of Arts, and playing Harlequin himself under the name of Lun. From this evolved the earliest form of English pantomime and, whether the intellectuals approved of it or not, there were few London playgoers who did not thoroughly enjoy it.

Sure of his own public, Rich could afford to look down on the more serious art of straight acting; and actors in their turn resented an attitude of superiority from a man whose lack of culture could hardly be distinguished from illiteracy. His mispronunciations of words and proper names were too fantastic not to have been partly deliberate. He made a practice of calling his actors by a mangled version of their correct names, which irritated them beyond endurance. Samuel Foote, maddened by being habitually addressed as 'Muster Footseye' asked him sharply why he did not call him by his name. 'Don't be angry,' said Rich. 'I sometimes forget my own name.' 'That is extraordinary indeed,' remarked Foote. 'I knew you could not write your own name, but I wonder you should forget it.' But Footseye he remained, just as Garrick had to answer to 'Muster Griskin' whether he liked it or not. 'No, you are unfit for the stage,' said Rich to a beginner, 'and I won't larn you.' Another he advised to lay the 'empharsis' on the 'adjutant' and referred to a turban as a 'turbot'. It is probable that his hatred of actors had its origin in his conviction that he alone knew how to act tragedy, and his resentment at the barely concealed laughter of those who heard him attempting to declaim. 'You should see me as Richard III,' he said to a young man, and proceeded to give an extraordinary demonstration of how not to act. In general, however, he left the production of plays to his leading actor, and his honesty in carrying out his side of a contract, which in those days was often only verbal, went some way towards reconciling the company to the crudeness of his manners. In the summer of 1746 he had to admit that Londoners had tired of light opera; a revival of interest in acting was already well on the way. Putting his personal preferences aside for the moment, he secured Garrick's services for the coming season, and, with Quin, Mrs. Cibber, Mrs. Pritchard, Ryan, Hippisley, and Woodward, Covent Garden opened one of the most brilliant seasons in the history of that theatre.

The rivalry throughout the winter between Quin and Garrick, the two leading exponents of the formal and the naturalistic styles of acting, aroused all the interest of a modern sporting event. It could not have been easy for them to act in the same theatre, but with good sense and good temper they came to a friendly understanding on the parts each was to play. The season opened with an ignominious defeat for Quin, when he recklessly chose to appear as Richard III. The audience barely tolerated him, and greeted Garrick eleven days later in the same part with tumultuous applause. As Cato and Sir John Brute, Quin recovered some ground, but Garrick kept the lead with his renderings of King Lear, Hamlet, and Bayes. Then came that tremendous evening when they appeared together in Rowe's *Fair Penitent*, Quin as the noble Horatio and Garrick as the gay Lothario. At first it seemed as though Quin would have the advantage, for not only was he representing the cause of virtue against vice but his technique harmonized with that of the rest of the cast. Mrs. Pritchard, it is true, inclined towards the naturalistic, but her part was a small one, and both Ryan as Altamont and Mrs. Cibber as the heroine sang out their lines in the good old way. The curtain rose and Quin, a stout, elderly figure, immensely dignified in his full-bottomed wig and embroidered velvet coat, began rolling out his heroics with a few mechanical ges-

75

tures to Ryan who chanted back in reply. Meanwhile a schoolboy in the audience sat waiting impatiently for his first sight of Garrick. At last, 'I beheld little Garrick,' relates Richard Cumberland in his memoirs, 'young and light and alive in every muscle and every feature, come bounding on the stage—heavens, what a transition!— it seemed as if a whole century had been stepped over in the transition of a single scene.' In the second act the old and the new met on the stage for the first time, and during the applause that held up the action of the play for several minutes, the two actors looked equally embarrassed. 'Faith, I believe Quin was as much frightened as myself,' remarked Garrick after the ordeal was over, but Quin's pride prevented him from ever making any allusion to his feelings that evening. And now Quin's slow utterance and long pauses began to irritate a section of the audience. When Garrick as Lothario challenged him, Quin, instead of accepting it promptly with the line 'I'll meet thee there,' waited so long that a man in the gallery had time to call out, 'Why don't you tell the gentleman whether you will meet him or not?' Yet there were still many who liked to hear moral sentiments in blank verse formally declaimed, and Cumberland recalls that in the dialogue between Horatio and Lothario, Quin, as the champion of purity, received much louder applause than Garrick.

In Shakespeare's *Henry IV*, it was Quin's acting that dominated the evening. His Falstaff has never been bettered, for the part was a projection of his own robust personality. Garrick, on the other hand, as Hotspur, was physically incapable of giving the impression of a fiery, rough-mannered soldier, and the illness that obliged him after five performances to give up the part released him from a humiliating position. A month later, the tables were turned when they appeared together in Rowe's pseudo-Shakespearian tragedy, *Jane Shore*. Both played villains, but Garrick as Hastings had all the action. He made dishonourable love and assaulted the heroine, leapt all over the stage in the course of an exciting duel, and, after many heartrending speeches in verse that reads to-day like a burlesque of Shakespeare, allowed himself to be carried to the scaffold; whereas Quin as Gloster, in what he used to call one of his whisker parts, had little to do but strut up and down, breathing malevolence—an emasculated Richard III.

With two successful farces to his credit, Garrick was already established as a playwright when on the 17th of January 1747 Rich allowed him to present *Miss in her Teens*. Both plot and characters are frankly derivative but, as usual, he took the stage personalities of certain well-known actors and actresses and blended them into a play—the tastiest of all recipes for a contemporary palate. Captain Flash suited Woodward to perfection, and when he swaggered on, saying 'Look at me now, miss, what do you think of me now, damme,' the audience looked at his handsome figure and wondered how any woman could resist him. Mrs. Pritchard, buxom and spirited, and Hippisley, who specialized in amorous dotards, were equally well served, and for himself Garrick chose the ever-popular part of a coxcomb. As the overdressed, effeminate Fribble, wearing a tiny hat to accentuate his littleness (a character unblushingly lifted from Baker's *Tunbridge Walks*), he filled Covent Garden night after night, and the five-act play that came earlier in the evening received no more attention than the curtain-raiser of a later age. Quin, finding that the audience hardly listened to him, refused to act again in the same programme, swearing that he would not 'hold up the tail of any farce'; with the result that he found himself unemployed for four or five weeks.

It has become a platitude to remark on the trashiness of the plays made famous by the great actors of stage history; given situations in which the actors can display their own particular accomplishments, the audience is easily satisfied. Dr. Hoadley's *Suspicious Husband,* performed for the first time in February 1747, reads badly and is unlikely ever to be revived; yet it ranked as one of the best comedies written in Garrick's lifetime, and Ranger, the honest young rake, was added to his repertory of characters. Foolish misunderstandings and disguises, eloping couples and endless entrances and exits through a window (enough, it was said, for a pantomime) make up the plot; and Ranger's crude advances to three young women, as he mistakes the character of each in turn, provide its rather smutty humour. His essential good nature and loyalty to his friends gradually reveal themselves to the audience, and virtue triumphs as usual. The play was repeated sixteen times that season, and for the rest of the century kept its place among the stock plays of both theatres.

The season came to an end, bringing Rich the very considerable profit of £8,500. Yet far from being pleased, he seemed disgusted with the success of his actors, and would have preferred, it was said, to see them play to empty benches so that he could humiliate them by bringing out a new pantomime and filling the theatre himself. Sometimes he would peep through the curtain at the crowded house and mutter angrily, 'What, are you there? Well, much good may it do you!' and then, going into the green-room among the actors, the old man would vent his spite against Garrick by getting down on his knees and repeating Lear's curse to his daughters in a silly burlesque of his manner. He made no attempt to engage Garrick for the next season; on the contrary, he seemed uncommonly glad to be rid of him.

As it happened, he could not have done Garrick a better service; since he left him free in the spring of 1747 to consider Lacy's offer of a half-share in the management of Drury Lane. For some time past, ever since Lacy's backers had declared themselves ready to sell their controlling shares of the patent, Garrick had been hesitating over various suggestions for raising the money and forming a new management. For Drury Lane, in spite of Lacy's heroic efforts to coax back its patrons, was in a desperate way. To compensate himself for Garrick's desertion, he had brought over Spranger Barry from Dublin and, with Macklin, Yates, Kitty Clive, Peg Woffington, Mrs. Furnival, and the Giffards, had formed a good, though rather ill-balanced, company. In October Barry made an excellent impression as Othello; his rich Irish voice and splendid figure gave the part a new glamour, and for the first time Desdemona's love for a Moor seemed credible. But in less romantic parts his acting lacked subtlety; and Drury Lane suffered another disastrous season.

Meanwhile Lacy had managed to scrape an acquaintance with the Duke of Grafton, the Lord Chamberlain, who promised him a renewal of the patent at its expiration in 1753. This concession Lacy secured, it is said, by riding close to him in the hunting-field with a supply of 'elegant and savoury refreshment', which he offered at suitable moments. Whether or not the story is true, he certainly extracted the promise, which made it impractical to exclude him from the ownership of the existing patent. But without Garrick no scheme could prosper; the two men were equally indispensable to Drury Lane. Putting his pride into his pocket, Lacy wrote to Garrick and laid the situation before him. Would Garrick, he suggested, join with him, buy out his two partners and share the management of the theatre? After talking it over with two City friends, Garrick accepted the offer, and his thrifty habits are justified when we find that at the age of thirty, after five years as an actor, he was somehow able to raise £8,000 for his share of the new management. Lacy, on the strength of the Duke's promise, contributed only half that sum. The two men agreed to draw £500 a year each in their capacities as managers, and in addition Garrick, as leading actor, claimed his usual salary of £500 with a clear benefit. They arranged to divide the work in such a way that their duties would not overlap. Garrick was to have the chief say in all that concerned the production of plays, while Lacy, assisted by Garrick's younger brother, George, would take charge of the accounts and the practical details of the management. On the 9th of April 1747 the agreement was signed, and in the autumn the greatest of all actor-managers began his career.

CHAPTER VI

THE MANAGER

1747

COMPARED with Covent Garden, Drury Lane in 1747 was shabby and out of date. Seventy-three years had passed since Sir Christopher Wren had designed it (the second of the four buildings that have stood on the site of the present theatre in Drury Lane), and during that time Vanbrugh had built a magnificent opera house in the Haymarket, which in its turn had inspired the architect of Covent Garden. Drury Lane had changed very little from the 'plain built House' described by Dryden in his prologue for its opening night in 1674. His reference, half satirical, half apologetic, to a 'mean, ungilded Stage' was directed at those who might compare it unfavourably with the much more richly decorated interior of Wren's earlier theatre in Dorset Garden, then the home of the rival patent company. After that gilded proscenium arch, ornamented with formal designs and Grinling Gibbon's voluptuously carved figures, a stage framed by Corinthian pillars and severely classical entablature might appear a little prosaic. Nevertheless, Drury Lane marked an advance in the new art of theatre planning, and its acoustics, the weakness in all early theatres, seem to have been fairly good.

The original design resembled the Elizabethan rather than the modern theatre in that the stage extended seventeen feet beyond the proscenium arch, which to-day serves as a picture-frame for the actors. Thus the stage, built with an incline from front to back, had two sections: the area that stretched back fifteen feet behind the proscenium arch and which was hidden from the audience by

80

the fall of the curtain; and the front stage, or 'apron', which was flanked on each side by a pair of doors, set obliquely to the audience. The four proscenium doors served as places of entrance and exit for the actors, who stood well forward so that their voices carried to every part of the theatre. The back stage held the scenery, which was treated as a tableau to illustrate the action of the play rather than as an integral part of it; for although a character might be 'discovered' there in a garden on the rise of the curtain or the opening of a shutter, he invariably came forward to speak his lines. By Garrick's time, however, the apron had been shortened by four feet in order to enlarge the pit, and the two proscenium doors nearest the audience had been converted into stage boxes. In consequence, the actors, driven back at least ten feet, found it much more difficult to make themselves heard; with bad acoustics, and incorrigibly noisy audiences, it is not surprising that Garrick and his contemporaries often shouted themselves hoarse.

The stage of Drury Lane, then, had been modernized but the rest of the house was unchanged. The pit with its fixed benches sloped upwards, and enclosing it in the form of an ellipse were two tiers of boxes. A top gallery faced the stage, but was not carried round the sides. The auditorium, like the stage, remained evenly lit throughout the course of the play. Candles, arranged at intervals along the edges of the galleries, flickered over a restless, chattering crowd; for human beings in mass, whether in church, concert hall or theatre did not learn to keep absolutely quiet until, with the introduction of gas, the lowering of lights hushed them into good behaviour. Much of the actors' technique at this time, moreover, can be traced to the exigencies of candlelight. The apron was comparatively well lit by chandeliers hanging from the roof, by wall brackets and by the footlights, which consisted of a row of unshaded candles. But the back stage had no lighting of its own, and it was to get into what was a little later called the focus that actors stepped out of the picture-frame on to the apron. The candles once lit at the beginning of each act remained so for all its scenes, and thus, suspended in the midst of a moonlit grove, a dark forest, or a street at midnight, were always, inevitably, those six chandeliers in the foreground.

Scenery consisted of little else than paint and canvas: a painted backcloth and three side wings or flats created an illusion of garden, street or even the interior of a room. For the box set had not yet been invented, and the problem of imparting a third dimension to seven flat pieces of canvas inspired all those wonderful feats of perspective that distinguish the pictorial art of this period. The scenic artist, moreover, had to provide the actors with much of the stage property; real objects, not actually handled in the course of the play, and even 'extras'—angry crowds or soldiers in battle—made their only appearance in paint. Scene-shifting took place in view of the spectators, since the curtain, which rose after the prologue, often remained drawn through the five acts. Its rise and fall had no dramatic significance until the illuminated picture-frame stage came into its own. To clear the stage at the end of an act, corpses were carried off and the surviving characters audibly recalled pressing engagements elsewhere.

Players wore what they fancied, regardless of the general effect. Actresses, concerned only to look their best, invariably wore contemporary dress of the richest quality they could procure, with a few modifications symbolic of their rôles. Thus a tragic queen or empress called for a black velvet dress and a plumed headdress, and in eastern plays an elegant turban transported the audience to Turkey, Egypt, or Asia. Another thirty years were to elapse before Mrs. Siddons appeared on the stage correctly dressed for her part. Actors, on the other hand, made occasional half-hearted attempts to achieve historical and geographical accuracy, and they generally satisfied their audiences however ridiculous their clothes may appear to us in their portraits. All fancy dress inevitably reflects the contemporary mode, but it is not until that mode is itself out of date that its influence becomes apparent. The subjects of Queen Anne saw nothing incongruous in the full-bottomed wig worn with breast-plate and helmet by Booth as a noble Roman, but Quin, carrying on the tradition unthinkingly, looked absurd to a younger generation; by then a tie-wig seemed the natural and necessary covering for the human head. Fixed on to his wig or helmet, the stage Coriolanus or Brutus sported two or three towering feathers, the tragic hero's insignia since the early days of the Restoration. For near-Eastern and Asiatic parts alike, the actor assumed a composite disguise—an Indian turban, a loose robe like a dressing-gown edged with fur, an Arabian sash, Turkish trousers, Russian boots and perhaps a curved scimitar—and no tiresome pedant raised any objections. Illustrated books of travel had yet to be published, and no one could have distinguished between a Turk and a Chinaman by his dress any more certainly than he could have visualized that of a medieval English nobleman. So it seemed safest in Shakespeare's historical plays to wear ordinary up-to-date clothes—with the exception of certain characters, such as Falstaff, Henry VIII and Richard III, who, surrounded by figures in mid-eighteenth-century costume, were themselves more or less correctly dressed.

The interpretation of a rôle, no less than the clothes that went with it, was in every detail the player's responsibility. The manager or leading actor conducted the rehearsals and made sure that the players were word perfect, but he left everything else to their discretion. All that an early eighteenth-century actor asked of his fellows was that they should give him his cues, keep out of his way and not distract the attention of the audience during his speeches. Stage production, as we know it, did not exist, and it was no one's concern if Kitty Clive chose to nod to her friends between her speeches, or if Garrick fidgeted with his buttons in the less important scenes in *Macbeth*. It is questionable whether, could we transport ourselves back through the centuries, the individual genius of the principal actors would compensate us for the raggedness of the general effect. Each actor competed against the others for the attention of the spectators, who came not so much to spend an evening in a new and imaginary world or to consider the literary purpose of the dramatist—for every line of the play would be familiar to them—as to criticize the technique of the actor. An actor who displeased his audience was soon drowned in catcalls and driven from the stage; the more fortunate were applauded after every telling speech. At the end of the century Mrs. Siddons was finding it more tiring to act in the country, for in London the bursts of applause that frequently interrupted her acting gave her time to rest. Each rôle was thus considered as a solo performance, and the more physically unsuited to the performer the more merit in a successful rendering. An audience would rather see a vigorous young man take the part of King Lear than an elderly man; it ranked as a greater achievement. And when Quin and Mrs. Pritchard, two mature, barrel-shaped figures, intoned in

piteous accents, 'Two unhappy orphans, alas, we are!' the excellence
of their elocution brought home to the audience the pathos of
their situation and protected them from laughter.

The performance began at six, but the audience could not have
left the theatre much before half-past ten. The play lasted three
hours; after it, came an interlude of songs, dances, or recitations,
and then a farce or a pantomime brought the evening to a close.
For all this, the spectators paid from one to five shillings apiece,
and a full house brought in a little over two hundred pounds. The
doors opened at five and no seats were reserved; at the end of the
first act the doorkeeper went round taking the money, and between
the third and fourth acts he made a second tour, charging newcomers half-price.

The arrangements for each season followed a recognized pattern.
The theatre opened in September for three performances a week,
and throughout that month the manager presented new members
of his company to the public in plays of established popularity. As
the season wore on, the weekly performances increased to six,
novelties were cautiously introduced, until January and February
—the best months for new plays—marked the climax of the year. By
March interest had waned; benefit nights attracted only the friends
and patrons of the actor concerned, and in May the theatre closed
down for the rest of the summer.

As the entire playgoing public numbered, according to a contemporary estimate, only twelve thousand, no new play, however
much admired, ran for more than about nine consecutive nights,
although it might have another short run later on in the season.
Two or three novelties a year were often as much as the managers
of each patent theatre could offer. For the rest they drew on their
common stock of old favourites, a stock that had been accumulating
since the reopening of the theatres after the Restoration, and which
included, as a legacy from an earlier period, corrupt versions or
adaptations of the tragic and historical plays of Shakespeare. At
a time when every man with literary ambitions, every playgoing
clergyman, physician and schoolmaster, liked to fancy himself a
dramatist and had at least one play in his desk, very few of the
manuscripts that reached the managers' offices were worth serious
consideration. None of the comedies submitted to Lacy or Rich
could compete with those by Vanbrugh, Steele and Farquhar,

written earlier in the century; Aaron Hill's adaptations of Voltaire's tragedies were being well received, but no one had appeared to take the place of Rowe as a writer of tragedies. Old Colley Cibber had written his last play, and Hoadley could not repeat his one success. Garrick, with three popular farces already to his credit, was himself writing better comedies than any of those submitted to him in his first years of management, and his courteous refusals to produce inferior plays were to earn him the bitter resentment of his fellow-dramatists.

From the time Lacy signed his agreement with Garrick in April 1747, little more is heard of him. He retired into the background, and with quiet competence looked after the scenery and the wardrobe, made himself responsible for the accounts, and kept a restraining hand on the expenditure. Garrick had a free hand in the choice of plays, the engaging of actors and the conduct of the rehearsals. Each of them kept strictly within his own province, with the result that, on the whole, they worked together in harmony.

By June, Garrick's engagement at Covent Garden had come to an end, and, after a holiday at Lichfield, he was free to make preparations for the autumn. First of all, the theatre had to be redecorated, and while he was still in the midst, as he put it, of alterations and mortar, he began to get together a company which he determined should be the best in England. And there was nothing to prevent him from doing so. After a long period of confusion at Drury Lane, his firm handling of its affairs inspired fresh confidence, and there were few actors whose services were not his for the asking. Rich made no attempt to compete with him; indeed, he bestirred himself so little that it looked as though he would be left high and dry that year.

To begin with, a little trouble arose with Mrs. Pritchard, or rather her husband on her behalf, after she had signed an agreement for the season. It was being said that Garrick intended to act only with Mrs. Cibber; this would, Mr. Pritchard wrote, injure his wife's professional reputation, and he asked Garrick to promise him that Mrs. Cibber would not be shown preferential treatment. In an irritable and long-winded reply, Garrick assured Mr. Pritchard that the rumour was absurd; that he had not even engaged Mrs. Cibber yet, and if he were to do so, he certainly would not be stupid enough to promise to act only with her. If Mrs. Pritchard's professional reputation were to suffer, would not he, as manager, be a loser? He had a great stake, he pointed out, and he must serve his own interests. He intended to do justice to everyone in his company, but if Mr. Pritchard had any doubt left in his mind, he could cancel the agreement altogether and offer the services of his wife and himself to Covent Garden.

The breeze died down, and with Mrs. Cibber and Mrs. Pritchard for tragedy, and Mrs. Clive and Mrs. Woffington for comedy, Garrick had secured the four outstanding actresses of the day. To alternate with himself in the lead, he chose Barry, the only rival he was ever to know in tragedy, and to support them he engaged Macklin, Havard, Yates, Delane, Sparks, and Shuter, all competent and experienced actors, many of whom were to be re-engaged every season. From this company—the strongest ever known in the history of the stage—only two star actors were missing: Woodward, an excellent comedian and harlequin, had engaged himself in Dublin and did not join Garrick until the following season; and Quin, who had retired to Bath in disgust at Garrick's success. At last, in November, Quin thought that perhaps it was time to go back to Covent Garden, but his laconic letter, 'Dear Rich, I am at Bath, yours James Quin,' received the reply, 'Dear Quin, Stay there and be damned, yours John Rich.'

Garrick began his career as manager full of ideas for stage reform and, overcoming his natural timidity and self-distrust, he proceeded boldly to put them into practice. He insisted on far stricter rehearsals, and penalized those who forgot their lines on the night of performance and tried to cover their lapse of memory by gagging. For the first time casting received serious consideration; minor rôles, which hitherto had been handed out indiscriminately, were carefully examined and allotted to those whose personality and gifts best fitted them. He discouraged intoning and taught his actors to speak accurately and as naturally as was compatible with the emphatic style of acting he had made his own. Before putting a new play into rehearsal, he would read it through to the assembled company, imparting so much interest to the minor rôles that actors who would have scornfully refused them had they seen their few lines on paper were hoodwinked into accepting them. It cannot be said that Garrick fulfilled all the functions of the modern producer, but in the plays he rehearsed he achieved a greater unity of effect than had hitherto been seen on the stage.

Some unevenness of performance was inevitable in the cheerful, quarrelsome, family-party atmosphere of an eighteenth-century theatre; the sympathy between actor and audience, much more strongly felt and more frankly expressed then than now, would stimulate him at moments to performances of great power, but if that sympathy were withdrawn, or if the attention of his listeners were to wander, his efforts would flag correspondingly. In the evenly lit house he could not but be acutely conscious of the audience which almost literally surrounded him; when he turned away from the benches in the pit he met the eyes of those seated on the side of the stage, and even when he made his exit through the wings he had to push his way through little groups of privileged onlookers who stood there gossiping and getting in the way. The sound of Johnson's loud voice in the wings used to exasperate Garrick as he tried to concentrate on his part. 'Punch has no feelings,' was Johnson's reply when someone remonstrated with him for his discourtesy. Occasionally a drunken beau would stray on to the stage itself, and interrupt the action of the play by kissing the leading actress, or by getting mixed up with the extras. Even the green-room itself was cluttered up with young men about town who shut out the fire from the players as they played 'heads or tails' against the mantelpiece. Peg Woffington, dressed as Cleopatra, could not sip her pint of porter in the Covent Garden green-room in peace without a disturbing gaze from the astonished Duchess of Queensberry. No member of the audience felt shy at the sound of his own voice echoing through the theatre, as he shouted encouragement or criticism; or scrupled, if bored, to re-open a conversation with his friends in an ordinary tone of voice. 'Rumps and Burrs,' shouted out a lady incomprehensibly from the gallery one evening as she awoke from a dream, so disconcerting Garrick in one of his tragedy rôles that for a while he could not go on with his part.

It was beyond Garrick's power to keep his audiences in order. Players, if no longer literally His Majesty's servants, were kept very much in their places as servants of the public, and to propitiate his patrons Garrick had often to adopt what seems to us an undignified servility of manner. For, if displeased, they might (and frequently did) rise as one man, hurl benches and mirrors at the stage, break up the harpsichord and smash the viols over the heads of the musicians. Only tentatively could he print on his first play-bill the words: 'As the Admittance of Persons behind the Scenes has occasioned a general Complaint on Account of the frequent Interruptions in the Performances; 'tis hop'd Gentlemen won't be offended that no Money will be taken there for the future.' And in an epilogue he wrote himself on the first night, he apologized for his audacity with the sprightly facetiousness that only too often served him for humour:

> Sweet doings truly! we are finely fobb'd
> And at one stroke of all our Pleasures robb'd.
> No Beaux behind the scenes! 'tis Innovation!
> Under the specious Name of Reformation.
> Public Complaint, forsooth is made the Puff,
> Sense, Order, Decency, and such like Stuff. . . .
> Each actress now a lock'd up nun must be,
> And priestly managers must keep the key.

Thus Garrick drove the audience back to their proper side of the footlights, and kept them there on all but benefit nights when the rule was relaxed and an amphitheatre erected on the stage itself. At the same time he removed another abuse; he obliged the boxholders to pay as they came in. Hitherto, the noise of collecting the money at the end of the first act and of chasing the young gentlemen as they dashed in and out of the boxes to evade payment had disturbed the rest of the house and delayed the next act. 'No other manager but himself,' wrote a friend to Peter Garrick, that autumn, 'would have dared to attempt such a thing. But he had all the people of fashion strenuously for him—as, indeed, they are in everything.'

The season opened on the 15th of September 1747 with Macklin's now popular rendering of Shylock in *The Merchant of Venice*. But it was the prologue, spoken by Garrick, that dominated the evening. On special occasions these short recitations before and after the full-length play provided the actor with an opportunity of making a direct appeal to the audience on matters of topical interest. He spoke as a rule in his own character, whether or not he appeared dressed for a part in the ensuing play. His listeners found nothing incongruous or destructive of stage illusion about that,

5. MRS. CIBBER

from a painting by T. Hudson

since they never for a moment would have forgotten his own personality in the imaginary rôle he was about to portray. For the epilogue, Garrick supplied Peg Woffington with some of the lively doggerel that flowed easily from his pen, but the writing of the prologue he entrusted to Samuel Johnson, to whose genius he was thus the first to pay public tribute.

It was now ten years since the two young men had arrived in London together; to one had come prosperity, to the other, unrelieved misery. While Garrick's name echoed throughout England and Ireland, Johnson, with his immeasurably superior intellectual powers, was known only to a few lovers of good literature as the author of a poem on London. The want of a university degree stood in the way of a professional career, and, in a time of political excitement, the booksellers hesitated to publish the translations for which they had paid Johnson barely enough to keep him from starvation. An ambitious plan for compiling a Dictionary of the English language had already taken shape in his head, but, as yet, the problem of finding the means to live while at work on it had not found a solution. To save those dependent on him from complete destitution, he was sometimes driven to borrow money from his friends, but it is significant that never once in his distress did he turn to Garrick for help, although in after years he frequently approached him on behalf of other people and always met with a generous response. 'Last night, I was behind the scenes at Drury Lane, and met Davy dressed for his part,' he once remarked bitterly. 'I was glad to see him, but I believe he was ashamed to see me.' But shame and embarrassment betray themselves by much the same signs, and if Garrick, the rich and fashionable actor, felt embarrassed at the sight of his friend's poverty, his reaction was surely as natural as Johnson's sense of injustice at the contrast between their situations.

Intimacy was impossible. Yet, on the whole, both men behaved well, and remained loyal to their early friendship. Johnson criticized Garrick, it is true, but never with the venom displayed by those who had real or fancied grievances against him; Garrick, on his side, poked fun at Johnson in private, but never wavered in his respect for his judgment and erudition. The prologue, written for him by Johnson, may be taken as the expression of Garrick's own views and ambitions. He willingly associated himself with

Johnson's reverence for Shakespeare, and agreed that since his time drama had steadily deteriorated. He too disapproved of the obscenity and false sentiment of Restoration playwrights, although in fact he belonged too much to his age not to enjoy much that seems intolerable to us. He deplored the popularity of foolish entertainments (an ever-recurrent lament) and he appealed to the audience for their support in bringing about a revival of the drama. There was nothing startlingly new about all this: Jeremy Collier had written his pamphlet against the immorality of the English stage before either Johnson or Garrick was born; Colley Cibber, whose private life was not remarkable for its austerity, had already written his plays which had as their avowed purpose the exposure and reform of 'the licentious irregularities that too often break in upon the Peace and Happiness of the Married State'; and the rediscovery of Shakespeare was well under way before Garrick and Johnson had ever left Lichfield. But the prologue represents the first clear expression of a change in taste that dates from the beginning of the century, and consequently led to a more general acceptance of the new literary values.

After the first night, Garrick went down with one of the slight illnesses that, even then, constantly interrupted his career, and the prologue went unspoken. The few who had heard it pronounced it the best ever written—a verdict that posterity has upheld—and to compensate later audiences for its omission from the programme it was printed and sold for sixpence a copy.[1]

Henceforth, Garrick paraded his admiration for Shakespeare on every possible occasion until their two names became linked together in contemporary thought. Every season he presented at least ten plays generally accepted as Shakespeare's, although most of them were in fact adaptations which contained a remarkably good part for himself. It may be said that his appreciation of Shakespeare did not go very deep; nevertheless, by popularizing certain rôles he sent many of his contemporaries back to the original text to discover its beauty for themselves. To the ordinary playgoer in the first half of the century, it did not matter in the least whether Macbeth, Lear or Richard III spoke the lines Shakespeare had written or not—so long as the situations remained fundamentally the same. And Garrick, whatever he may have said

1 See Appendix II.

to the contrary, held much the same point of view. After all, it was within living memory that the original plays had appeared in print for the first time, and these early editions had never circulated widely. The players relied on manuscript copies of their respective parts, handed down among themselves for generations, many of them altered nearly out of recognition. When Garrick played Macbeth, more or less as written by Shakespeare, Quin, who unknown to himself had always used Davenant's version, listened with amazement to the lines:

> *The devil damn thee black, thou cream fac'd loon*
> *Where gott'st thou that goose look?*

He asked Garrick afterwards where he had found such strange and out-of-the-way expressions. According to Garrick's biographer, Quin received the reproof his ingenuous question had invited. Yet Garrick himself is supposed to have preferred acting copies to the printed text. Indeed, Johnson went so far as to doubt whether he had ever read any single play right through in the original.

It may be argued that Garrick was perfectly right to present Shakespeare's plays in the form that his audience could best appreciate. The eagerness with which they followed the plot of Cibber's *Richard III* and Tate's *King Lear* would have gratified Shakespeare much more than the respectful boredom of a puzzled audience at a production of scholarly accuracy. But when Garrick revived *The Tempest* in December, why did he use Dryden and Davenant's adaptation, the worst ever made of any Shakespearian play? The original happens to conform to the unities of time and place and has a plot neat enough for the tidiest eighteenth-century mind. It does not depend on strong dramatic situations, but on its poetic charm—or so it seems to us—and this he sacrificed for the sake of giving the audience the rubbishy concoction that had held the stage ever since the time of Pepys, on the strength of its trap-door magic, its catchy tunes and the rollicking dances of the sailors.

The honours that season went to Mrs. Pritchard, whose success as Lady Macbeth is all the more astonishing when we know that she had never read any other part in the play but her own. Her massive figure and vigorous personality, in contrast with Garrick's vacillations as Macbeth, threw a new and lurid light on the murder, and the play gripped the audience as never before. Henceforth the rôle of Lady Macbeth belonged unquestionably to Mrs. Pritchard, and Garrick, knowing how much the dramatic effect of his own performance depended on her, never attempted the part with any other actress.

Yet according to Johnson, Mrs. Pritchard acted mechanically. She was a vulgar idiot, he declared, and talked of her 'gownd'. He wondered how little mind she had. And Garrick's only recorded comments on her are no more flattering. She was clumsy, he said, and in her stage grief blubbered tiresomely. We know from other sources that her humble origin betrayed itself in every word and gesture, and that no matter how richly dressed she never looked other than a fat fishwife on holiday. All this is difficult to reconcile with the indisputable fact that she was the best all-round actress the English stage had yet seen. To Garrick as manager of Drury Lane she was invaluable, and proved the mainstay of his company for the rest of her life. She played comedy and tragedy with equal ability; she never disappointed her public at the last moment by real or pretended illness, and no scandal or indiscretion in her private life interrupted her career. Perhaps this was as much as an eighteenth-century manager expected of any actress. In seventy years, the novelty of seeing a woman on the stage had worn off; nevertheless, an actress's personal charms and the bestowal of her favours still attracted more attention than her achievements. No Mrs. Siddons had yet arisen to demonstrate by her genius that acting is an art that women can practise as brilliantly as men.

CHAPTER VII

MARRIAGE

1748–1749

THERE are no dark secrets in Garrick's private life awaiting disclosure. On the day he broke with Peg Woffington his wild oats were sown, and henceforth the record of his daily life reveals an asceticism not usually credited either to his generation or his profession. He did not drink for the sake of getting drunk, he did not gamble, and, whether from social ambition or from natural fastidiousness, he preferred to seek feminine society in the drawing-rooms of the aristocracy rather than in the taverns and lodging-houses of Covent Garden. The unvarying, sometimes mechanical, gaiety of manner that made him an ideal dinner guest hid a sobriety of temperament that puzzled and antagonized his fellow-actors. They acknowledged his gifts, but never really liked him or felt at ease in his presence. They might have forgotten how touchy he could be and laughed good-humouredly at his vanity; they might even have forgiven him for his success, had he been able to let himself go, get drunk or be arrested for debt like the rest of them. But he was incorrigibly temperate and offensively cautious in his expenditure.

Mrs. Cibber and he had the most in common and they naturally gravitated together. She admired him, indeed she was probably in love with him, but, although he found her soft, wheedling ways very delightful, the gallantries with which he answered her eagerly affectionate letters meant no more to him than the elegant verses he could turn out by the dozen to flatter ladies of social distinction. Their long calm friendship never, so far as is known, disturbed

93

Mr. Sloper's peace of mind, or prevented him from giving Garrick a warm welcome in the summer holidays to the home he shared with Mrs. Cibber near Buxton. During the season Garrick and Mrs. Cibber met every day. He never cured her of intoning, yet, in spite of that, he liked acting tragedy with her better than with anyone else. Her small slender figure made him feel tall in comparison, and her passionate sincerity helped him to give his best. On Sundays he would go round to her house in Scotland Yard where he could be pretty certain of finding someone worth talking to among the writers, actors and musicians who made it their meeting-place. Sometimes, to be sure, the atmosphere was rather too musical for his taste; for Mrs. Cibber, a singer herself, gathered round her the musicians of the day, and Garrick, although less outspoken about it, cared no more for fiddling than Johnson. He had nothing much to say to her brother, Tom Arne; he saw him every evening leading the orchestra at Drury Lane and thought (if he thought at all) of his charming compositions as light, ephemeral entertainment on a level with ballet or pantomime. Handel, gross and surly, made no impression on him, but there was a young organist, a pupil of Tom Arne, whom Garrick found more congenial. Charles Burney, he discovered, had far wider interests than the average musician, and, with a distinct turn for mimicry, could tell a good story. He soon learned to take off Garrick himself, and, after he went to live with Fulke Greville, used to entertain his patrons by getting up comedies and giving imitations of Garrick in his popular rôles.

At this time private theatricals, elaborately produced, were becoming popular among those rich enough to afford them, and Garrick gained the entry into many great houses by his readiness to help in procuring the scenery and supervising rehearsals. And one invitation led to many more, for his hosts found him the perfect guest, talkative and amusing, with a fund of anecdotes which he told with the skill of a professional entertainer. If conversation flagged at the dinner table, he took very little pressing to get on his feet and give the company a sample of his acting. These turns were usually in dumb show—studies in facial expressions ranging from tragedy to comedy in rapid succession. The dagger scene from *Macbeth,* too, was frequently called for, and the story that it was once interrupted at its climax by Speaker Onslow's audible, 'Was you at the last turnpike meeting?' to his neighbour only serves to emphasize the rapt silence in which his fellow-guests habitually watched him. Acting was no effort to him; on the contrary, he could not stop acting. From the moment he entered a room full of people to the closing of the door behind him he was giving a performance—and it was one that made him a delightful guest. In a sense he had no private life; with more invitations than he could accept, he had not the leisure to make intimate friends.

His fellow-actors used to say of him that he was 'all submission in the presence of a peer', and despised him for not being, as they were, equally rude to everyone. But his attentiveness to rank, which now suggests the obsequiousness of a flunkey, counted then as good manners in a man who, for all his personal charm and culture, earned his living as a player. When he was staying at a great house, it amused his enemies to send him grubby little notes addressed to *Mr. Garrick, Player.* But he needed no reminder of his status. He never took a liberty or was guilty of the slightest impertinence, and this partly explains why the aristocracy singled him out for attention. He was still a young man when he wrote to the large but handsome Lady Rochford, asking her permission to dedicate some verses to her, and at the same time he sought to be reassured on a matter about which he had, in fact, very little doubt. 'You say you are little versed in the delicacies of good breeding,' she replied. 'I'm sure that you are safe with me, for I own it's the last thing I should lay to your charge, and I'm sure of this, you may err in some court forms but your good nature will always give you a title to politeness so you need never fear transgressions of that sort.'

Garrick stands convicted of toadying to rank. But there is this to be said in extenuation: he chose for his personal friends intelligent men and women with tastes akin to his own, and he never wasted time on a fool or a good-for-nothing just because he happened to have a title. The truth is that he felt at his best in the company of such well-bred intellectuals as George Lyttelton, the Earl of Bath, William Pitt and Mrs. Montagu, and at Bath and Tunbridge Wells, where he frequently went for his health, he enjoyed their suave exchange of compliments and cultured platitudes. He felt safer among them than among the rough-tongued wits at the Bedford Coffee-house; for in company, as on the stage, he was easily disconcerted. A joke at his expense would silence

95

him for the evening. As a conversationalist he tended to monologue, and did not like to be interrupted; when he argued he did so timidly, taking care not to go out of his depth or to offend his antagonist. No scruples of politeness or even of truth stood in the way of a joke in the coffee-houses of Covent Garden, and actors who disliked Garrick, and knew how to embarrass him, did so without mercy.

Garrick was no match for Samuel Foote, who made it the first business of his life to plague Garrick whenever and wherever they met. It was always the same old joke, Garrick's meanness (Foote had picked it up from his friend, Macklin), and no matter how feeble or far-fetched the witticism it always raised a laugh. Garrick, vexed and discomfited, would give a wry smile, unwilling to admit that he had been scored off by the man who was mimicking him with so much success at the Little Theatre in the Haymarket. It was in Garrick's first year of management that Foote, after a short and disastrous career on the stage, thought of using his gift for satirical mimicry in sketches of his own invention. He took the small theatre used by Fielding for his comedies before the passing of the Licensing Act drove him from stage management. To evade that Act, Foote disguised the character of his entertainment by issuing an invitation to his friends to take a Dish of Tea with him every afternoon at 6:30. Tickets for admission were sold at a neighbouring coffee-house. He began by taking off well-known actors: Quin, Ryan, Woodward, Peg Woffington, and Garrick all suffered at his hands. Garrick he impersonated in a dying scene, and exaggerated his tendency to drag out his last words by a hesitation in speech that came very near to a stammer. It was not that Foote's imitations were in the least like their originals, for he had no command over his sharp, nasal voice, but his implied criticisms were cruelly apt and the lines funny in themselves. In preparing these sketches he discovered where his real talent lay, and before many years had passed he was rivalling Garrick as a writer of satirical comedies. His humour, whether on the stage or in private life, was generally aimed at some particular person, and Garrick was too much afraid of him to take open offence.

In his second year of management, Garrick had to compete with a stronger company at Covent Garden. Mrs. Woffington, professionally jealous of Mrs. Cibber and Mrs. Pritchard, and hating the sight of Mrs. Clive, went over to the enemy and played her breeches parts for Rich with never-failing gusto. Mrs. Ward, a new discovery from Edinburgh, had a brief vogue as a tragedy actress, although she must have made a curious Cordelia as she was obviously going to have a baby. However, no one worried very much about that. Indeed it is difficult to decide, on looking through Mrs. Ward's list of appearances that season, just when her baby was born. (Presumably she was luckier than the provincial actress who, according to Gilliland, 'in the fifth act of *The Mourning Bride* became a joyful mother'.) Quin bestirred himself and went through his repertory of noble heroes and drunken profligates with George Anne Bellamy as his leading lady. With her tantrums and complicated love-affairs, George Anne often gave more trouble than she was worth; Garrick had, indeed, refused her an engagement that autumn. But, on the whole, she behaved fairly well until one evening, fortunately late in the season, when she eloped between the fourth and fifth acts of *The Provok'd Husband,* leaving Quin to discover her absence for himself and break the news to the audience. At the Little Theatre, Foote with a small company of his own must now be counted as a competitor, and there were few playgoers who missed seeing his burlesque of the Italian opera rendered by two actors mewing like cats.

At Drury Lane the season which opened in the autumn of 1748 was marked by two Shakespearian revivals. As Benedick and Beatrice, in *Much Ado about Nothing,* Garrick and Mrs. Pritchard made an ideally matched pair and the play was repeated year after year for the rest of her career. As far as we know, they played it as written by Shakespeare. A fortnight later, Barry and Mrs. Cibber almost eclipsed them in *Romeo and Juliet,* but this time, alas, Garrick made some 'improvements'. In the first scene he suppressed the reference to Rosaline, for a truly romantic hero must only be in love once in a lifetime. But he did something worse than that. To prolong Romeo's death agonies—Garrick's skill in simulating physical pain always warped his aesthetic judgment—he made Juliet regain consciousness in the tomb. 'Bless me,' she cries, 'how cold it is! Who's there?' 'Thy husband,' answers Romeo. ''Tis thy Romeo, rais'd from despair to joy unutterable.' But presently Romeo feels the poison working. 'My powers are blasted. 'Twixt death and love I am torn—I am distracted.' He dies slowly but effectively,

97

and Juliet falls fainting on his body. 'No play ever received greater advantage from alteration than this tragedy,' wrote Francis Gentleman, a distinguished critic of the day, 'especially in the last act. Bringing Juliet to life before Romeo dies is undoubtedly a change of infinite merit. The whole dying scene does Mr. Garrick great credit.' And generation after generation of playgoers agreed with him. It was not until 1845 that Garrick's additions to the play were scrapped.

But, seen in retrospect, the most interesting event of the season was Garrick's production of Johnson's *Irene,* under the title of *Mahomet and Irene*—a painful episode, perhaps, but one that shows Garrick in an amiable light. He must have known that Johnson's friends were absurdly sanguine to think that his tragedy might repeat the success of Addison's *Cato.* Even if *Irene* had been a better example of its kind, contemporary taste had tired of pseudo-classic tragedy as well as the formal style of acting its presentation demanded. *Irene* is dry and lifeless, but Garrick, as a good and loyal friend, did his very best to get it across. He thought it would liven up the play if Mrs. Pritchard, as Irene, were strangled in view of the audience instead of off-stage as befitted a play written in the classic tradition. When he put his idea into words Johnson could hardly believe his ears. The care with which he had written the play!—the years he had been obliged to keep it unacted!—and now it was to be criticized and altered at the pleasure of an actor! He exploded with rage and Garrick was obliged to appeal to the Rev. Dr. Taylor, Johnson's old school friend, to reason with him. 'Sir,' cried Johnson indignantly, 'the fellow wants me to make Mahomet run mad that he may have an opportunity of tossing his hands and kicking his heels'—a jibe that for once was undeserved, because Garrick had already allotted the part of Mahomet to Barry and was proposing to take the smaller part of Demetrius himself. In the end, Johnson gave in, and Garrick added a bow-string to the splendid new scenery and magnificent oriental dresses that were being held in readiness for the first performance on the 6th of February 1749.

When the evening came, Johnson made something of a stir by appearing in a scarlet waistcoat richly braided with gold and a gold-laced hat; as a dramatic author he considered that his dress should be gayer than that he had hitherto worn. Meanwhile the spectators were taking their seats in a sceptical mood and Johnson's friends heard with some dismay unmistakable catcalling from the gallery. The prologue, however, written in Johnson's grandest and most sonorous manner, soothed them into silence and when the curtain rose they listened politely. Cali's speech, with its reference to the British Constitution, went down particularly well, although it seemed rather odd that a Turk, particularly one who lived three centuries earlier, should know much about it. The first four acts went tolerably well but, alas, Garrick's alteration wrecked the play. When Mahomet put the bow-string around Mrs. Pritchard's neck, the audience shouted, 'Murder! Murder!' Again and again she tried to make her last two lines heard; at last she was obliged to go off alive. On the next night she was carried away to be executed behind the scenes, but the audience did not like the play much better. Garrick kept it on for as long as he could, and, financially, Johnson did well. Indeed, he made more money in a week than he had ever made before in a year. He received the profits of three performances as well as one hundred pounds from the booksellers for the manuscript.

The play ran for nine nights, not at all a bad run for those days of repertory, but as it was never revived the production must be counted a failure. Johnson took his defeat stoically; he blamed no one for it, and, when asked how he felt, replied 'Like the Monument'. But he never wrote another play. He put away the gold-laced hat and scarlet waistcoat, explaining humorously that when in that dress he could not treat people with the same ease as he did in his usual plain clothes, and he did not want his gold-laced hat to make him proud. Years afterwards, when told that a gentleman called Pot pronounced *Irene* the finest of modern tragedies, he replied shortly, 'If Pot says so, Pot lies'. All the same, he remembered his finery with considerable satisfaction and, looking back in later life, his appearance in it represented to him, as it does to us, not the least remarkable moment of that evening.

By this time Garrick had met his future wife, but as he never confided in anyone we know very little about his courtship. It was Horace Walpole who, in May 1749, first noticed that Garrick was in love, when he caught sight of him at the Duke of Richmond's riverside garden-party at Whitehall given in honour of the Duke of Modena. It was the prettiest entertainment in the world, wrote

Walpole to a friend. After a concert of water music, rockets were sent up from lighters, and then a dazzling variety of wheels, rockets and set pieces illuminated the sloping lawns of the garden. King George II and his daughter, Princess Emily, sat watching the show from their barge, under the curious gaze of hundreds of sightseers on both banks of the river. On the terrace, the Duke of Cumberland, fat and unwieldy, wheezed away asthmatically to the guest of honour, who to hide a disfigurement had painted his face in vivid red and white; and round them stood nearly the whole of the English aristocracy as well as a great many distinguished foreigners. And now Sabbatini, Secretary of State to the Duke of Modena, was asking Horace Walpole one question after another. Who was this? Who was that? But he did not get much in reply, for Walpole was watching a small group of people with cynical amusement. Lady Burlington he saw, had brought with her the young Austrian dancer in whom she took a strange maternal interest, and she was glaring disapprovingly at David Garrick, whose lovesick expression was plain for everyone to see. He stood there wrote Walpole, 'ogling and sighing the whole time'. It was 'an admirable scene.' Sabbatini looked at the graceful figure, the object of the young man's admiration, and asked who she was. 'Mlle Violette,' replied Walpole after a little hesitation. 'But what Mlle Violette?' persisted Sabbatini. Walpole changed the subject. A few months later she became Mrs. Garrick.

Nothing more than this is known for certain about their early acquaintance, and Mrs. Garrick's extraordinary reticence about everything that happened to her before she met her husband has inspired a number of romantic legends. Who was she?—and why did the Burlingtons take possession of her? 'Lord Burlington was not my father,' she is reported to have said in old age, 'but I am of noble birth.' And that was all she ever said about herself. So we must dip into the memoirs of an eminent Scottish divine to learn how she arrived in England disguised as a boy.

In the spring of 1746, three years before the Whitehall fireworks, three young Scots boarded a packet at a Dutch port bound for Harwich. They carried with them a cold ham, a couple of fowl, a sirloin of beef, nine bottles of wine, and three of brandy, which they had bought on the advice of an innkeeper who assured them that the voyage might well last several days if the ship were becalmed. As they paced the quarter-deck in the optimistic mood that prevails while land is still in sight they noticed three foreigners of varying ages, who had under their care a young person of about sixteen—'very handsome indeed', they thought—whom they took for a Hanoverian baron coming to pay his court at Saint James's. But before they had time to scrape an acquaintance with them, the breeze freshened and the three Scots retreated hurriedly to the berths reserved for them in the cabin below. They were soon joined by the supposed Hanoverian baron, who took the bunk immediately opposite Alexander Carlyle, the narrator of the story. The three older men never reappeared; and Carlyle thought it probable that they could not afford cabin fare. Preoccupied by their sufferings, the four invalids lay there in silence, while the little ship pitched and tossed in the storm. As the gale reached its climax, the young foreigner became thoroughly frightened and called out to Carlyle in French to know whether they were in danger. The voice was unmistakably feminine and, for a time, surprise and curiosity got the better of his nausea. Reassuring her as best he could, he began to question her, and learned that she was a dancer on her way to try her luck at the Opera House in the Haymarket, Her stage name, he understood, was Violetti. Then conversation languished and they lay there, hardly moving their heads for the sixteen hours of the voyage, ruminating bitterly, as they eyed the expensive hampers with distaste, on the rapacity of innkeepers and their own foolish credulity.

After they had landed, one of the foreigners, who represented himself as the girl's father, called on Carlyle and his friend and expressed his hope that they would come to his daughter's début and, in due course, her benefit. The two parties of travellers hired separate coaches to take them to London, but they met again in the evening at an inn in Colchester. Here Mlle Violetti, or Mlle Violette as she came to be called, would have been roughly handled but for her new friends, for the servants objected to a girl who wore breeches, particularly as all four travellers proposed to occupy one bedroom. But before the servants had made up their minds what to do, the young men came forward and saved her from insult. The next day they continued their journey in separate coaches as before, but when they stopped for dinner, the Scotsmen persuaded Mlle Violette to be their guest, so that they could make sure that she was treated with respect. A few weeks later Carlyle saw her dance at the Opera House and pronounced her performance 'exquisite'.

At this time the Opera House was under the capricious management of Lord Middlesex, an intimate friend of Frederick Prince of Wales, but it does not appear that Mlle Violette owed more than her initial engagement to their favour. At her début she created a mild sensation by revealing, as she kicked up her legs, a neat pair of black velvet breeches with rolled stockings. Finding that they attracted a disproportionate amount of attention, she discreetly changed them the next night for a pair of white drawers. Her success was immediate, and by June her dancing was the talk of London. The Prince, who considered himself a connoisseur, invited her to come twice a week to Leicester House for lessons from his private dancing master, Desnoyer. When she wisely ignored the compromising honour, he took no more interest in her, and let it be understood that he thought poorly of her dancing. Lord Middlesex, too, felt bound to belittle her in order to allay the jealous fears of his mistress, whose position as first dancer was imperilled by the newcomer. By December, Mlle Violette had transferred herself to Drury Lane.

To account for her ease in securing these engagements and for the fact that King George II attended her first performance, it is said that she brought with her from Vienna letters of recommendation from the Empress Maria Theresa. Eva Maria Veigel, for that was her real name, had been trained, like her brother Charles, as a ballet dancer but had not as yet appeared in public when she was taken to Court to dance with the royal children. Her fresh young beauty caught the Emperor's eye and the Empress, to get her out of the way, suggested the journey to England. In London, her perfect manners and irreproachable private life brought her many invitations not usually extended at that time to ballet dancers.

In Lord and Lady Burlington she inspired an especial interest. Lady Burlington fussed over her with the fond anxiety of a mother; she waited in the wings with a shawl to throw over her shoulders lest she should take cold after dancing; she commissioned an artist to paint her portrait; she took her to dine with the Duke of Bedford; to sup with Lady Cardigan, and at the weekends drove her down to rest at her elegant Palladian villa at Chiswick. Lord Burlington, too, gradually came to regard her as a permanent member of his household in Piccadilly; he arranged that her benefit tickets should be designed by his protégé, Kent, and engraved by Vertue; and when he visited the rebel prisoners at the Tower on the day before they were executed, he allowed her to come with him. Eva Maria accepted their protection, and fell in with all their plans for her with the docility of an ideal daughter. Soon it was whispered that she must in fact be his natural daughter, and gossip invented for him a Florentine mistress during a period when he was known never to have left England.

But it was Lady Burlington, rather than her husband, who assumed the responsibility of a parent, and protected the young dancer in difficult situations as fiercely as though she had been her own flesh and blood. At a masquerade she kept the girl safely tucked under her arm, and when she saw that Lord Coventry was following them with a hopeful look on his face, she pulled off her gloves ostentatiously and moved her wedding ring up and down her finger to make it clear that no other terms would be accepted. And fortunately for the future Mrs. Garrick, the elderly widower found them too high.

Garrick was still acting in Dublin when Eva Maria made her début at the Opera House, and her engagement at Drury Lane coincided with his at Covent Garden. Professionally, their paths never crossed, but they must often have met as fellow-guests in those great houses where a few privileged artists and players were received with gracious condescension. At first Lady Burlington received Garrick coldly; she had hoped for a much better match, and she expressed her disapproval clearly. Garrick, however, was not to be discouraged, and it is said that he went to the length of disguising himself as a woman in order to slip a letter into Eva Maria's sedan chair. The two young people were deeply in love and Lady Burlington had to give way. On the 22nd of June 1749 David Garrick and Eva Maria Veigel were married in Bloomsbury at eight o'clock in the morning and, since the bride belonged to the Roman Catholic faith, a second ceremony followed later on the same day at a chapel in South Audley Street.

The marriage settlements, signed two days before the wedding, aroused intense curiosity, and suspicions were renewed when it was rumoured that Lord Burlington had given the bride six thousand pounds. But Mrs. Garrick's will reveals that her dowry came not from the Earl, but from Lady Burlington, and took the form of a mortgage for five thousand pounds on one of her estates. She paid Mrs. Garrick a yearly interest on the sum and, after her death, the payments were continued by her son-in-law, the fourth Duke of Devonshire. Lord Burlington did not, therefore, pay Garrick to marry his natural daughter, as malicious people said at the time, and, in short, there is no reason why he should be regarded as her father. If Mrs. Garrick's claim to noble birth is to be taken seriously, and as representing more than a little innocent vanity, then the clue to the mystery lies buried and forgotten in Vienna.

After a honeymoon spent mostly with the Burlingtons at Chiswick, the newly married couple settled into their first home at No. 27 Southampton Street. Here, a few minutes' walk from Drury Lane, they lived comfortably but unostentatiously; the only sign of wealth lay in the profusion of pictures and china which Garrick, without claiming to be a connoisseur, liked to have round him. Mrs. Garrick's gentle ways endeared her to all Garrick's friends, and with her exquisite manners she was as welcome as her distinguished husband in all the great houses to which he was cordially invited. It can never be easy for the wife of a star actor not to feel neglected and ignored, and when she has been something of a celebrity herself the outlook for such a marriage seems gloomy indeed. But Mlle Violette, 'the finest and most admired dancer in the world,' according to Horace Walpole, gave up her career to become Mrs. Garrick and devoted herself to him wholeheartedly. In consequence, there is not in all history a more perfectly happy marriage. She identified herself with him in all that he did, attending the final rehearsal of each new play or revival so that she could help him by criticizing the dresses. Even in his office during an interview, a cough or a laugh behind the screen might betray the presence of his wife. 'I'll speak to Mrs. Garrick,' he would say in a difficulty, so often, that some people imagined that she ruled him. '*He* durst not do such a thing. His wife would not *let* him,' remarked Johnson many years later, after Garrick had jokingly

6. GARRICK AND MRS. PRITCHARD AS MACBETH AND LADY MACBETH
from a painting by Zoffany

remonstrated with him for his frisk with Langton and Beauclerk at three o'clock in the morning. But Johnson knew perfectly well that Garrick stayed at home with his wife because he chose to do so. After a long, exasperating day at Drury Lane, he wanted nothing better than to go home to Mrs. Garrick and pour out his grievances. He was never robust, nervously or physically, and the responsibilities of theatrical management told on his temper as he grew older. He became increasingly prone to see ingratitude and malice in those whose careers depended on his favour, and Mrs. Garrick's uncritical admiration soothed him as he fulminated against the latest offender. Sometimes she went to sleep before he had finished scolding, but he did not mind. She is like a good sailor, he used to say, she can sleep under fire.

Even Foote spoke with respect of Mrs. Garrick. Fortunately, neither he nor any of Garrick's enemies realized that the reluctance to waste money they made so much fuss about in Garrick was far more characteristic of her. She never accustomed herself to the casual attitude of English women towards household expenditure; to her Austrian mind it was both a duty and a pleasure to make money go as far as possible. She liked looking for bargains at private auctions and would bid for them in guttural accents which the auctioneer found difficult to understand. In this way she once secured a large quantity of damaged linen, and when asked for her name cautiously gave that of her maid, Betty Price. Or rather she intended to, but it sounded like 'Potty Brice' and Betty herself was obliged to repeat the name more clearly.

There were a few evenings in the year that Garrick set aside for dining with the merchants in certain city taverns, so that he could find out what they were thinking of him in the east end of the town; and there were necessarily many others he spent in the coffee-houses of Covent Garden, picking up stage gossip and persuading his newspaper friends to give him some useful piece of publicity. But generally speaking, Mr. and Mrs. Garrick went about everywhere together, and in all the thirty years of their married life they were never to spend a night apart. Consequently their romance is not one that can be told by quoting love letters, for they were never apart from each other long enough to necessitate writing. But we know that he fully appreciated her. Soon after their marriage a poem aimed at Garrick (and probably written or inspired by him) appeared in the press. It ended with the couplet:

> *Who is the paragon, the marvellous she,*
> *Has fixed a weathercock like thee?*

He replied with a word portrait of her, and everything that we know about her from other sources testifies to its excellence.

> *'Tis not, my friend, her speaking face,*
> *Her shape, her youth, her winning grace,*
> *Have reach'd my heart; the fair one's mind,*
> *Quick as her eyes, yet soft and kind.*
> *A gaiety with innocence;*
> *A soft address, with manly sense.*
> *Ravishing manners, void of art,*
> *A cheerful, firm, yet feeling heart.*
> *Beauty that charms all public gaze,*
> *And humble amid pomp and praise.*

CHAPTER VIII

PANTOMIME

1749 — 1751

G ARRICK went back to Drury Lane that autumn to face a difficult season. He had exploited the publicity value of his marriage to the full, and his choice of Benedick for his first appearance as a married man delighted the gallery but did not increase his popularity in the green-room. His craving for publicity—a weakness a later age might have viewed more tolerantly—and the puffs he was suspected of giving himself in the press were a constant source of irritation to his fellow-actors. In time he came to control the theatrical policy of all but two of the London newspapers, or so it was said, and just as Johnson's hand was later to be seen in almost every important literary enterprise of the day, so Garrick was already believed to write or inspire every unsigned pamphlet, squib or lampoon that referred to himself. His facility with his pen gave him an advantage over his rivals which they felt to be unfair.

Both Barry and Mrs. Cibber were out of humour with their manager. Mrs. Cibber, in spite of being under contract to Drury Lane, did not act at all that season, and her absence has suggested the theory that she was angry with Garrick for marrying someone else. But there is not the slightest reason to suppose that she had any cause for complaint, or that he was not morally free to marry whom he chose. Her defection did not improve Barry's temper, for without her support he found his favourite parts much less effective than usual, and he began to plead hoarseness—a weakness to which he was genuinely prone—as an excuse not to appear. He complained, moreover, that Garrick asked him to act on days when the fashionable world was already engaged elsewhere. Garrick immediately invited him to choose his own days, but no matter when Garrick acted he drew by far the greater crowds. To make up for the loss of Mrs. Cibber, Garrick encouraged Mrs. Ward to break her agreement with Rich and act for him at Drury Lane. He soon wished her back at Covent Garden. During one of his most impassioned speeches, he was exasperated to see her busying herself in doing up her glove, and from that moment he took an intense dislike to being on the stage with her. She was cold and insensitive, and Barry refused point-blank to play Romeo to her Juliet.

With little support or co-operation from his company, Garrick yet managed to draw larger audiences than Rich, and there were no rival attractions to consider. The Little Theatre in the Haymarket gave no plays and had closed down for the time being. Foote, having inherited a fortune, was dazzling London with a great display of wealth before taking himself off to Paris to squander it as rapidly as possible. Before he left, he wrote a characteristically disagreeable letter to Garrick. He had heard, he said, that Woodward was planning 'to dress at him' in a revival of Otway's *Friendship in Fashion* at Drury Lane, and he threatened Garrick with reprisals if he did not interfere. Foote had in mind a farce, he hinted, that would be wormwood to Garrick, entertaining to the public and highly profitable to himself. In a postscript he added that he was returning the free pass to Drury Lane given him by Garrick, and would in future pay his five shillings, 'a sum,' he said, 'not very contemptible to you.' Garrick replied with the mildness he always displayed towards Foote no matter how much provoked. He had no idea, he said, what Woodward was planning to do, but he had his full permission to imitate anyone he liked, not excepting the manager. The part in question was that of a very smart conceited little fellow and a good mimic, and he advised Foote to regard the story as a compliment. As for the five shillings, if it were indeed true that he valued the money, then the favour he had shown Foote in giving him the pass had been all the greater. Foote need not have concerned himself; the play failed, and the subject was dropped and forgotten.

By the end of the summer of 1750 the grumblers were in open revolt, and Barry, Mrs. Cibber and Macklin went over to Rich.

With Quin, Barry, Mrs. Cibber, Macklin, Peg Woffington and Ryan ranged against him at Covent Garden, with the perennial attractions of Rich's harlequinades behind them, Garrick felt a little daunted, and many people prophesied his ruin. He even tried to tempt Quin from his allegiance—he had no scruples about poaching on other managers' preserves—but Quin, supreme at Covent Garden and entrusted by Rich with the power of an actor-manager, had no desire to take orders from Garrick at Drury Lane, and remained faithful to his master. He made good use of the offer, however, to extract a salary of £1,000 from Rich, then the largest ever paid to an actor. Old-fashioned or not, Quin still had a following, and, moreover, his already great prestige had been recently increased by royal patronage. Eighteen months earlier, Frederick Prince of Wales had invited him to supervise the rehearsals of *Cato* at Leicester House, and coach the royal children in the correct intoning of their parts. Years later, when King George III made his first speech to the two Houses of Parliament, Quin, thinking of those days, remarked with satisfaction, 'I knew he would do it well, *for I taught the boy.*'

When the season opened in the autumn of 1750, Covent Garden was overwhelmingly strong on the tragedy side, but at Drury Lane the troops were under better discipline, and with Woodward, Kitty Clive, Shuter, and Mrs. Pritchard to support him, Garrick could offer much better comedy. For tragedy he had, besides the versatile Mrs. Pritchard, Miss Bellamy, soon to be known as Mrs. Bellamy,[1] whose refreshing youth and sincerity did much to compensate for her lack of experience, and, finally, stimulated by the competition, he was a host in himself, playing comedy and tragedy with equal vigour and ease.

The prologue, written and spoken by Garrick on the opening night, was clearly intended as a declaration of war. He referred to the desertions from his ranks and, speaking for the rest of the company as well as for himself, told the audience that they were ready and anxious for the fray. Barry, in an answering prologue three weeks later, described his friends and himself as refugees from managerial tyranny and selfishness, and appealed for public

[1] George Anne Bellamy never married, but in England actresses were given the title of a married woman. In France they were professionally known as Mademoiselle.

sympathy and support. Garrick guessed that Barry's first choice would be Romeo now that he had Mrs. Cibber to act with him, and when a revival of the play was announced for September 28th at Covent Garden, it was immediately capped by a similar announcement for Drury Lane with Garrick as Romeo, a part he had hitherto left for Barry, and Miss Bellamy as Juliet. The contest lasted for twelve successive nights until Mrs. Cibber's strength failed, and Barry was obliged to throw in his hand. Garrick triumphantly gave a thirteenth performance with the added attraction of a funeral procession before laying it aside for a while.

Such a contest had never been known before in the history of the stage, and the merits of the rival Romeos were discussed and compared for many years afterwards. Either presentation of the play was almost certainly better than any other of which we have records. Barry had all the natural advantages as well as a great gift for tragedy; with his magnificent physique, romantic profile and rich musical voice, he was ideally suited to the part. That Garrick, short and heavy-featured, could nearly equal him was a triumph that indicates more clearly than any other in his career the extent and quality of his genius. The easy grace of his movements, his effective attitudes, his youthful vitality and masterly portrayal of physical and mental suffering almost made up for the glamour of Barry's love scenes. The Juliets, too, were evenly matched and the style of each suited their respective Romeos. Mrs. Cibber's soft plaintive voice blended perfectly with Barry's rich tones. Miss Bellamy's more natural style of acting suited that of Garrick, and she listened to his ardent speeches with amorous rapture. At Drury Lane, Woodward's tendency to overdo pantomimic gesture—the effect of his Harlequin rôles—did not prevent him from scoring as Mercutio, one of his greatest successes. Although silent and even solemn in private life, on the stage he was second only to Garrick for vivacious charm. Macklin in the same part at Covent Garden was tolerably well received, but his sour cadaverous face, which no make-up could disguise, contrasted oddly with Mercutio's attractive personality. He was miscast, yet incapable, like so many actors, of seeing where his real talents lay, he always spoke of Mercutio as one of his best parts, and liked to enlarge on his excellencies in it during that famous run. Financially, both managers lost; the public tired of the contest long before the protagonists, and on the last nights both houses were thin. Visitors from the country, dependent on the two houses for their entertainment, found themselves restricted to one play; the only other diversions London could offer them were an occasional opera at the Opera House in the Haymarket, or an inferior Harlequinade at Sadlers Wells. Their irritation found vent in an epigram which appeared in *The Daily Advertiser:*

> *'Well, what's to-day?' says angry Ned,*
> *As up from bed he rouses.*
> *'Romeo, again!' and shakes his head,*
> *'Ah, pox on both your houses!'*

Garrick next attacked Rich in his own stronghold by presenting a new pantomime, *Queen Mab,* on Boxing Day, which ran for forty nights (a long run for those days), and made Rich tremble for his throne and the tragedians for their livelihoods. In this deliberate choice of a pantomime instead of a farce for his afterpiece, it seemed to the lovers of drama as though Garrick had betrayed his ideals. The struggle between Harlequin and Shakespeare, between pantomime and straight drama, dominates the history of the eighteenth-century stage, and to many people it often looked as though Shakespeare were fighting a losing battle. Fleetwood and Rich had depended very largely on the attraction of Harlequinades to fill their theatres for the plays their licences demanded of them. Then Garrick's break with tradition revived popular interest in acting, and Shakespeare's plays, newly interpreted, acquired a deeper meaning; even the bombastic tragedies and drearily monotonous comedies of intrigue of more recent origin came to life under his invigorating influence. And now, after three years of management, having ranged himself on the side of drama and having pledged himself to its service, Garrick was descending to pantomime. His critics would not recognize that both Johnson's famous prologue and the one Garrick wrote himself for the opening night of the season made it clear that the necessity to eat came first, and that if the public would not pay to see plays he must give them pantomime. But his concession to popular taste needs no apology, for the humour, ingenuity and imagination of the age found a happy expression in pantomime. Its demands gave an impetus to every branch of stage production, while the revival

111

of miming had an unexpectedly far-reaching effect on acting and ballet.

The invasion of London fairs after the Restoration by French and Italian Harlequins and Scaramouches met with weak resistance from the native clowns and tumblers, although insults were freely hurled at the foreigners in print. They rapidly established themselves, became naturalized, ousting the fools of Elizabethan descent and even edging the players off their own stages. Insinuating themselves into the play-bill by giving a tumbling dance at the end of the evening, they began to suggest a story in dumb show, calling in Columbine, Pantaloon, Punch, and Pierrot to their aid until their entertainment acquired the proportions of a short play. Thoroughly anglicized, they added songs and dialogue; they introduced magic into the plot, thereby providing the excuse for ingenious transformations effected mostly by trap doors and 'machines'; and with scenery, costumes and spectacle far more elaborate and expensive than were ever provided for straight plays, the English pantomime came into being.

The personalities of Harlequin and Scaramouche, though undergoing a gradual change through the years, differed little from pantomime to pantomime, and their adventures, involving a good deal of horseplay, followed a traditional pattern. From a stupid, mischievous country servant, Harlequin, as interpreted by Rich (or Lun, as he called himself), became a romantic magician, and his wooden sword changed from a slapstick to a magic wand. Harlequin was invariably chased and invariably allowed to escape, taking with him Pantaloon's daughter, Columbine, whose morals were traditionally light. Within this framework the plot could be almost anything—a classical myth, a fairy story or a crime. At the unlicensed theatres it was often a thinly disguised satire on contemporary events in which Harlequin would have a double identity, and, as the dialogue was seldom written down, the most scurrilous libels passed unpunished.

There were no topical allusions in Rich's pantomime, each of which consisted of two parts, one serious and the other comic. 'By the help of gay scenes,' wrote Tom Davies, 'fine habits, grand dances, appropriate music and other decorations, he exhibited a story from Ovid's Metamorphosis, or some other fabulous history. Between the pauses or acts of the serious representation he inter-

112

wove a comic fable consisting chiefly of the courtship of Harlequin and Columbine, with a variety of surprising adventures and tricks, which were produced by the magic wand of Harlequin; such as the sudden transformation of palaces and temples to huts and cottages; of men and women into wheelbarrows and joint stools; of trees turned to houses; colonnades to beds of tulips; and mechanics' shops into serpents and ostriches.' Rich's own share of the performance was always in dumb show, and his acrobatic dances with marvellous leaping and the exquisite detail of his miming made him the best Harlequin of all time. Born a century later, he might have been no less supreme as a ballet dancer. That Garrick fully appreciated him is apparent from the following lines written some years later:

> *When Lun appeared, with matchless art and whim,*
> *He gave the power of speech to every limb;*
> *Tho' masked and mute, conveyed his quick intent,*
> *And told in frolic gesture what he meant.*

In his costume, Rich was midway in distinctiveness between the rather nondescript loose jacket and trousers and cat's mask[1] of the seventeenth-century Italian Comedy of Arts, and the vivid lozenge-patterned tights of the black-masked Regency Harlequins. His short jacket and trousers of criss-cross design were obviously based on those of the older Harlequins, but they fitted him more closely. With a cap that hid his hair, he wore the mask of a youth. Thus clad he could be seen silently scratching his ear with his foot, chasing and catching a butterfly, gracefully taking leave of Columbine, as a statue coming to life, performing a dance in which he executed three hundred steps in an advance of ten yards, and best of all as the first Man being hatched from an egg by the heat of the sun. 'From the first chipping of the egg,' wrote Johnson, 'his receiving motion, his feeling the ground, his standing upright, to his quick Harlequin trip round the empty shell, through the whole progression every limb had its tongue and every motion a voice, which spoke with most miraculous organ to the understandings and sensations of the observers.'

It may well have been the effectiveness of Rich's miming that first brought home to Garrick the sterility of the classical style of

[1] Harlequin's mask denoted his invisibility.

113

; at any rate, it is certain that he owed much of his power
pressing thought by gesture and byplay to the inspiration of
lequin. 'Even his back has expression,' said Garrick of Carlin,
the French Harlequin, whom he saw in Paris in 1751 and pronounced a genius. 'Even the skirts of his coat acted,' said Dr. Burney of Garrick as he watched him in a comedy. At first Garrick,
like many of his followers, introduced rather too much Harlequin
into his acting for contemporary taste. When, as Benedick, he said,
'If I do, hang me in a bottle like a cat, and shoot at me,' he went
through the motions of clapping the cat into the bottle, hanging
it up and then shooting at it—or so Theophilus Cibber asserted.
The criticism was intentionally destructive, but it had a foundation
of truth. His over-realistic death scenes, in which, according to
Noverre, he simulated a death rattle, were as pure Harlequin as
Rich's hatching from an egg. Again, reacting against the old tragedians' studied immobility, he darted about the stage rather too
often and too athletically. Finally, his striking 'attitudes', the subject of varied comment, were directly suggested by pantomime, of
which they were a recognized feature.

Rich in his prime had no equal, but in 1750 he was too old for
a part that needed great agility. In Harry Woodward, Garrick had
the second best Harlequin of the century, and the prosperity of
Drury Lane during the ten years of Woodward's engagement there
was largely due to the success of the Harlequinades devised and
acted in by him. He had been trained from boyhood by Rich himself, who allowed him to appear on his programmes as Lun, Junr.,
until he almost equalled his master as a mime. He would sit by a
bare table, pick up a bunch of imaginary currants by the stalk:

'Then, holding high his hand, with the points of finger and
thumb compressed, he seemed to shake the stalk, and to strip off
the currants with his mouth. In like manner he would appear to
hold up a cherry by the stalk, and after eating it, to spurt the stone
from his lips. Eating a gooseberry, paring an apple, sucking an
orange or peach—all were simulated in the same marvellous fashion.
In short, the audience perfectly knew what fruit he seemed to be
eating by the highly ingenious deception of his acting.'

Woodward was known as the 'attitude Harlequin'. Each attitude represented some emotion, and he would change from one
to another to the rhythm of music. When he came to be chased,

he would go through the traditional routine of jumping through normally impenetrable objects. In a certain pantomime he jumped through apparently solid walls, and to create this illusion he employed a second Harlequin. One night the two Harlequins by some mistake met in the centre of the stage and were greeted by a howl of delight from the audience. It must have been hard work pretending not to enjoy these delicious entertainments.

As the season wore on, Garrick had the satisfaction of knowing that the enemy forces were quarrelling among themselves, and that never again was he likely to have such a powerful combination against him. Mrs. Cibber and Mrs. Woffington had a long-standing contempt of each other; Quin disliked Barry; Barry disliked Quin; they all despised Rich, and Rich hated the whole lot of them. Mrs. Cibber's indispositions necessitated frequent postponements of tragedies—the poor woman was genuinely ill, although no one believed it, with a chronic internal complaint only diagnosed after her death—and Mrs. Woffington, who never disappointed her public, resented being asked again and again to fill the gap with Sir Harry Wildair. In revenge, she waited one day until five o'clock, and then sent a message to the manager to say that she was too unwell to apear that evening. Rich cursed both actresses equally for putting him into such a difficult position, calling Mrs. Cibber his Katherine Hayes and Mrs. Woffington his Sarah Malcolm—two women recently hanged for murder. To this Quin replied that it would be wronging the ashes of the dead to call Mrs. Woffington Sarah Malcolm. Then Barry and Quin were not on speaking terms, and could not be induced to rehearse together. The decisions made by Quin on one day would be reversed by Barry on the next, and the company did not know what they were expected to do. Finally, Mrs. Woffington packed up in disgust and went back to her native Dublin. Quin, old for his fifty-eight years and his health impaired from a life of self-indulgence, retired to Bath. He made his last appearance two years later playing Falstaff for his old friend Ryan's benefit night. When Ryan's benefit night came round again he asked for a repetition of the favour. But Quin had lost two of his front teeth, and refused, saying that he would whistle Falstaff for no man.

In May 1751, after Drury Lane had closed down for the summer, Mr. and Mrs. Garrick spent a few weeks in Paris. It was Garrick's first holiday abroad, and, as a sightseer, he was tireless; churches, palaces, gardens, public buildings, picture galleries—even the people in the streets interested him and invited comparisons. The women he thought 'very ugly and disagreeably painted', on the other hand, the sight of two well-dressed women with perfectly clean, unpainted faces astounded him more than anything he had seen since landing at Boulogne. At Versailles, where he and Mrs. Garrick stayed for a few nights at an inn, he stood and watched King Louis XV enter the Palace. This His Majesty did with great haste, observed Garrick, and with a very dirty retinue. A few days later, the Garricks shared with many others the privilege of staring at the Dauphine while she dined. 'As I was hungry myself,' he wrote in his Diary that evening, 'the sight was not very agreeable, so after *she* had picked a bit, I gave a wink to my wife and we retired to the same ceremony.'

In Paris, Garrick called on the English Ambassador, and paid his respects to various members of the English aristocracy who happened to be staying there. He found time to sit for his portrait to Liotard, and made many new friends among the French actors and men of letters. Unlike many Englishmen abroad who then, as now, kept together and returned more insular than ever, Garrick liked while in France to mix with the French, and his name was sufficient to ensure him a welcome into literary circles. He thought of himself as completely English, and his French, though fluent, was by no means perfect, but with his essentially French temperament he was immediately more at ease in Parisian society than the most travelled Englishman. His vivacity, his lack of English reserve, his flow of graceful compliments proclaimed his Gallic blood, and his eagerness to please met with a warm response. After dinner, he would give his new friends the dagger scene from *Macbeth* in dumb show, filling them with terror. His face expressed all the emotions one after the other, and his audience, accustomed only to the impassive faces of their tragedians, whose style had remained more stilted than the English had ever been, were astounded by his genius, and completely won over to the new naturalism. He told them frankly that he considered all their actors equally bad, and they agreed with him. Then reluctant to appear ungracious, he made two exceptions: Le Kain, the new tragic actor, had feeling and spirit, and Mlle Clairon, he prophesied, had a great future.

In private, however, Garrick admitted that he thought her cold and artificial.

In addition to the theatres, each of which he visited at least once, he attended the Opera. He could not hide his detestation of the singing, but he thought the dancing excellent. Indeed there is reason to suspect that he explored the possibilities of procuring recruits for the ballet at Drury Lane. Although the best ballets were those at the Opera House in the Haymarket, classical dancing was an essential part of pantomime, and Garrick had not a large enough *corps de ballet* to compete with the brilliant spectacles at Covent Garden. With him in Paris was his *maître de ballet*, Levié, a Frenchman who had originally occupied that position at Covent Garden. To assist them in their search for new dancers they had Jean Monnet, a theatrical manager with an extraordinary flair for discovering talent,[1] anxious to repay Garrick for his kindness to him in London when he was in trouble. Two years ago, Monnet had brought over a company of French comedians and, with the permission of the Lord Chamberlain, had hired the Little Theatre in the Haymarket for a season of French comedy. Although welcomed by the aristocracy, whose cultural sympathies with the French went deeper than any passing national prejudices, the visitors were met with a hail of apples and oranges from the pit and galleries, and sustained catcalls and whistling reduced them to silence. The disturbances were repeated at each performance until the Lord Chamberlain, in the interests of public order, was obliged to close the theatre. Monnet was then in distress; his actors demanded their salaries, and the owner of the theatre his rent. He was arrested for debt, and owed his release only to the generosity of the Lord Chamberlain, who made him a present of £100 from his private purse, and Garrick, who raised a similar sum by giving him a benefit night at Drury Lane. Garrick was often to be disgusted with the ingratitude of men whom he helped out of difficulties, but in this instance he had no cause for complaint. During a friendship that lasted for thirty years, Monnet acted as Garrick's unpaid representative in Paris, performing every kind of service from engaging dancers for Drury Lane, keeping him informed of any novelties in lighting and scenery, looking after members of the

[1] Amongst those discovered by Monnet were Rameau, the composer, Boucher, the painter, and Noverre, the most famous of all *maîtres de ballet*.

Drury Lane company on holiday in Paris, to shopping for Mrs. Garrick and sending instructions on how to dress her hair in the latest Parisian style. He seemed to live for Garrick, writing him long letters which Garrick preserved among those he evidently intended for the eyes of his future biographers.

It was probably through Monnet's agency that a dancer called Dévisse, engaged at the Opera, had slipped away to London to join the Drury Lane ballet. Garrick, scrupulously fair in every other way, saw nothing underhand in tempting members of a rival manager's company to desert to his colours. In England this carried with it no penalty, but Monnet should have known, if Garrick did not, that in France actors and dancers were servants of the King in a more literal sense than in England, and in inciting one of them to break his engagement Garrick was guilty of a political crime. Soon after Garrick arrived in Paris the missing dancer was seen in the city, and his reappearance, coinciding with the visits of Garrick and his *maître de ballet,* excited the suspicion that the deserter had returned in order to help Garrick carry off more members of the ballet. A meeting between Garrick and Dévisse seemed highly significant. The police, accordingly, issued a warrant for the arrest of Dévisse, and officers were sent to interrogate Garrick. But someone must have warned Garrick of his danger, for he was nowhere to be found, and a week or two later we hear of him and Mrs. Garrick comfortably settled at Chiswick as the guests of Lord and Lady Burlington. Garrick never referred to this episode; indeed, his reticence on the whole subject of his first visit to Paris is too marked to be without significance, and had not a letter from one high French police official to another come to light giving the facts about Dévisse we should never have known anything about it.

CHAPTER IX

PROSPERITY

1751 — 1755

WITH Woodward as his right-hand man, Garrick settled down to several years of steady prosperity. As manager, he made all the decisions and exacted unquestioning obedience from his actors, but he had confidence in Woodward's judgment and often asked his advice in a difficulty. Moreover, he could leave the pantomimes entirely in his hands, knowing that he could count on him to devise a popular Harlequinade in the traditional manner at least once every season. It proved impossible to surpass Covent Garden in any form of entertainment that depended on spectacle; Rich had more elaborate stage machines, spent greater sums on trick performers, dancers and novelties of all kinds, and, although too old himself for Harlequin, knew how to impart his technique to others. Woodward's *Queen Mab* had shaken him for a while, but by February 1752 he was ready with a revival of *Harlequin Sorcerer*,[1] in which a young Harlequin, hatching from the egg under Rich's tuition, recaptured all the old magic. It was the great success of the season. The doors of Covent Garden had to be opened three hours before the performance, and so intense was the excitement that sometimes they were broken in by the crowds. During the run, Drury Lane could only hope to attract those who had failed to get in to Covent Garden—an audience little in the mood to enjoy one of the dreary and pretentious new tragedies Garrick thought it his duty to produce that season. 'The grown Masters and Misses,' remarked Garrick bitterly after failing to rouse them from their

[1] First produced in 1717.

119

apathy, 'are disappointed of their puppet show and are deprived of their rattle.'

In comedy as in pantomime, Woodward was invaluable to Garrick, approaching him more nearly than any other actor of his time. Without being an Adonis like Barry, he had a handsome stage appearance with a perfect figure, a sense of dress and a natural swagger that fitted him admirably for fine gentlemen parts. His stage and private personalities were entirely different. Behind the scenes on pantomime nights he made himself thoroughly disagreeable, terrifying the stage carpenters and scene shifters with his violent language. He was well read, and could talk intelligently enough with those who shared his intellectual interests, but among his fellow-actors his serious temperament did not make for popularity. He had no taste for conviviality, and, as a companion, the best that could be said of him was that he was inoffensive. Seeing him sitting glum and silent in the tavern adjoining the theatre, no one would have taken him for a comedian. The lines of his face would have suited him for tragic parts, and it was those that he longed to play, but there was something in the quality of his voice that made serious utterance impossible. As he stepped on to the stage, his personality, even his appearance, seemed to change in spite of himself; his face lighted up, his voice took on the inflexions of comedy, and his whole being radiated humour and gaiety.

To Woodward alone among his actors, Garrick allowed the privilege of interpreting his parts as he pleased. When he revived Ben Jonson's *Every Man in his Humour* in the winter of 1751, he summoned the company as usual, read through the play with his own alterations and additions, allotting the parts and giving his instructions. It was many years since the play had been acted, and he took great pains with his part of Kitely as well as explaining to Woodward his conception of Bobadil. But Woodward had his own ideas which Garrick allowed him to carry out, and when the night came the applause was equally divided between them. On the only occasion when Woodward went against his own judgment to please Garrick, the result did not encourage a repetition—although in fact Garrick was perfectly right. In the spring of 1754 Garrick played Hamlet to Woodward's Polonius, a part that, like many others difficult to understand, was habitually buffooned. Garrick, talking it over with Johnson, thought it had been misrepresented, and saw it as dotage encroaching on wisdom. He persuaded Woodward to play it seriously with that interpretation in mind. But the audience, disappointed of their laugh, found his performance flat and insipid, and Woodward was no better pleased with it himself.

As a comedian, Woodward could not expect a very high salary, but Garrick gave him more than had ever been paid to any actor in his line. In addition to a basic salary of £500 for the season, he received extra for pantomime, and his benefit night brought him another £200 or so. Austere in his tastes, he lived well below his income, and at the end of ten years on those terms had saved a considerable sum of money. Had he remained at Drury Lane he might have died a comparatively rich man, but, like the others, he became discontented, and considered himself underpaid. It was natural that when the actors saw Garrick driving in his carriage with a nobleman by his side, and heard of the style in which Mr. and Mrs. Garrick were entertaining in Southampton Street while they struggled to keep the bailiffs out of their lodgings, they should feel that the profits of the theatre were unequally divided. If they dared to ask for a raise in salary, they were treated with great severity, and made to feel guilty of the grossest ingratitude; if they left his management for any other without a good excuse, they were branded as traitors. On the other hand, no actor in a financial difficulty was refused help on a generous scale, although Garrick's businesslike methods in transacting a loan aroused more indignation than gratitude.

Was Garrick a harsh employer? A tabulated list of salaries would not supply the answer. More significant is the fact that no actor or actress who left Drury Lane found better fortune elsewhere, and we have his own word for it that every one of them of any consequence directly or indirectly sought re-engagement. George Anne Bellamy, privileged by her youth and beauty, alternated between the two theatres; Mrs. Cibber came back to Drury Lane in 1753 and remained there for the rest of her career; Woodward and Barry came financially to grief when they left his company; Macklin and Foote never lost an opportunity of saying something malicious about Garrick, but were glad enough to accept an engagement from him whenever they were in difficulties. Peg Woffington was the exception. Her continued absence from Drury Lane is usually put down to a reluctance to meet her old lover in the presence of

ife, and Garrick's dislike of being reminded of their liaison.
ther such delicacy of feeling is likely to have survived in the
boisterous atmosphere of an eighteenth-century green-room is open
to discussion. But, apart from any possible awkwardness between
them, she must have known that Garrick did not like male impersonations, and that her gifts had fuller scope under Rich's management. George Garrick's salary of £250 for his services on the business side arouses some misgivings; considering that his brother died
worth £120,000 it sounds disproportionately small. One is apt to
forget that Lacy, whom he was primarily supposed to assist, though
less in the public eye than his famous partner, actively shared the
responsibilities of management and in all matters of finance took
a very firm line. On two occasions we find Garrick approaching some
influential friend in the hope of finding a better post for George,
and his failure suggests that the young man's abilities did not merit
a higher reward. George gave his brother a lifetime of devoted
service; in return, David made himself responsible for his welfare,
gave him wise elder-brotherly advice, and later on paid for the
education of his children.

That Garrick was vain would be hard to deny with the whole
weight of contemporary opinion against us, but his vanity had
nothing in common with complacency. It would be too much to
say that a nervous fear of losing his hold over his audiences poisoned
his life, for he was on the whole a happy man, but for his peace
of mind he needed to be continually reassured that he was not in
any danger of doing so. Any suggestion, however, that he kept the
best parts for himself for fear of being overshadowed, as some of
his actors complained, is utterly false. Every actor of promise was
tirelessly coached by him, and presented to the public in the rôles
that best suited him. When Garrick set out to compete with Barry
in the acting of Romeo, he suffered from the disadvantage of having
already given Barry all his best ideas. It was not his fault that most
of his pupils did not fulfill their promise, and that only Barry in
tragedy and Woodward in comedy ever approached him in power.

In the autumn of 1751 he engaged three young actors from
Dublin—Ross, Dexter, and Mossop. David Ross proved himself a
competent all-round actor, but laziness and intemperance limited
his usefulness. Dexter's superb self-assurance and the report that
Garrick hoped great things from him ensured him a rapturous wel-

come, but with each successive performance his powers of pleasing waned, and after two or three seasons he went back to Dublin. Of the three, Henry Mossop was the best discovery, and as a tragedian he was to rank third after Garrick and Barry. He had a tremendously powerful voice, which some found 'harmonious' and full of 'force, fire and fury', while others said that he 'bellowed in unnatural rants' and that his favourite attitude of left hand on hip and right arm outstretched reminded them of a teapot. His shambling walk and clumsy movements unfitted him for the juvenile leads he hankered after; he was best in character parts of vehemence and rage, particularly in Richard III, which Garrick made over to him. Within his narrow range he was a good copy of his master, and for the next few years Garrick and he carried the tragedy between them.

Disappointed playwrights—of whom there was a plentiful supply, for never in the history of the drama have more bad plays been written—used to say that Garrick gave the public adaptations or revivals of old plays rather than new ones in order to make easy money. But the very reverse is the truth. In the years covered by this chapter he produced seven new tragedies and one new comedy; only one—a tragedy—approached what we should now call a box-office success, and the losses incurred by the others had to be made good by putting on the old favourites. Another complaint was that, in making his choice, he was guided by considerations other than the merit of the play. This, alas, is true. Sometimes he would reject the work of an author whom he suspected of writing or talking against him; at others, he would accept a play to please a person of social consequence. In 1754 Lady Coventry drove to Drury Lane in her carriage and, calling him out from a rehearsal, put into his hands the manuscript of a tragedy written by her husband's kinsman, Samuel Crisp (Fanny Burney's 'Daddy Crisp'), urging him to accept it and telling him that Mr. Pitt thought well of it. Garrick obeyed her, said Arthur Murphy, who had his own reasons for feeling bitter, as if she had been a tenth muse, and produced the play with the utmost dispatch. The tragedy was probably no worse than many others he had nearly accepted, and to Garrick her patronage was the deciding factor.

The comedies of these early years were little better than the tragedies. In his vain search for good new plays Garrick asked Cibber, now well on in his eighties, whether he had an unacted comedy of two of his own in his desk. 'What then?' asked Cibber. 'I should be glad to have the honour of bringing it into the world.' 'Who have you to act it?' 'Why,' said Garrick, 'there are Clive, Pritchard, myself,' and he mentioned some other names. 'No,' said the old man, taking a pinch of snuff with great nonchalance, 'it won't do.'

Far more to the public taste than any contemporary tragedy in blank verse, however noble its sentiments and academically correct its construction, was *The Fairies*, a light opera produced in the spring of 1755 based on *A Midsummer Night's Dream*, and its popularity foreshadowed the coming vogue for musical plays. Two Italian singers, Signor Curioni and Signora Passerini, took the parts of Lysander and Hermia, and a prologue written by Garrick made a reference to Signor Shakesparelli. At the time it was assumed that Garrick had himself rewritten the whole of the play, but from his subsequent denial it appears that only the bad taste of the prologue can be laid at his door. A year later he allowed *The Tempest* to be subjected to the same treatment.

When Garrick was in Paris he had the dubious pleasure of meeting Foote, and on his return could contradict the extraordinary rumours that had long been circulating about him. Some said that he had been killed in a duel; others that he had died of drink; while a few declared cheerfully that he had been hanged. But he turned up again safe and sound in the autumn of 1751 and, having run through the whole of his fortune (his third, by the way) as the result of profligate living, felt particularly censorious about the comparatively harmless follies of other Englishmen abroad. His farce, *Taste*, produced by Garrick early in 1752, was aimed at the rich collectors who gave immense prices for mutilated pieces of statuary and faded paintings from abroad for the sake of their supposed antiquity, while neglecting the living artists of their own country. But those who were priding themselves on their rich collections of Greek and Roman art brought home from their Grand Tours, or acquired for them by their agents abroad, did not relish the suggestion that many of their antiques were spurious, and the stay-at-homes could not fully understand the point of the joke. It was not until much later, when the aptness of his criticisms became apparent, that the satire was appreciated.

Considering Foote's habitual impertinences to Garrick, it is surprising to find him in and out of Drury Lane as though nothing ever had, or ever would, cast a shadow between them, and even borrowing money as though he were somehow entitled to it. It was not that Garrick was either long-suffering or forgiving by temperament. He flared up quickly, and an actor who displeased him was made to smart for it before being taken back into favour. Indeed, Kitty Clive was the only one at Drury Lane who was not afraid of him. But Foote was irrepressible; nothing short of personal violence could have silenced him, and as no one took anything he said seriously, it was wiser to appear deaf. The two men had known each other since very early days at the Bedford Coffee-house, before either of them had thought of going on the stage, when Foote was a little beau in green and silver, with a large bag-wig and a muff, and when Garrick with three quarts of vinegar, as Foote used characteristically to say, was calling himself a wine merchant.

Foote, like Garrick, fell under the influence of Macklin; he listened to his ideas on acting and even submitted to his instruction. For Macklin, with very little knowledge to support or develop his theories, and incapable of putting them into practice, was always looking out for pupils. It so happened that he expounded his views to talented beginners who would have succeeded without help from anyone, and when they became famous Macklin, recalling the advice he had given them, claimed much of the credit for himself. He could point with pride to Garrick, Barry and his own daughter, Miss Macklin, all of whom could in a sense be described as his pupils. Of Foote as a pupil he preferred not to speak; but it was under his management at the Little Theatre in the Haymarket that Foote made an unfortunate first appearance as Othello. IIis alternations between shrillness and a miserable whining were exceedingly comic, and Macklin took pains to let it be known that it had been against his advice that Foote had attempted tragedy at all.

Macklin was only fifty-four years old when he decided to leave the stage and open a tavern, where refreshment and instruction were to be profitably combined. In December 1753 Garrick allowed him the use of Drury Lane for a farewell performance and, with a readiness too cheerful to escape Foote's malicious tongue, wrote a prologue suitable for the occasion. A few months later Macklin opened his tavern in the Piazza next door to Covent Garden Theatre, offering a public ordinary at the unusually low price of three shillings a head with wine included. As the clock struck four every day, the tavern bell rang and the diners took their places at the long table. At ten minutes past, the outer door was closed and no one else admitted. Macklin himself always brought in the first dish, placed it on the table, and after a low bow retired a few paces back. During dinner carefully drilled waiters, directed by a pre-arranged code of signals from Macklin, attended to the guests in unbroken silence. The meal over and the wine and glasses laid on the table, Macklin walked gravely to the table, passed the bell rope round the back of the chair at the head of the table, bowed low and made a dignified exit. This novel formality had a sobering effect on the company, and, during the short time the tavern flourished, fewer blows were exchanged there than at any other place of refreshment in the neighbourhood.

By seven o'clock the diners were assumed to be in the mood for instruction, and expected to repair to a lecture-room near by to be known as *The British Inquisition*. Admission was a further shilling per person, and every night Macklin opened the proceedings with a lecture. The ground he proposed to cover in his course of instruction indicates a vanity bordering on madness. He was to run through the whole range of human thought and knowledge from the arts and sciences to politics and philosophy, and, after his discourse, the audience would be invited to take part in a free debate on some subject chosen by himself. In particular, he would trace the history of Comedy from earliest times; he would compare the modern stage with those of Greece and Rome; he would discuss each of Shakespeare's plays, considering how the leading parts had been played, and how they should be played; how far French influence on English culture had been beneficial—and many more equally ambitious themes. As he knew no language but his own, and had read little or nothing in that, the level of his discourse was laughably low. When he came to *Romeo and Juliet* he told Garrick beforehand that, as the critics had not properly decided which was the better Romeo, Barry or he, his lecture would decide the question. Garrick cocked up his ears. 'Ah! my dear Mac,' he exclaimed, 'how will you bring that about?' 'I'll tell you, sir,' said Macklin, 'I mean to show your different merits in the garden scene. Barry comes into it, sir, as great as a Lord, swaggering about his love, and talking so loud, that by God, sir, if we don't suppose the servants of the Capulet family almost dead with sleep, they must have come out and tossed the fellow in a blanket. Well, sir, after having fixed my auditors' attention to this part, then I shall ask, "But does Garrick act thus?" Why, sensible that the family are at enmity with him and his house, he comes creeping in upon his toes, whispering his love, and looking about him *just like a thief in the night* . . .' At this Garrick thanked him kindly but begged him to drop the idea, saying that after all it was best to leave the decision to the audience.

The most regular attendant at the lectures was Foote, who could hardly be expected to resist such a heaven-sent opportunity for ridiculing an old friend. By his questions and interjections he kept the audience convulsed with laughter, and Macklin's attempts to snub him into silence only drew from him still more damaging repartees. For a time, the contest between the two amused their audiences, and Macklin, though annoyed at being scored off in public, was not financially the loser for it. But Foote, who never knew where to draw the line, reproduced the whole scene on the boards of his theatre in the Haymarket, where the mimic contest between lecturer and student had none of the spontaneity that had made it amusing in real life. Macklin, losing his temper, retorted with a clumsy charge against Foote of stealing his portmanteau, abusing him with the coarsest epithets in his vocabulary. The public tired of the quarrel, and soon Foote in the Haymarket and Macklin in his Covent Garden lecture-room found themselves attacking each other to empty benches. Their anger evaporated. 'Macklin,' said Foote in a low voice one evening, looking cautiously about him, 'as we are left alone, suppose we take a beefsteak together,' and the two old friends went off happily together.

Nor was the tavern any more profitable. In his preoccupation with the arts and sciences, Macklin left the practical side of the catering in the hands of his servants with the result that he was robbed in every direction. By the end of the year he was made bankrupt, and London lost its first Academy of Dramatic Art. A few years later he returned to the stage for nearly another half-century.

CHAPTER X

BALLET

1755 — 1761

GARRICK's liking for spectacle and ballet was regarded as a streak of vulgarity in a man of otherwise cultured tastes, and the failure of an ambitiously staged ballet at Drury Lane in 1755 aroused no sympathy and caused no regret. But the production is of great interest to us, for it brought Jean-Georges Noverre, the greatest name in the history of ballet, to London for the first time, and led indirectly to the invention of the modern ballet form. Watching Garrick's performance, the young *maître de ballet* noticed its pantomimic quality and saw the possibilities of combining the art of miming with that of dancing. In later life, he placed no value on those of his ballets composed before he saw Garrick.

It had long been assumed that the art of the theatre on its highest plane should rely on human speech for its effects, and spectacle and ballet should be relegated to the lighter forms of entertainment such as pantomime or opera. In 1755 there was some justification for this point of view; spectacle usually implied little more than a procession, and ballet a disconnected series of dances at the end of an act to assist the audience in imagining a change of scene. Not only was there no attempt to outline a story, but the dances did not even reflect the mood of the opera or pantomime in progress. As Paris was the home of dancing, formalism reigned as supreme in that art as in the acting of Racine and Corneille. Like the heroes of classical dramas, the men wore plumed headdresses and the eighteenth-century stage version of a Roman officer's uniform, the women, wide paniers and ankle-length skirts,

128

and the large wigs and masks worn by both sexes made their heads look more than life-size. Free and graceful movement was impossible to achieve, and dances consisted mostly of complicated steps and high jumps, with a few routine movements of the arms.

It can be safely assumed that Garrick heard of Noverre from his friend Monnet, under whose management in Paris Noverre had just scored a sensational success. It was to Monnet that he owed his first chance when, in 1743 at the age of sixteen, he had been allowed to appear in a *pas de trois* at the Opéra Comique. There he came across Rameau, who was leading the orchestra, and Boucher, who was designing the scenery and costumes, and the meeting of these three men of talent was to have the happiest results. In addition, Monnet secured the services of the great dancer, Dupré, as *maître de ballet,*[1] Simon Favart as reader of plays, and an obscure actor from Rouen called Préville who came to be acknowledged as the greatest French comedian of the century. Now the relationship of the Opéra Comique to the Comédie Française and the Comédie Italienne was somewhat similar to that of the Little Theatre in the Haymarket to the two patent theatres, and so strong a company excited the jealousy of the regular players. Achieving a success disproportionate to its standing, the Opéra Comique found itself ordered to close down. In 1752, however, Monnet re-established himself there, and two years later he invited Noverre, by then well known in the provinces, to become his *maître de ballet*. In July 1754 Noverre achieved his first great success with *Les Fêtes Chinoises,* a ballet which, in the splendour of its *décor,* the ingenuity of its round-dances, and the perfect training of its *corps de ballet,* marked a considerable advance on all previous productions of the kind. The scenery was painted by Boucher and the costumes designed by Boquet. The music may have been by Rameau, who was to provide the music for many of Noverre's later ballets, but it is typical of the period that the composer's name does not appear on the contemporary references to the ballet. In after life Noverre took no pride in recalling this early work, and he has left us no scenario. In his more mature judgment, he thought the colour scheme dazzling and confusing to the eye, and the set dances by masked figures cold and inexpressive in comparison with the more romantic style he

1 The *maître de ballet* fulfilled the functions of what we should now call the choreographer in addition to training the dancers under him.

evolved after he took off his dancers' masks, simplified their costumes, and taught them to dance with their whole bodies. But a contemporary account in the *Nouveau Calendrier des spectacles de Paris* has survived, and we give the translation that appears in *David Garrick and his French Friends*, by F. A. Hedgcock:

'The scene represents at first an avenue ending in terraces and in a flight of steps leading to a palace situated on a height. This first set changes, and shows a public square decorated for a festival; at the back is an amphitheatre, on which sixteen Chinamen are seated. By a quick change of scene, thirty-two Chinamen appear instead of sixteen, and go through a pantomimic performance on the steps. As they descend, sixteen other Chinamen, mandarins and slaves, come out of their houses and take their places on the steps. All these persons form eight ranks of dancers, who, by bending down and rising up in succession, give a fair imitation of the waves of a stormy sea. When all the Chinese have come they begin a characteristic march. In this is to be seen a mandarin, carried in a rich palanquin by six white slaves, while two negroes drag a car in which a young Chinese woman is seated. They are both preceded and followed by a crowd of Chinamen, who play divers instruments of music in use in their country. When this procession is finished the ballet begins, and leaves nothing to be desired, neither for the variety nor for the neatness of the figures. It ends by a round-dance, in which there are thirty-two persons; their movements form a prodigious quantity of new and perfectly planned figures, which are linked and unlinked with the greatest ease. At the end of this round-dance the Chinamen take up their places anew on the amphitheatre, which changes into a porcelain shop. Thirty-two vases rise up, and hide from the audience the thirty-two Chinese.'

It was the sensation of the season, and Garrick not unreasonably supposed that it would do equally well at Drury Lane. Londoners, with an innate appreciation of dancing, had never seen the best. Despite the large salaries offered them by the managers of the Opera House in the Haymarket, dancers from abroad shrank from crossing the Channel until they had passed their prime and had ceased to please the fastidious audiences in France and Germany. Yet even second-rate dancers had been received in London with enthusiasm, and Garrick saw in Noverre's elaboration of the ballet form an effective counter-blast to Rich's pantomimes. Noverre, he had heard, was a Protestant of Swiss extraction, and, though born in Paris, had neved liked the French. The *maître de ballet* was as indispensable a member of the company as the leader of the orchestra; the post at Drury Lane was vacant, and Garrick hoped that, if all went well, Noverre might make London his home. Elated by his success, Noverre placed his value high. He refused an offer of £ 200 for the season with a benefit, and demanded 350 guineas with the stipulation that Garrick should himself perform at his benefit. The contract was signed in January 1755, and arrangements went forward to produce *Les Fêtes Chinoises* at Drury Lane early the next season. Noverre was authorized to engage dancers at 40 guineas each, Boquet was commissioned to design the scenery and costumes for a fee of £ 150, and by November preparations had been completed for a production even more splendid than the original.

From the first Lacy had misgivings. He did not share Garrick's enthusiasm for Noverre's gifts, and did not approve of the large sums that were being lavished on the ballet. Moreover, he watched with growing concern the deterioration in the relations between France and England. knowing that the pit and the gallery, never friendly to foreigners, would resent the presence of French performers in a London theatre. By the time the ballet was announced under its English title, *The Chinese Festival,* war was imminent, and Garrick thought it advisable to insert a paragraph in the newspapers explaining that M. Noverre was Swiss and that the dancers were nearly all English. As a final insurance against disorder, the King was persuaded to honour the first performance with his presence, and by royal command the evening of November 8th opened with *The Fair Quaker of Deal,* a comedy whose rough humour appealed to King George II. Throughout its five acts all went well, but as soon as the curtain rose on the ballet the whistling and catcalling began. From their places on the stage the French dancers were amazed to see how little in awe the English were of their King, and could hardly believe their eyes when they saw the old gentleman laughing heartily at the uproar. At each succeeding performance the opposition increased. Lacy was in favour of withdrawing the ballet at once, but large sums had been spent on it and Garrick hoped that the audience would relent. He tried to humour them by appearing in their favourite rôles, but nothing would mollify them. On the sixth day a free fight broke out between the occupants of the boxes, who, as usual, championed the foreign performers, and those in the pit and the gallery. Benches were torn up, scenery and chandeliers smashed; finally an angry crowd went to Garrick's house in Southampton Street and, breaking his windows, would have set fire to the building had not the military intervened. The experiment had failed, and Garrick and Lacy were four thousand pounds out of pocket.

Far more to British taste were the mangled versions of Shakespeare produced later in the season. *A Winter's Tale,* drastically cut down and altered, was followed on the same evening by *The Taming of the Shrew,* renamed *Katherine and Petruchio* and reduced to the dimensions of an afterpiece. In a prologue Garrick declared unblushingly:

> *'Tis my chief wish, my joy, my only plan*
> *To lose no drop of that immortal man.*

A new production of *King Lear* in October 1756, with many of Tate's alterations scrapped in favour of the original, was more to his credit, but he lacked the courage to restore the Fool and give the play its tragic ending. *Antony and Cleopatra,* produced in January 1759 for the first time since the Restoration, suffered no great injury from his pen, but it failed to arouse any interest. The stage at that time could not provide a Cleopatra; Mrs. Yates, then at the beginning of her career, was not equal to it, and Garrick did not look important enough for Antony. The play was laid aside until 1830.

Had Garrick shown a little tact at the right time and been willing to compromise, Woodward might have remained at Drury Lane for the rest of his career to the great advantage of them both. But he left in the summer of 1758 and, with the exception of a benefit night in 1768, never appeared there again. The season was already well advanced when Barry, tired of acting, under Rich's management, was fired by an ambition to build a new theatre in Dublin in opposition to Sheridan, under whose management the two theatres in Smock Alley and Aungier Street had for some years been united. Needing help, financial and professional, Barry approached Woodward with an offer of partnership. Their lines of acting, he pointed out, were too different to clash, and between

them they were sure to succeed. Woodward considered the prop-
osition carefully: he had always worked amicably with Garrick,
his position was secure and his salary higher than that of any other
comedian; on the other hand, the suggestion that a fortune awaited
him elsewhere unsettled him. He took Garrick aside and, telling
him of Barry's proposal, offered to stay at Drury Lane on one condition: that Garrick and Lacy should sign an undertaking to pay
him as large a salary as they then gave, or thereafter would give,
to any other actor or actress. This Garrick thought unreasonable.
They could not shut the door, he explained, upon unexpected
merit; he warned Woodward of the danger of losing his hard-
earned savings, and advised him to be content with his present
salary which, in the managers' opinion, was an adequate reward
for his admittedly valuable services. He expressed himself with the
severity habitual to him when any actor had the temerity to ask
him for more money, and Woodward did not persist in his demand.
He was still reluctant to take the plunge, and, moreover, his wife
was unwilling to leave London. A very small concession might have
tipped the scale. But Garrick, loath to admit Woodward's value to
him, made no gesture, while Barry, who according to Rich was
capable of wheedling a bird from the tree and squeezing it to death
in his hand, flattered Woodward into saying that he would join
in the venture. They left for Dublin together at the end of the
season. Garrick, deprived of his first comedian too late in the season
to engage another of equal standing, had no redress; he had so
relied on Woodward's loyalty that nothing but verbal promises had
passed between them. And Woodward did not go alone; with him
went many of Garrick's small part actors, and at the end of the
following season he enticed away Mossop from Drury Lane. Garrick never forgave him; four years later the adventurer returned
sadder, wiser, and poorer by three thousand pounds to find Drury
Lane closed to him. Yet Garrick would not admit that Woodward
had outstanding gifts, or that the loss of his services mattered to
him. 'It was all beaten into him,' he would say when Woodward
was praised in his hearing, and he professed to regard Shuter, a
leading actor at Covent Garden, as the best comedian he had ever
seen on the stage.

To take the parts played by Woodward, Garrick engaged
William O'Brien, a young Irishman unknown to London playgoers,

whose style, by a happy coincidence, strongly resembled that of
Woodward. He is described as uncommonly genteel, and, as the
son of a fencing-master, knew how to draw his sword with a swift-
ness and elegance that made everyone else on the stage look clumsy.
He might in time have equalled Woodward in fame had not his
elopement a few years later with Lord Ilchester's twenty-year-old
daughter brought his stage career to an end. Meanwhile in the
autumn of 1758 he was a useful addition to the company, and Garrick could safely have entrusted him with all of Woodward's parts.
But, anxious to prove to himself and the world that he could eclipse
Woodward in one of his most popular rôles, he kept Marplot in
Mrs. Centlivre's *Busybody* for himself. For once he failed; the character required a vacant expression which Woodward assumed to
perfection, whereas Garrick, despite his success as Abel Drugger,
could not help looking intelligent.

The first Christmas appears to have passed by without any
pantomime, but by December 1759 Garrick had ready one of his
own devising in which Harlequin, for the first time for many years,
had the use of his tongue. A battle between Harlequin and Shakespeare, ending with the triumph of Shakespeare, provided the
theme of *Harlequin's Invasion,*[1] which was based on a pantomime
produced at Goodman's Fields in the year of Garrick's first appearance there. It may well have been the very pantomime in which
Garrick, unknown to the audience, played Harlequin in place of
Yates.

A novelty in the autumn of 1758 was the joint appearance of
those two oddities, Foote and the youthful Tate Wilkinson, in
their imitations of contemporary actors. Garrick had himself given
the public their first taste of this form of entertainment at Goodman's Fields when he had offended the leading actors in the west
end by mimicking them in *The Rehearsal,* and Foote had more
recently given his impersonations at the Little Theatre, but this
was the first time anything of the kind had been seen at Drury
Lane. Most people assumed that the newcomer was Foote's discovery, but Garrick had known of Wilkinson's gift for mimicry
long before Foote met him and it was, in fact, Garrick who had
brought them together.

[1] Garrick wrote the famous sea song known as 'Heart of Oak' with a setting
by William Boyce for this pantomime. See Appendix VI.

Wilkinson was a plain-featured, shabbily dressed youth of seventeen when, armed with a letter of introduction, he knocked nervously at Garrick's house in Southampton Street. He had already idled away many months hanging about behind the scenes of Covent Garden in the hopes of finding an opening there, but Rich would not be bothered with him, and he had only succeeded in getting himself thoroughly disliked by his mimicry of the actors behind their backs. Garrick was now his last hope. The door opened. Yes, Mr. Garrick was at home; the young gentleman could come inside. For ten minutes he waited while Garrick studied Lord Mansfield's letter. Wilkinson was a name that must have made Garrick feel slightly uncomfortable, for he had been instrumental in bringing tragedy into that family. Some months ago, it had come to his knowledge that two members of his company had been granted a marriage licence by Dr. Wilkinson of the Savoy Chapel in defiance of the Marriage Act. Garrick sent for the newly married pair, cross-questioned them, insisted on examining their marriage certificate and, although it could not have concerned him in any way, informed the authorities—with the result that Dr. Wilkinson, who had been doing a brisk trade in illegal licences for some time, was arrested and sentenced to transportation. He was to have sailed in March 1757, but weakened by many weeks of distress and imprisonment died (or, it was said, committed suicide) before the ship left Plymouth. And now, two months later, his young son, whose only assets were a natural turn for mimicry and a craving to appear on the stage, sat waiting for the great man to speak. 'Well, sir,' said Garrick, looking up from the letter. 'Now you are a stage candidate? Well, sir, let me have a taste of your quality.' The wretched youth, shaking with fear, stumbled through a speech from *Richard III*. After a few minutes, Garrick stopped him, saying that he was much too frightened to give a true impression of his abilities, but that nervousness by no means indicated a want of merit, rather the contrary. He went on making conversation until Wilkinson, feeling more at ease, asked if he could give him a few imitations of well-known actors. 'Nay, now, sir,' said Garrick, 'You must take care of this, for I used to call myself the first at this business.' Luckily Wilkinson happened to start with Foote, giving an astonishingly exact, yet ludicrous, imitation of his mannerisms. Garrick's face glowed with satisfaction, and when Wilkinson had

135

finished Garrick asked him to do it all over again. 'Hey, now! Now —what—all,' stammered Garrick, as he always did when some favour was being asked of him. 'How—really this—this—is—Do call on me again on Monday at eleven, and you may depend upon every assistance in my power. I will see my brother manager, Mr. Lacy, to-day and let you know the result.'

On Monday a greatly inflated Wilkinson presented himself again. Garrick greeted him with outstretched hand, speaking kindly to him about his mother, and giving him the impression that he was the subject of his especial interest. He had talked it over with Mr. Lacy, said Garrick, and they had decided to put him on the books at thirty shillings per week for the following season. He would think of some suitable parts for him later on—to-day his time was short, he could not wait, but would Wilkinson oblige him by giving him a repetition of last Saturday's performance? Wilkinson, now full of self-assurance, was only too happy to do so. After his impersonation of Foote, which went down better than ever, he passed to Barry and Peg Woffington in a scene together as Macbeth and Lady Macbeth. Without a single physical characteristic in common with Peg Woffington, he somehow contrived to look like her, and the harsh voice which unsuited her for tragedy lent itself admirably to burlesque. Garrick laughed so much that Wilkinson had to stop and laugh too. When they had recovered their gravity, Wilkinson was surprised to hear the sound of feminine laughter continuing from behind a baize door. Suddenly it flew open, revealing a little breakfast parlour, and in the doorway stood an elegantly dressed lady, who smilingly apologized for her intrusion. It was Mrs. Garrick, who had been posted there to give her opinion of his performance, and her laughter at his version of Peg Woffington's Lady Macbeth had in it, Wilkinson thought, a particularly happy note.

With Garrick's approval, Wilkinson took a summer engagement at Maidstone to fill in the time before the opening of Drury Lane, and, before he left, Garrick gave him some excellent advice. After earnestly stressing the need for sobriety, he urged him always to be word-perfect. An actor, he said, was not the best judge of his own natural bent, and could more easily discover it from the feelings of his audience. This he could not do if he had to be

7. GARRICK AS KING LEAR

from a mezzotint by J. McArdell from a painting by B. Wilson

thinking of his words. Often a lucky hit would indicate to him where his real genius lay, and it might be the very character in which he had expected to fail.

Garrick had his own means of getting information about promising young actors playing in the country theatres, and he was not pleased with what he heard of Wilkinson that summer. He was showing little talent, wrote his observer, and would play truant rather than act parts he considered beneath his dignity. This was not at all the attitude Garrick expected beginners to take, and, consequently, when the company mustered on the stage for the opening rehearsal in September, he determined to put Wilkinson in his place. The first business of the day was to allot the parts, and this was done by the prompter, who informed Wilkinson curtly that by the manager's express orders he was to go on the stage as a Waiting Gentleman in every play. Then Garrick went up to him and, in front of the whole company, added severely, 'This, sir, is my command, and, if not complied with, I shall take your coat off and do the business myself; and you, sir, will immediately be dismissed my theatre.' Wilkinson, unaware that his behaviour that summer had been reported to Garrick, stood petrified with astonishment at Garrick's change of manner.

Some weeks went by, and Garrick softened a little towards him. One day, Garrick and Foote happened to be discussing imitations in the manager's office. 'Egad, Foote,' said Garrick, 'there is a young fellow engaged with me who I really think is superior to either of us at mimicry. I used to think myself well at it, but I actually give him the preference. He has tried to resemble me, but that will not do, though Mrs. Garrick says she is sure he will be like me.' 'Damn it,' said Foote, 'I should like to hear it.' So Wilkinson was sent for to give his impersonations, and, as a result, Foote invited him to come to Dublin for six weeks to act with him at Sheridan's theatre. Wilkinson, thinking that any change from Waiting Gentlemen must be for the better, accepted his offer providing that he could obtain a leave of absence. Garrick gave his permission willingly enough, telling Wilkinson that he was glad of an opportunity of doing him a service and that he hoped it would turn out well. But as it was probable that the expedition would fail, he had from motives of friendliness for him consulted with Mr. Lacy and they were giving him a contract for two years. Wilkinson understood him to say that it was to come into effect that day, the 20th of October 1757.

Mrs. Woffington prophesied from a sick-bed that if Wilkinson dared to mimic her in her native town he would be stoned to death. But she was wrong; Smock Alley rocked with laughter to see her mannerisms burlesqued, and Wilkinson could not make himself heard in the uproar. Many other well-known actors were victimized, and Dublin could not have enough of the new joke. It was March before Wilkinson, proud, happy and with £130 in his pocket, started for home and Drury Lane.

As he had been absent with Garrick's permission, Wilkinson supposed himself entitled to his arrears of salary. He called on the treasurer, who looked surprised to see him and told him that without instructions from the managers he could not make any payment. In his opinion, Wilkinson could not justly claim it. A few days later, Wilkinson met Garrick, who rebuked him sharply for being so audacious, as he called it, as to ask for money, telling him that he had repaid his kindness with impudence and ingratitude. Wilkinson, believing himself to be in the right, stood his ground and produced his copy of the two years' agreement with the date 24th October 1757 on the outside. Garrick, looking at him contemptuously, advised him to go home and ask his mamma to read it to him. He would then learn that inside it stated clearly that the two years were to date from September 1758. To his astonishment, Wilkinson discovered that it was just as Garrick had said, and felt, rather unreasonably, that he had been outwitted.

When the season of 1758 opened it looked as though Wilkinson, in spite of his success in Dublin, was as far as ever from making his London début. The truth is that Garrick regarded him as worse than useless; he was a nuisance. He could not be trusted to take any part without mimicking some other actor, with the result that the laughs came in the wrong places, upsetting those on the stage with him. He drew his thirty shillings a week, but would probably have stood idle for the rest of his two years' engagement had not Foote asked Garrick to revive *Diversions of the Morning,* the farce in which Wilkinson and he had delighted Dublin. Garrick, an inveterate mimic himself in private life, disapproved of stage impersonations—he knew from experience that quarrels followed in their train—and no one but the dreaded Foote could have persuaded him into allowing them on his stage.

The trouble started before the farce was even put into rehearsal, when Colonel Caesar, with whom Mrs. Woffington had for some years been living, called on Garrick and threatened him with a duel should he allow her to be impersonated. Garrick assured him in all sincerity that he detested such performances and willingly promised to protect Mrs. Woffington from annoyance. It is difficult to believe that Colonel Caesar need have resorted to threats on this occasion, for Garrick must have known that Peg Woffington was lying seriously ill, and would never have refused her a small favour. Eighteen months earlier, she had collapsed on the stage while playing Rosalind, interrupting the performance with a scream of terror, and was still lingering, half-paralysed and changed beyond recognition, with only enough of her old spirit left to resent being ridiculed. She died in 1760.

One quarrel at least was averted; but there were many other people who felt like murdering Wilkinson when they saw themselves being burlesqued on the stage. Garrick had hardly finished breakfast when he was called on by a furious actor from Covent Garden, who declared that he was being ruined by what he described as an illiberal attack on him. On his arrival at Drury Lane for the noon rehearsal, Garrick found that sympathy was all on the side of the victim. He sent for Wilkinson and scolded him publicly; when he had finished, Kitty Clive added a little on her own account, rating the culprit for his impudence to his betters. 'Now I can and do myself "take off",' she explained, 'but it is only —' (and she named an opera singer) 'and a set of Italian squalling devils who come over to England to get our bread from us. And I say curse them all for a parcel of Italian bitches.' Then Mossop, who carried into private life the tragedy manner that had brought him fame on the stage, advanced breathing heavily, his hand on the hilt of his sword, 'Sir, if you were to take such a liberty with me, sir,' he declaimed, 'I should draw my sword and run it through your body,' and slowly made his exit. This exhibition proved too much for Garrick's gravity; as soon as Mossop was out of sight he fairly exploded with laughter, and the rest of the company followed his example. Presently in came Foote, and Garrick, recovering his composure and trying to look stern, explained the situation to him, saying that in future the imitations must be omitted altogether. When evening came the farce opened as usual, but here, as in Dublin, Wilkinson's entrance was eagerly awaited, and when he failed to come on, the gallery and pit called loudly for him. Foote's excuses only increased their impatience, and, in the end, Garrick, fearing a riot, actually pushed Wilkinson on to the stage. In the excitement of the moment, he rashly offered himself as a victim. Wilkinson, who had been longing for just such an opportunity, took him at his word, and, to the intense delight of the audience, proceeded to give his version of Garrick as Lear, Biron,[1] and Hamlet, cruelly parodying his hesitations and pantomimic gestures. Wilkinson had never enjoyed any evening more, but it does not surprise us to learn that Garrick refused to look at or to speak to him for the rest of the season.

Wilkinson, with little reason to think that he was a favourite with Garrick, was astonished to find himself treated almost like a son when they met at Portsmouth in the summer. Away from the theatre Garrick was a different man and, as a holiday companion, wholly delightful. He was staying with friends in the neighbourhood and, hearing that Wilkinson was acting in Portsmouth, sent a messenger to invite him to breakfast at a tavern. All the coldnesses of the past vanished in the warmth of his handshake, and after breakfast they walked arm in arm on the ramparts. Mrs. Garrick and their host, Dr. Garney, Garrick told the flattered young man, were anxious to have the pleasure of his company for the inside of a day, and over a mid-morning bottle of hock, Garrick fixed on a date, dropping a hint to his guest to come in his best clothes. And so Wilkinson presented himself dressed to the nines and Garrick, looking him up and down with the freedom of an old friend, passed all but his buckles, which he said were too large and more suitable for a sailor. Mrs. Garrick and the Garneys gave him the kindest of welcomes, and Garrick took him all over the house and garden, running and skipping like a boy. When Wilkinson left at ten that evening after a day devoted to his entertainment, it was settled that the whole party would attend his benefit. A night or two later, twelve of them took their places in the most expensive seats in the house, rather late, but in the mood to applaud generously, and afterwards Garrick came round behind the

---

1 In *The Fatal Marriage*, by Thomas Southerne.

scenes and insisted on carrying off his young protégé to supper with the rest of his party at the tavern. At midnight Mrs. Garrick was ready for bed, and Garrick, with the gallantry he always displayed towards her, rose to escort her home, borrowing Wilkinson's handsome sea-captain's cloak for the walk. Having delivered his charge he returned to the party, and they all sat chatting together until three o'clock in the morning.

After this happy interlude it is sad to record that when the two men got back to Drury Lane exactly the same quarrels and misunderstandings happened all over again. Wilkinson went to Dublin for a second visit with Garrick's permission, and when he returned in the spring of 1760 his request for arrears of salary met with the same indignant refusal; the fact that his engagement had still a few months to run did not in Garrick's opinion affect the issue.[1] When it expired, he did not offer to renew it, and Wilkinson went over to Covent Garden. There he took his revenge by mimicking Garrick to his face as he sat in a front box, thereby forfeiting his goodwill for ever.

Wilkinson was not an attractive young man; his successes were all gained at the expense of far better actors than himself, and his manner to Garrick, even on his own showing, was impertinent. Even so, the story of their relationship helps to explain why it was that Garrick was not liked or respected by his actors. He was too changeable; they never knew where they were with him. They did not realize—as did his friends in private life—that he was not as angry as he often appeared; at the other extreme, his naturally high spirits and anxiety to please everyone often led him into demonstrations of warmer cordiality than he felt. In the greenroom he would join in the general talk, making deliberately coarse and rather feeble jokes in his wish to be accepted as one of them, but an actor approaching him for a rise in salary was quickly made aware of the gulf between them, and to feel that an unwarrantable liberty had been taken.

If London was short of leading actors during these years, it was because Dublin was overweighted with them. At the new theatre in Crow Street, Barry and Woodward regardless of expense

---

[1] In 1765 with find Kitty Clive smarting under a similar grievance. 'You stopped four days' salary when I went to Dublin,' she wrote him angrily, 'though you gave me leave to go.'

had collected a brilliant company, including Mossop, Dexter, Macklin, Foote and Mrs. Dancer, against which the older house could not compete. Sheridan, knowing that Dublin could not support two companies, and that this cut-throat competition would bring ruin to both, gave up the management of Smock Alley and engaged himself to Drury Lane for the season of 1760–1761. The arrangement worked fairly well. Garrick did not like Sheridan, but, looking back on his years as a manager, he admitted that, with the exception of Barry, he was more useful to him as a member of his company than any other actor. He knew that Sheridan, like Barry, could draw a good house on the nights he did not himself appear, whereas no one else could do more than half-fill the theatre. This is hard to reconcile with the poor opinion of Sheridan's acting expressed by those qualified to judge, but at least his style was his own—he did not imitate Garrick—his elocution was good, and sheer hard work and persistence had done the rest.

Unfortunately, he was rather too successful for Garrick's peace of mind. At first, they appeared on different nights—Garrick in some of his most popular comedy rôles and Sheridan as Richard III, Cato, and Hamlet. Then, in Rowe's *Fair Penitent,* they shared the applause, the grave dignity of Sheridan's Horatio making a perfect foil for the liveliness of Garrick's Lothario. But Garrick should have been warned by previous experiences to avoid Shakespeare's *King John,* for neither as King John nor as Faulconbridge had he ever been wholly successful, and it had been Mrs. Cibber's performance as Constance that had dominated the evening. Mrs. Yates in her place (Mrs. Cibber was too unwell to act that week) had not her power, and in consequence the male parts acquired more importance. Garrick began by rehearsing King John, leaving Faulconbridge for Sheridan; then he wavered and persuaded Sheridan to exchange parts. In the interests of the production as a whole, his final decision was the right one, since Sheridan was more seriously handicapped for Faulconbridge by his stiffness than Garrick by his small physique. But while Garrick made a passable Faulconbridge Sheridan achieved one of the outstanding successes of his career as King John, and this was more than Garrick had bargained for. He could not hide his mortification when some mischievous person told him that the young king, before whom the play was performed, had been uncommonly pleased with Sheridan, but considered

142

that Garrick had over-acted, and, according to Tom Davies, the play was promptly and prematurely withdrawn. It was foolish of Garrick to attach so much importance to the opinion of a monarch for whom all Shakespeare was 'sad stuff', but, in the years to come, Garrick often allowed himself to be damped by the lack of royal appreciation. The truth was that King George III, having been taught by Quin, did not care for Garrick's romantic style of acting, and was one day to find the classicism of Mrs. Siddons much more to his liking.

CHAPTER XI

AWAY FROM THE THEATRE

1755—1761

GARRICK in the manager's office, harried and pestered by discontented players and authors, was not always a likeable figure —he was too highly strung to come through the ordeal unscathed— but at home in the country, surrounded by his friends, he was all kindness and good humour. In 1754 he bought a house at Hampton with a few acres of garden extending for about a hundred feet along the Thames, but intersected by the main road from London to Hampton Court. Here he spent every moment he could spare from the theatre, using the house in Southampton Street as a *pied à terre* for the nights he was obliged to spend in London. Here he became the perfect country squire, entertaining the parson, and distributing coals to the old people and cakes to the young. Robert Adam, then at the beginning of his career, refronted the house, adding a portico supported by four Corinthian columns, and down on the lawn by the water's edge he designed a small octagonal brick temple with a dome and Ionic pillared portico.[1] 'Capability' Brown, the famous landscape gardener then employed at Hampton Court, laid out the grounds, connecting the garden round the house with the lawn on the riverside by a tunnel which had about it the romantic flavour of a grotto, and by various ingenious devices making the whole appear much more extensive than its six acres. It was in the garden that Mrs. Garrick's interest centred, and, with her husband's assistance, she planted with her own hands cypresses

---

[1] Garrick's Villa, as Hampton House is now called, has been converted into flats. The temple is the property of the Hampton Urban District Council.

144

which she was to live long enough to see grown into great trees.

Now at last Garrick had room to display all the delicate china-ware he had been collecting ever since he first came to London, and enough wall space for the pictures he had bought from the men who had painted them; for, influenced perhaps by the out-spoken views of his friend Hogarth, he preferred the work of living artists to the faded paintings and mutilated statues so often indis-criminately collected by eighteenth-century lovers of the antique. A large proportion of the portraits and conversation-pieces com-missioned by him naturally had him as their subject, but that every one in the house represented himself was the malicious exaggera-tion of his enemies. In the great bow-windowed room on the ground floor, Hogarth's four Election pictures hung on each side of the fireplace, and the drawing-room above, as well as the Garricks' bedroom, was decorated and furnished *à la Chinoise*. Another room housed Garrick's library, with its collection of rare old plays in splendid new bindings.

In 1758 he conceived the idea of dedicating the little temple by the riverside to the memory of Shakespeare, and of placing inside it a life-sized statue in marble. 'Lo, the Bard of Avon!' ex-claimed Garrick, striking an attitude to show Roubiliac what he wanted, and the statue that resulted is more suggestive of Garrick impersonating Shakespeare than of the poet himself, despite the fact that Roubiliac took the Chandos portrait for his model. Dur-ing the progress of the work Garrick frequently visited the studio. 'How's Shakespeare, eh?' he asked, meeting Roubiliac in the street. 'I shall go and pay my respects to him,' and Roubiliac went back to the studio with him. As Garrick entered the marble yard, a practical joke occurred to him. 'See now,' he whispered to the sculptor, 'how I shall frighten that great red-headed Yorkshireman sawing the stone.' He fixed his eyes on the man, assumed a dia-bolical expression and drew from his pocket what he hoped would be mistaken for a pistol; it was, in fact, the footrule he always carried in his pocket for correcting the work of the Drury Lane car-penters. But every humorist has his failures. The burly stonemason looked down on Garrick indulgently, squirted some tobacco juice from the corner of his mouth and said as though to a child, 'What trick will you be after next, my master?'

The first version of the statue did not satisfy Garrick. The block of marble chosen by Roubiliac was full of faint veins, which crossing the face imparted to it a sinister expression. 'What!" cried Garrick, 'was Shakespeare marked with mulberries?' Roubiliac, admitting the justice of the implied criticism, hewed the head from the shoulders and replaced it with another of a purer marble. The joint can be seen just above the collar.[1]

The temple with its statue and Shakespearian relic provided the Garricks and their guests with an object for an after-dinner stroll, and on a summer's evening they would sit outside it taking their wine or their tea, while Mrs. Garrick's pet dog, Biddy, an important member of the household, chased imaginary rabbits or barked at the swans on the river. Before leaving, guests would sometimes lay at Shakespeare's marble feet complimentary verses coupling him with Garrick, and the best of these would appear anonymously in the monthly periodicals. Among many agreeable neighbours there was Horace Walpole, who often came over from Strawberry Hill for dinner, and never ceased to marvel at the number of peers and ministers of state he saw sitting at the table of a player. But the two men never became more than friendly acquaintances; they had few tastes in common, and Walpole, like Johnson, found Garrick's mimicry and buffoonery irritating. He much preferred what he described as Mrs. Garrick's sweetness and good sense. A very different sort of neighbour was Johnson's friend, the unclubbable knight, then plain Mr. John Hawkins the attorney, who lived two miles away, and used to ride over in the holiday season for an afternoon call. One August day he found the Garricks in the garden eating figs. Garrick complained of the wasps, and said that he had heard lately of a man who had swallowed one and died of the sting. Hawkins told him that it was perfectly true, for he had been assured so by the apothecary in charge of the case. 'I believe it,' said Garrick, 'and have been persuading this lady,' pointing to Mrs. Garrick, 'to do so; but I cannot convince her and yet she can believe the story of Saint Ursula and the eleven thousand virgins.' Garrick often teased her gently about her religion, but between her discretions and his lack of strong religious feeling their differing beliefs never disturbed the tranquillity of their married happiness.

[1] Garrick bequeathed the statue to the British Museum, where before the second world war it could be seen standing in the vestibule.

One afternoon in 1758 a group of Scots could have been seen there trying to teach their host golf. One of them aroused Garrick's astonished admiration by hitting a ball right through the tunnel and into the river. It was Alexander Carlyle's first visit to Hampton, and on being introduced by his friend, John Home, to his host and hostess, he looked at Mrs. Garrick with curiosity. Many years had passed since they had shared a cabin on that rough voyage from Holland, when her soft high voice had belied her boy's breeches. She had grown much stouter, he noticed, and did not seem to recognize in the grey-haired clergyman the young Scotsman in a bag-wig who had shown her so much courtesy on the road to London.

The Garricks were ascetic in their tastes, and when by themselves the simplest fare contented them. Garrick, a moderate drinker at any time, was particularly abstemious on the days he was going to perform. One experience of going on the stage drunk had so frightened him that a crust of bread and a single glass of white wine was often all that he would take before the performance. But for their guests at Hampton they kept a good table; in Garrick's later days it could even be described as splendid, and those who envied his prosperity would count the dishes with as much indignation as though they had never laughed at fantastic stories about his meanness. Nothing delighted Garrick more than to try and satisfy Quin's gargantuan appetite during the visit he habitually paid Hampton House in the autumn. Calling Quin his 'butler', Garrick would give him the keys of the cellar and invite him to choose the best Burgundy to go with the high-seasoned venison and fat turtle especially provided for him.

Their friendship had only become possible since Quin's retirement from the stage brought their rivalry to an end. It was Quin who had taken the first step when they met as fellow-guests of the Duke of Devonshire at Chatsworth. Finding himself alone with Garrick one evening, he went up to him and asked after Mrs. Garrick's health, assuring him of his affectionate regard for her. This was the surest way of pleasing Garrick; after that evening they got on famously, chaffing each other like old friends, and Quin's Falstaffian appetites and Garrick's small physique provided the themes of their rather laborious jokes.

The year 1755 can be seen as a turning-point in the fortunes of

Garrick and Johnson; after it, Johnson could meet Garrick with less cause for secret bitterness. For Garrick, the year brought the *Chinese Festival* riot—the first of a series of annoyances and defeats that in the end drove him from the stage; for Johnson, it saw the triumphant publication of his Dictionary, and the award of a pension seven years later freed him from the necessity of earning his bread. Those intervening seven years were among his most poverty-stricken, but by no means his unhappiest; for he enjoyed now the fame to which his scholarly writing had long entitled him. Twice he was arrested for pitifully small debts and twice those debts were paid for him; first by Richardson, and secondly by a bookseller. Considering Garrick's many acts of generosity to persons who had no claim on him, it is surprising that he did not find some way of helping Johnson in his distresses without injuring his pride.

But at least he never went long without seeing his old friend, and inviting him to Hampton. Indeed, Johnson must have been one of his first visitors, for he was present when the making of the tunnel was under discussion. Garrick was in favour of building a bridge over the road, but 'Capability' Brown suggested digging under it. Johnson was all for the tunnel, remarking gleefully that what could not be overdone could be underdone. Living in a London garret (the delights of Streatham were as yet unknown to him), he saw Hampton House as an earthly paradise. 'Ah, David,' he sighed, looking around him, 'it is the leaving of such places that makes a deathbed terrible.' Only the library failed to please him. He took down one book after another, dropping them on the floor in disgust until Garrick remonstrated with him.[1] 'Silly plays in fops' dresses,' was all that Garrick got in reply.

In 1760, we find Garrick entertaining Johnson, Burke[2] and Arthur Murphy for dinner on Christmas Day, and in the absence of evidence to the contrary are free to imagine them at Hampton. They spoke of Foote and how he had been horse-whipped in Dublin by an apothecary for mimicking him on the stage. 'But I wonder,' remarked Garrick, 'that any man would show so much resentment to Foote. Nobody ever thought it worth his while to quarrel with him in London.' 'I am glad,' said Johnson, 'to find that the man is *rising in the world*.' Foote came back from Dublin to find

[1] The same story has been told of Johnson in Garrick's house in Southampton Street.　　[2] The first recorded meeting between Burke and Dr. Johnson.

148

this story going the rounds of the coffee-houses, and in revenge gave out that he would shortly impersonate the Caliban of literature on the stage. Hearing of this, Johnson sent word to Foote that as the theatre was intended for the reformation of vice, he would on such a night go from the box on to the stage and *correct* him before the audience. Nothing more was ever heard from Foote on the subject, and, although Johnson was probably more cruelly mimicked behind his back than any man who had ever lived, no one dared make fun of his physical peculiarities on a public stage.

It must have been about the time he bought Hampton House that Garrick became friendly with Dr. Messenger Monsey, whose acquaintance he made by chance in curious circumstances. At the Old Bailey, where Garrick sometimes went to watch comedy and tragedy in real life, and to study the facial expressions of men and women in moments of great emotion, he heard a man ask a burly fellow just in front of him to move a little to one side so that he might see the bench. The big man refused to budge. The request was repeated; again it was ignored. Finally the smaller of the two men in a voice just above a whisper said, 'If I were not a coward, I would give you a blow even in the court.' The oddity of the remark made Garrick smile and he looked at the stranger more closely. He saw a middle-aged man, with a tousled wig and slovenly clothes; but when he discovered that he was looking at Dr. Messenger Monsey, Lord Godolphin's friend and physician, whose crude, blunt humour he had heard described by Lord Bath and Mrs. Montagu, he determined to make his acquaintance. The two men took to each other and Dr. Monsey became a regular visitor to Hampton. IIis conversation, too rough and blasphemous for Johnson's taste, amused Garrick; and he, in his turn, found Dr. Monsey a good audience for the practical jokes nearly all actors like to play.

One day, the story runs, they were walking home from the city when, at the top of Ludgate Hill, Garrick suddenly left him. He strode into the middle of the street and, looking upwards, repeated several times to himself the words, 'I never saw two before.' A man talking out loud to himself naturally attracted attention, and soon a crowd collected round him. Several people asked him what it was that he saw. He made no reply, but repeated the same words. Someone then observed that the gentleman must have seen two storks, as those birds were rarely seen in pairs. This seemed to satisfy the crowd until another man said, 'But who sees one besides the gentleman?' Garrick affected an insane stare, and Monsey hurried away for fear of getting into trouble. Another day, they were walking past Old Somerset House behind a porter, who was humming cheerfully to himself. 'I'll get a crowd around that man before he reaches Temple Bar,' said Garrick. He then went in front of the man, turned his head and gave him a piercing look. The man's gaiety was checked in a moment; he kept his eye warily on Garrick, who stopped at an apple stall until the man came near, then gave him another penetrating glance and went on again. The man began to wonder whether there could be anything strange about him and, as Garrick went on repeating his performance, he became more and more self-conscious. He turned himself in all directions to see if anything ridiculous were stuck on to him; he even pulled off his wig and examined it. His restless anxiety became evident to the passers-by, and by the time they reached Temple Bar Garrick had carried out his promise.

Then there was the occasion when Dr. Monsey was himself the dupe. One afternoon, Garrick was expecting a visit from him in Southampton Street; it was on a day that Garrick was billed to play King Lear. When Monsey arrived, the servant ushered him into the bedroom, and there on the bed lay Garrick in his night-cap, the quilt drawn up over him and looking the picture of misery. Dr. Monsey expressed his surprise; the play had not been cancelled, and by this time Garrick should have been ready to start for the theatre. In a languid, whining tone of voice, he told Monsey that he felt much too ill to perform himself, but that there was an actor called Marr, extraordinarily like him in figure, face and voice, and a most accomplished mimic. He had entrusted the part to him, and he was sure that no one would see the difference. Dr. Monsey was horrified; he begged Garrick to think better of it; the trick could not possibly succeed and the audience would never forgive him. At this, Garrick became much worse, and asked his friend to leave the room so that he might get a little sleep. But, just as Dr. Monsey was getting up to go, Garrick asked him as a favour to attend the performance and let him know the result. The moment the doctor had closed the door behind him, Garrick jumped out of bed fully dressed, and hurried off to Drury Lane. Monsey, partly to please his friend, and partly to satisfy his curiosity, took his seat in the theatre. The curtain went up and Monsey was bewildered by what he saw on the stage. Sometimes he doubted; at others he marvelled at the likeness between Garrick and Marr. But, finding that the audience was convinced of Garrick's identity, he became suspicious and, as soon as the play was over, rushed back to Garrick's house. But Garrick was home first and back in bed, the quilt drawn up over the clothes he had worn as King Lear, and looked more pathetic than ever. It was not until the next day that Dr. Monsey discovered the truth.

Mrs. Garrick and he did not always get on very well together. He ruffled her usually sweet temper by correcting her English, and laughing rudely when she assured him that nobody took her for a foreigner. Once when they were driving back to London from Hampton, after the weekend (Garrick having ridden on ahead), relations became so strained that he got out of the carriage at Turnham Green and walked the rest of the way. But as a rule she put up with him for Garrick's sake, and they often invited him to dinner on evenings when they were not expecting fine company. When Dr. Monsey found out that they were giving a party for the Duke of Argyll and several ladies of social distinction, he was furious at being left out. 'I would have asked you,' Garrick assured him, 'but you are too great a blackguard.' 'Why, you little scoundrel!' exclaimed Dr. Monsey, 'Ask Lord Godolphin, one of the best-bred men in the world, if I do not behave as well as the politest of his visitors.' 'Well,' replied Garrick, 'if you'll promise to behave properly, you shall come.' Monsey promised. Garrick, however, took the precaution of warning the Duke what to expect and begged his indulgence. All went well until Mrs. Garrick began to help her titled guests, and in her deference to them did not seem to notice Dr. Monsey's plate which he kept handing up again and again. After being disappointed several times in this way, he burst out with, 'Will you help me, you bitch, or not?' Garrick fell back in his chair with laughter; the Duke, though prepared for some display of oddity, looked astounded. But Dr. Monsey, apparently unconscious of the impression he had made, began to tell some amusing stories and the incident was soon forgotten in laughter.

CHAPTER XII

QUARRELS

1755 – 1763

GARRICK always had at least one private war on hand, and, although he was usually in the right, he cuts a very poor figure as a fighter. Physically he was no coward; he would face an angry audience like a man, and speak to them with a firmness and dignity that surprised them into silence. But in a duel with pens his courage varied inversely with the literary stature of his opponent. Third-rate pamphleteers, who attacked and even libelled him for the sake of earning a few sorely needed pounds, he would charge vigorously, knock out, and then, the quarrel over, behave with generosity, often lending or giving money to help them out of their difficulties. These payments may have been made out of sheer kindness of heart, but unfortunately they looked a little like hush-money. On the other hand, when the dangerous satirist, Charles Churchill, and at a later period the terrible Junius, turned on him, he was ready to make peace on any terms. Between these two extremes, there were the men approximately his own size; when it came to a fight they found him fiery and timid in turns.

A detailed relation of all his quarrels with authors would make monotonous reading. Many were with men obscure in their own day and unworthy of serious consideration now, and injured vanity lies at the root of each one. The story, however, has three variations. In the first, A dislikes Garrick's acting. Dramatic criticism at that time knew no half-way house between adulation and venomous disparagement, and consequently A's faultfinding, when it appears in print, is malicious in tone. Garrick declares war. In

8. GARRICK AND MRS. GARRICK ENTERTAINING FRIENDS AT HAMPTON

from a painting by Zoffany

the second, B's play is rejected by Garrick, or, if produced by him, fails. B blames Garrick, and the battle begins. In the third, C is dissatisfied with Garrick's treatment of his play, and after a lapse of time revenges himself by publishing a general attack on Garrick. Garrick takes up his pen.

In addition to these paper wars, in which a great deal of ink was spilt and no good purpose ever served, there was always a number of men with whom Garrick was not on speaking terms because of some remark they were supposed to have made about him. It was one of his weaknesses that he could not help asking what was being said against him, and those who wished to curry favour with him readily satisfied his curiosity. But these squabbles, unpleasant as they were, should not be magnified into vendettas. Again and again, after learning from the pages of one of his contemporaries that Garrick and So-and-so have had a dreadful quarrel and will never speak to each other again, we look elsewhere and discover them a year or two later, dining together and cracking jokes as though nothing had happened. In private life as on the stage, Garrick easily worked himself into a semblance of fury, but, as he once said himself, he was too happy to bear malice for long.

More interesting than to follow in detail the course of any one quarrel is to try and determine from a general survey whether Garrick served the public and the dramatists faithfully, or whether his policy was prompted solely by motives of self-interest. That on the whole he gave the public what it wanted is evident from the fortune he left behind him; that he gave the dramatists their chance is equally evident from his record of twenty-nine years' management, during which he produced seventy-five new plays, exclusive of pantomimes, farces and afterpieces, and twenty-five adaptations or revivals of plays extra to his repertory. Seventeen of these adaptations and revivals were produced before 1760; after that, the level of playwriting rose and, with it, his proportion of new plays to old. It was not his fault that a great many of them failed. At the same time, it is a curious fact that he refused or failed to appreciate the only important plays written during his management. His most serious mistake belongs to a later period than that covered by this chapter, when he missed the opportunity of producing Goldsmith's *Good Natur'd Man,* and in consequence *She Stoops to Conquer.* But in 1756 and 1758 he successively rejected

Home's *Douglas* and Robert Dodsley's *Cleone,* and in 1759 made difficulties over the production of Murphy's *Orphan of China*— tragedies much admired at the time by men whose opinions must be respected. 'I am greatly struck with *Douglas,*' wrote Gray to Walpole. 'The author seems to me to have retrieved the true language of the stage which has been lost for these hundred years.' David Hume preferred it to Shakespeare.

The play had already had a successful first performance in Edinburgh when it was offered to Garrick, and it had the backing of the young Prince of Wales.[1] But Garrick did not like it, and could not be persuaded to produce it. He paid heavily for misjudging popular taste, for after its success at Covent Garden he could not refuse Home's next two tragedies, which were inferior in quality and failed.

Dodsley's *Cleone* came to Garrick with Johnson's approval. Johnson's praise, it is true, was lukewarm; the play had more blood in it than brains, was the opinion he expressed privately, but 'Doddy' was his publisher and patron and he had to stand by him. Garrick did not like the play at all; he thought it 'cruel, bloody and unnatural', and returned it to its author. Then, as so often happened, he wavered; he asked to have the manuscript back, and promised that if on a second reading he thought better of it, he would reverse his decision. But he disliked it rather more, and, after telling everyone at the Bedford Coffee-house that the failure of *Cleone* was inevitable, had the mortification of seeing it succeed at Covent Garden. Perhaps it was true, as some people said at the time, that he refused these two plays because he would have been overshadowed in them by Mrs. Cibber. But Mrs. Cibber, though still a superb tragedy actress, was in a precarious state of health, and could never be relied upon to appear. Garrick was risking his own money when he produced a new play; surely it was natural that he should wish to bear the heaviest responsibility himself. His attempt to ruin Dodsley's first night is more difficult to justify. It was just at the time that he was showing his public how well he could get on without Woodward, and was planning to eclipse him as Marplot. The nights on which Garrick appeared in a new character were important dates in the theatrical calendar, and it could not have been by accident that he chose for his first

1 Later George III.

appearance the date in November for which *Cleone* had already been advertised. Dodsley, alarmed for the fate of his play, secured a postponement to December 2nd. Garrick promptly followed suit, and the two first nights coincided. When, in spite of his manœuvrings, *Cleone* succeeded, Garrick wrote to Dodsley congratulating him, and expressed his concern to hear that he was being accused of trying to entice away Dodsley's audience by acting on the same night. While ridiculing the idea with an affectation of modesty, he offered to make any amends within reason. He received a very cold reply.

In the end, after a long wrangle, Garrick produced *The Orphan of China* himself, and its reception justified Murphy's persistence. It took the united efforts of Henry Fox, Horace Walpole and William Whitehead to overcome Garrick's objections to the play, but, from the moment he gave in, he put his whole heart into making it a success. He delighted even the author with his acting of the lead, and provided the play with a magnificent setting recognized by one of his biographers as that designed for the ill-fated *Chinese Festival*. Mrs. Yates, in the part Mrs. Cibber would have taken had she been in better health, made her name that night as a tragedy actress, and Garrick went out of his way to express satisfaction at her triumph.

In his failures to foresee the popular appeal of three dreary tragedies Garrick has our sympathy, but at the time they were regarded as grave errors of judgment. In comedy his instinct was surer, for here his long experience as a writer of farces guided him. When reading a script he saw at a glace how situations could be made more effective, and could foretell accurately where and for how long the play would be held up by laughter and applause. Many well-known dramatists owed more than they cared to admit to Garrick's judicious alterations of their plays. His emphasis on spectacle, for which he was mercilessly criticized, was his duty to an age that demanded it. Only once did he disappoint his public. After the coronation of George III in 1761, the patrons of Drury Lane expected to see a similar scene enacted on the stage—a custom that dated from the accession of James I. Garrick, aware that Rich was planning a representation far beyond his own resources, contented himself with reviving the production that had been seen in 1727 with the original dresses now shabby from use. It served as an interlude between Shakespeare's *Henry VIII* and the after-piece. His only novelty was to open the back of the stage on to Drury Lane, where a real bonfire, with a crowd drinking porter to the health of Queen Anne Boleyn, was revealed to the audience. Within a few minutes the stage dukes, duchesses, archbishops and heralds were choking in the smoke that poured in from outside, and shivering in the raw autumn air. Night after night this absurdity was repeated until the occupants of the pit rose up and drove the performers, many of them miserable enough already with colds, rheumatism and swelled faces, right out into the street.

Garrick had hoped that if he forestalled Rich and brought out his Coronation a fortnight earlier, the Covent Garden version would misfire. He was wrong; the playgoers flocked in their hundreds to see Rich's production, his most splendid—and his last. He died in the middle of the run. There were few who mourned the old Harlequin manager or appreciated his lifelong service to the stage, yet many stories suggest that he was kinder-hearted than his misanthropic mutterings implied. Some of the expedients to which Garrick resorted to get the better of him would not be in accordance with the theatrical ethics of to-day, but Rich did not expect soft treatment from his rival and their relations were amicable. Not long before his death, hearing that Garrick wished to inspect the alterations at Covent Garden, he invited him to come over, and showed him round the theatre with great courtesy. To a question about its maximum capacity, he made the graceful reply that if Mr. Garrick would favour his theatre with a personal performance an exact calculation would be possible.

It was not Garrick's fault that his public preferred to see Shakespeare, Otway, Rowe, Congreve and Farquhar brilliantly acted than the adaptations of lesser known Restoration plays that often passed for new, and which provided fewer opportunities for good acting. Nor should he be held responsible for the deterioration in the art of playwriting that had set in before he was born. But it was natural that the dramatists of his day, prolific as they were mediocre, should feel that he was in some way to blame for their failure. They never could understand the principles on which he refused or accepted their plays. They complained that he toadied to the aristocracy and cared more for pleasing his noble patrons than producing good drama. They would not recognize that the prosperity of Drury Lane depended on the goodwill, not of the pit, but of the boxes, and Garrick could not afford to give offence. Interference from outside was one of his many difficulties in management. Yet when he refused to oblige Lord Chesterfield he made an enemy of Smollett.

'I have now with me a play,' he wrote to John Hoadly, in 1746 when he was on the eve of going into management, 'sent to me by my Lord Chesterfield, and wrote by our Smollett. It is a Scotch story, but it won't do, and yet recommended by his Lordship and patronized by Ladies of Quality, what can I say or do? Must I belie my judgment, or run the risk of being thought impertinent and disobliging the great folk?' After thinking it over, Garrick could not bring himself to have anything to do with the tragedy, an immature work of little merit, and, in consequence, found himself pilloried in *Roderick Random* and again in *Peregrine Pickle*. Too appreciative of Smollett's genius not to make allowances (or too wise to measure his strength against so powerful an opponent), Garrick ignored the attacks, and in 1757 a successful production of Smollett's farce, *The Reprisal,* at Drury Lane laid the foundation of a friendship that lasted until Smollett's death. Both men come out very well from the story. Garrick took as much trouble with the play as though he had never recognized himself as 'Mr. Marmozet', and when he found that Smollett had not been paid enough for his benefit night, hastened to refund the money with the fairness and generosity characteristic of his dealings with authors. The following letter was written on the 26th of November 1757:

'Sir,

'There was a mistake made by our office-keepers to your prejudice, which has given me much uneasiness. Though the expense of our theatre every night amounts to £ 90 and upwards, yet we take no more from gentlemen who write for the theatre, and who produce an original performance than sixty guineas; they who alter only an old play, pay eighty guineas for the expense, as in the instance of "Amphytrion"; this occasioned the mistake which I did not discover till lately. Though it is very reasonable to take fourscore pounds for the expense of the house, yet as we have not yet regulated this matter, I cannot possibly agree that Dr. Smollet shall be the first precedent. I have enclosed a draught upon Mr. Clutterbuck for the sum due to you.

'I am, most sincerely,

'Your most obedient, humble servant,

'D. GARRICK.'

Smollett responded with equal generosity. He did all he could to make amends for the past, acknowledging himself at fault and paying a tribute to Garrick's acting in his *History of England*.

Whatever else the dramatists found to complain of, they could not say that Garrick treated them with incivility. The trouble was that he carried his politeness too far. In his anxiety to please, he promised more than he could perform, and disappointment often led to a quarrel that a firm refusal might have avoided. He never gave a dramatist an opportunity to accuse him of deliberately dishonourable conduct, but the effect of his hesitancies, evasions and changes of mood was that they found him a little slippery. His evasions over *The Orphan of China* would alone fill several pages, and Arthur Murphy, with his impetuous Irish temperament, was not the man to suffer them in silence. Indeed, he made himself disproportionately unpleasant, and his letters, carefully preserved by Garrick for posterity to judge between them, suggest that there were faults on both sides. It is easy to see that Garrick did not find his plays worth the trouble they gave him, and that he regretted the contract that obliged him to buy their production rights.

Some seven years before he wrote *The Orphan*, Murphy joined the Drury Lane company, and, failing as an actor, turned his attention to playwriting. Like Garrick, he took his plots from older plays and manipulated his borrowed material with skill. Self-confident and persistent, he induced Garrick to substitute for the usual concession of a benefit night a promise to pay him for a stipulated number of plays; on the understanding that he wrote only for Drury Lane. His comedies—straight comedies, nearer to Farquhar in manner than to the sentimental comedies of more recent years —were successful, and Garrick had no reason to regret his bargain until he met George Colman. This young man's plays were rather better than Murphy's (*The Jealous Wife*, produced at Drury Lane

158

in 1761, was the most successful comedy since Hoadly's *Suspicious Husband*), and, in addition, he was prepared to help Garrick in his secret schemes for discrediting his critics; while Murphy, as Garrick must have known, was writing anonymous pamphlets against him. All that Garrick could do was to try and goad Murphy into breaking his side of the agreement, and it is evident from one of Garrick's letters that Colman knew what was going on.

In the early days of their association Garrick liked Murphy well enough to take Dr. Monsey to see him. After the first night of Murphy's *Apprentice* in 1756, they paid the young author a morning call. Garrick entered a room on the first floor, but Monsey went straight on upstairs. Running to the door, Garrick called out, 'Dr. Monsey, where are you going?' 'Upstairs to see the author,' was the reply. 'Come down,' said Garrick, 'the author is here.' 'You scoundrel!' said Monsey, using his favourite mode of address, 'I was going up to the garret. Who could think of finding an author on the first floor?' After their first quarrel over *The Orphan of China*, Murphy and Garrick made great efforts to bury the hatchet. Garrick asked Murphy to Hampton, and in 1760 Murphy took Garrick to Streatham to be introduced to his friends, Mr. and Mrs. Thrale. It was a very easy house, he assured Garrick, and he need not fear heavy drinking. Five years later he performed the same friendly office for Johnson, and by so doing changed the whole course of his life.

But Murphy and Garrick could never agree for long at a time; as soon as one of Murphy's plays came up for consideration, there would be another exchange of long angry letters, until their common interest demanded a half-hearted reconciliation. 'Prithee,' said Johnson, presiding at one of these meetings, 'do not talk of plays; if you do, you will quarrel again.' He liked the young Irishman, and thought more highly of his plays than did Garrick. He is said to have fulfilled Johnson's ideal of a fine gentleman—a distinction he earned by never directly contradicting him in an argument. Instead, he would hesitatingly quote a learned writer on the other side, and wait deferentially for the scornful comment that inevitably followed. He was a welcome addition to those tavern suppers that later became famous, because, without approaching his more distinguished fellow-guests in originality or depth of thought, his well-informed remarks helped to keep the conversational ball rolling.

And, as a sign of great favour, Johnson would invite him to come with him for late tea with Mrs. Williams, his blind pensioner, before they separated for the night.

The dissatisfaction, felt by those who wrote for and about the theatre, with the state of the drama, resulted in a split into two factions; one held Garrick responsible and nothing he did could be right, and the other flattered him in the hope of getting their plays accepted. Each faction praised the achievements of its members and belittled those of the other, so that before judging contemporary taste from a printed criticism, or accepting its statements of fact, the circumstances of its publication must always be considered. The prejudices, motives and even the politics of its authors must be taken into account; for, remote as the connection may now appear, those who supported Lord Bute's administration were inclined to be critical of Garrick's theatrical management, and those who opposed it were satisfied. The war was carried on chiefly by pamphlet, and the author's name, though known to the frequenters of coffee-houses, seldom appears on the title page, and has in many instances been forgotten. This pretence of anonymity makes the controversy difficult to follow, and Garrick's habit of writing anonymous damp squibs against himself adds to the general confusion.

Theophilus Cibber's death at sea in the autumn of 1758 on his way to Dublin relieved Garrick of a bitter enemy who had openly attacked him throughout his career. But there were many others to take his place, whose methods were more tortuous. 'Sir' John Hill, the quack doctor and self-styled knight, James Ralph, and Dr. Paul Hifferman were all authors of plays rejected or unsuccessfully produced by Garrick, eager in consequence to injure him in the eyes of his public. Murphy alternated between flattering him, scolding him, borrowing his money, and writing anonymous pamphlets against him, and Smollett, although he did not himself attack Garrick after his farce was produced, helped the other side for a while by opening to them the columns of *The Critical Review*, of which he was the editor. To defend his own interests and those of Drury Lane, Garrick enlisted the help of a number of pamphleteers, including such men as George Colman, Robert Lloyd and Bonnell Thornton, and his enemies gradually became aware of a powerful combination ranged against them. In 1761, Garrick,

Colman and Thornton acquired the controlling interests in *The St. James's Chronicle,* a newspaper which appeared three times a week. Its lively gossip on the topics of the day soon attracted a wide circle of readers, and the control of its policy enabled Garrick to manipulate public opinion on theatrical affairs, and undo the work of mischief-makers.

In March of that year, *The Rosciad,* a scathing attack in verse on contemporary acting, stole into a world ill prepared for it by the bare announcement of its title in a list of forthcoming publications. It did not need advertisement. No satire since Pope's *Dunciad* had displayed so keen an edge, and its effect on the actors has been compared to the discharge of a gun into a rookery. Onlookers thoroughly enjoyed the consternation behind the footlights, and noticed with amusement that those who had received the deadliest wounds pretended to suffer least, but were distressed only for the injuries inflicted on others. 'Why should this man attack Mr. Havard?' said one. 'I am not at all concerned for myself, but what has poor Billy Havard done that he must be treated so cruelly?' 'And pray,' asked his companion, 'what has Mr. Havard done that he cannot bear his misfortunes as well as another?' Only Garrick among the actors escaped punishment; it was, in fact, an elaborate tribute to him at the expense of most of his rivals. According to the scheme of the poem, Shakespeare and Ben Jonson are appointed judges of a contest to fill the chair left empty by Roscius. The actors come forward in turn to demonstrate their powers, and the couplets describing their performances deal exclusively with their mannerisms and limitations and ignore the gifts we know that many of them possessed. Finally, Shakespeare, speaking for his fellow-judge as well as for himself, awards the honour to Garrick with an appreciation of his genius which in the circumstances embarrassed rather than pleased him.

No one could suspect Garrick of having written it himself. Its venom was foreign to his nature, and, moreover, the puffs he was in the habit of writing of himself were always oblique in their praise. It was assumed to be the work of one or more of his satellites, and, in its style and complimentary allusions to Colman and Lloyd, a writer in *The Critical Review* saw evidence that these two young men were themselves its joint authors. This, Colman and Lloyd instantly and emphatically denied, and within a month *An*

Apology, a poem written by the same hand and addressed to the Critical Reviewers, appeared under the name of Charles Churchill. The actors then recalled having noticed a clergyman of large athletic build sitting night after night in the first row of the pit, and being told that his name was Churchill. The references to Colman and Lloyd were explained when it was discovered that they were, all three, old school friends.

Meanwhile Garrick, who had in fact never met Churchill and knew nothing of the poem until he saw it in print, felt bound in loyalty to his company to express disapproval and contempt of the author, and in so doing gave offence. In the *Apology,* Churchill ridiculed acting as a profession, depicting the poverty-stricken life of a strolling player with stinging contempt. This the actors minded much less than his damaging descriptions of their individual faults, and their old wounds ceased to smart when they saw that their manager had himself come under the lash. Four lines in particular brought comfort to them and agitation to Garrick:

> *Let the vain tyrant sit amidst his guards,*
> *His puny green-room wits and venal bards,*
> *Who meanly tremble at the puppet's frown,*
> *And for a playhouse freedom lose their own.*

Garrick, tremblingly anxious to pacify the satirist, made overtures to him through Lloyd, and the following letter, intended for his eyes, shows how far Garrick would go in flattery and self-abasement when he wished to placate an enemy whom he regarded as dangerous:

'I see and read so much of Mr. Churchill's spirit, without having the pleasure of his acquaintance, that I am persuaded that his genius disdains any direction, and that resolutions once taken by him will withstand the warmest importunities of his friends.

'At the first reading of his *Apology,* I was so charmed and raised with the power of his writing that I really forgot that I was delighted when I ought to have been alarmed. This puts me in mind of the Highland officer, who was so warmed and elevated by the heat of the battle that he had forgot, till he was reminded by the smarting, that he had received no less than eleven wounds in different parts of his body.

'All I have to say, or will say upon the occasion is this:—if Mr. Churchill has attacked his pasteboard majesty of Drury Lane from resentment, I should be sorry for it, though I am conscious it is ill-founded. If he has attacked me merely because I am the Punch of the puppet-show, I shall not turn my back upon him and salute him in Punch's fashion, but make myself easy with this thought— that my situation made the attack necessary, and that it would have been a pity that so much strong, high-coloured poetry should have been thrown away, either in justice or in friendship on so insignificant a person as myself.

'In his *Rosciad* he raised me too high; in his *Apology* he may have sunk me too low. . . . He has thought fit, a few weeks ago, to declare me the best actor of my time (which, by the by, is no great compliment, if there is as much truth as wit in his *Apology*) ; and I will show the superiority I have over my brethren upon his occasion, by seeming at least that I am not dissatisfied and appear, as I once saw a poor soldier on the parade, who was acting a pleasantry of countenance, while his back was most woefully striped with the cat-o'nine-tails.'

Lloyd's intervention succeeded in its object, and for the few remaining years of Churchill's life he was on friendly terms with Garrick. Before his death in 1764, the man whom Garrick had taken so much trouble to propitiate was writing thus:
'My dear Mr. Garrick,

'Half drunk, half mad, and quite stripped of all my money, I should be much obliged if you would enclose and send by the bearer five pieces by way of adding to the favours already received by
'Yours sincerely,
'CHARLES CHURCHILL.'

Garrick's quarrel with Thaddeus Fitzpatrick is worth recalling because it led to a riot at Drury Lane, and prevented the managers from carrying out a theatrical reform. Fitzpatrick was an idle young man about town of no importance, and had Garrick treated his earliest impertinences with the contempt they deserved, instead of paying him the compliment of a laboriously written satire, Fitzpatrick might never have attracted any attention, and Garrick and his fellow-manager would have saved themselves considerable expense and annoyance. At first, Garrick rather liked the tall young

Irishman when he met him at the Bedford Coffee-house, and found his conversation agreeable. With enough private means to please himself in the employment of his time, Fitzpatrick attended every play at both patent houses, and posed as a man of letters on the strength of occasional contributions to the newspapers on theatrical subjects. The admiration subtly conveyed in every tone of his soft Irish voice gratified Garrick, and earned him a free pass to Drury Lane theatre.

Just why Fitzpatrick suddenly turned on Garrick, no one can say. Tom Davies, at that time a member of the Drury Lane company and hearing all the coffee-house gossip of the day, says that the applause of Fitzpatrick's friends for his literary efforts turned his head, and made him think that he knew all that there was to be known about the drama. To emphasize his own superiority, he professed to see in the great actor only an impudent impostor and took it upon himself to undeceive the public. He astonished his coffee-house acquaintances by speaking of Garrick with contempt, wrote a series of letters for a weekly newspaper attacking Garrick's action and elocution, and, finally, issued a collection of these letters in pamphlet form. No one was in the least impressed by his arguments, and the pamphlets and its writer would soon have been forgotten had not Garrick taken fright and opened a wholly unnecessary counter-offensive with a poem directed against Fitzpatrick and his friends. *The Fribbleriad* takes its name from that of the traditional stage fop, and, although unsigned, was immediately recognized as his. But the ruthlessness essential to good satire was lacking, and the feebleness of his attack was made more apparent when, a few weeks later, Churchill followed it up with fifty searing lines in *The Rosciad*. Fitzpatrick, thus brought into public notice, swelled with self-importance. That he was nothing more than a moneyed corner-boy should have been evident from that day many years earlier when he threw an apple at Woodward on the stage of Drury Lane, and had the further impertinence of declaring himself affronted because Woodward responded by pulling off his hat and bowing in his direction with the words, 'Sir, I thank you.' He now saw himself as the chosen representative of the playgoing public, and, bestowing the title of 'The Town' on his small gang of roughs, began to organize a faction of playgoers hostile to Garrick.

In the autumn of 1762, the Drury Lane managers had quietly introduced a reform designed to prevent young gentlemen like Fitzpatrick from making nuisances of themselves in the theatre, and carried it through without meeting any opposition. It was fifteen years since Garrick had announced his intention of refusing admittance to members of the audience behind the scenes, but the rule had not always been enforced. On benefit nights it had been waived, and the actors' friends swarmed into the green-room, the wings, and on to the stage itself, where they sat during the performance in an amphitheatre erected for the evening. Mrs. Cibber used to die in the Capulet vault with at least two hundred of her admirers immediately behind her. When Quin returned to Covent Garden for Ryan's benefit night, he took several minutes to force his way through the crowd of spectators who, in full view of the audience, hemmed in the actors on the stage. But the best story is that of Charles Holland when he played Hamlet for his benefit. On the appearance of the Ghost, Hamlet's hat by the usual stage device flew off, and came to rest at the feet of a young country girl, who sat at the end of the amphitheatre on the stage. Having heard the actor complain of the cold night air and seeing him shiver, she stole from her place and, with the best intentions, replaced the hat on his head. Unfortunately, she put it on back to front, and gave the Prince of Denmark a most unsuitably rakish appearance. Holland finished the scene unconscious of the absurdity, and the spectators suppressed their amusement until he was well off the stage. Then they let themselves go in one of the loudest laughs ever heard in a theatre. The managers were perfectly aware of the incongruities that arose from this custom of having seats on the stage but as it brought in an additional hundred pounds they could not abolish it without making compensation to the actor. Accordingly, Garrick and Lacy enlarged the seating accommodation in the body of the theatre during the summer of 1762, to a receipt of £335 from £220, and, when they announced at the beginning of the new season that in future they would not erect any seats on the stage, the actors had no cause for complaint and the audience no excuse for leaving its rightful side of the footlights.

It was during the same season that Garrick tried to make another change, and might have carried it through had not Fitzpatrick taken his revenge for *The Fribbleriad* by organizing a public demonstration in defence of what he claimed as a public right. It had long been the custom to charge half-price for admittance at the end of the third act, but in the course of the last fifty years the costs of production had trebled, and the concession now appeared disproportionate to the managers of both patent theatres. Full prices were charged at Drury Lane for the first time at a new production of *Two Gentlemen of Verona,* and for five performances all went quietly. On the sixth night, Fitzpatrick got up and harangued the audience. He abused the managers for their extortionate charges, and insisted on the audience's right to half-price admittance to the last two acts of every play excepting only on the evenings of a new pantomime. When Garrick came forward to address the house, he was shouted down and ordered to do as he was told. When he refused, Fitzpatrick and his gang wrecked the theatre, tearing up the benches and smashing the chandeliers. On the next night, Garrick thought it prudent to give in, but the audience would not be mollified until some of the actors who had supported the management on the previous evening had done penance. John Moody was singled out to apologize for having restrained a rioter from setting fire to the building. Hoping for a laugh, the actor said in an assumed brogue that he was sorry he had 'displeased' them by saving their lives in putting out the fire. Tempers flared up again, and he was ordered to go down on his knees and apologize. This Moody stoutly refused to do, and coming off the stage he was met and embraced by Garrick, who assured him that while he had a guinea he would pay him his salary, but that had he submitted he never would have forgiven him. On the following nights, the audience made it impossible for Moody to come on to the stage, and he was forced to seek out Fitzpatrick and appeal to his sense of fair play. In the end, Fitzpatrick withdrew his opposition and, in a condescending letter to Garrick, promised to overlook the actor's misdemeanour. Moody was then reinstated in the public favour.

Having gained his point at Drury Lane, Fitzpatrick and his friends took the next opportunity of repeating their demands at Covent Garden, and, on being refused, smashed everything within reach. John Beard, the new manager, a stronger personality than Garrick, had the ringleaders arrested and brought before Lord

Mansfield. Fitzpatrick's naturally pallid face turned livid with fear when the Lord Chief Justice told him sternly that if, in the course of these riots, a life were lost, he would have to answer for it with his own. After this warning, Fitzpatrick and his followers contented themselves with drowning the actors at Covent Garden with hisses and catcalls, until Beard was obliged to fall into line. Thus late-comers regained their privilege of paying half-price for admittance, and the custom continued until well into the following century.

It was no wonder that Garrick began to feel tired and in need of a long holiday. The strain of persuading the members of his company, each as highly strung and egotistic as the next, to work together harmoniously, of trying in vain to heal the wounded vanities of his authors, of providing a varied repertory of plays as well as keeping his own acting up to its high level of perfection, told on his health, and a falling off in the profits of his management discouraged him. It was not that any actor had arisen to challenge his supremacy, but, after twenty years, playgoers had grown accus-tomed to his Ranger and Benedick, his Richard III and King Lear, and preferred the musical plays at Covent Garden. John Beard was an excellent singer himself and, on taking over the manage-ment of his father-in-law's theatre, had decided to specialize in the form of entertainment he understood best, A new Polly in the person of Miss Brent had revived all the old enthusiasm for *The Beggar's Opera,* and inspired Dr. Arne and other musicians to com-pose music for new plays which proved hardly less popular. Miss Brent might have made her first appearance at Drury Lane, for Arne had warmly recommended her to Garrick's notice. But Gar-rick did not care for music and would not heed him, with the result that Arne took his young pupil to Covent Garden, where she at-tracted even greater crowds than the original Polly Peachum. In the summer of 1763, Garrick had the novel experience of playing to empty benches; one evening, Mrs. Cibber and he performed to a house of £ 20, and on another, he played Abel Drugger to a house of £ 5.

A temporary retirement was clearly advisable, and the state of his health, as well as that of Mrs. Garrick, provided a legitimate excuse for a holiday abroad. He began to make preparations for a year's absence from Drury Lane. He engaged and coached a promising young actor called William Powell for a first appearance in London, expecting him to draw audiences for as long as he remained a talented newcomer, but never dreaming that his popularity would provide any cause for jealousy; he arranged that Colman should look after his publicity and advise Lacy in matters of stage policy; and, finally, with many injunctions to write frequently and in detail, he entrusted his personal interests to his brother George. He promised to keep in close touch with them at every stage of his journey, and if his presence in London proved absolutely necessary he would return home with all speed. On the 15th of September 1763, Mr. and Mrs. Garrick set out on their travels, and it was eighteen months before London saw them again.

9. HAMPTON HOUSE

from an engraving by Medland from a drawing by Metz in the Enthoven Collection,
Victoria and Albert Museum

CHAPTER XIII

TRAVELS IN FRANCE AND ITALY

1763 — 1765

GARRICK had long been wanting to revisit Paris, and only the war had kept him in England. He had, indeed, felt tempted to slip over during the hostilities, but was warned of the danger of doing so by a friend in Paris, who reported that even French nationals returning home from England were being arrested and kept in prison on suspicion. But now at last the war was over, and Garrick could join the great exodus of English travellers to the Continent. Driving in their own postchaise to Dover, the Garricks crossed the Channel by sailing-packet to Calais, and arrived in Paris after a four-day journey. There they spent a fortnight visiting the theatres and renewing old friendships, and then, with the intention of making a longer stay on the way home, resumed their journey southwards towards the Italian frontier.

By the time they had left the dreaded Mont Cenis behind them, with the inevitable mishaps on the rough mountain road, Garrick had recovered all his old high spirits. The reception given him by the actors in Paris, and the tributes paid him by France's most distinguished men of letters, had restored his self-confidence. He could even hesitate with complacency over an invitation to Ferney from the great Voltaire. He was angry with the damned fellow, he said, for what he had written about Shakespeare, but he would take him in on the way home. Now and then he felt uneasy about Drury Lane and Hampton, and would write to Colman and George, plying them with questions and giving them fresh instructions. How was Powell shaping in Philaster (the part in the tragedy of that

name by Beaumont and Fletcher chosen for his first appearance)
and was the play as a whole being properly rehearsed? Did his
public miss him, and what were the newspapers saying about him?
He hoped that the gardener was not being too much of a fine
gentleman. Hogarth's pictures would be ruined if they were not
protected from the sun. Would George take a peep at Hampton
and see how things were going? But his worries faded from his
mind as they crossed the frontier, and came down from the snows
on to the plains of Piedmont, golden in the autumn sunshine.

At Turin, the travellers visited the Opera, where Garrick
thought the dancing the worst he had ever seen, and where the
contrast between the magnificence of the theatre and the barbarous
behaviour of the audience defied description. The spectators did
not attempt to lower their voices during the performance, and
even the actors engaged their friends in the audience in animated
conversation in between their lines. During these first weeks abroad,
Garrick was in a perpetual state of astonishment—the grandeur
of the Alpine scenery, the squalor and discomfort of the inns, and
the manners of the natives all amazed him. He would write down
some of the things he had seen with his own eyes, and Colman
could read them aloud to his friends after dinner. At Florence,
Garrick visited the dying poet, Algarotti, and urged him—unavail-
ingly—to take tar-water, an English panacea much in vogue. As
they approached Rome, Garrick could not sleep with excitement,
and his disappointment on entering the city from the north was
acute. Could these crooked dirty streets really be the capital of
Imperial Rome? And those muddy yellow waters Horace's Tiber?
Disillusioned, he had to be dragged out that afternoon to see the
ancient monuments, but as he entered the Pantheon its beauty
stunned him. He gasped, and for a few moments could not speak.
For the next fortnight he feasted his eyes on statues, pictures,
palaces and ruins, and willfully neglected an opportunity of seeing
the Pope and his Cardinals in all their splendour.

They spent Christmas in Naples, basking in the flattering attentions of the English aristocracy wintering in the south. 'We are
continually with Lady Orford, Lady Spencer, Lord Exeter, Lord
Palmerston and the Nobility of the country,' he wrote to George,
and every letter reflects his delight in the fine company around him.
The King of the Two Sicilies paid him the compliment of inviting

him to supply the Court actors with the outline of a short play so that they could demonstrate their powers of improvisation. Lord and Lady Spencer took him to Herculaneum to see the antiquities recently uncovered there. Hardly a day passed without its ball or its banquet. Mrs. Garrick, whose charms made her gratified husband the subject of arch innuendoes, kindly and innocently intended, was no less happy than he; until a sudden attack of sciatica, brought on perhaps by getting very wet on the way from Rome, kept her a prisoner in her room. The moment her pain eased she was out and about again, and, in her determination not to miss any of the fun, declared her intention of going to a carnival masquerade in the character of a lame old woman. 'I have scolded and phy'zed about it,' wrote Garrick, 'but if she can wag, she goes.'

By February they had had their fill of pleasure-parties, and were ready to go back to Rome. Their stay in Naples had been saddened at the last by the grim signs of famine, and stories of emaciated men and women being picked up dead in the streets. In Rome, the situation was less serious, and Garrick could smile with Protestant scepticism at the expedients to which the Pope was resorting in his attempts to ward off disaster from his State. Mrs. Garrick was by no means well, but she hobbled bravely after her husband on his antiquity hunts. It may well have been in his search for bargains that he came across young Nollekens, at this time deeply engaged in the not over-scrupulous traffic in antiquities. As Scheemaker's pupil in London, he had shown promise, winning several money prizes for his models in clay, and was now spending the period in Rome necessary for his prestige as a sculptor. But the gullibility of the English traveller proved too tempting, and he was making more money than his sordid way of living suggested. A mutilated marble head and some skilfully chosen fragments of torso, arms and legs underwent dexterous 'restoration' in his studio, and in due course a complete 'antique' statue would take an honoured place in the collection of some rich English nobleman. The moment Garrick set eyes on the unprepossessing young man he realized he had seen him before. 'What, let me look at you!' he exclaimed. 'Are you the little fellow to whom we gave the prizes at the Society of Arts?' 'Yes, sir,' replied Nollekens, and the next morning Garrick, with his usual kindness to youth, was giving him breakfast and offering to sit for him. A few weeks later, the young man who was to model every well-known Englishman of his day was the proud recipient of twelve guineas in gold for the first portrait-bust ever commissioned from him.

But Garrick, whose real love and knowledge of the visual arts is evident from his quick recognition of genius however immature, preferred the work of another student, the brother of one of his actors, and the son of George Dance, the architect of Mansion House. He liked Nathaniel[1] personally much better than James, who, under his stage name of Love, was at that moment directing the Drury Lane pantomime with, Garrick feared, very little humour. This young painter working in Rome had great talent, in Garrick's opinion, and would have London at his feet whenever he chose to return. All that London had so far seen of his work was the large canvas of mythological figures he had sent for exhibition the previous summer, and if, as we are free to suppose, he began his painting of Garrick as Richard III that April in Rome, Garrick once more sat for the first of a series of famous portraits.

By May the Garricks were in Parma, where they came in for the festivities given for the Duke of York on his tour of the Italian States. Garrick had the honour of dining with the Duke, and was presented by him to the Duke of Parma, who expressed in fairly good English his deep admiration for Shakespeare. Before this select audience Garrick gave some of those scenes from Shakespeare that enabled him to display his astonishing variety of facial expressions, and the performance so delighted the Duke of Parma that he sent the actor a handsome gold snuff-box. Garrick was tremendously proud of this sign of royal favour, and showed it to his actors when he came home. 'So you went about the Continent mouthing for snuff-boxes,' remarked Holland, but Garrick wisely ignored him.

In Venice, he was still following in the royal wake, and a regatta held in the Duke's honour on the Grand Canal realized his idea of fairyland, and put to shame every spectacle he had ever seen on the stage. He bought pictures and books, watched the proceedings in the Courts of Justice, which struck him as more fantastically funny than the Italian Comedy itself, dozed away the hot afternoons in a gondola, and in the evenings walked in sober fact on the Rialto he had often trodden in fancy on the stage. But he

[1] Later Sir Nathaniel Dance-Holland.

172

was growing homesick, and the steaming heat of the Venetian summer took all the energy out of him. It was high time he was back at Drury Lane, planning the next season's productions, and it was only his concern for Mrs. Garrick's health that prevented him from setting out at once for home. Her lameness had increased alarmingly since their arrival in Venice, and Garrick, distressed to see her a cripple, decided to take her to the mud baths near Padua for treatment. After a fortnight there she had sufficiently improved to start on the long journey northwards over the mountains to Munich.

And then it was Garrick's turn to fall sick. For five weeks he lay seriously ill with abdominal trouble which he accepted as a penalty for over-indulgence in rich Italian dishes and wines; whatever its cause, it was followed by an attack of acute pain in the region of his kidneys, which left him with a weakness he was never wholly to overcome. Mrs. Garrick, by no means fully recovered herself, forgot that she had ever been ill in her anxiety for her husband, and, under the orders of an English physician, whose services she felt herself fortunate to procure, made a devoted nurse. By the middle of September, Mrs. Garrick and the doctor were trying to instil into a sceptical invalid their own comfortable belief that in future he would be all the better for the 'scouring' his inside had received.

Already in low spirits, Garrick took the news of the Duke of Devonshire's death very badly. As Lady Burlington's son-in-law and trustee under her will, the Duke would anyhow have taken a friendly interest in the Garrick's, but, with a common love of literature and the arts, the two men had struck up an independent friendship and were warmly attached to each other. Garrick had been looking forward to joining him at Spa, and delivering in person the prints he had been buying at the Duke's own request. He had hardly recovered from the shock when he opened a letter from Colman and read that Hogarth was dead. This second blow was no less shattering. In Hogarth he had lost one of his oldest and staunchest friends—one with whom he had never had any of those foolish little misunderstandings that often clouded his relationships with other men. Only a year ago he had begged Churchill as a personal favour to himself not to tilt against Hogarth, whom he loved as a man, he said, and reverenced as an artist, but Churchill paid no attention and, in his *Epistle to Hogarth,* ridiculed the great painter's physical infirmities in a pamphlet that Garrick described as a bloody performance. The death in wretched circumstances of the satirist himself that autumn meant comparatively little to Garrick, but the spate of bad news made it difficult for him to throw off the nervous depression of convalescence.

They left Munich without regrets, and travelled by easy stages through Augsburg and Frankfort to Nancy. Their plans were now a little uncertain. Garrick was too unwell to think of going back to the theatre that winter, and, without the Duke, Spa held no attraction for him. Voltaire's home near Geneva lay within a few days' journey, and Garrick thought uneasily of the invitation he had received from the great man—an invitation which in the eyes of French intellectuals amounted to a royal command. He did not wish to be thought lacking in respect, but he did not feel equal to the tiring journey into the Jura, the irritating arguments about Shakespeare, and the performances he would be expected to give in Voltaire's private theatre. After some hesitation, he wrote excusing himself on the grounds of ill health and, packing as much as possible about Shakespeare into a short letter, expressed his deep regret for the lost opportunity of trying to convert the first Genius of Europe to the English Dramatic faith. Then breathing a sigh of relief, he took the road for Paris, and arrived there at the end of October.

'*L'exercice à cheval et beaucoup de dissipation*' was the French doctors' advice, which Garrick followed with excellent results. His hollow cheeks filled out, his skin took on a healthier hue, his waistcoat recovered its customary rotundity, and all his old vivacity returned. But it took very little to tire him, and the doctors united in forbidding him to do any kind of work. He had no inclination to disobey them. For the time being, he was content to rest on his laurels; and, indeed, there were days when he seriously contemplated retiring from the stage altogether. He had already made more than enough to live on in comfort for the rest of his days, and Drury Lane was getting on unexpectedly well without him. It mortified him to discover how well. Lacy, Colman and George, despite some wrangling among themselves, made a good team, and had shown a profit of £ 9,000 for their first year of management. For much of this renewed prosperity, they could thank Powell, who had more than justified their hopes for him. Even Garrick in his most famous parts, wrote Lacy with rather too much satisfaction to please his correspondent, had not attracted greater crowds, and Garrick need not deny himself any of the delights of travel on account of the theatre at home, for everything, he assured him, was going on smoothly and happily.

Garrick, in normal circumstances, was not the man to stand down willingly for anyone however talented, still less for a raw young actor whom he had himself taken from a stool in a City counting-house and taught many of his tricks. But now he accepted the situation calmly, and wrote a cordial letter to Powell congratulating him on his success, and giving him advice that is of interest to us since it clearly represents his own policy. He cautioned him against undertaking a larger number of parts than he had time to study carefully; he must never let Shakespeare out of his hands or his pockets; and, above all, he must not waste time in clubs and coffee-houses with idlers and flatterers under the customary pretence he was doing so in order to fill the theatre on his benefit night. Only by good acting and hard work could he win public favour, and then he could choose his own friends. But he would find that none but the best company would be of any real service to him. The letter sealed and dispatched, Garrick put him out of his mind and proceeded to conquer French society as easily and completely as he had his first audiences at Goodman's Fields. Without giving a single public performance and relying only on dumb shows, he impressed fellow-actors, philosophers and men of letters alike with the power and beauty of English naturalism in the theatre, and, at the same time, established a reputation for himself that has never disappeared from French literature.

In theory, the French tragedians had long abandoned the sing-song declamation and formal gestures of Racine's day, and were priding themselves on their naturalism. Voltaire, after his years of exile in England, had striven hard to infuse into his actors some of the fire and verve that a study of the English barbarian, Shakespeare, had inspired in him, and the technique of their delivery was founded on speech. Mlle Dumesnil, rather *passée* now and very uneven in her performance, portrayed passion and fury with a realism Garrick himself could not surpass. Mlle Clairon, from the time she had first seen Garrick act in 1751, had declared herself

175

his most ardent admirer, and would have been astonished had she known that he thought her artificial. Molé flung himself about the stage, shouted, raved, stopped and took up his part again in what he thought was the English style, but was a caricature of it from which Garrick learnt to correct his own excesses. Even Le Kain, who strongly reminded English visitors of Quin, was admired by his countrymen for his close imitation of nature, and Voltaire went so far as to call him the Garrick of France. But Garrick had only to give his three famous scenes from Shakespeare—the Ghost scene from *Hamlet*, the dagger scene from *Macbeth*, and King Lear's madness—and his French audiences knew that nothing like it had even been seen on their stage. After one of these demonstrations in a private house, Mlle Clairon threw her arms round his neck and kissed him in her enthusiasm. Then, turning to Mrs. Garrick, she apologized for having taken the liberty.

Garrick's relations with the French actors were particularly happy; no feelings of rivalry or jealousy entered into them, and many of the friendships he made that winter lasted for the rest of his life. Their admiration for him was generous and whole-hearted, and he in return paid them graceful compliments to hide his dislike of their mannered style. He pleased them by saying how much he regretted that he could not learn their language well enough to have the honour of appearing with them on their own stage. Nothing, he said, would have given him greater pleasure. Taking him seriously and assuming him willing and able to act with them, we can be sure that he would have chosen comedy rather than tragedy, for here the national styles of acting did not conflict. The only actor whom he genuinely admired was Préville, whose versatility within the range of comedy was second only to his own. The two men enjoyed each other's company, and there are many anecdotes of the practical jokes in which they were associated.

They were out riding in the country, runs one story, when Préville began pretending to be drunk. Garrick congratulated him on his performance, but pointed out that his legs had remained sober. In showing him what he meant, Garrick carried his fooling so far that he fell off his horse and lay apparently unconscious on the ground. When Préville dismounted and ran back to him in alarm, Garrick sat up and laughed in his face.

Another day, they set out together for Versailles, and took their

176

places in the public diligence, but the driver refused to start until he had four other passengers. Garrick slipped out unobserved, retired to a distance, and then returned with a gait totally unlike his own. Hailing the coachman in a disguised voice, he got in again. He repeated the trick three times, assuming a different character each time. The driver, satisfied that his coach was full, cracked his whip and started off with the two actors inside.

The eternal schoolboy in Garrick enjoyed playing pranks with his *compagnon en ivresse,* as he afterwards addressed Préville in a letter, alluding to their many mock contests in drunkenness, but stories like these, of which there are legion, give a false impression of the way he passed his days in Paris. Much of his time was, in fact, spent in the company of that illustrious group of men known as the *Philosophes,* whose sceptical writings, challenging authority and tradition, were preparing the way for open and bloody revolution. To find Garrick, the gay and amusing social butterfly, in almost daily companionship with such intellectual giants as Diderot and D'Alembert, joint editors of the *Encyclopædia,* and the no less distinguished Holbach, Helvetius, Raynal, Morellet and Grimm is at first sight surprising. There were those in England who considered his association with avowed atheists discreditable as well as surprising, but he only laughed when he heard that he was said to be keeping bad company. Accepting with comfortable, if unthinking, assurance the dogmas of the Church of England, he is unlikely to have taken part in the metaphysical discussions of the French philosophers or to have been swayed by their reasonings. We know that whenever Garrick saw Morellet arguing with Diderot, he would sit down near him, fold his arms and watch in fascinated silence. But it was not the subject of the learned men's discourse that interested him. It was Morellet's frenzied gesticulations which Garrick was committing to memory for future reproduction.

The importance of Garrick to French men of letters was his interpretation and championship of Shakespeare, round whom the Anglomania of these years was centred, and his development of a style of acting that the tragedians demanded. Through the medium of a bad prose translation, published in 1745, the enthusiasts were struggling manfully to understand and assess the qualities of a dramatist whom they were nationally incapable of appreciating. They admired his tragic force, the beauty of his sentiments,

177

and his telling situations, but his ignorance of the unities and his deliberate introduction of buffoonery into tragedy they could not and would not forgive. Many, like Voltaire and Le Blanc, decided that his defects outweighed his merits. Criticism of his idol roused Garrick to fury. He could not treat Voltaire with open disrespect, but he flatly refused to meet Le Blanc in Paris because of what he had said about Shakespeare, and he could not have been touchier on the subject had he written the plays himself. 'He used to watch me out of the corner of his eye,' recalled Morellet, 'when I read Shakespeare and he noted the smallest signs of disapprobation expressed on my face. Then he would come at me like a madman. calling me French dog and pressing me with questions and vindications, in order to make me approve peculiarities which our taste cannot support.'[1] Looking back, Garrick's sensitiveness seems very absurd. His own alterations to Shakespeare's plays were made in deference to the unities, and little but the greater outspokenness and honesty of the French critics separated him from them.

To Diderot, Garrick was of especial interest, for their intimacy enabled him to analyse the relation between an actor's own emotions and those simulated by him on the stage, a problem which had long excited his curiosity, and there is little doubt that his famous *Paradoxe* was the outcome of their meeting. It was probably an early draft of the essay that Suard sent Garrick in 1773, pressing him to give him his comments in writing. But Garrick, whose feelings must have been mixed when he read that the actor who can play all characters does so because he has none of his own, and that an actor should have penetration and no sensibility, remained obstinately silent. Until Diderot met Garrick, he took the opposite point of view; he deplored the lifelessness of contemporary French acting and urged the need for more feeling in the actor and a greater dependence on the impulse of the moment. This was Mlle Dumesnil's system, and she carried it very far. While she acted her servant stood in the wings with a bottle from which she surreptitiously drew liquid inspiration. Sometimes, the effect was electrifying; at others, disastrous. Garrick, on the other hand, Diderot noticed, left nothing to chance; every detail was carefully rehearsed. The tremble in the voice, the shuddering of the limbs, the shaking of the knees, Diderot saw as a lesson learnt beforehand and de-

[1] Quoted in *David Garrick and his French Friends,* by F. A. Hedgcock.

livered without emotion or variation. 'Punch has no feelings,' Johnson used to say. Garrick naturally did not agree. How much he depended on technique is suggested by his remark that a good actor should be able to make stage love as well to a table as to the finest woman in the world. But genius, in his opinion, needed something more. 'The greatest strokes of genius,' he once wrote, 'have been unknown to the actor himself till circumstances and the warmth of the scene has sprung the mine, as it were, as much to his own surprise as that of the audience.'

So far as is known, Garrick never went to the French court,[1] or received any hospitality from the aristocracy, and in a country where a player enjoyed fewer rights as a citizen than an English footman and was finally denied Christian burial, he could hardly expect anything else. But at least the Duke of Orleans paid him the compliment of commissioning Carmontelle to paint his portrait —a task Garrick deliberately made more difficult by imperceptibly changing his expression until the artist despaired of getting a true likeness.[2] Despite the vagaries of the sitter, however, painters and sculptors here as elsewhere clamoured for the honour of portraying him, and, since he genuinely enjoyed their society and was not averse from seeing himself through their admiring eyes, he never refused a sitting. Thus many portraits by French artists commemorate his visit, and, in addition, engravings of portraits by Wilson, Zoffany and Reynolds were sent to him from England for distribution among his personal friends. Some of these gifts were accompanied, rather surprisingly, by copies of Johnson's Dictionary.

As the winter wore on, Garrick grew stronger, and by January felt able to fix the date of his return for April. Then began the tortuous business of exciting public interest in his doings to ensure himself a good welcome, and he would send Colman rough drafts for the paragraphs he wanted to insert into *The St. James's Chronicle*. His great concern was that he should not be suspected of writing or inspiring them himself. Supposing, he said, Colman were to concoct a 'letter from Paris' giving all the gossip of the day (and Garrick gave him a sample dispatch which began, arrestingly enough, with an account of a hermaphrodite's marriage and the complications that ensued), and slipping in a casual reference to

[1] Except as an ordinary sightseer in 1751. See page 116.

[2] This story, however, has been told of many actors and may be apocryphal.

him. Or would it be better to begin boldly with, 'Our little stage hero looks better than he did'? Colman could speak of him as he pleased, gravely, ludicrously, jokingly or how he liked, so long as Garrick was not suspected of writing it himself. Colman carried out his instructions to the best of his ability; he was too wary to accept Garrick's invitation to speak disrespectfully of him—he knew how that would end—and, instead, stressed London's woeful need of him as a manager and actor. Garrick read the newspaper with extreme displeasure; it would almost certainly, he thought, be attributed to him, and he would be accused both of praising himself and of ingratitude to his public for deserting them in order to enjoy himself abroad. He begged Colman to do all that he could to prevent suspicion from falling on him. 'I never in my life praised myself knowingly,' he wrote, 'except a little matter in *The Fribbleriad*, which always pinched me.'

In the end, Garrick decided to do the job himself, and sat down in all seriousness to write a satire on himself, which he called *The Sick Monkey*. Choosing La Fontaine as his model, he presents himself in the title rôle surrounded by animals who rail at him ill-humouredly. This poem, the silliest that ever came from his pen, he sent off to Colman with elaborate instructions to take it to some printer not usually associated with either of them, and swear him to secrecy. But the poor little squib, when it appeared a few days after his return, failed to explode. In the general rejoicing, which had needed no artificial stimulus and in which there was no discordant note, *The Sick Monkey* fell still-born from the press. No one took the slightest notice of it, and, but for the curious light it throws on Garrick's character, it would long since have been completely forgotten.

CHAPTER XIV

BACK TO THE STAGE

1765 — 1769

THE season was nearly over by the time Garrick reached home at the end of April, and there was no need yet for him to go back to Drury Lane. He could spend the summer pretending to himself that he had retired, with nothing to do for the rest of his life but entertain his friends at Hampton House—a day-dream he thoroughly enjoyed until a Royal Command from King George III to appear before him in the autumn awakened him to reality, and brought home to him the impossibility of withholding his gift from the world for longer than the state of his health made necessary. His holiday had lasted two years, and this break in his career provides an opportunity to consider the changes that had taken place in the theatre since he first came to London, twenty-eight years ago.

In the first place, the playgoing public was steadily increasing, and there were more opportunities for a young actor. Theatres were springing up all over the country, and the hard life of a strolling player was not now the only alternative to a London engagement. No longer would a promising young actor like King be obliged in one evening to speak a prologue, take the part of Richard III, sing two comic songs, play in an interlude, dance a hornpipe and finally play Harlequin for threepence and two pieces of candle. He could gain experience and a small salary at one of the many provincial theatres; Richmond, Bath, Tunbridge Wells, Portsmouth, Bristol and many other towns each supported a company, and an actor who showed talent would soon be noticed and recommended to the London managers. Edinburgh, now fully equalling Dublin

181

in prestige, served as an easy stepping-stone to London, and many of the actors at Drury Lane and Covent Garden had already been well known to their audiences when they made their first appearances in London. The two patent theatres kept their monopoly during the winter season, but as the century wore on the old cut-throat competition between them diminished, as each could attract a full house without necessarily emptying the other. The King's Theatre in the Haymarket[1] continued to present Italian opera with varying success, and up till 1766 the Little Theatre, generally, but not always, under Foote's management, gave its dramatic performances thinly disguised as lectures or concerts. In the July of that year, Foote was granted a life patent to present plays during the summer months, in compensation for the loss of a leg following a practical joke played on him by the Duke of York—a misfortune he met with great courage. Henceforth, there was no need for camouflage, and from May to September Foote presented a variety of plays in a new theatre built on the site of the Little[2] and authorized to describe itself as a Theatre Royal.

Audiences had not lost their preference for comedy rather than tragedy, and the quality of the new comedies was improving. Shakespeare's plays were increasingly appreciated, romanticism was gaining ground, but pseudo-classic tragedies were still administered to the public in regular doses, and swallowed with wry faces. For there was no one left of the old school to declaim the classic rôles —Quin, Ryan[3] and Colley Cibber[4] belonged to the past—and the Garrick manner, which now dominated the stage, did not suit the rhymed couplets of a noble Roman in a bag-wig. Of Garrick's contemporaries, Thomas Sheridan and Macklin appeared only occasionally; Mrs. Cibber was in bad health and died in 1766, Mrs. Pritchard was to retire in 1768, and Mrs. Bellamy had dissipated too much of her energy in the tangles and excesses of her private life to fulfill the promise of her youth. Barry, with the talented Mrs. Dancer whom he later married, was on the eve of returning from Dublin and, although a somewhat gouty Romeo, had not lost the melting tones of his voice. Holding the tragic stage at Covent Garden were Ross, soon to leave London for theatrical management

1 On the site of what is now His Majesty's Theatre.
2 On the site of what is now the Haymarket Theatre.
3 Ryan died in 1760.　　　　4 Cibber died in 1757.

in Edinburgh, Mrs. Ward, Garrick's *bête noire*, and Miss Macklin, the competent daughter of the actor. Drury Lane, as usual, carried heavier guns with Powell, a gifted young man though not the genius he appeared to be in the absence of competition, Holland, a conscientious imitator of his master, Havard, a useful actor of secondary parts, and Mrs. Yates, the best tragedy actress between Mrs. Cibber and Mrs. Siddons. In comedy, some of the old stagers lingered and many talented newcomers had joined them. At Covent Garden, the sixty-year-old Woodward gave a wonderful illusion of youthful charm and vivacity, and Shuter's twin preoccupations, the bottle and Whitefield's Tabernacle, had not yet robbed him of his lively sense of humour. At Drury Lane, Yates's long and varied experience made him an invaluable standby, and Kitty Clive, after thirty-seven years on the stage, could still fill a house with her comic chambermaids and low comedy matrons. Among the younger members of the company, Mrs. Abington, who returned from Dublin in the summer of 1765 to rejoin the Drury Lane company, Miss Pope and Thomas King were making theatrical history. ·

In methods of production—scenery, lighting and costume—the stage had made little progress. Three side wings arranged laterally still represented the interior of a house, and actors, making their entrances through walls meant to be solid, advanced to speak their lines on what remained of the apron in much the same way as the Elizabethans. The introduction of the drop scene in the early fifties, however, foreshadowed the use of the falling curtain for dramatic effect. In all but their stage machines, the English lagged behind the Continent. The best scene painters in London were foreigners, and the French, despite the greater formalism of their acting, had a stronger feeling for realism in their settings. Garrick brought back with him from Paris the setting for a palace, the walls of which consisted of painted stones, put together with handles at the back. When the stones at the bottom were drawn away, the edifice came down in ruins—a triumph of ingenuity for its day. Lighting, again, was better abroad, and as soon as he returned to Drury Lane Garrick discarded the rings of candles that hung conspicuously across the stage, and installed the French system of side lighting, hidden from the audience and thrown on the stage by means of reflectors. For the old footlights of candles, he substituted a line of oil-lamps sent him by Monnet.

'I have carried out your two commissions,' wrote Monnet in the summer of 1765, 'and with M. Boquet's designs I will send you a reflector and two different samples of the lamp you want for the footlights at your theatre. There are two kinds of reflectors: those that are placed in a niche in the wall, and which have one wick; and those which are hung up like a chandelier, and which have five; the first, which are, I fancy, the more suitable for the illumination of your hall, cost twelve shillings and sixpence, and the others from thirty shillings up to three pounds according to the size and the ornaments applied to them. As to the lamps for lighting your stage, they are of two kinds; some are of earthenware, and in biscuit form; they have six or eight wicks, and you put oil in them; the others are of tin, in the shape of a candle, with a spring, and you put candles in them. The first are less costly, and give more light. But for them not to smell, you must use the best oil and keep the lamps very clean.' [1]

Much Ado about Nothing was the play chosen by the King in honour of Garrick's return, and from the moment he stepped on the stage that day in November 1765 to the day he made his last exit in 1776 he had no reason to complain of any lack of public appreciation. His Benedick to Miss Pope's Beatrice was greeted with thunderous applause, and the craze for Powell was forgotten in this fresh revelation of genius. His manner was easier, he played less to the gallery, and, as the season wore on, it was noticed that he had corrected many of the extravagances that had marred his early performances. The unconscious burlesqueing of his style by his followers on the French stage had taught him more than all the destructive criticism of English pamphleteers, and, although his state of health was henceforth to prevent him from appearing oftener than twenty or thirty times a season, his greatest period as an actor began from this moment. He never again attempted a new part; he discarded his less successful ones, and chose rather to keep his rare performances up to a level of perfection beyond the reach of actors obliged continually to master new parts. The tributes paid him are too numerous to record, and if he became increasingly vain it is hardly surprising. 'If this had happened to me,' remarked Dr. Johnson to Boswell after Garrick had retired from the stage, 'I should have had a couple of fellows with long

1 Quoted in *David Garrick and his French Friends*, by F. A. Hedgcock.

10. GARRICK RECITING THE ODE AT THE SHAKESPEARE JUBILEE
from a print in the Enthoven Collection, Victoria and Albert Museum

poles walking before me to knock down everybody that stood in the way. Consider if all this had happened to Cibber or Quin! They'd have jumped over the moon'—adding with a smile—'yet Garrick speaks to *us*.' Every distinguished foreigner visiting this country made a point of seeing him act, and many of them paid him the compliment of calling on him at Hampton. In 1766 the great Rousseau, understanding little or no English, sat with Mrs. Garrick through a comedy, and in his anxiety to be seen himself by the audience leaned so far over the ledge of the box that Mrs. Garrick had to hang on to the skirts of his coat to prevent him from over-balancing. Two years later, the King of Denmark, taking his seat in the royal box just as Garrick came on to the stage, shared with him the applause of the audience, and, although he dropped off to sleep during the performance, sent Garrick a snuff-box set with diamonds as a token of his appreciation, and paid him the honour of visiting him at Hampton House.

With a company strong enough to attract good houses without him, Garrick could devote more time to writing; prologues, epilogues, burlesques and adaptations flowed from his facile pen, and, however ephemeral most of his work proved to be, it served its purpose at the time as light entertainment. Even during his holiday he had been working on a comedy in collaboration with Colman, and this was produced in February 1766, under the title of *The Clandestine Marriage*. It met with outstanding success. The apportioning of the credit led to a quarrel between the two men, and it is impossible to say now which of them was in the right. One of the few comedies of its period that would bear revival to-day, it is so much better than Garrick's own plays that it is natural to infer that Colman, the author of the almost equally successful *Jealous Wife*, was responsible for the greater part. For Garrick by himself never attempted to write a full-length play—his powers of invention, it would seem, could not be sustained for five acts—and his satire had not the keenness of either *The Jealous Wife* or *The Clandestine Marriage*. On the other hand, it is equally possible to argue that *The Clandestine Marriage* is greatly superior to Colman's other plays with the exception of *The Jealous Wife*, which Garrick revised for him when he produced it. Moreover, the resemblance of Lord Ogleby, the play's most effective character, to Garrick's Lord Chalkstone in his farce, *Lethe*, is too marked to be fortuitous. Thus the only decision it is reasonable to make is that the play was a true collaboration of two writers whose gifts were complementary to each other. It seems probable that Garrick suggested the rough outline of a plot,[1] Colman wrote the play and Garrick revised it, doing most to the scenes in which Ogleby appeared. The play was so much worked over by both men that they may well have forgotten in the process which of them thought of the ideas first.

The trouble began when Colman discovered that Garrick did not intend to take the part of Ogleby, the vain old fop who imagines that the virtuous Fanny is in love with him. Each part had been written with a particular player in mind, and the skill with which the comic powers of a brilliant company was exploited largely accounted for its success. Mrs. Heidelberg, who in her illiterate vulgarisms foreshadowed Mrs. Malaprop, was admirably made to fit Kitty Clive; Yates could do full justice to the money-loving old city merchant; Miss Pope as the heroine's haughty elder sister, Powell as the likeable young hero secretly married to Fanny, Holland as Ogleby's nephew ready to marry beneath him for money, and Mrs. Palmer as the warm-hearted heroine, were all equally well catered for. Colman had assumed that Garrick, the creator on the stage of his own Lord Chalkstone, would take Lord Ogleby himself and he thought he had his promise to do so. When Garrick told him of his intention not to undertake any more new rôles, Colman went off to Bath in a rage. All those in the secret sympathized with Colman, and Garrick, on being pestered to change his mind, let fall an unfortunate remark which, on being repeated, gave offence. 'Since my return from Bath,' wrote Colman to Garrick, 'I have been told, but I can hardly believe it, that in speaking of *The Clandestine Marriage* you have gone so far as to say, "Colman lays great stress on having penned this character on purpose for me—suppose it should come out that *I wrote it.*" ' Garrick declared that he had been misquoted, and angry letters were exchanged. By Christmas, however, they were friends again, and King's brilliant rendering of the part and the play's long run to packed houses

[1] In 1801 a claim was made that three of the characters and certain of the scenes had been taken from Townley's *False Concord*, which was performed at Covent Garden in 1764. As this play was never printed, the claim cannot be substantiated, and, even if it could, adaptation of older plays without acknowledgment was a common practice and would not have been regarded as discreditable.

reconciled Colman to his disappointment. It was, alas, characteristic of Garrick that King's success did not altogether please him. 'I know that you all take it as granted,' he said in later years, 'that no one can excel, if he can equal, King in Lord Ogleby, and he certainly has great merit in the part; but it is not MY Lord Ogleby, and it is the only character in which I should now wish to appear.'

Garrick was not at all well during the winter that followed his severe illness, and in April 1766 a sharp attack of gout obliged him to go to Bath for treatment. Sometimes he doubted whether he would ever be fit to lead a strenuous life again, and whether in any case he could go on working with Lacy. Their association had been happy enough until George Garrick began to irritate Lacy. He could not see why David and he need burden themselves with an assistant whose ineptitude for the theatre only increased with the years, and whose main activity was to carry mischief-making tales to his brother. In the end, Lacy must have said as much, for we find David writing angrily that, if George went, he went with him.

The truth is that Garrick had tired of theatrical management and hankered after a life of greater ease. He even thought of going into politics and standing for Lichfield, but that ambition soon faded. While abroad he had made cautious inquiries as to the value of his share of the patent, only to discover that, unless he acted, the sum would be less than he felt inclined to accept. He had a vague scheme for getting Colman into the management, either instead of Lacy or instead of himself, but he could not find a way of putting it into effect. Colman's literary gifts were invaluable to him, and consequently he was not at all pleased, in the summer of 1766, to hear that Colman was putting out feelers for a share of the Covent Garden patent. It was particularly galling since Garrick had himself told Colman that the patent might come into the market. Early in the following year Lacy heard a rumour—and passed it on to Garrick—that Colman was negotiating for a fourth share, and then that Powell was preparing to join in the enterprise. Now Colman was a free agent, and Garrick, though hurt by his secretiveness, could not openly object, but Powell was bound to Drury Lane, and Garrick angrily insisted on his paying the full forfeit of a thousand pounds laid down in his contract before giving him his release. To take his parts he re-engaged Barry, who brought

with him Mrs. Dancer, and, as Powell died two years later, Drury
Lane did not in the long run lose by the exchange. After a brief
coldness with Colman, during which they pulled off their hats, in
Garrick's words, but did not smile, Garrick forgave him, and in
1760 London playgoers had the unprecedented experience of seeing
two parts in *The Clandestine Marriage* played on the stage of
Covent Garden by two actors borrowed for the occasion from Drury
Lane by friendly arrangement between the rival managers. Had
Colman been given as free a hand at Covent Garden as Garrick
enjoyed at Drury Lane, his success in management might have been
comparable. He certainly possessed many of the necessary gifts,
and, even as it was, the profits of Covent Garden began to rise substantially under his rule. Three years' quarrelling with his associates,
however, who accused him of arbitrary acts detrimental to their
financial interests, culminated in a legal action, and although he
emerged victorious he severed his connection with Covent Garden.

As the acknowledged head of the theatrical profession, Garrick
was extremely annoyed on his return from abroad to discover that
a theatrical fund had been established at Covent Garden for the
relief of sick or aged actors without any communication with him.
Hitherto, players in distress could at best only hope for a benefit
night—that is, if they were lucky enough to have influence with the
management—otherwise, they depended on the private charity of
their fellows. A fund had been under discussion for some years, and
during the summer of 1765 a workable plan was formulated and
put into practice by Beard and Mrs. Rich, then joint patentees of
Covent Garden. Garrick, mortified not to be the first, immediately
opened a similar fund at Drury Lane, paying in a considerable sum
and establishing the custom of giving it an annual benefit. In the
year of his retirement, he paid the expenses of an Act of Parliament
for the legal establishment of the fund. In all it has been calculated
that his own contributions amounted to £4,500—a creditable sum
for a man whose meanness was an article of faith for his contemporaries.

CHAPTER XV

A COLDNESS WITH JOHNSON

1765–1769

AFTER two years of social triumphs abroad, Garrick came back to find himself pointedly excluded from the small supping club formed during his absence by two of his oldest friends, Johnson and Joshua Reynolds.[1] 'I like it much,' remarked Garrick to Reynolds, on hearing of the weekly meetings at the Turk's Head. 'I think I shall be of you.' *'He'll be of us!'* exploded Johnson when the unlucky phrase was repeated to him. 'How does he know we will *permit* him? The first Duke in England has no right to hold such language.' 'If Garrick *does* apply, I'll blackball him,' he said to his new friend, Mr. Thrale. 'Who, sir? Mr. Garrick, your friend, your companion—blackball him!' exclaimed Thrale in astonishment. 'Why, sir, I love my little David dearly,' said Johnson rather more mildly, 'better than all or any of his flatterers do, but surely one ought to sit in a society like ours

Unelbow'd by a gamester, pimp or player.

'He'll disturb us by his buffoonery,' was the reason he gave Hawkins, one of the original nine members of the Club, and for ten years Johnson managed to prevent Garrick's name from being formally proposed for election. Garrick took the snub very well, betraying his disappointment only by a rather wistful curiosity as to the doings of the Club. He would stop at Hawkins's house in Twickenham on his way to and from Hampton and bombard him with questions. 'Were you at the Club on Monday night? What did you

---

[1] Sir Joshua was not knighted until 1769.

189

talk of? Was Johnson there? I suppose he said something of Davy—
that Davy was a clever fellow in his way, full of convivial pleasantry,
but no poet, no writer?' Yet ten years later, Johnson warmly supported Garrick's election, and after his death refused to consider
filling his place until a year's mourning had elapsed.

Boswell, seeing for himself that Johnson was genuinely fond
of Garrick, could not believe that he had ever been serious in his
opposition. In 1764, however, Boswell had only recently been introduced to his hero, and may not have known how near the two men
were to an open quarrel. When we last saw them together at Hampton they were on the happiest terms. It was to Garrick that Johnson poured out his grievances against Lord Chesterfield who, after
seven years' neglect, tried to associate himself with the Dictionary
by recommending it to the public in the columns of *The World.* 'I
have sailed round the world of the English language,' runs Johnson's bitter phrase preserved for us by Boswell, 'and does he now
send out two cockboats to tow me into harbour?' No one was more
delighted than Garrick with the success of the great work, and in
an epigram[1] he congratulated Johnson on his prowess in performing single-handed for the English language a service it had recently
taken forty French Academicians to perform for theirs. As they sat
together after dinner, Johnson asked Garrick to tell him what people were saying about his Dictionary. Some objections were being
made, replied Garrick, to his use of authorities beneath the dignity
of such a work, and he gave Richardson as an example. 'Nay, I
have done worse than that,' said Johnson smiling. 'I have cited
thee, David.' Now 'giggle' happens to be one of the two words[2]
the use of which Johnson illustrated by a quotation from Garrick,
and, in view of the innumerable sly jokes which can be found
hidden in the Dictionary, it is doubtful whether the association of
ideas can be regarded as altogether a compliment.

It was kind of Garrick to give 'Mrs.' Williams, the blind poetess,
two benefit nights (one in 1755 from which she received £ 200,
and another in 1763) ; for she had no claim on him save as Johnson's friend and dependant, and Johnson fully appreciated his
generosity. When Johnson aired his small grievance in Tom Davies's
bookshop in front of Boswell on the occasion of their first meeting,
he was only half-serious. 'What do you think of Garrick?' he said,

1 See Appendix IV.　　2 The other is 'nowadays'.

addressing himself to Davies and ignoring the young Scot whom he had just stunned into silence. 'He has refused me an order for the play for Miss Williams, because he knows the house will be full and that the order would be worth three shillings.' Boswell, eager to recover his attention, stumbled in with, 'Oh, sir, I cannot think Mr. Garrick would grudge such a trifle to you.' 'Sir,' said Johnson sternly, 'I have known David longer than you have done, and I know no right you have to talk to me on the subject.' It was many years later that Boswell ventured to say to him, 'It is observed, sir, that you attack Garrick yourself, but will suffer nobody else to do it.' 'Why, sir,' replied Johnson with a smile, 'that is true.'

Nevertheless, admirers of Dr. Johnson will regret that he stooped to make the stale old joke, and in Davies's bookshop of all places; for most of its frequenters were, for one reason or another, hostile to Garrick, and in Garrick's opinion met there for the chief purpose of abusing him. Davies had not long left the stage in order to devote his whole attention to bookselling—or so he let it be understood by his customers, but he told Dr. Johnson that Garrick's ill-temper at rehearsals had made the stage intolerable to him. Garrick, informed of this by Davies himself in the course of a quarrel, retorted that a more likely explanation for his retirement was his discomfiture at the lines devoted to him in *The Rosciad*.[1] It had been noticed, wrote Garrick, that after its publication the mere sight of Churchill sitting in the pit was enough to confuse him for the whole evening, and if he had indeed betrayed any warmth at rehearsals, Davies's want of preparation in his parts had justified it. Whatever the reason for Davies's retirement, the stage suffered little from it; his pompous manner, which made him ridiculous in private life, limited him to tragedy kings, and had it not been for his pretty, accomplished actress wife, his engagement at Drury Lane might have terminated much earlier. Superficial in his learning and pretentious in his display of it, he was nevertheless a friendly, hospitable man, and Johnson liked to sit in the back-parlour in Russell Street, finding some of the innocent satisfaction in Mrs. Davies's feminine charms he was soon to find in those of Mrs. Thrale.

[1] *With him came mighty Davies. On my life,*
That Davies hath a very pretty wife:
Statesman all over; in plots famous grown,
He mouths a sentence as curs mouth a bone

Johnson's frequent visits there at this time were in themselves an indication that he was not feeling kindly disposed towards Garrick, and the cold formality of his letters to him strengthens this impression. Their friendship had, in fact, cooled from the day Johnson undertook to edit Shakespeare, and made it clear that he set no value on Garrick's knowledge and interpretation. Garrick, in his opinion, was like any other actor, incapable of taking in the full significance of his lines. To say that he brought Shakespeare into notice was to lampoon the age, Johnson told Boswell a few years later. Many of Shakespeare's plays—*Macbeth,* for instance—were, in Johnson's view, the worse for being acted, and had he mentioned Garrick, he would have felt obliged to mention Mrs. Pritchard, Mrs. Cibber, and even Colley Cibber, for he too, added Johnson, altered Shakespeare. Garrick, on his side was shocked—like many others in their circle—to find that Johnson did not look upon his task as a labour of love, nor apply himself to it with any enthusiasm. He was, indeed, more than a little bored by it, telling Hawkins frankly that he regarded the undertaking as he had the Dictionary—as a means of making money. After dawdling over it for nine years, he completed the edition in 1765—the year, by the way, that the University of Dublin made him a doctor of laws—and his coolly critical attitude towards the divine Shakespeare exasperated Garrick. It was blasphemy to Garrick to put into words the offences against contemporary taste that his own alterations to Shakespeare's plays were expressly designed to obscure. 'All that he writes', he said of Johnson indignantly, 'comes from his head. Shakespeare, when he sat down to write, dipped his pen into his own heart.' Yet Johnson's edition, though it fell short of what was expected of him, cleared the text of many impurities, and his critical comments are the logical reactions of the eighteenth-century classicist to Elizabethan romanticism. To Garrick, who had grown accustomed to seeing his name coupled with Shakespeare, Johnson's failure to make the briefest reference to him was a deliberate slight. He was the only living writer, Garrick complained, who had never paid him any tribute in print. There was one passage, moreover, that gave him the deepest offence.

'I collated such copies as I could procure,' wrote Johnson in his Preface, 'and wished for more, but I have not found the collectors of these rarities very communicative. Of the editions which chance or kindness put into my hands I have given an enumeration that I may not be blamed for neglecting what I had not the power to do.' Garrick, as most of his friends knew, had been collecting early editions of Shakespeare for years, with some idea of bringing out one of his own, and it was generally assumed that Johnson was referring to him. If so, and Johnson never made any denial, it was unfair, for Garrick was always ready to give writers access to his library. Before he went abroad he left orders with his manservant to let Johnson have whatever books he wanted; and he did so knowing Johnson would maltreat those he despised and appropriate the others. Johnson, however, never applied for any, regarding the offer as a bribe—or so it was thought at the time.

Garrick was much too much in awe of his old schoolmaster to make any complaint to his face, and after the edition was published the usual courtesies were exchanged. When William Kenrick made a violent attack on Johnson in a review of the work, Johnson, taking for granted Garrick's sympathy, sent him a copy of an answer written by a well-intentioned, if ill-informed, undergraduate. But Garrick's comment on the affair in a letter to Colman has in it a hint of malicious glee at Johnson's evident soreness on the subject under his show of unconcern. Far from dissociating himself from Kenrick in loyalty to Johnson, Garrick took especial pains over the production that season of his play, *Falstaff's Wedding*—a service Kenrick repaid a few years later with a gross libel on Garrick's private character causing him great distress and agitation.

Johnson's coldness to Garrick covers the period during which the manager's relations with men of letters were at their worst, and when many of Johnson's closest friends had real or fancied grievances against him. It was then that Garrick seemed to justify the complaints made against him by the dramatists of discouraging talent when he refused Dodsley's *Cleone,* made difficulties over Murphy's *Orphan of China* and, by his failure to recognize the promise in Goldsmith's first play, missed the opportunity a few years later of producing *She Stoops to Conquer,* the best play written during his management. Goldsmith, one of the nine original members of the Club and for whom Johnson had an especially warm affection, was still smarting under an injury done him by Garrick when Johnson refused to consider adding Garrick to their number, and some years were to elapse before the two men made friends.

In the first place Goldsmith was to blame. There was no reason for him to attack Garrick's management in the pamphlet he wrote in 1758; as a newcomer to London, he had no personal experience of its theatrical managers, and was only echoing James Ralph, a dramatist of no ability who owed much to Garrick's generosity, and had taken his revenge for the failure of a play by sneering at the manager in an anonymous pamphlet. Soon after these two pamphlets appeared, the post of secretary to the Society of Arts fell vacant, and Goldsmith was persuaded by his friends to apply for it. They told him that Garrick was a leading member of the body, and that it would be necessary to enlist his support. Calling on the manager in his office and apparently expecting a welcome, Goldsmith asked him for his vote; Garrick not unnaturally refused it. He pointed out that Goldsmith by his unprovoked attack on him had forfeited his goodwill. Goldsmith, far from expressing any regret, made matters worse by retorting that he had spoken his mind and what he said was right. Whereupon Garrick dismissed him with cold civility, and the post fell to a Dr. Templeman while Goldsmith continued to starve in his garret.

Goldsmith had nothing but a few essays and pamphlets to his credit when Johnson and Reynolds befriended him, recognizing the gifts that lay hidden under an unprepossessing exterior. Garrick saw only a slovenly, awkward Irishman, whose vanity and foolish simplicity were making him the laughing-stock of the coffee-houses. As an adversary, Garrick did not consider him worth appeasing, and in their first encounter treated him with the severity he usually displayed towards those whose literary abilities he despised. It was Reynolds who, some nine years later, arranged another meeting between them, hoping that Garrick would interest himself in a comedy Goldsmith had just finished, and in which Reynolds. Burke and Johnson saw great merit. By this time, Goldsmith, as the author of *The Vicar of Wakefield* and *The Traveller,* was entitled to respect, and, considering how quick Garrick was as a rule to recognize good writing, it is astonishing that, despite the immaturity of *The Good Natur'd Man,* he did not think its author worth encouraging.

But their vanities clashed; the successful manager treated the inexperienced playwright with condescension, and Goldsmith, conscious of being the better writer, took offence. Garrick made it appear that his production of the play would be a favour, and this

Goldsmith would not admit, seeing no kindness in a bargain intended to benefit both parties. Nor was he prepared to admit for a moment that he had anything to learn in stage-craft from a playwright and producer of over twenty-five years' experience, and he received Garrick's criticisms on his play with indignation. He could not suffer such airs of superiority from one who was only a poor player, he told Reynolds, who remarked mildly that 'poor' was hardly the right adjective. Garrick, after making Goldsmith vague promises of an early presentation, assured Johnson and Reynolds privately that the play could not succeed, and at subsequent meetings with Goldsmith made one difficulty after another until the summer of 1767 came to an end with matters no further forward. Finally he refused positively to accept the play as it stood, and suggested that William Whitehead, the poet laureate, who was at this time reader of plays for Drury Lane, should arbitrate between them. For Goldsmith this was the last straw, and in the furious quarrel that followed it took the united efforts of Burke and Reynolds to quieten the two men. By a fortunate coincidence it was just at this time that Colman, having taken over the management of Covent Garden, was looking out for novelties with which to rival Drury Lane. Making the excuse that the play had been half-promised to that theatre before his friends offered to use their influence at Drury Lane on his behalf, Goldsmith took it out of Garrick's hands and sent it to his rival. Colman accepted it unconditionally, and it was put into rehearsal before Christmas.

So far in their quarrel we can sympathize with both of them. Goldsmith, at the beginning of his playwriting career, should have submitted to criticism from an experienced man of the theatre, and Garrick should have seen in *The Good Natur'd Man* a freshness that comedy had lacked for several decades, and treated Goldsmith with more tact and tolerance for the sake of the better work sure to come from his pen. But their gifts were too dissimilar for them to appreciate each other. Garrick wrote skilfully constructed farces round groups of well-contrasted stock characters at whom playgoers had been laughing for two or three generations, and their invariable success justified him in thinking that he knew what the public wanted. *The Good Natur'd Man* had a weak plot, some of the characters were misty in outline, and the whole play lacked stagecraft. On the other hand, two of the characters, the lugubrious

195

Croaker and the bragging Lofty, were not only amusing in conception and effectively drawn, but they had never been seen on the stage before,[1] and had Goldsmith allowed Garrick to do for his play what he had done for many other men's, *The Good Natur'd Man* might have met a better fate.

But after the manuscript was taken out of his hands Garrick resorted to those tactics in his war with Covent Garden that, by modern standards of behaviour, are so difficult to defend. As soon as he knew approximately when Colman intended to present Goldsmith's play, he busied himself in preparing a counter-attraction to ensure the failure he had predicted. Hugh Kelly's *False Delicacy* was the play he put up against Goldsmith's comedy, and nothing was too much trouble to prove himself right. The two plays represented conflicting tendencies in contemporary taste, and the success of one militated against that of the other. *False Delicacy* was genteel, artificial and sententious—an example of the sentimentalism introduced much earlier in the century as an antidote to the coarseness of the Restoration, and which had permeated the French comic stage more thoroughly than our own; *The Good Natur'd Man,* robust, realistic and humorous, followed the mood of Shakespeare's early comedies, and was essentially English in feeling. The first performance of *False Delicacy* on the 23rd of January 1768, with a prologue and epilogue by Garrick, forestalled that of *The Good Natur'd Man* by one week; its advance publicity, if one may use so modern a term, had been handled with Garrick's customary skill, and a brilliant production, with Mrs. Dancer and King at their best, won the day for sentimentalism before their opponents had opened fire. Three thousand copies of the play were sold on the day of publication, and Kelly's profits exceeded seven hundred pounds.

Meanwhile nothing had gone right for *The Good Natur'd Man,* and poor Goldsmith was in despair. Long before its last rehearsal, Colman had lost faith in it, Powell had made it known that he could do nothing with the title rôle, and it was only Johnson's unfailing kindness, writing a prologue and even attending the rehearsals, that gave Goldsmith the courage to go through with it. 'It is the best comedy since *The Provok'd Husband,*' declared John-

1 Croaker is, however, strongly reminiscent of Suspirius in Johnson's *Rambler,* No. 59.

son stoutly. 'There has not been of late any such character exhibited on the stage as that of Croaker. *False Delicacy* is totally void of character.' But few people shared his enthusiasm. The first night was not a Club night, but its members agreed to attend the performance together and meet afterwards at the Turk's Head. The evening opened badly. The first two lines of Johnson's prologue held out little hope of hilarity

> *Prest by the load of life, the weary mind*
> *Surveys the general toil of human kind.*

When the curtain rose, Powell made no effort to infuse life into an insipid part, and it was only when Shuter as Croaker and Woodward as Lofty came on to the stage that the audience awoke from its apathy. As they warmed to their parts, however, the atmosphere of the house changed for the better, and there were moments when even Kelly's supporters in the pit, who had come for the purpose of damning the play, were surprised out of their gentility into boisterous laughter. The scene where the bailiffs are introduced as the hero's friends was too badly acted to bring out its humour, and the indignation of the pit at its 'lowness' found noisy expression. The comedy seemed doomed to failure when Shuter's Croaker saved the day by his reading of an ambiguously worded letter intended for his son, which he misconstrues as a demand for money under threat of violence, and his ludicrous exhibition of terror put the audience into a good mood for the rest of the play.

When the curtain fell, Goldsmith, convinced of his play's complete failure, hurried round to the green-room and, in front of all the actors, thanked Shuter for his fine performance in the most generous terms. Then, avoiding congratulations he suspected of insincerity, he went off by himself to the Turk's Head. By the time he got there he seemed to have recovered his spirits; he took no supper, but talked noisily and gaily, even treating the company to his favourite song. But some time afterwards, in front of Dr. Johnson, he told Mrs. Thrale exactly what had happened that night. 'All this while,' he said 'I was suffering horrid tortures; and verily believe that if I had put a bit into my mouth it would have strangled me on the spot, I was so excessively ill; but I made more noise than usual to cover all that, and so they never perceived my not eating, nor I believe at all imagined to themselves the anguish of my heart. But when all were gone except Johnson here, I burst out a-crying, and even swore by God that I would never write again.' Dr. Johnson listened in astonishment, and then confirmed his story 'which I thought,' he said, 'had been a secret between you and me; and I am sure I would not have said anything about it for the world.'

Although *The Good Natur'd Man* did not act well, its good qualities were more apparent in print, and, on the whole, Goldsmith gained in prestige as well as in pocket by giving it to the world. Whether Garrick suddenly began to see merit in work he had hitherto disparaged (he had thought little of *The Vicar of Wakefield* when it first appeared), or whether they both found it uncomfortable and inexpedient to carry on a war while meeting constantly as fellow-guests of Sir Joshua Reynolds, Burke, Topham Beauclerk and all the rest of those associated more particularly with the name of Dr. Johnson, it is impossible to say, but their undisguised hostility gradually gave way to a semblance of cordiality. Then each found himself enjoying the gaiety and high spirits of the other, and their contests in disrespectful mimicry of Dr. Johnson became a favourite entertainment for those evenings when the great man's absence rendered learned discourse unnecessary.

They first came together in a friendly way in their efforts to help Baretti, an Italian of their acquaintance, when he was arrested and charged with murder. No one liked this disagreeable, ill-mannered foreigner, and it was only to please Dr. Johnson, whom Baretti had helped with his Dictionary, and who, in consequence, considered himself under some obligation to him, that Baretti was tolerated by Dr. Johnson's friends. But he was no murderer, and as soon as Goldsmith heard of his plight he went to his assistance, offering him every shilling in his purse. He stood by him when Sir John Fielding committed him for trial, and even insisted on going with him in the coach to Newgate. Then Baretti's friends, Johnson, Reynolds, Burke, Garrick and Goldsmith among them, met to arrange his defence. Baretti, it appeared, had been on his way to a meeting of the Royal Academicians, for whom he acted as secretary for foreign correspondence, when he was solicited by a woman; repulsing her roughly, he was set upon by three men with whom she was subsequently proved to be connected. Baretti ran away, but, being pursued, turned to fight, and instinctively drew from his pocket the fruit knife he habitually carried there. In his excitement, he gave one of his assailants a fatal wound. He could not evade responsibility for the man's death; he could only plead self-defence, and call upon his friends to bear witness to the 'quietness of his general character'. At the trial, Garrick testified that everyone abroad carried such a knife; for in foreign inns, he explained, only forks were provided. On his travels he had himself carried such a knife. 'I never knew a man of more active benevolence,' he lied unblushingly in answer to a question. 'He is a man of great probity and morals.' And Reynolds, Johnson, Burke, Beauclerk and Goldsmith in turn attested to Baretti's amiable qualities with so much apparent sincerity that the prisoner was acquitted, and lived to be the bane of Mrs. Thrale's life as tutor to her children.

Four days before the trial, which took place on the 20th of October 1769, Boswell gave a dinner-party in his rooms in Old Bond Street, but for him the date had no particular significance; indeed, he was rather hoping Baretti would be hanged. Dr. Johnson, Sir Joshua Reynolds, Murphy, Goldsmith, Garrick, Isaac Bickerstaffe and Tom Davies took their places round the table, and no reader of Boswell's account of that evening would ever suspect that his guests had not always been the best of friends. It was just at this time that Boswell was transferring his allegiance from Paoli, the Corsican patriot, to Dr. Johnson, or, as his father chose to express it, from the 'landlouping scoundrel of a Corsican to the auld dominie', and Jamie listened and observed that evening with an intentness born of a newly formed resolution. While they were waiting for the last guest to arrive, 'Garrick,' he tells us, 'played round [Dr. Johnson] with a fond vivacity, taking hold of the breasts of his coat and, looking up in his face with a lively archness, complimented him on the good health which he seemed to enjoy; while the sage, shaking his head, beheld him with a gentle complacency.' Then Goldsmith attracted their attention by strutting about, showing off his clothes. 'Come, come,' said Garrick, 'talk no more of that. You are, perhaps, the worst . . .' but before Goldsmith could interrupt him, he went on, laughing ironically, 'Nay, you will always *look* like a gentleman; but I am talking of being well or ill *dressed*.' 'Well, let me tell you,' said Goldsmith, 'when my tailor brought home my bloom-coloured coat, he said, "Sir, I have a favour to beg of you. When anybody asks you who made your clothes, be pleased to mention John Filby, at the Harrow, in Water Lane." ' 'Why, sir,' said Dr. Johnson, 'that was because he knew the strange colour would attract crowds to gaze at it, and thus they might hear of him, and see how well he could make a coat of so absurd a colour.'

Dr. Johnson was in his most characteristic mood that evening, dogmatic, argumentative and throwing brickbats in every direction. After genially calling his young host a dunce for no particular reason, he mentioned Congreve's *Mourning Bride,* which contained the finest poetical passage, he contended, that he had ever read; he recollected nothing in Shakespeare, he went on with one eye on Garrick, equal to it. 'But,' said Garrick, swallowing hook, line and rod, 'we know not the extent and variety of his powers. We are to suppose there are such passages in his works. Shakespeare must not suffer from the badness of our memories.' Johnson, diverted by the signs of personal injury always displayed by Garrick whenever Shakespeare was attacked, warmed to his theme, almost persuading his listeners that he genuinely preferred Congreve to Shakespeare. 'No, sir, Congreve has *nature.*' At this point, the sight of Garrick's tragic earnestness was too much for his gravity, but composing his features again with an effort, he went on, 'Sir, this is not comparing Congreve on the whole with Shakespeare on the whole, but only maintaining that Congreve has one finer passage than any that can be found in Shakespeare. You can show me no passage where there is simply a description of material objects, without any *intermixture of moral notions,* which produces such an effect.' It was this subtle distinction that enabled him to dispose one after another of the examples from Shakespeare brought up against him by his antagonists, while Garrick, who never had the smallest skill in argument, could only sit in exasperated silence. Later on that evening, however, when Dr. Johnson spoke disparagingly of Mrs. Montagu's *Essay on Shakespeare,* Garrick spoke up with, 'But surely, sir, it shows how much Voltaire has mistaken Shakespeare, which nobody else has done.' 'Sir, nobody else has thought it worth while,' was the crushing reply. 'And what merit is there in that?' continued Dr. Johnson, 'You may as well praise a schoolmaster for whipping a boy who has construed ill. No, sir, there is no real criticism in it; none showing the beauty of thought,

11. GARRICK AND MRS. GARRICK IN 1773
from a painting by Sir Joshua Reynolds

as formed on the workings of the human heart.' Here Johnson was saying what he thought, for he had disliked the *Essay* before its authorship was known, and could not understand why Reynolds admired it.

No matter what was said that evening, Dr. Johnson contradicted the speaker. It was probably Boswell himself who, knowing how much Johnson despised Thomas Sheridan, remarked wickedly that a certain barrister with a bad delivery should have studied oratory under Sheridan.[1] Johnson was rising nicely when Garrick spoiled Boswell's sport by agreeing with Johnson. 'Sheridan has too much vanity to be a good man,' remarked Garrick, with the result that Johnson swiftly changed sides and proceeded to defend Sheridan. 'No, sir,' he said. 'There is, to be sure, in Sheridan something to reprehend and everything to laugh at; but, sir, he is not a bad man. No, sir, were mankind to be divided into good and bad he would stand considerably within the ranks of the good. And, sir, it must be allowed that Sheridan excels in plain declamation though he can exhibit no character.'

And so the evening passed pleasantly for Garrick and Johnson, their trifling grievances forgotten in good fellowship, and never again do we hear of any serious misunderstanding between them. Equally famous now, though in very different spheres, each came to look on the other's failings and eccentricities with indulgence; Garrick, with all the rest of the world's playgoers at his feet, could smile at his old schoolmaster's criticism, and Johnson, no less revered by scholars and men of letters, could contemplate the fame of a mere player without secret bitterness.

[1] Sheridan lectured on elocution at the Oxford, Cambridge, London and Edinburgh universities and was awarded a civil pension for his services to education and literature.

CHAPTER XVI

THE SHAKESPEARE JUBILEE

1769

UNTIL the great Shakespeare Jubilee of 1769 brought Stratford-upon-Avon into the headlines, few Londoners had visited the small country town in the Midlands. Its pride as Shakespeare's birthplace had kept pace with the increasing popularity of his plays, but, outside Warwickshire, little curiosity was shown about the poet's early environment or the house[1] with its large garden in which he spent his last years. Garrick and Macklin had made an expedition to Stratford together in their young days, but, generally speaking, no sightseers from any great distance, other than a few scholars and antiquaries, had visited Shakespeare's birthplace; pilgrimages, relics and shrines were as yet the prerogatives of saints, and it was only with the growth of romanticism that the history of more recent times began to stimulate popular imagination. It was Garrick who suggested and planned the festival, but, although it brought the town fame and prosperity, it brought nothing but annoyance and humiliation to him. At least, however, he never fully realized why in the first place he was presented with the freedom of Stratford—an honour he found highly gratifying and which gave him the idea of the Jubilee.

In 1767 a new town hall was nearing completion, and on its north side was an empty niche. A statue of Shakespeare was to be the finishing touch, but the problem of how to obtain it without further expense awaited solution. Nothing was more natural than that Francis Wheeler, one of the town councillors who often came

[1] Only the garden of New Place was as Shakespeare had known it.

to London, should mention it to his friend, George Steevens, the editor of Shakespeare's plays. Steevens remarked in the course of conversation that if Garrick (whom he hated for all the usual reasons) were sufficiently flattered, he would probably be only too pleased to present the town with a statue. Steevens would, if Wheeler liked, introduce him to Garrick. 'In order to flatter Mr. Garrick into some such Handsome present,' wrote Wheeler to the Town Clerk in November 1767, 'I have been thinking it would not be at all amiss if the Corporation were to propose to make Mr. Garrick an honorary Burgess of Stratford, and to present him therewith in a Box made of Shakespeare's mulberry tree.' As a reward for his help Steevens, added Wheeler, should be rewarded with a tobacco-stopper made from the same sacred wood.

The suggestion was well received in Stratford, but the matter needed delicate handling and could not be hurried. Three months passed, no steps had been taken, and Wheeler wrote again to ask for the measurements of the niche. Garrick, hearing from his new acquaintance of the honour likely to be conferred on him, had seemed delighted enough to offer anything. Another eight months elapsed before the resolution was officially passed by the Town Council, and then Garrick, on being privately notified, offered, just as Steevens had foretold, to provide the town hall with a statue and, in addition, a painting of Shakespeare. Twice that autumn Wheeler wrote to the Town Clerk, trying to hurry on the completion of the box in which the freedom was to be formally presented. 'He knows that we have made him a Free Burgess,' wrote Wheeler at the end of November 1768, 'and is very well pleased with it, and his presents are finishing. I did not write to him, rather choosing to deliver his freedom with a verbal message.' By May 1769, everything was ready for the ceremony, and Garrick, who had just returned to London from Bath where he had been recuperating from a sharp attack of stone now unhappily recurrent, formally received a delegation from Stratford. He accepted with evident pleasure the carved box containing the document that made him an honorary burgess of Stratford, and suitable speeches were exchanged.

Garrick already possessed a sample of the mulberry tree. In 1762 he placed among his important papers a receipt for 'four pieces of Shakespeare's mulberry tree lately cut down', which were subsequently made into a carved armchair. Garrick's scribbled note on the bill, however, is misleading; the Reverend Francis Gastrell had, in fact, made his shocking blunder in 1756, but the walls of New Place were high, sightseers were irritably discouraged, and several years passed before the full horror of what the miserable man had done came home to the public.

It had long been locally known that the mulberry tree—the first of the species in the neighbourhood—had been planted in the garden of New Place by Shakespeare himself, in obedience to the royal instructions to grow more mulberries for the breeding of silkworms. A century and a half later the tree had grown to enormous proportions, overshadowing the house and rendering it damp —or so the culprit pleaded, but nothing could excuse such vandalism. Astonishment and grief at the sight of the tree lying on the ground at first struck the townspeople dumb; it was as though the tomb of the Unknown Soldier had been desecrated. Then in an ugly mood they surrounded the house, shouting threats of death and destruction to all inside it. The wretched clergyman fled in terror, and never ventured to brave the warning that no one bearing the name of Gastrell would be allowed in Stratford again. What happened to him, or where he hid his shame, will never be known, but some years later we find his widow living quietly in Lichfield. By a coincidence less strange in the tiny social world of those days than it would now appear, Gastrell had married one of the Misses Aston, and was thus brother-in-law to Gilbert Walmesley.

One man, however, owed Gastrell a fortune. Thomas Sharp of Stratford, variously described as watchmaker, silversmith and carpenter, purchased the tree, and from its wood made small ornamental articles, which he sold for substantially profitable sums. The number of these relics was prodigious: just as ten or twelve skulls of the same holy saint could at one time have been seen in different convents, and enough wood in the world for a forest in the various fragments of the true Cross, so an orchard of mulberry trees might have gone to make all the ink-horns, tobacco-stoppers, snuff-boxes and tea-chests that circulated England as relics of Shakespeare's tree. This, then, is the history of the wood out of which Garrick's box is made. On one side of it was carved a likeness of Shakespeare, and, on the other, Garrick as King Lear.

Garrick sent a warmly appreciative letter of thanks to the Mayor and Corporation, and soon a picture of *Shakespeare in his Study* by Benjamin Wilson and a leaden figure of the poet were on their way to Stratford. The statue was a version of Scheemaker's Shakespeare in the Poets' Corner of Westminster Abbey, in the commissioning of which Garrick in 1741 had been concerned. Twenty-four years later Scheemaker executed a revised version of the statue for Lord Pembroke, and the leaden figure at Stratford is, except for one detail, an exact copy of this later version at Wilton. It was cast by John Cheere, the brother and assistant of Scheemaker's well-known pupil, Sir Henry Cheere, whose leaden figure factory at Hyde Park Corner was the joy of contemporary satirists. When the coatings of white paint, which disfigured it for many years, were removed in 1930, the fine quality of the statue was revealed to testify to Garrick's unerring connoisseurship. In this same Jubilee year, the Corporation of Stratford acquired from Gainsborough a painting of Garrick standing by a bust of Shakespeare, and for this masterpiece—the best portrait, in Mrs. Garrick's opinion, ever painted of her Davy—they paid sixty guineas. Alas, both this painting and that by Benjamin Wilson were destroyed in the fire of 1946.

Garrick purred with contentment: this association of himself with Shakespeare must receive the fullest possible publicity. Would it not be fitting, he suggested to his fellow-burgesses while visiting Stratford later that May, to make the opening of the new hall the occasion for a festival in honour of Shakespeare, to which all the world should be invited? Thenceforth the fame and prosperity to which the poet's birthplace was entitled would be ensured to it for ever. The festival had better be called a Jubilee, and he would undertake its stewardship. His enthusiasm carried the day, and an announcement of the Jubilee to be held that summer appeared in *The London Magazine* for May 1769. The date chosen for the Jubilee appears to be arbitrary, and does not commemorate any particular event in the life of the poet.

All that summer Garrick busied himself with elaborate preparations, sending down to Stratford carpenters and painters from Drury Lane to erect a gigantic wooden rotunda on the bank of the river, in imitation of that in Ranelagh Gardens, for the public performances and balls he was planning. As Lacy had been partly responsible for the famous amphitheatre in London some twenty-seven years before, this part of the proceedings suggests some measure of co-operation from him. If so, it was unwillingly given; he grudged the expense for what he angrily called an idle pageant, and grumbled at his partner incessantly. Garrick found himself obliged to shoulder all the responsibility himself, for offers of help were noticeably lacking. Not a single man of letters of any distinction came forward, and only two leading actors, Thomas King and 'Gentleman' Smith, volunteered their services; the others found it impossible to break their summer engagements. Sometimes Garrick's courage almost failed him, and it needed all his wife's sympathy and encouragement to counteract his nervously exhausting dread of the fatigue he saw ahead of him.

Only at the Angelos' house in Carlisle Street could he be sure of finding an enthusiastic audience, and it was here that the details of the Jubilee were planned. Mrs. Garrick came along too, for she and Mrs. Angelo were friends, and in the background young Henry Angelo would sit eagerly listening. Soon he would be going back to Eton and telling his schoolmates, Carrington and Nathan, George Garrick's young sons, all that he had heard their uncle say. Here in family conclave the firework display for the festival was discussed, and Angelo undertook to superintend the arrangements for the crackers, squibs, rockets and Catherine wheels. 'Our friend Angelo,' remarked the humourless Lacy, rashly attempting a joke, 'is to make the most *brilliant* figure of the undertaking.'

It was to Dominico Angelo that Garrick always took his problems of stage production, because, although Angelo owed his present prosperity to his teaching of riding and fencing, it was his interest in scenery, costume and stage machinery that appealed to Garrick. Angelo's recollections of what he had seen his friend Canaletto doing in Venice gave Garrick ideas to pass on to French, the Drury Lane scene-painter, and Garrick's few timid reformations in stage costume were largely inspired by Angelo's strong views on the subject. When Garrick was planning his first speaking pantomime, *Harlequin's Invasion,* Angelo made a useful suggestion for the setting of an enchanted wood. Brightly coloured screens could reflect their hues, he said, by means of judiciously placed lights on to a transparency, behind which figures could flit dimly across the stage. This device with ingenious elaborations was the basis of many stage illusions in subsequent pantomimes. Transparencies were now designed for the Jubilee, and lamps from Drury Lane sent down to Stratford to render them effective by night. In front of the rotunda, elegantly painted and gilded, hung one on which were painted figures suggested by Sir Joshua Reynolds—Time leading Shakespeare to Immortality with Tragedy on one side and Comedy on the other. Over the windows of the new town hall were five more in the same style, and the tiny house, associated by local tradition with Shakespeare's infancy, was almost hidden by yet another, designed to show the sun breaking through the clouds as the great genius made his first appearance on earth.

But this transformation of a shabby, evil-smelling country town into a vast stage was only achieved in the face of obstinate non-co-operation on the part of the simpler-minded members of its community, who had never heard of either Shakespeare or Garrick, and could not understand the purpose of so much activity. They stared at the strange workmen from London with deepening distrust, seeing in their stage machinery a dangerous defiance of the laws of nature. As the time of the festival approached, and the half-Christian, half-pagan rites were rehearsed, their worst suspicions seemed confirmed, and many were afraid to leave their homes lest the Devil himself should be raised by the necromancers. The more sophisticated inhabitants were hardly less fearful: like the Londoners of 1851 before the opening of the Great Exhibition, they dreaded the influx of strangers and expected rioting and looting. At the same time, however, all those with spare rooms, attics, floor space and even vacant sheds made the most of an opportunity never likely to recur, and the visitors, for the most part wealthy members of the aristocracy, on being offered wretched accommodation at a guinea a night for themselves, and half a guinea for the stabling of each horse, were too thankful for the certainty of a roof over their heads to protest against the rapacity of their hosts.

It was hoped at one time that the Jubilee would open on August 6th, and the nature of the festivities assumed summer weather, but as the date drew near it was evident that it would need at least another month to complete the preparations. Everything that could go wrong, went wrong; the Drury Lane lamps arrived smashed to pieces, the rotunda could not be completed for lack of timber, and the local carpenters refused point blank to lend their tools. Even the weather misbehaved, and after weeks of heavy rainfall the Avon began to rise with ominous speed.

At last everything was ready and, in spite of darkening skies, zero hour was fixed for 8 a.m. on Wednesday, September 6th. Visitors poured into the town until arrivals at the one and only inn found the street too full of loose horses for the ladies to alight in safety from their carriages, and they were obliged to drive round to a private entrance at the back. By Tuesday, Mr. and Mrs. Garrick were installed in their rooms in the Mayor's house, and Mrs. Garrick, having supervised the unpacking of all the fruit and provisions she had brought with her from Hampton, went with Dr. Arne's young niece to decorate Shakespeare's grave with flowers, while Garrick held last-minute conferences in an agony of nervous excitement.

The aristocracy was well represented in Stratford that week: the Duke of Dorset, Lord Spencer, Lord Carlisle, Lord North, Lord Hertford, Lord Craven and the Duke of Manchester are only some of the names that appear in the accounts of the Jubilee. But Garrick could not help being aware that his audience was not wholly a friendly one, and that several pairs of satirical eyes were on him noting every mishap with satisfaction. The presence in the town of George Colman and Arthur Murphy was disquieting enough, but the sight of Foote, stumping about on his wooden leg, terrified him. It was perfectly apparent that he had come there for the express purpose of teasing him to his face and satirizing the whole episode afterwards. 'Well, Sam,' said Garrick, hailing him in the public breakfast room of the inn as they sheltered from a very heavy shower of rain, 'what do you think of all this?' 'Think of it!' replied Foote, in a loud voice for everyone to hear. 'Why, as a Christian should do. I think it is God's revenge against vanity.' To this impertinence Garrick characteristically made no reply, and throughout the festival Foote took every opportunity in public and private to ridicule his activities.

At dawn on Wednesday a sudden burst of cannon-fire roused the visitors from their beds. Soon afterwards singers in costume appeared in the streets and, to the accompaniment of guitars, carolled under the windows of the more important visitors, distributing as they went from one house to another printed programmes of the entertainments that had been planned for the following three days. At daybreak Garrick hurried to the Town Hall to settle the final details of the public breakfasts to be held there each day at 8 o'clock, but, before the company arrived, a little ceremony took place. The Mayor and Corporation, in a speech delivered for them by the Town Clerk, formally appointed Garrick Steward of the Jubilee, investing him with a medal of Shakespeare carved on a piece of the mulberry tree. This he exhibited on his breast throughout the festival, while visitors, servants and country-people wore favours, the most popular being rainbow-coloured to symbolize Shakespeare's achievements. 'Each change of many-colour'd life he drew,' Johnson had written, but, far away in Brighton enjoying the hospitality of the Thrales and with no thought of the Jubilee in his mind, he would have been astonished to know that his line was appearing on handbills to advertise the sale of a ribbon.

After breakfast, Dr. Arne conducted a performance in the church of his oratorio, *Judith,* to a bewildered audience, who could not see the relevance of its subject to Shakespeare and did not listen with any appreciation. Then, headed by Garrick and singing a chorus, performers and audience marched in procession to the rotunda. There, after some songs of a cheerful character, all of which had been written for the occasion by either Garrick or Isaac Bickerstaffe (Garrick's chief writer at this time) and set to music by Dr. Arne or Charles Dibdin, six or seven hundred ladies and gentlemen sat down to three o'clock dinner. The afternoon passed with the singing of glees and catches until it was time to go home and dress for the ball, and, while the visitors were adorning themselves, hundreds of hands were employed in decorating and illuminating the rotunda for the evening's festivities.

On the whole, the first day of the Jubilee passed off pretty well, but from the time Garrick left his bed on Thursday things began to go wrong. His barber, a little off colour from the previous night's celebration, gave him a great gash on the chin, and Mrs. Garrick had the utmost difficulty in stanching the blood. It was evident, too, that the weather was worsening, and he could not get Lacy to agree to the use of the Drury Lane costumes in the Shakespearian pageant planned to start at eleven o'clock. 'Who the devil, Davy,' exclaimed Lacy ill-temperedly, 'would venture upon the procession under such a lowering aspect? Sir, all the ostrich feathers will be spoiled, and the property will be damnified five thousand pounds.' And so there was nothing for it but to cancel the pageant, and to hurry through the rain to the rotunda for the *Ode to Shakespeare* written by Garrick and set to music by Dr. Arne—the high-spot of the Jubilee. Garrick had felt dubious of the wisdom of giving a performance in the cold light of day, but no one who saw him taking up his position in front of the orchestra guessed his misgivings. In the songs that came first, he was all life and spirit, joining in the choruses and making expressive gestures, and the audience settled down to enjoy themselves in a genial and uncritical mood.

The *Ode* was applauded with rapture, but its success owed much to the life infused into it by Garrick, who seemed in ecstasy, according to Boswell, as he declaimed it, giving the impression of a mortal transformed into a demigod. Every now and then he directed a reverential glance in the direction of Shakespeare's statue, which idol-like towered over the assemblage. Never had his face expressed more emotion—joy, triumph, tenderness and sly humour followed each other in quick succession—with the result that the audience shared his emotional excitement.

At best, Garrick's verses have a charm and sparkle of their own, but the *Ode* was too ambitious for the slightness of his muse. That it defied criticism was all Dr. Johnson allowed himself to say, but Warburton, unhampered by kindly feelings towards its author, compared it unfavourably to Cibber's odes in which, he said, nonsense occasionally sounded like sense while Garrick's occasional sense always sounded like nonsense. Its only interest for us, apart from Dr. Arne's delightful musical setting which is still sometimes performed by itself, is the fact that for the first time the words were declaimed, instead of sung, to a musical setting—an innovation that many of the listeners wished could be introduced into oratorio to take the place of recitatives, often badly and carelessly rendered.

After the *Ode,* Garrick made a speech, and with laboured modesty apologized for what he called his weak abilities, paid tribute to Dr. Arne's musical gifts, and finally invited anyone in the audience to stand up and say a few words for or against Shakespeare. The incident that followed was accepted by many as spontaneous but, in fact, it was stage play devised by Garrick, who used in it his favourite damp-squib technique with even less than its usual efficacy. King, well known by sight to the audience for his performance of Lord Ogleby and dressed foppishly in blue and silver as though for the part, stood up and, in a strain intended as satire but mistaken by many for genuine abuse, delivered a tirade against Shakespeare. He was a vulgar author, an execrable fellow, who inspired snivellings and horse-laughs instead of ennui, the only desirable sensation for a gentleman, and the speech ended on a note of deliberately feeble ridicule of the Jubilee and its Steward. Garrick, in reply, thanked the gentleman in the audience for what he sarcastically described as a panegyric, and then, addressing the ladies with much gallantry, recalled that it was a Society of Ladies who early in the century had been the first to rediscover Shakespeare's genius, and appealed to them in verse to protect their Bard. At the conclusion of the poem, the audience, puzzled and fatigued by all this speechifying, heard with relief the sound of a dinner-bell, and adjourned for a substantial meal, which included a turtle weighing a hundred and fifty pounds, to restore its flagging enthusiasm for Shakespeare.

As night fell, the rain came down in torrents, and, although some attempt was made to light the set piece erected by Angelo on the other side of the river, the Catherine wheels and rockets failed to go off. Cold, wet and disappointed, the spectators went back to their lodgings to put on their fancy dress for the evening's masquerade ball. The river now began to overflow its banks, and by eleven o'clock the low-lying ground on which the rotunda had been built was a swamp, through which the horses had to wade knee-deep and planks were laid down from the carriages for the ladies to reach dry ground. Such a flood had never been known in the history of Stratford.

Once inside the ballroom, a brilliant scene met the eye, and, although a good deal of grumbling was heard from the gentlemen until supper-time, and some of the ladies were too frigid and generally British in temperament to accept with good humour the freedoms invited by their Venetian masks, the evening as a whole went tolerably well. Lady Pembroke, the Hon. Mrs. Bouverie and Mrs. Crewe made an effective trio as the Three Witches, and the skill with which they had concealed their outstanding good looks was universally admired. Kenrick, who in everyday life bore a marked resemblance to the portraits of Shakespeare, stalked through the revels as the poet's ghost. But the surprise of the evening was provided by young James Boswell, who, as a tribute to his hero, General Paoli, wore the striking get-up of an armed Corsican chief with the words VIVA LA LIBERTA inscribed in large gold letters across his feathered cap. Into the belt of his cartridge pouch he had stuck a stiletto on one side and a pistol on the other; across his back was slung a musket, and he carried a long vine stalk as staff. He wore no mask, saying that disguise was not proper for a gallant Corsican, and, taking a long poem from his pocket, would have read it aloud to the whole company had not those round him, who had heard quite enough poetry already that day, firmly prevented him from doing so. A few weeks later this poem, in which the Corsican struggle for freedom was oddly mixed up with Shakespeare's Jubilee, appeared in *The London Magazine* prefaced by an enthusiastic description of the elegant and warlike appearance of Mr. Boswell at the masquerade in a literary style strongly reminiscent of that young gentleman himself.

On the third and last day, the weather improved sufficiently for the running of the Jubilee Gold Cup horse race, which was won by a groom who rode his own colt and confessed frankly that he knew very little about Master Shakespeare. A successful firework display and a final ball brought the first festival of its kind to a close —a festival, by the way, during which no word of Shakespeare's had been uttered from beginning to end.

The expenses of the Jubilee had greatly exceeded Garrick's calculations, and, although most of the money came out of his own pocket, the wear and tear of costumes and destruction of stage property put Lacy into a very bad humour. To appease him, Garrick promised to re-enact the Jubilee on the Drury Lane stage as an afterpiece, which would indemnify them for the loss they had jointly sustained. By the middle of October he was ready with a show, which, combining spectacle, farce and music, hit off popular taste to a nicety and, in spite of Colman's efforts to forestall him at Covent Garden with a similar production, scored the hit of the season and the record run of a hundred nights. 'Davy is an able projector,' said Lacy, now completely mollified, as he rubbed his hands with satisfaction. 'This was a devilishly lucky hit.' The scene was laid in the courtyard of the inn in Stratford, and King as a frightened, ignorant countryman, and Moody as the Irish visitor obliged by the overcrowding of the little town to sleep in his postchaise, supplied its simple humour. Admirably suited to popular taste were the catchy tunes composed for the Jubilee by Dr. Arne and Charles Dibdin to Garrick's words which were interspersed with the dialogue. Some of the ballads—'The pride of all nature was sweet Willy O,' for instance, and, 'For the lad of all lads was a Warwickshire lad'—seem to fall naturally into a tune as they are spoken, and suggest that Garrick was not quite so insensible to music as his contemporaries would have us believe.

Finally the grand pageant, which had been cancelled at Stratford because of the weather, brought down the house. Preceded by sixteen drummers and a band, every available actor and actress marched across the stage in richly brocaded silks and satins, glittering with tinsel and coloured glass, acting in dumb show the Shakespearian characters whose costumes they wore. Each play was represented by its leading characters, and differentiated by means of painted banners. Garrick personated Benedick to Miss Pope's Beatrice, King Touchstone, Holland Richard III, Reddish Lear, and so on. After the comedies a magnificent car drawn by satyrs conveyed Mrs. Abington across the stage as the Comic Muse, and the tragedies were followed by a triumphal car in which sat Mrs. Barry as Shakespeare's Tragic Muse surrounded by the nine muses of ancient Greece. The ghost-like figure of Shakespeare himself from his monument in Westminster Abbey closed a procession described by *The London Magazine* as splendid beyond conception.

Financially, then, the Jubilee justified itself in the end, but Garrick never recalled it with any satisfaction. It gave his enemies an advantage over him they were quick to seize, and the volley of satirical letters, poems, odes and epigrams discharged from the printing presses would have daunted a man far more thick-skinned than poor Garrick. William Warburton and George Steevens, whose editions of Shakespeare entitled them, in their own opinions, to criticize, were tireless in their attacks, but, as usual, it was Foote who displayed most cruelty. The success of the Drury Lane show gave him the idea of following it up at his own theatre with a mock procession in which a counterfeit Garrick as Steward of the Jubilee, with wand, white gloves and mulberry-tree medal, would be the principal figure. Some ragamuffin in the procession was to address him with Whitehead's well-known couplet:

> *A nation's taste depends on you,*
> *Perhaps a nation's virtue too.*

To this the mimic Garrick was to make no answer but would clap his arms like the wings of a cock and crow out:

> *Cock-a-doodle-doo!*

Long before it reached the stage of rehearsal, Garrick got wind of the scheme, and could not hide his consternation. But for some reason or other, Foote relented. One story has it that Lord Stafford interceded with him, and persuaded him to give up the idea. Soon afterwards, it was added, the two actors, invited to dine with Lord Stafford, happened to meet at his front door. They stood looking at each other in silence for a few tense seconds, and Garrick was the first to speak. 'Is it peace or war?' he asked. 'Oh peace, by all means,' replied the unaccountable Foote, and the rest of the evening passed with great cordiality between them. At heart, however, Garrick agreed with his enemies, and in one of his letters of a later date there occurs the significant phrase, 'that foolish hobby horse of mine, the Jubilee'.

CHAPTER XVII

THE OLD AND THE NEW

1769 – 1776

I F Garrick had been a little slow off the mark to recognize the growing appeal of musical plays, he soon made up for lost time, and now, for a while, Drury Lane was to surpass Covent Garden in plays that depended on music and spectacle. In Isaac Bicker-staffe, Garrick had the best comic-opera writer of the day; in Charles Dibdin, a composer of tunes second only, in contemporary opinion, to Gay; and in Loutherbourg, a stage designer far superior to any hitherto employed in England, and from whose knowledge of light-ing and mechanical devices gained on the Continent the English theatre was greatly to benefit.

In 1769, however, Garrick had not met Loutherbourg, and spectacle in its simple sense of a procession, rather than elaborate stage effects, had been the attraction of *The Jubilee,* but it was used in a way that represented an advance. Instead of being inter-polated into a play regardless of its relevance, spectacle now formed an integral part of the whole, and thus prepared the way for the extravaganza and melodrama of a later period. The Coronation of George III, for instance, had had little to do with Shakespeare's *Henry VIII,* or his *Henry V,* both of which had been followed by a representation of the ceremony at the time of his accession; and, eleven years earlier, Garrick had added a funeral procession to *Romeo and Juliet* for the sole purpose of having the last word in his contest with Barry at the other house. But the Shakespearian pageant through a street in Stratford—the *raison d'être* of *The Jubilee*—was anticipated in the dialogue and, in short, provided

215

the entertainment with something like a plot. Four years later this new tendency resulted in Garrick's *Christmas Tale,* a play spectacular in itself with novel and romantic pictorial settings by Loutherbourg. In place of the old conventional set consisting of back shutter and triangularly arranged side-wings that had served as a mere background for pageantry, Loutherbourg broke up the scenery to give the effect of distance and devised transparencies with hidden lights to simulate moonlight, sunshine or fire, and although the critics poured scorn on the *Christmas Tale* as a play, its many innovations ensured good houses for nineteen performances—a moderately good run for those days.

In later years it came to be believed that it was Loutherbourg who invented transparencies, and opened Garrick's eyes to the importance of varying the illumination of his scenes, but, although his improvements were of the greatest value, Garrick and his scene-painters had been experimenting with transparencies and lighting long before Loutherbourg came to England. We find Garrick applying to Gainsborough for advice in about the year 1772, and the painter's reply suggests that he found the productions at Drury Lane rather crude, and emphasizes the almost insuperable technical difficulty of creating stage illusions with candlelight. Garrick, he said, had used so much 'glare and noise' that 'the return to modest truth will seem very gloomy for a time, and I know you are cursedly puzzled how to make this retreat without putting out your lights, and losing the advantage of all our new discoveries of transparent Painting and how to satisfy your tawdry friends whilst you steal back into the mild evening gleam and quiet middle term. Now I'll tell you my sprightly genius how this is to be done—maintain all your light but spare the poor abused colours (red, blue and yellow) till the eye rests and recovers. Keep up your Music by supplying the place of Noise by more Sound, more harmony and more tune, and split that cursed Fife and Drum.'

It must have been soon after this that Garrick met Loutherbourg among the foreign painters and musicians who frequented Angelo's house in Carlisle Street. After dinner, the talk turned— as it often did when Garrick was there—to the problems of stage effects, and he was struck by the value of the Alsatian painter's suggestions. As a result of this meeting, Loutherbourg was engaged in 1773 as stage designer to Drury Lane at the salary—unprece-

12. GARRICK AS DON JOHN IN 'THE CHANCES'

from a painting by P. J. de Loutherbourg in the Victoria and Albert Museum

dented for such a post—of £ 500 a year. Hitherto, French had been responsible for the scenery, but, like all his fellow scene-painters, he was poorly paid and did not, in consequence, always exert himself to produce the good work of which he occasionally proved himself capable. When Loutherbourg was placed over him, he remained on with his assistants to execute the scenery from Loutherbourg's designs.

Loutherbourg's efforts were generally concentrated on the settings of pantomimes or other forms of spectacular entertainment, for little money was expended on revivals of the old stock plays. Hardly any progress in historical accuracy was made under Garrick's management, and all that mattered was that an actor's clothes should conform to the recognized stage tradition for his part, if any such tradition existed; if not, a contemporary style was quite good enough. It is true that Garrick is credited with getting rid of the towering plumes worn by tragic heroes in classic dramas, but this reformation needed little courage to carry out, as the necessity for it was already patent to all. In one of his anonymous satires against himself, written as early as 1744, he ridicules the custom of wearing a tie-wig in Shakespeare's plays, but continued notwithstanding to do so himself. The truth is that, in his more considered opinion, period clothes savoured of a masquerade, and would have disturbed his audiences just as *Hamlet* in modern dress jarred those of a generation or so ago. 'Quin dressed it so,' he said, when scolded by Benjamin West, the painter, for playing Horatius in a dressing-gown and a bag-wig, 'and I dare not innovate.' In Paris, he had seen the efforts Le Kain and Mlle Clairon were making to achieve historical accuracy, but another eleven years passed before he found the courage to present the male characters of *King Lear* in 'old English dresses'. By then, the ice had been broken by old Macklin, who in 1773, actually played Macbeth in Highland dress instead of the uniform of an English general in the time of George II, worn by Garrick and his more immediate predecessors.

Away from Drury Lane, Garrick, if Sir John Hawkins is to be believed, did not always conduct his affairs with wisdom, but in the manager's office he was essentially a practical man of business. He knew exactly when a liberal expenditure on the staging of a play would pay dividends in the form of full houses, and when, on the other hand, rigid economy was the more prudent policy to be carried out no matter how unpopular. He had started his career with high ideals, and the intention of educating his audiences to appreciate the best, but as the years went by he grew more and more cynical until, to use his own words, if the town had required him to exhibit *Pilgrim's Progress* in a drama, he would have done so. In defending the sentimental comedy against the challenge brought against it by Goldsmith's realism, he was influenced by its 'box-office' appeal as much as his own natural preference. Following closely certain recognized conventions for human behaviour, it was easy to write, and the acceptance by almost everyone, however cynical and worldly-wise, of the false sentiments expressed by the delicate Clarissas of literature guaranteed a sympathetic reception. Thus, after the success at Covent Garden in December 1769 of *The Brothers*, Garrick lavished on its author, Richard Cumberland, a vain, ill-tempered and stupid man, all the help and patience that posterity would have regarded as better expended on Goldsmith.

Garrick had already refused two of Cumberland's plays when he attended the first night of *The Brothers* at Covent Garden and was certainly not expecting the fulsome compliment paid him by the author in the epilogue. But Cumberland was determined to succeed as playwright, and only with Garrick's goodwill could he hope ever to realize his ambition. *The Brothers* is grandiloquent nonsense about the sufferings of a sweetly innocent heroine at the hands of a hardened villain who eventually repents. 'I am struck to the heart,' he cries in the last act. 'I cannot support my guilt. I am married to Violetta. Save me the confusion of relating it. This dishonourable engagement for ever will I renounce, nor will I rest until I have an atonement to an injured wife.' It is impossible to believe that Garrick genuinely admired such trash, but it was in tune with the age, and Cumberland's obvious anxiety to please, his facility with his pen and tireless industry all combined to hold promise of future usefulness to Drury Lane. Gratified by Cumberland's publicly-made tribute, Garrick cultivated his acquaintance; Mrs. Garrick and Mrs. Cumberland became friends, and many visits were exchanged between Southampton Street and Queen Anne Street.

In the following autumn, Garrick undertook to produce *The West Indian* before the end of the year, and for many weeks he worked with Cumberland on the manuscript. According to the dramatist, only one passage was radically altered at Garrick's suggestion, although he acknowledges his debt for many lessons in stagecraft, but the finished version has all the slickness that characterizes the plays written, adapted or revised by Garrick, and it was probably largely owing to his help that audiences all over Europe and America were to enjoy it for more than a century. The casting presented some difficulties but, as usual, Garrick did the best that could be done with the actors at his disposal. King, a little old at fifty for the juvenile lead, had nevertheless the debonair gaiety needed for Belcour, the good-hearted rake. Mrs. Abington's modish appearance and lively manner gave interest to the somewhat thin part of Charlotte Rusport. Major O'Flaherty, however, whose overhearing of a soliloquy rather oddly provides the *dénouement* of the plot, gave Garrick the most trouble. Now that he had forsworn new parts, Barry had the right to it, but Garrick did not feel confident that he had enough humour; whereas Moody, who had made his name as the comic Irishman in *The Jubilee,* had not shown himself capable of assuming the manners of a gentleman. In the end, Garrick's choice fell on Moody, on the grounds that being less firmly established in popular favour, he would be more amenable to criticism. Garrick was right, and Moody's performance proved the hit of the evening.

'He is a man without a skin,' said Garrick of Cumberland, pot-like calling the kettle black without moving a muscle of his face, and when the dramatist called at Southampton Street one morning during the run of *The West Indian,* Garrick played on him one of his good-humoured practical jokes. 'I found him with the St. James's evening paper in his hand,' relates Cumberland, 'which he began to read with a voice and action of surprise most admirably counterfeited, as if he had discovered a mine under my feet and a train to blow me up to destruction. "Here, here," he cried, "if your skin is less thick than a rhinoceros's hide, here is that [which] will cut you to the bone. This is a terrible fellow; I wonder who it can be." He began to sing out his libel in a high declamatory tone, with a most comic countenance, and pausing at the end of the first sentence, which seemed to favour his contrivance for a little ingenious tormenting. When he found he had hooked me, he laid down the paper, and began to comment upon the cruelty of newspapers, and moan over me with a great deal of malicious fun and good humour.

219

"Confound these fellows, they spare nobody. I daresay this is Bickerstaffe again; but you don't mind him; no, no, I see you don't mind him; a little galled, but not much hurt: you may stop his mouth with a golden gag, but we'll see how he goes on." He then resumed his reading, cheering me all the way as it began to soften, till winding up in the most professed panegyric of which he was himself the writer, I found my friend had had his joke, and I had enjoyed his praise, seasoned and set off in his inimitable manner, which to be comprehended must have been seen.'

So far, Garrick had no cause to regret his patronage of Cumberland, and when, a year later, he put another of his comedies, *The Fashionable Lover,* into rehearsal he had great hopes of its success. Cumberland, who by this time had gained complete confidence in himself as a dramatist and did not seek advice from anyone, followed his favourite recipe of a rich, aristocratic villain, an impoverished hero and a virtuous heroine in distress, with a happy ending for the innocent and repentance for the wicked, the mixture well seasoned with the dialects of subsidiary characters. (This use of dialect to heighten the characterization of a serious figure instead of to raise laughter in a farce is his sole claim to originality.) He contemplated the result with a satisfaction that approached reverential awe. 'I have an internal plaudit,' he wrote to Garrick, as he put the finishing touches to his opus, 'that sanctifies my efforts,' and when he re-read the play many years later he thought it realized his ideal of true comedy. But it never enjoyed the popularity of *The West Indian,* and henceforth the comedies and tragedies that poured unceasingly from his pen grew ever more sententious and unnatural until Garrick's interest in him turned to boredom and dislike, and Cumberland's recommendation of an actor or an artist was quite enough to put Garrick against him. 'Damn his dish-clout face,' remarked Garrick to Sir Joshua Reynolds in exasperation, 'his plays would never do if I did not cook them up and make epilogues and prologues too for them so that they go down with the public. He hates you, Sir Joshua,' he went on, 'because you do not admire the painter whom he considers a second Correggio.' 'Who is that?' asked Sir Joshua. 'Why, his Correggio,' replied Garrick, 'is Romney the painter.'

It was a year or two before this conversation that Cumberland had taken Garrick to see the portrait Romney was painting of him.

At this time the artist was still painting portraits at eight guineas apiece, and Cumberland hoped that Garrick, who had brought fame to many obscure young painters and sculptors by commissioning his portrait, would do the same for his protégé. But whether it was Romney's association with Cumberland, his openly expressed contempt for the newly founded Royal Academy in which Garrick took a great interest, his hatred of its first President, Sir Joshua Reynolds, whom Garrick loved and admired, that alienated Garrick, or whether his early work did not appeal to Garrick, it is difficult to say. At any rate, the visit was a failure, and Romney was the only well-known portrait-painter of the day who never numbered Garrick among his sitters. If Cumberland is to be believed, Garrick did not hide his poor opinion of a conversation piece on which they found the painter at work. In this family group, father, mother and six children sat gazing at them with wooden expressions, and as soon as Garrick caught sight of it he assumed the posture and vacant look of the gentleman depicted. Then, turning to Romney, he said, 'Upon my word, sir, this is a very well-ordered family, and that is a very bright well-rubbed mahogany table at which that motherly good lady is sitting, and this worthy gentleman in the scarlet waistcoat is doubtless an excellent subject of the State (if all these are his children), but not for your art, Mr. Romney, if you mean to pursue it with that success which I hope will attend you.' Accepting the criticism good-humouredly, Romney turned his family with their faces to the wall, and brought out Cumberland's portrait. But Garrick was hardly less crushing. 'It is very well,' he said. 'This is very like my friend, and that blue coat with a red cape is very like the one he has on, but you must give him something to do; put a pen in his hand, a paper on his table, and make him a poet; if you can set him well down to his writing, who knows but in time he may write something in your praise?' And these words proved prophetic adds Cumberland, with characteristic lack of humour, for very soon afterwards he printed some complimentary verses on Romney in *The Public Advertiser*.

Garrick's health did not allow him to act very often now (he appeared 29 times during the season of 1772-1773 as compared with 101 times ten years earlier), but when he made the effort to act at all he wanted to occupy the centre of the stage throughout the entire play. If a speech delivered by any other character received much applause, it would somehow be incorporated into his own part before the next performance of that play; for no dramatist, living or dead, was safe from Garrick's pen when one of his star rôles needed strengthening. It was because the part of Hamlet as a vehicle for his genius fell short of perfection that he started tinkering with the play in the winter of 1772. Hamlet had always been one of his favourite parts and, with all its drawbacks, had provided many opportunities for the display of his particular gifts: Hamlet's terror at the sight of the Ghost, his simulation of madness (which was treated as comic relief),[1] the scenes of violence and death, and the varied emotions his features must express, Garrick rendered superbly. But temperamentally restless and vigorous himself, he found it difficult to identify himself with Hamlet in his moods of irresolution and inaction. With a little more attention to the unities, a clear-cut plot and a man of action for a hero, the play could be as effective for him as Cibber's *Richard III*—thus Garrick might have reasoned as he prepared to mutilate the text, without realizing that in so doing he was playing into the hands of Voltaire, whose attacks on Shakespeare he passionately resented.

'It is a vulgar and barbarous drama,' Voltaire had written four years earlier, 'which would not be tolerated by the most ignorant audiences in France or Italy. Hamlet becomes crazy in the second act, and Ophelia becomes crazy in the third; Hamlet mistakes Ophelia's father for a rat and kills him; in despair she throws herself into the river; her grave is dug on the stage, and the gravediggers, holding skulls in their hands, make coarse jokes; Hamlet responds with equally disgusting sillinesses. Meanwhile another of the actors conquers Poland. Hamlet, his mother and stepfather carouse together on the stage; they sing drinking songs, they quarrel, fight and kill—one would imagine this piece to be the work of a drunken savage. But amidst all these vulgar irregularities there are sublime passages, worthy of the greatest genius.' This, coming from a foreigner, was offensive; nevertheless, there were few of Garrick's compatriots who did not secretly think that there was a good deal in it, and that some attempt should be made to free Hamlet from what they termed its impurities. The trouble was that, vulgar and irregular as Shakespeare's plays might appear to a purist, any change always proved to be for the worse, and Garrick's

[1] 'The pretended madness of Hamlet causes much mirth.' Dr. Johnson, 1765.

version of Hamlet pleased no one. It held the stage for several years on the strength of his acting, but he never ventured to print it, and would not even allow the prompt copy to be examined by anyone outside Drury Lane.

Piecing together the evidence of eyewitnesses, it appears that Garrick made no great changes until the fourth act. Then he omitted the painful fate of Rosencrantz and Guildenstern, Hamlet's later soliloquy and the whole of the Gravediggers' scene (the rubbish of the fifth act, as he called it), did not tell the audience of Ophelia's fate, sentimentalized the character of Laertes and did not allow him to plot Hamlet's murder with the King. The revised play ended much more simply than the original. In the third act Hamlet, as before, kills Polonius by mistake. Then, reproached by Laertes and the King on his return, he attacks the latter, who, instead of being, as Garrick put it, stuck like a pig, defends himself bravely with a sword and is only overcome after an exciting duel; Laertes falls on Hamlet to avenge his King, and, after another good skirmish round the stage, wounds him mortally; Horatio is on the point of killing Laertes when Hamlet stops him, assuring him that Heaven, not Laertes, has brought him death, 'that precious balm for all his wounds'. Writhing in Garrick's best death agonies, Hamlet joins the hands of Laertes and Horatio and commands them to unite their virtues (as a coalition of ministers) to 'calm the troubled land'. The Queen, instead of being poisoned on the stage, is led off it insane with remorse, and the play ends with the traditional couplet to facilitate the removal of dead bodies from the stage.

In the battle between the sentimentalists and the realists in comedy, Garrick did not care much who won. The sentimentalists, it is true, owed much of their vogue to his patronage; his own work betrays a slight leaning towards their conventions; and he did not have sufficient faith in the popular appeal of Goldsmith's 'low' humour to take any trouble to secure his next play for Drury Lane. But he did not work against him, as he had against other dramatists whose plays were produced at the rival theatre. On the contrary, he listened with some show of sympathy when Dr. Johnson, Burke and Sir Joshua warmly praised Goldsmith's new play, for whose title they 'were all in labour', and even contributed a prologue for the production Colman, as manager of Covent Garden, had reluctantly promised for March 1773. And when, a few weeks before the first night, Foote struck the sentimentalists a mortal blow in a human puppet show, entitled *The Handsome Housemaid, or Piety in Pattens,*[1] Garrick sat in full view of the audience in the Theatre Royal, Haymarket, as Foote was now entitled to call the Little Theatre, laughing as loudly as though he had never supported the victims of the satire. With so many sentimental comedies in the Drury Lane repertory, his carefree enjoyment of this exposure of their absurdities struck some people as curious, and gave rise to the rumour that, having bribed Foote to leave him alone, relief at his escape from a greater evil, rather than amusement at the satire, was the cause of his happy laughter.

While the farce was in rehearsal, it appears, Foote, making a great show of secrecy and assuming an air of malicious glee, went about whispering that he had something very novel in store for the public. To a favoured few he showed a mask, with features closely resembling those of Garrick, to which was attached a pasteboard figure. A man was to be hidden behind this shell, and at appropriate intervals would clap his sides and crow like a cock—the joke Foote had planned but never carried out at the time of the Jubilee. The rumour that his old enemy was hatching another plot against him reached Garrick's ears, as Foote had foreseen, and made him uneasy. He tried by every means in his power to discover its nature, but without the slightest success. Finally, Foote, having kept him on tenterhooks for as long as possible, pretended to take pity on him, and promised to let him into the secret if he would make one of a party for dinner on a certain day. Garrick, who was always easy game for Foote, agreed to go, and waited impatiently for the revelation. When the great moment came, Foote told him with a look of suppressed triumph that he was about to introduce a performer, of most singular talents, who would do everything in a new way. 'What's his name?' asked Garrick in surprise. 'That I'm not at liberty to mention yet,' replied Foote, 'but he's a near relation of your old friend, Dr. Birch[2]—will you be introduced to him?

[1] In derision of the genuine puppets in Panton Street which had been the rage that winter.

[2] Presumably a pun on the name of Dr. Thomas Birch, the historian, of whom Dr. Johnson said that he was as brisk as a bee in his conversation, but no sooner did he take a pen in his hand than it became a torpedo to him and numbed all his faculties.

He is now, I understand, in my study—but ask him no questions, for he'll make you no answers.' The mystified Garrick nodded agreement, and presently in came Foote's manservant carrying a large well-dressed Punch. 'Ah,' said Garrick, a good deal relieved. 'Now I understand you—what, a puppet show, I suppose?' 'Nothing more or less.' 'Well, but—let me see,' said Garrick slowly, his fears reviving. 'What are these puppets to do?' 'Now, damn it, David,' said Foote, looking at him full in the face, 'you are not jealous of Punch already? Come, part the rivals. I am determined to have no noble blood spilt in my house,' and the company had their promised laugh at Garrick's discomfiture. The news that Foote intended to give a puppet show spread fast, and he had many questions to parry. 'Will your figures be as large as life, Mr. Foote?' asked a titled lady a few days later. 'Oh, no, my lady,' replied Foote, 'not much larger than Garrick.' When, after all this teasing, no reference was made to Garrick in the final version of the farce, it was generally supposed that a substantial sum of money must have changed hands.

Garrick often gave offence by keeping dramatists in suspense, but once he made up his mind to produce a play no one could justifiably accuse him of not doing his best with it. Goldsmith might have been spared much misery had he pocketed his pride and gone to Garrick in the first place with his new comedy, instead of taking it to Colman, who not only tortured him with delays, but would not spend any money or take the slightest trouble over a play in which he had no confidence. At one point, Goldsmith, in despair over Colman's objections, sent the manuscript to Garrick, but recalled it the next day after Dr. Johnson had pointed out to him the folly of offending Colman without the certainty of Garrick's acceptance. In the end, Colman had to be browbeaten by Dr. Johnson into settling a date for the first performance, but nothing would induce him to supply a single new piece of scenery or dress, so great was his distrust of the play. His misgivings communicated themselves to the players, and one by one they refused their rôles. 'Gentleman' Smith would have nothing to do with Young Marlow, Woodward threw up Tony Lumpkin, and, worst of all, Mrs. Abington, whose part Goldsmith had boasted of having written especially for her, declined Miss Hardcastle—with the result that three comparatively unknown players, Lee Lewes, Quick and Mrs. Bulkley, had the honour of creating those immortal parts in the play that was finally entitled *She Stoops to Conquer.*

Garrick's name does not appear among the group of Goldsmith's friends who, led by Dr. Johnson, entered a side box on the fateful evening, but, as he attended most first nights, it can be assumed that he came to hear his satirical prologue against the sentimentalists spoken by Woodward. More significant was the presence of Dr. Johnson, a majestic figure in black, who, it was said, had the same effect on actors and audience as Cato on the Romans; when he applauded, the members of his party followed suit, and when he laughed, they dutifully roared. Among them was a Scotsman, who had been invited for the sake of his loud and infectious laughter. Frankly admitting that he knew no more when to give his fire than a cannon, he agreed to obey Cumberland's signals. Unfortunately, as the evening wore on, he became carried away by his own performance, and made so much noise in the wrong places that he was nearly thrown out. But the play needed no *claque,* and when Goldsmith crept into the theatre at the opening of the fifth act, his mouth parched with misery, he found the audience rocking with spontaneous laughter, and his place as a dramatist was secure for all time. After that night, Garrick never again spoke or wrote of his work with contempt, and when, soon afterwards, Goldsmith composed an indignant reply to a stranger who accused him of introducing a real-life character into the play, Garrick did him the friendly service of persuading him not to post the letter.

The gap between Garrick and any other performer was wider now than at any period in his career, notwithstanding the improvement in the general standard of acting he had himself brought about. His contemporaries had declined rather than gained in power, and none of those who had since appeared had the slightest chance of catching up with him. The veteran Sheridan had dwindled, according to Foote's kindly pen, into a mere cock-and-bottle Chelsea pensioner, and could not draw even a summer audience. Barry, gouty, hoarse and generally infirm, would not have been engaged at all by either management had not the services of his wife been invaluable. Yates, now over sixty, as the husband of Mrs. Yates, was similarly privileged. Woodward leapt bravely about the stage of Covent Garden, looking wonderfully young for his years, but his range, even in comedy, had never equalled that of Garrick.

For the Benefit of Mrs. CLIVE.

(Being the laſt Time of her Appearing on the Stage.)

At the Theatre Royal in *Drury-Lane*,

This preſent MONDAY, the 24th of *April*, 1769,

The WONDER,

Don *Felix* by Mr. GARRICK,

Col. *Briton* by Mr. JEFFERSON,

Don *Lopes* by Mr. BADDELEY,

Don *Pedro* by Mr. BURTON,

Liſſardo by Mr KING,

Frederick Mr. PACKER, *Gibby* Mr JOHNSTON,

Violante by Mrs. BARRY,

Iſabella by Mrs. STEPHENS,

Inis by Mrs. BRADSHAW,

Flora by Mrs. CLIVE,

End of the Play, a Dance called The WAKE,

By Sig. *Giorgi*, Mrs *King*, &c.

To which will be added

LETHE.

Lord *Chalkſtone* (1ſt time) Mr. KING,

Æſp Mr. BRANSBY, *Fine Gentleman* Mr DODD,

The *Drunken Man* by Mr. LOVE,

Mercury by Mr. VERNON,

Frenchman Mr. BADDELEY. *Old Man* Mr PARSONS,

The *Fine Lady* by Mrs. CLIVE.

PIT and BOXES laid together

N. B. No Tickets have been given out, but to theſe Ladies and Gentlemen who have their Places ſecured, in the Pit or Boxes, and to prevent any Miſtakes, or Confuſion, no Box Tickets will be admitted into the Gallery; Mrs. CLIVE begs the Favour of thoſe who have Places in the Pit, to be there by half an hour after Five, and to let their Servants come to keep them a quarter before Four.

To-morrow, The JEALOUS WIFE, with a Farce and Entertainments,

For the Benefit of Mr. BRANSBY, and M. BURTON.

King and Smith, both useful members of the Drury Lane company, were competent but uninspired actors. Holland and Powell had died before reaching their prime, and since then no new male star of any magnitude had risen. Of the actresses, none remained from the old days: Mrs. Woffington, Mrs. Cibber and Mrs. Pritchard were all dead; Mrs. Clive, after forty years on the stage, was enjoying well-earned leisure in her Twickenham cottage; and Mrs. Bellamy, her looks and wits destroyed by drink and dissipation, was keeping house for Woodward in involuntary retirement. But their places had been well filled; indeed, the women were now more outstanding than the men. Mrs. Abington gained as many laughs in her line of comedy as Mrs. Clive and Mrs. Woffington had in theirs, and Mrs. Barry, Miss Younge and Mrs. Yates proved themselves worthy successors to Mrs. Cibber and Mrs. Pritchard. None of them, however, could compare for a moment with Garrick, who, unsurpassed in certain rôles and with thirty years' experience of playing them, enjoyed triumphs unbroken by a single murmur of disapproval.

'If I were to begin life again,' he said one day to Boswell, with a great show of sincerity, 'I think I should not play those low characters.' Boswell, astonished that he should regret playing the parts many people regarded as his best, repeated the saying to Dr. Johnson, who assured him that Garrick had only been fishing for a compliment. 'He seemed to dip deep into his mind for the reflection,' said Boswell doubtfully. 'He had not far to dip, sir. He had probably said the same thing twenty times before.' And, no doubt, Dr. Johnson was right. To Garrick, as to all normally constituted creative artists, compliments were meat and drink, but, unfortunately, he did not know when he had had enough. The praise lavished on him was fulsome enough to send most men clean out of their minds, and if occasionally he was betrayed into dropping all pretence of dissatisfaction with his own acting—dissatisfaction no one could reasonably expect him to feel—his contemporaries must surely take some of the blame. 'More pains have been taken to spoil the fellow than if he had been heir-apparent to the Emperor of India,' said Dr. Johnson of him. No Emperor, indeed, had more power over his domain than Garrick had over the London stage, and even his bitterest enemies considered it necessary to write him obsequiously flattering letters to further their own ends, while circulating the latest and most fantastic story of his vanity. One night when he was acting Lear, ran a typical anecdote, one of the two soldiers who stood on guard in front of each proscenium door[1] blubbered like a child. Garrick gave him half a crown. On another evening, a 'celloist in the orchestra emitted a yawning noise as Garrick, in the character of Sir John Brute, fell asleep on the stage, to the audible amusement of the audience and the annoyance of Garrick, who, always easily put off, was liable now to forget his lines when anything unexpected occurred to disconcert him. The 'celloist's explanation the next day that he always yawned when particularly amused was said to have entirely satisfied Garrick.

'I have no vanity about me,' he wrote about this time to a friend, '*whatever* you may think,' and there are many indications that he knew perfectly well what was being said about him. His encounter some years earlier with Bridge Frodsham, the Yorkshire tragedian, who regarded himself as Garrick's equal, would hardly have become known had not Garrick related it himself, and he could not have been blind to its comic implications. During a fortnight's holiday in London, this provincial actor left a card on Garrick. Its simple inscription, *Mr. Frodsham of York,* aroused Garrick's curiosity and led to a meeting between them. Frodsham's happy self-possession in telling Garrick that he thought his Hamlet clever in parts, but that he was unimpressed with his interpretation as a whole, took Garrick aback; it was many years since an actor had spoken to him as an equal. He did not, as one might have expected, take offence; on the contrary, he gave Frodsham an order for the pit to see him as Sir John Brute, and invited him to come and discuss it with him at breakfast the next morning. Frodsham seemed better pleased with Garrick in this part; then, reverting to the acting of Shakespeare—a subject on which he expressed himself with confidence and freedom—he proceeded to give Garrick a demonstration of how Hamlet's soliloquy should be rendered. Discerning great gifts despite the overweening conceit, Garrick offered him an engagement—only to discover to his astonishment that Frodsham had no such object in view. He regarded himself as the Garrick of the North, and was merely paying a social call on a brother genius.

This story, related by Wilkinson, the last person likely to invent

[1] A custom that dated from the beginning of the reign of George II to symbolize the armed force that might (but never did) come in time to quell a riot.

it, shows Garrick in a generous light, but, on the whole, an increasing preoccupation with his own achievements led to a correspondingly greater slowness in recognizing talent in others, and, with a company well stocked with experienced actors, he had little incentive to go looking for it. How it was that he failed to see rare promise in Henderson and Mrs. Siddons needs fuller explanation, but the facts do not warrant the belief, widely held at the time, that he deliberately put obstacles in their way in order to keep all eyes focused on himself. The worst that can fairly be said of him is that he did not wish to be outshone and could not disguise his uneasiness when any other actor was praised in his presence. But he never refused to give a promising young actor a chance, providing always that he was himself treated with the deference he regarded as his due, and that the salary he offered—not always generous, but never below the average—was accepted without dispute and with becoming gratitude.

John Henderson was about twenty when he procured an introduction to George Garrick and gave him a sample of his acting abilities. Now Garrick did not, as a rule, pay much attention to what George said about acting, and even went so far as to advise the younger members of the company not to heed him, but when George told him that the weedy-looking young man he had seen hanging about had too feeble a voice to make an actor, he accepted his opinion and began to regard Henderson as a nuisance. George was, in fact, justified in what he had said: Henderson was a delicate youth and his voice did not develop its full power until a couple of years later when his general health improved. Meanwhile his determination to go on the stage only increased with the years; he haunted the green-room, trying to attract attention, until, perhaps in the hope of getting rid of him, Garrick agreed to give him an interview. As Henderson went through a variety of scenes, Garrick listened patiently, but after some hesitation told him that 'he had in his mouth too much wool, which he must absolutely get rid of before he was fit for Drury Lane.' Not to discourage him altogether, he gave him a letter of introduction to John Palmer,[1] the manager of the Bath theatre, who, as a result, engaged him for the winter season of 1772-3 at a salary of one guinea a week. This salary, low by modern standards, was a usual one for a beginner, and the

[1] Father of the better-known actor of that name.

230

advantages he gained by making his first appearance as the protégé of the great London manager were considerable; Garrick had, indeed, done him a great service.

Outstandingly successful as Hamlet, Henderson passed on to Richard III, Benedick, Macbeth, Bayes, Hotspur, Bobadil and Lear, until by the end of the season he had, according to Tom Davies, appeared in no less than thirty different parts. Nearly all of these, it will have been noticed, were favourites of Garrick's, who, hearing how closely his every trick of manner and tone of voice was being imitated by the Bath Roscius, as Henderson was now called, did not altogether relish this form of flattery. Soon London visitors to Bath were writing to Garrick about Henderson, urging him to give the young actor an engagement. Cumberland's enthusiasm almost procured Henderson an offer, but George Garrick, in Bath for his health, saw him act and gave a poor account of him, with the result that Garrick cooled. Every summer Henderson came to London in the hope of an engagement for the winter, and every autumn he was obliged to return to Bath. 'The young fellow,' said Garrick to those who praised Henderson, 'is destitute of every requisite for a London theatre—he will do mighty well in a confined and a small stage—vastly so for *Bath*; but give me leave to tell you, sir, that the boards of Drury Lane are quite another thing.' And Garrick was not the only one to think so: the other London managers just as regularly and persistently refused Henderson engagements, without, moreover, showing him any compensating kindness. As Colman and Foote were always on the look-out for some way of scoring off Garrick, we can only assume that Henderson really had some serious defect in his elocution which he afterwards remedied.

After three brilliantly successful seasons at Bath, Henderson, aggrieved at his exclusion from London, approached Garrick with a confidence that bordered on arrogance. He would give two performances at Drury Lane without pay, he suggested through an intermediary, one of Hamlet and the other of Shylock, and he would accept the decision of the audience as to his good or ill success in those parts. A favourable verdict, he implied, would entitle him to an engagement. Garrick never took kindly to offers from actors: he thought that they should wait for him to dictate the terms, and trust him to do his best for them. Without pausing to consider whether there would be any harm in accepting the offer as it stood, he wrote off at once picking holes in it: the plan was most unwise, two performances were not nearly enough, and failure would do Henderson irreparable harm. A dozen performances, he suggested, in at least four different parts would provide a better test. Henderson replied with a caution that came as an unwelcome surprise: the young man was hardly more than a strolling player, and here he was actually making a fresh offer more advantageous to himself! Then began a haggling over terms which led to a quarrel. Henderson's refusal of a three years' engagement at a salary of not less than £5 a week and not more than £10, and his attempt to extract a definite promise of certain leading parts usually falling to King and Reddish, enraged Garrick. He accused him of attempting to take the management of the theatre out of his hands, and to render him a mere cipher in his own dominions.

In the end, Henderson was introduced to a London audience by Colman, not on the stage of Covent Garden, the management of which he relinquished in 1774, but on that of Foote's theatre in the Haymarket, the patent of which he had bought. By that time—the summer of 1777—Garrick had retired, and his continued dislike of Henderson cannot be put down to jealousy. The truth is that he knew that Henderson was mimicking him; that he was impersonating him in the manager's office, interviewing ladies of social distinction, interfering on their behalf at the box office, showing them to their carriages in an absurd bustle of anxiety, importance, eagerness and politeness, and, again, calling on his old master, Dr. Johnson, to recite the Jubilee Ode for his approval, covering by his brilliant recitation the literary defects of his verses—all to the great delight of the green-rooms and taverns. Moreover, Henderson was displaying a letter of advice, written to him some years earlier by Garrick, for the purpose of ridiculing it. This letter, a copy of which Garrick had placed among his papers for the benefit of posterity, contained much the same advice as he had given Powell: Henderson was not to waste time idling and drinking, not to have his head turned by success, to seek good company away from the stage, and to enlarge his knowledge of literature and life. The letter, kindly intended and carefully composed, was obviously Garrick's advice to all young actors. But as it happened, it did not apply to Henderson, who, naturally steady and hard-working, and, regarding himself as a genius whose career had been nearly ruined

13. ADELPHI TERRACE

from an engraving by B. Pastorini in the Print Room, Victoria and Albert Museum

by the older man's jealousy, resented and made fun of the advice. When an intermediary tried to reconcile them, Garrick replied that he would have nothing to do with a man who had ridiculed him and exposed and laughed at his letters.

Mrs. Siddons made her début at Drury Lane at the age of twenty during the last year of Garrick's management, and he did not think well enough of her acting to advise his successor to re-engage her for the following season. He remembered her as a young girl of fifteen who had recited to him some of Jane Shore's speeches (later to be one of her most famous rôles), and her tragedy manner impressed him so little that, with one exception, the parts he allotted to her during her first season were in comedy or farce. It was natural, therefore, that in after years the great tragedienne did not recall with pleasure her brief experience of Garrick's management, and would relate how he instructed her where to stand on the stage so that he could keep his full face to the audience the whole time, and how his look of reproach in her scene as Lady Anne to his Richard III made her too miserable to do herself justice. But there is no need to assume, as did her later admirers, that he was jealous and wished to keep her in obscurity.

The winter season of 1775-6 was the worst she could have chosen for her début. Garrick, taking his leave of the stage in one after another of his great rôles, necessarily drew all eyes, and at such a time of emotional stress could hardly be expected to concern himself overmuch with the future of a young, inexperienced player. Moreover, Drury Lane had never been better stocked with leading actresses: Mrs. Abington, Mrs. Yates and Miss Younge were tearing Garrick to pieces with their tempers, grievances and jealousies—one of the causes, it was rumoured, of his decision to retire —and the best rôles were theirs by the unwritten laws of the theatre. In these circumstances, Mrs. Siddons was lucky to be chosen by Garrick to play Mrs. Strickland to his Ranger, and Lady Anne to his Richard III, and it was not his fault that the critics decided that she 'spoke sensibly but that her powers were not equal to a London theatre.' Woodward told her bluntly that she had better go back to the small country theatres where she could be sure of being heard, and she had no alternative but to take his advice. After six years' hard work at Bath, she tried again at Drury Lane, and this time astonished the house with a display of gifts never revealed before by a woman. But her style was much quieter, more formal and restrained than that of Garrick, for she reflected the neo-classicism of her age as he the romanticism of his, and, even had he lived to see her triumph, it is doubtful whether he would have appreciated a genius so unlike his own.

CHAPTER XVIII

FAREWELL PERFORMANCES

1769 – 1776

G ARRICK had the fright of his life in the autumn of 1771 when he received a letter from the dreaded Junius, threatening him with ruin if he did not keep what he knew to himself. Here was an enemy far more dangerous than any he had ever encountered; one who could not be intimidated, appeased or bribed. The letter was brief and to the point:

'I am very exactly informed of your impertinent inquiries, and of the information you so busily sent to Richmond, and with what triumph and exultation it was received. I knew every particular of it the *next day*. Now mark me, vagabond. Keep to your pantomimes, or be assured you shall hear of it. Meddle no more, thou busy informer! It is in my power to make you curse the hour in which you dared to interfere with

JUNIUS.'

Four years had passed since the first of the *Letters* had appeared in *The Public Advertiser*, and, although there is reason to believe that at least half a dozen persons had by this time correctly guessed their source, Junius had not made the slightest slip in the guarding of his secret. But nothing can be stated with any certainty, for the most curious fact in this controversy is that, with only one exception,[1] none of those who are believed to have suspected Philip

---

[1] Lady Francis did not reveal her suspicions until many years after Sir Philip's death. Her proofs are negative in nature.

Francis of writing the *Letters* ever, so far as can be proved, committed their suspicions to paper. All of them—Lord Chatham, Lord Temple, John Calcraft,[2] Edmund Burke, John Wilkes and Philip's father, Dr. Francis—were Garrick's intimate friends, and nothing seems more likely than that he should have discussed the mystery with them, particularly as he happened to be one of the proprietors of the newspaper in which the *Letters* were appearing. His interest in politics did not go very deep, and Dr. Johnson might have said, as he did of Foote's infidelity, that Garrick was a Whig as a dog may be said to be a Whig. When Garrick asked him laughingly why, since they had lived so much together, he had never made a Tory of him, Johnson merely replied by taking out a handful of halfpennies from his pocket and asking him why the King had not made them guineas. As far as Garrick had any political bias, however, he shared the admiration of his great Whig friends for the general tenor of the *Letters*, and he would never have brought ruin on their author by helping to expose him. Or so it seems to us, but Junius was not so sure: from his private letters to H. S. Woodfall, the publisher and printer of the newspaper, it is clear that he believed that Garrick either had already guessed, or was on the verge of guessing, his identity, and was perfectly capable of betraying him in order to curry favour at Court.

What had happened was this: Junius, in one of his private letters to Woodfall written in a disguised hand and left at a coffee-house to be called for, told him without any appearance of confiding a secret that he did not intend to write any more *Letters* for publication. Woodfall, always loyal to his mysterious correspondent (his old schoolfellow had he but known it), saw no harm in repeating his words to Garrick. At this time, Garrick was ill, and had occasion to write to an official of the Court, then at Richmond, to say that he could not obey His Majesty's command to perform in a certain play. Knowing that Junius's decision would greatly relieve the King, who was still smarting from his lash, Garrick passed on the good news, and it all went back to Junius with the rest of the Court gossip that reached him through the unwitting agency of Lord Holland.

Garrick, in a long, agitated letter to Woodfall (his letters were always too wordy to be effective), protests against what he describes

2 Natural son of the first Lord Holland.

as scurrility unworthy of the celebrated Junius, and declares that, however much provoked, he will not retaliate with equally foul language. 'I beg you will assure Junius, that I have as proper an abhorrence of an informer as he can have,' he writes, forgetting the little episode of Dr. Wilkinson,[1] 'that I have been honoured with the confidence of men of all parties, and I defy my greatest enemy to produce a single instance of any one repenting such confidence. I have always declared that were I by any accident to discover Junius, no consideration should prevail upon me to reveal a secret productive of so much mischief, nor can this most undeserved treatment of me make me alter my sentiments.'

When the circumstances were explained to Junius, he accepted Woodfall's interpretation of the facts, and expressed himself satisfied with his correspondent's integrity. But there must have been some reason for the sudden fear which led Junius to warn Woodfall so earnestly against Garrick, to beware of his curiosity, to call at a different coffee-house for letters and to let no mortal know the change, and above all to send Garrick only a copy of the menacing letter and not to let him see his penmanship. Could it be that Garrick knew Francis's handwriting and might compare it with that of Junius? Had Francis read recognition in Garrick's eyes as they faced each other at his father's dinner table?

Garrick's next attack came from a man of a very different stamp and he might safely have ignored his existence. Kenrick was hardly more reputable than the poor wretch whose disgrace he openly hinted that Garrick should in justice have shared, the unfortunate Bickerstaffe, whose flight abroad in 1772 to escape from what was then a capital crime surprised no one but Dr. Johnson. 'By those who look close to the ground, dirt will be seen, sir,' was his lofty reply to Mr. Thrale's remark that Bickerstaffe had long been a suspected man. 'I hope I see things from a greater distance.' Garrick must have known that the private life of his chief writer would not bear inspection, but all that mattered to him before the exposure was that Bickerstaffe could turn out popular comic operas with fresh and engaging lyrics, adapt old comedies to contemporary taste and, particularly important since Colman's defection, express Garrick's views in the newspapers. It was probably through Garrick that Bickerstaffe consorted with men of such high

[1] See page 135.

moral character as Johnson, Reynolds and Burke, but there their friendship ended, and no one, not even Garrick's bitterest enemy, could possibly have taken seriously the libellous pamphlet written by Kenrick associating him with Bickerstaffe's offences.

William Kenrick was a man whose irrational theories (he claimed to have discovered the secret of perpetual motion), intemperance and senseless persecution of men who had never injured him suggest that he was not completely sane. He had already libelled Goldsmith who, after thrashing the wrong man by mistake, took no further steps when he discovered the truth. Johnson had not deigned to defend himself against Kenrick's attack on his edition of Shakespeare, and when, three years later, Kenrick turned his attention to Boswell, Johnson would not let Boswell hit back. In spite of Kenrick's behaviour to his friends, Garrick had taken great trouble with two of his comedies, both of which failed, and his refusal of a third was the cause of the attack. Garrick had one of two sensible courses open to him: to ignore the libeller, or to take strong action against him. Characteristically, he took neither course; he blustered, he appeased, he remonstrated, he began to take legal proceedings, and finally he forgave. We can only be thankful that he did not, so far as is known, pay hush-money. In anyone else but Garrick such panic would suggest that he had something to hide. In his excitement, he challenged Kenrick to a duel, which happily came to nothing, each side accusing the other of cowardice. Kenrick went about saying that Garrick was afraid to fight; he himself had a wife and children depending on him for support, but if Mr. Garrick would settle a sum of money on them in the event of their being left destitute, he would be happy to give him satisfaction.

'I am really sorry for the figure you made in the late transaction with me,' was the mild reply Garrick drafted with the intention of sending. 'Could not you have finished a little better, for the sake of that honour which so readily drops from your pen? Do you imagine I could have risked my reputation to have acted unlike a man, even to him who has been ungratefully vilifying me? No, sir. I would have honoured you by giving the satisfaction of a gentleman, *if you could* (as Shakespeare says) *have screwed your courage to the sticking place* to have taken it.' And the letter actually went on to apologize for his refusal of Kenrick's last play, saying that he would have acted it had it been sent him in time. On second thoughts, Garrick put this letter away in his desk with the comment, 'This not sent to that scoundrel, Dr. Kenrick. It was judged best not to answer any more of [his] notes; he had behaved so unworthily.' In a stiffer mood, he took the first step towards a libel action; weakening again, he withdrew after something approaching a public apology had been made, and the libeller went scot-free. After it was all over, Kenrick told Thomas Evans, the bookseller, that he had never believed in Garrick's guilt, but had 'only said it to plague the fellow'. Evans never spoke to Kenrick again.

In March 1772 the Garricks were busy moving from their house in Southampton Street into the centre house on Adelphi Terrace,[1] and a month later were sufficiently straight to show Dr. Burney and his young daughter, Fanny, all over it. Fanny pronounced the situation sweet and the house large and elegantly fitted up, but, although the Garricks were loath to admit it, they were not very comfortable there. It was damp; the cellars were often flooded, and the rooms facing north were small and dungeon-like. Those looking on to the river, on the other hand, let in too much sun for the welfare of Garrick's valuable paintings. There was only one satisfactory room in the house—the drawing-room—which, with decorations by Zucchi, Angelica Kauffmann's second husband, and a rich Italian marble chimney-piece, was really magnificent.

Garrick must have been among the very earliest residents of the Adelphi; for two years later when the tenancies of the other houses were being decided by lottery, their interiors had not even then been completed. In 1768, all that could have been seen on the site was a mass of tumbledown hovels sloping sharply down to the muddy, evil-smelling banks of the river, and here in Durham Yard, as it was called, Garrick had had his wine vaults when he first came to London. On this unpromising site the Adam brothers erected a terrace, and on it a building with side-wings and central classical pilasters, which was to inspire those groupings of town houses into one symmetrical whole characteristic of the later Georgian London. The Embankment, too, in a sense owes its origin to their project; before the terrace could follow a straight line along the Thames, it was necessary to encroach upon the river, and an Act of Parliament had to be passed in order that the frontage could be built

[1] No 5, later renumbered 4.

up on its series of arches. A hundred years later a more ambitious undertaking gave us the Victoria Embankment.

Soon after Garrick settled in, he wrote to his 'dear Adelphi', as he called Robert and James Adam, and begged them to let Becket, the bookseller, have the corner house. It would be a personal favour to him, he said, as he never now went to a coffee-house and seldom to a tavern (a statement he could not have meant to be taken literally), but if Becket's shop were at the corner he could go there at twelve and again at six to meet his friends. In addition to this pleasant rendezvous that grew up so close to his home, he had his friend Topham Beauclerk as a neighbour, and here Johnson, Boswell, Goldsmith, Walpole and Bennet Langton were often to be found in the evenings. It was here in front of a party of Beauclerk's friends that Garrick read aloud an ode by Cumberland. Beauclerk could not make head or tail of it, and asked Garrick to read it backwards to see if it would not sound equally well that way. Garrick performed the feat with amazing facility.

Garrick was now on the happiest terms with all the eight original members of the Club; Goldsmith and Johnson had forgotten their grievances against him, and his exclusion from the weekly meetings at the Turk's Head was becoming absurd, particularly as he often dined informally with many of them at the Saint James's Coffee-house. If he felt any annoyance in 1768 when George Colman was preferred to him as a member, he never expressed it, and in 1773 displayed becoming pleasure when, together with Vesey,[1] Lord Charlmont, William Jones and Boswell, he was finally admitted to the Club. He made an agreeable member; his gaiety never degenerated into buffoonery as Dr. Johnson had feared, and it was only when he arrived late, giving as his excuse that Lord So-and-so had kept him, or that he had been detained at the House of Lords, that the Doctor looked volumes. Judging from the few scraps of conversation that have come down to us, it is difficult to imagine Garrick contributing much of value to the discussions on politics, art, literature and morality that we are assured took place at the Turk's Head, but, to have kept the lifelong friendship of men prominent in all walks of public life, he must have had his more serious side that has gone unrecorded. Dr. Johnson, in one of his

[1] Vesey's Christian name, Agmondesham, is too magnificent to insert into a mere list of names.

kinder moods, professed to enjoy his conversation, and described it as gay and grotesque, but lacking in substance. 'It is a dish of all sorts,' he told Boswell, 'but all good things. There is no solid meat in it; there is a want of sentiment in it. Not but that he has sentiment sometimes and sentiment, too, very powerful and pleasing; but it has not its full proportion in his conversation.'

To see his old pupil assuming the airs of a great man sorely tried Dr. Johnson, and, in an attempt to put matters in their proper perspective, he would loudly recall their arrival in London from Lichfield, he with twopence-halfpenny in his pocket and Davy with three halfpennies in his. Garrick did not much like it but, entering into the spirit of the conversation, contributed the picturesque detail that with one horse between them they had 'rode and tied'. Then again the Doctor would score off Garrick by trapping him into admiring the wrong things by pretending to do so himself and then pouncing on him. Garrick was entertaining Dr. Johnson to dinner when he quoted twenty lines by Dryden in a voice vibrant with enthusiasm. He thought he remembered hearing the Master praise them only a day or two before. But Dr. Johnson promptly found sixteen faults in the passage, and Garrick could only look dumbfounded at such treachery. Mrs. Thrale, to whom Garrick had related the story, approached Dr. Johnson on the subject. 'Why what a monkey was David,' remarked the Doctor complacently, 'to tell of his own disgrace.' 'These fellows,' he said to Boswell, with Garrick in mind, 'know not how to blame, nor how to commend.'

All that Garrick could do in revenge was to mimic Dr. Johnson as he professed to remember him whispering sweet nothings to his Tetty, or to impersonate him with all his strange nervous tricks saying, 'Yes, yes, Davy has some convivial pleasantries. But 'tis a futile fellow.' There was nothing of Foote's grossness or cruelty in Garrick's mimicry, and when his listeners assured him that they had heard Dr. Johnson speak of him in very different terms, he was obviously touched and pleased. He made fun of Johnson's opinions on acting; the actor, whose courtly vivacity the Doctor admired, was, according to Garrick, the most vulgar fellow who ever went on the boards. But his respect for his old schoolmaster's judgment of poetry never wavered throughout their trivial misunderstandings. When dissatisfied with his epitaph on Hogarth in 1771, he took his problem to Johnson, who, appreciating always what was best in

241

Garrick's verses, did all he could to help him out of his difficulty.

Goldsmith and Garrick, now outwardly cordial, were both too egotistic and quick-tempered to make allowances for each other, and the course of their friendship never ran smoothly. When Garrick's name came up for election to the Club in 1773, it was Goldsmith who warmly seconded it. A few months later, Garrick was encouraging Goldsmith to persevere with his plan for *A Popular Dictionary of Arts and Sciences,* and, greatly to Goldsmith's satisfaction, persuaded his friend, Dr. Burney, to promise a paper on Music. Unhappily, the booksellers distrusted Goldsmith's staying-powers as an editor of so vast a work, and the scheme collapsed. Then another little breeze blew up between the two men when Goldsmith approached Garrick for a loan, on a security the shakiness of which he sought to remedy by offering the acting rights of his first two comedies, and the refusal of a third yet to be written. Garrick, as unprepared as ever to make concessions to those in his power, stipulated as before: Lofty must be cut out of *The Good Natur'd Man,* or he would not act it. Goldsmith would have refused just as obstinately as ever to tamper with his finished work had not the acuteness of his financial distress forced him to yield, and he accepted the loan on Garrick's terms. Garrick was probably right about Lofty, although Goldsmith's death some months later robbed him of the satisfaction of proving it, but it seems all wrong that a man of Goldsmith's achievements should have to go cap in hand to Garrick to procure his release from a sponging-house.

Recovering his courage, Goldsmith went back to his old haunts, squandering borrowed money in one last desperate fling, and, deceived by his noisy laughter, not one of his friends was aware of the ill health and distress he was trying to forget. In December, Garrick and he were invited with several others to dine and sup at Beauclerk's house in the Adelphi. It happened to be the first night of Kelly's *School for Wives,* and Garrick was in too much of a fidget during dinner to be his usual amusing self. Before hurrying off to Drury Lane, he promised his host that, on his return for supper, Goldsmith and he would give the company a very special entertainment, the nature of which he would not disclose. At ten o'clock he reappeared, greatly elated by the success of Kelly's play, and in just the right mood for the burlesque Goldsmith and he had prepared. Garrick, wrapped in a cloak, took a chair; Goldsmith sat

on his knees, and the cloak was so arranged as to cover them both
with the exception of Goldsmith's head and Garrick's arms, which
now appeared to belong to one body. Then from the head came
one of the most solemnly heroic speeches from *Cato,* sonorously
declaimed, while the arms made rubbish of it by flippantly inappropriate gestures. But, alas! the joke fell flat. The audience had
waited four hours for it, and, even had there been the semblance
of spontaneity necessary for such simple humour, Horace Walpole's
expression of boredom and disgust would have been quite enough
to kill any laughter. Yet it could not have gone better when they
repeated their performance at Sir Joshua's. Then it was Christmas
—the right time for such an entertainment—and the spectators were
of a better age to enjoy it. Sir Joshua's younger niece, recalling this
memory of her girlhood, said that Goldsmith and Garrick kept an
immense party laughing until they shrieked. This time the parts
were reversed. 'Garrick sat on Goldsmith's knee,' she continued. 'A
tablecloth was pinned under Garrick's chin and brought behind
Goldsmith, hiding both their figures. Garrick then spoke, in his
finest style, Hamlet's speech to his father's ghost. Goldsmith put
out his hands on each side of the cloth, and made burlesque action,
tapping his heart, and putting his hands to Garrick's head and
nose, all at the wrong time.'

While Dr. Johnson and Boswell were touring the Hebrides, the
coffee-house dinners and tavern suppers, if any took place, went
unrecorded, but by the New Year the weekly meetings were again
in full swing. Goldsmith, it was noticed, was noisier and ruder,
more childishly vain and touchy than ever before, and in his absence
his irrational changes of mood, their tragic cause unguessed, provided the subject for laughter among his friends. It was on such
an evening at the Saint James's Coffee-house that someone suggested that the diners should write a series of epitaphs on him, and
Garrick, whose gifts for extempore versifying had always been
remarkable, almost immediately came out with:

Here lies Nolly Goldsmith, for shortness call'd Noll,
Who wrote like an angel, but talk'd like poor Poll.

At their next dinner, several epitaphs were produced and read
aloud to the victim himself, who, during the general laughter at

his expense, grew very thoughtful. Some weeks later, he took from his pocket the first of the series of answering epitaphs he called *Retaliation*. His poem on Garrick,[1] the first of his tormentors to receive attention, is not only good literature, but is in itself a portrait of penetrating truth. Garrick's insatiable thirst for flattery, his unpredictably changeable temperament, his elaborate tricks for defending himself against imaginary enemies are candidly exposed but fairly set against his genius and personal charm, and the analysis as a whole is permeated with the humanity that earned Goldsmith, with all his faults, the warm affection of his friends. Handed about under a thin pretence of secrecy, the poem quickly became well known, and Garrick, stung into replying, wrote another epitaph on Goldsmith, imitating his in metre and conception. The comparison thus challenged is not a fair one; Goldsmith's lines are among his very best, while Garrick's are only up to his average standard. Unfortunately, however, it inevitably brings home to us Garrick's shallowness and poverty of ideas. The bad taste with which the irregularities of Goldsmith's private life are emphasized is uncharacteristic of Garrick, and is the only sign he ever allowed to escape him that he resented Goldsmith's satire. In the circumstances, it was particularly unfortunate. While Garrick's poem was still going the rounds of the coffee-houses, Goldsmith was lying dead in his squalid lodging with his graceful epitaph on Reynolds lying unfinished on his desk.

Both Garrick and Goldsmith loved and were beloved by children, and in comparing them it has been said, as though disparaging Garrick, that, whereas Goldsmith played and romped to amuse the children, Garrick did so to amuse himself. But many of the children concerned lived to write their memoirs, and not one of them shows any sign of having enjoyed himself less because their lively old friend was obviously enjoying himself too. It is true that in children he found a perfect audience for the mimicry of birds in which he delighted, and whenever he found himself in their company he would revel in the childish shrieks of delight as he impersonated in turn a turkey, a peacock and a water wagtail. It did not matter whether the laughter came from the young Cumberlands, prim and genteel in their papa's drawing-room, or the little black boy in the courtyard of an inn. Off the stage as on it, he acted

[1] See Appendix III.

244

to the gallery as well as to the boxes, and fellow-guests at the dinner tables of the great were often shocked to see him stealing a look at the footmen to see if he had made a hit. In the more homely atmosphere of the Burney's house, he even went so far as to chase the housemaid, broom and all, up a whole flight of stairs pretending, as they ran, to cane her for having laughed aloud at the droll attitudes he had struck while talking to little Miss Charlotte on the landing.

These eight children of his old friend, Dr. Burney, were his special pets, and they adored him. They saw him, not as a plump bustling little man with tired lines on his face, but as a handsome romantic figure with piercing black eyes, so expressive that Fanny was too shy to meet them with her own. And she admired Mrs. Garrick almost equally; she was the most perfectly well-bred woman in the world, all sweetness, softness and elegance, confided Fanny to her Journal, and her movements were so peculiarly graceful. When they went to Italy, the Garricks greatly delighted the children by entrusting their favourite black and white spaniel, Phill, to their care. One of the first things Garrick did on his return was to go and bring the dog home, but, finding that it moped for the children and knowing how sad they had been to part with it, Garrick sent it back to them as a present. He had only to hear that the children would like to see a certain play and he would straightway offer them Mrs. Garrick's private box, saying that he would sooner have them there than all the Lords and Commons, and on the night he watched them from his place in the orchestra, storing up their unselfconscious registering of indignation, amazement, disapproval and triumph in order to reproduce them the next morning for their father's amusement at breakfast.

Garrick liked a brisk walk before breakfast, and whenever he wanted to see Dr. Burney would walk out to his house in Queen Square enjoying its almost rural aspect and comparatively fresh air. He often arrived before eight to find the family just coming downstairs or sitting down to breakfast. Having delivered his message, he would indulge in some good-humoured bantering of each of the young people in turn, and then rush off again saying that Mr. Boswell or some other of his friends would be waiting for him at home. When the Burneys moved to their house off what is now Leicester Square, Garrick's strange choice of time for visiting them had some justification. He could not walk through the heart of London with comfort later in the day. Passers-by in the vicinity of the theatres recognized the little man in a dark blue coat and cocked hat laced with gold, and would crowd round him to satisfy their curiosity. Before breakfast, however, the streets were empty, and he could walk along unmolested from the Adelphi in the shabby coat and old scratch wig he always wore in the morning—the same wig that, worn with an old hat and loose greatcoat, led Lord Sandwich's servant to mistake him for his own coachman when he was sent with a message to Hampton House.

One spring morning in 1775, Garrick arrived at the Burneys so early that the housemaid was still washing the steps. Getting past her with difficulty, for she was new and reluctant to let in a visitor at this hour of the day, he ran upstairs to the study, where he found Dr. Burney having his hair dressed, his books and manuscripts spread out all round him. Charlotte was reading the newspaper aloud to him, Fanny was making the tea, and the others had not yet put in an appearance. Dr. Burney was beginning a laughing apology for the untidiness of the room and making ineffectual attempts to put things straight when Garrick stopped him with, 'Ay, now, do be in a little confusion. It will make things comfortable.' Then he began looking very gravely at the hairdresser, and assumed an air of admiring wonder at his amazing skill. Dr. Burney, seeing that his visitor had some fooling in mind, smiled and stopped talking. The hairdresser worked on, frizzing, curling, powdering and pomading, greatly set up to find himself the centre of attention, until he saw Garrick's face change from intelligent admiration to the vacant stare of envy and sadness he always assumed when playing the part of Abel Drugger. When the hairdresser had finished and was preparing to go, Garrick lifted his own frightful scratch wig from his head and holding it up high, squeaked out in a whining tone, 'Pray, sir, could you touch up *this* a little?' The man only grinned and left the room.

Garrick had lent Dr. Burney several books which the Doctor needed for writing his *History of Music,* and now asked him how many he had. 'I have ten of the *Memoirs of the French Academy,*' began Dr. Burney. 'And what others?' 'I don't know,' said the Doctor, and then turning to his daughter, 'Do you, Fanny?' 'Oh, what!' cried Garrick with humorous irony, 'I suppose you don't choose to know of any others; oh, very well! Pray, sir, make free with me! Pray keep them, if you choose it. But pray, Doctor, when shall we have the History out? Do let me know in time that I may prepare to blow the trumpet of fame.' He put his stick to his mouth, and in a showman's voice cried, 'Here is the only true History. Gentlemen, please to buy, please to buy. Sir, I shall blow it in the very ear of yon scurvy magistrate.' Here he was referring to Sir John Hawkins who was engaged on a similar work. With the same light humour, so ineffective in print, so diverting in life, he rattled on, mimicking one person after another, until he came to Dr. Johnson. To the welcome sound of youthful laughter, he began to take on the great man's authoritative manner, apearing as he did so to swell in circumference and even to grow taller. Carefully picking out a mark on the carpet, he gave it a thundering stamp with his foot, not from anger but from sheer eccentricity, and spoke in the impressive voice Dr. Johnson was supposed to have used to him recently when asking for the loan of a book. 'David, will you lend me your Petrarca?' 'Y-e-s, sir!——' 'David! you sigh?' 'Sir, you shall have it certainly.' Accordingly the book, finely bound in Russian leather, was sent that very evening. But scarcely had Dr. Johnson taken it into his hands, so Boswell was supposed to have reported, than, uttering a Latin ejaculation (which Garrick repeated), he lifted up his arms in a fit of enthusiasm and over his head went poor Petrarca, Russian leather, gold border and all. As Garrick walked about the study, giving them this imaginary scene, the Burney's greyhound, successor to the spaniel Garrick had given them, followed him, trying to attract his notice by licking his hands. 'Ah, poor Phill!' cried Garrick, looking at the greyhound contemptuously, 'You will never take his place, Slabber-chops!' Suddenly he caught sight of the clock and said he must run. Tearing downstairs, with the girls at his heels, he entertained them all the way to the door, telling them how cross their housemaid had been with him that morning, and how he had frightened her by saying sternly, 'Child! you don't guess whom you have the happiness to see! Do you know I am one of the *first geniuses* of the Age! Why, child, you would *faint away* if you knew who I am.'

No one would guess that the hero of this anecdote was in his fifty-ninth year, and on the stage he looked as young as many of his parts. He could dance as well as ever; his easy, graceful movements neutralized the middle-aged heaviness of his figure, and his face had grown plump instead of sharp, so that, skilfully made up, he could still play the young lover convincingly. It was only by daylight that the shadows under his eyes, the drawn lines on his face and unhealthy pallor were noticeable. He was constantly ill, sometimes with gout, but more often with attacks of stone and gravel, and the soap medicines he swallowed in generous quantities only made matters worse. 'I can play Richard,' he told a friend, 'but I dread the fight and the fall. I am in agonies afterwards.' The more tired he became, the more impossible he found it to rest. 'David begins to complain of the fatigue of the stage,' remarked Dr. Johnson to Cradock. 'Sir, a man that bawls turnips for his bread does twice as much.' For once the Sage was wrong: Garrick worked like a whirlwind—writing, revising, adapting, supervising every detail of each play, stage manager, producer and star actor all in one, as well as making the major decisions on the financial side of the management. In 1773 Lacy's death added to his responsibilities. He had not always seen eye to eye with his partner, but on the whole they had worked well together, and Willoughby Lacy, who took his father's place, proved himself worse than useless. The actors, and more especially the actresses, had never been so difficult to control. Their grievances against him, their quarrels with each other and their last-moment refusals to appear on the flimsiest pretexts exasperated him. He hated Miss Younge and Mrs. Yates, and as for Mrs. Abington, he never spoke to her except when he was acting with her.

Whether in London or Hampton, Garrick gave and received hospitality incessantly. Writing to him in 1773, Lord Camden expressed his doubts whether he and Mrs. Garrick had ever known the pleasure of a single day's solitude. The only time, scolded Lord Camden affectionately, that Garrick allotted for thought or reflection was from eight to ten in the morning in winter, and even those hours were generally interrupted by posts and boxkeepers. His entertaining became more magnificent as the years went by, and his enemies were hard put to it to know how to reconcile their accusations of meanness with those of ostentatious expenditure. In 1774 the Garricks gave a splendid fête at Hampton. The Temple and garden were illuminated with six thousand coloured lamps, Signor Torre gave a brilliant display of fireworks, and a concert,

14. FROM THE GARRICKS' CHINESE BEDROOM
IN HAMPTON HOUSE
now in the Victoria and Albert Museum

described at the time as elegant, provided the background for conversation. As a guest, Garrick was greatly in demand, and, when nothing jarred him, could be relied on to keep the company entertained. But he was not always an easy one: he could not read poetry aloud if a certain nobleman were in the room; he would not come if young Mr. So-and-so were there, for he had been talking against him. His nerves were overstrained, and his voice too easily took on a peevish tone.

Garrick had threatened to retire so often since his return from abroad that his friends had ceased to take him seriously, but before the theatres reopened in September 1775 he had definitely made up his mind to find a purchaser for his share of the patent before the year was out, and to retire from the stage altogether at the end of the season. With the idea of handing over the theatre to his successor in perfect condition, he had employed the Adam brothers during the summer recess to carry out extensive alterations. The façade was embellished with pilasters, pediments, balcony, and colonnade, and an ornamental trophy—a helmet and coat of mail—crowned the whole. The interior, completely remodelled and decorated with garlands and vases, had all the delicate charm characteristic of these architects.

Garrick offered Colman the first refusal of his share of the patent, but Colman, enjoying the prospect of being sole manager of the Haymarket Theatre, as the Little Theatre came to be called, which he had taken over from Foote, would not consider the proposal unless Willoughby Lacy sold out too. This Lacy was not yet willing to do, and the negotiations broke down. However, another bidder appeared, and after Christmas Garrick came to terms with the brilliant young son of Thomas Sheridan, the twenty-five-year-old Richard Brinsley, whom he had known since boyhood and in whom he had long taken a friendly interest.

Richard was as popular with the members of the Club as his father had always been the reverse, and, young as he was, had already made a name for himself with *The Rivals* and *The Duenna,* both of which had been produced at Covent Garden in 1775. His humour had much of the naturalness which in Goldsmith had been denounced as 'low', but Garrick gave him the support he had withheld from the other, and would have enlisted his pen for Drury Lane had not Sheridan considered himself under an obligation to write for Harris, the manager of Covent Garden. There was no one, Colman perhaps excepted, better fitted to take Garrick's place: the son of an actor and a successful dramatist (Garrick had produced two of Mrs. Frances Sheridan's plays), his knowledge of the stage was inborn; no actor himself, he accepted his father's offer to super-vise the rehearsals in return for a salary; and his father-in-law, Thomas Linley, the composer, was more than willing to advise on the musical side. Garrick's share of the patent was now valued at £35,000, three times what he had paid for it, and much too large a sum for young Sheridan to raise without associates. Accordingly, he offered a partnership to Linley for £10,000; a Dr. James Ford, who already held a large mortgage on the theatre, was ready to invest a further £15,000; and he made preparations to raise the remaining £10,000 himself on loans and mortgages. 'I have at last slipt my theatrical shell,' Garrick was writing in January 1776, 'and shall be as fine and free a gentleman as you would wish to see upon the North or South Parade at Bath.'

Rumours of the transaction leaked out in the newspapers almost at once, but Garrick did not announce his retirement until March 7th. Then, in a prologue, spoken by King in the character of a bookseller, he told the audience:

> *The master of this shop, too, seeks repose,*
> *Sells off his stock-in-trade, his verse and prose,*
> *His daggers, buskins, thunder, lightning and old clothes.*

Letters of appreciation now began to pour in from every quarter, ranging from intimate friends to complete strangers. Many of them were expressed in terms too fulsome and sycophantic to be of any real value, but a tribute from Kitty Clive, as unexpected as it was warm-hearted and sincere, pleased and touched him very deeply. Their long association on the stage had been a stormy one: wilful and quick-tempered, she had resented the strict discipline which he as manager had imposed on her, and her sharp tongue had engaged him in many hot disputes. Now her stage career was over, her posi-tion in society assured, and, with nothing to gain by flattery, her letter of affection and admiration is worth more than all the others put together.

'In the height of the public admiration for you,' she writes, 'when you were never mentioned but as the Garrick, the charming man, the fine fellow, the delightful creature, both by men and ladies; when they were admiring everything you did, and everything you scribbled, at this very time, I, *the Pivy*,[1] was a living witness that they did not know, nor could they be sensible, of half your perfections. I have seen you with your magic hammer in your hand, endeavouring to beat your ideas into the heads of creatures, who had none of their own. I have seen you, with lamblike patience, endeavouring to make them comprehend you; and I have seen you, when that could not be done, I have seen your lamb turned into a lion; by this your great labour and pains, the public was entertained; *they* thought they all acted very fine; they did not see you pull the wires.

'There are people now on the stage to whom you gave their consequence; they thought themselves very great; now let them go on in their new parts, without your leading-strings, and they will soon convince the world what their genius is. I have always said this to everybody, even when your horses and mine were in their highest prancing. *While* I was under your control, I did not say half the fine things I thought of you, because it looked like flattery; and you know your Pivy was always proud; besides, I thought you did not like me then; but now I am sure you do, which makes me send you this letter.'

Writing on this letter the words, 'My Pivy—excellent,' Garrick put it away among his most cherished papers.

For the remaining three months of the season, Garrick gave a series of farewell performances in his most celebrated rôles, and never has the retirement of an actor made so much commotion. Elsewhere, events of momentous importance were taking place— the year 1776 has associations other than theatrical for the historian —but, at the time, all that the man in the street cared about was that Mr. Garrick was retiring from the stage. Many of his distinguished French friends crossed the Channel on purpose to pay his genius a last tribute, the greatest and most powerful in English society begged, wheedled, bribed and, in exasperation, scolded for seats, while the ordinary Londoners came in their thousands and stood for hours in the vain hope of squeezing into the theatre. At

1 Garrick, like Johnson, had pet names for his friends based on their surnames. He called Mrs. Clive, Clivy-Pivy.

the end of each performance the house seemed literally to shake with applause, and one spectator felt that, not only was she taking leave of a great actor, but that she was attending the funeral service of each character in turn, for never would they come to life again so convincingly.

Garrick chose his last parts with a full sense of their significance to posterity, and an analysis of them is a guide, not only to contemporary taste, but to an understanding of where his real strength lay. Of the thirteen plays chosen, only two were written in his lifetime; the others are of Elizabethan or Restoration origin. Four are tragedies: *Hamlet, Lear, Richard III* and Aaron Hill's *Zara*, an adaptation of a play by Voltaire. The first three of these gave full scope to his powers of miming and his varied tempestuous style. The choice of Lusignan in Hill's *Zara* is less obvious; the tragedies of French derivation did not as a rule suit him, but in this rôle his elocution and air of distinction had been much admired. In three of the comedies he played strongly farcical characters: Abel Drugger the simpleton, Bayes the coxcomb, and Sir John Brute the drunkard, whose scene disguised as a woman was particularly comic when a middle-aged lady's feathered headdress adorned Garrick's large and essentially masculine features. The remaining parts were light comedy—the charming, high-spirited young lovers which Garrick in his sixtieth year still played to perfection. One of these, Benedick, was his only Shakespearian comedy part. Assuming that our records of his farewell performances are complete, Garrick played Richard III and Lear three times, Hamlet, Ranger and Don Felix twice, and the others once.

Garrick would have liked to end his career, as he began it, with Richard III, but, on thinking it over, he decided that the part was too exhausting and that after the stage fall he would be physically incapable of coming out in front of the curtain to take his last call. Accordingly, for the evening of June 10th, he chose Don Felix, in Mrs. Centlivre's *Wonder*, which he had played for the first time twenty years earlier and in which no actor was ever to equal him for charm and vivacity. The entertainment opened with a rhymed prologue written and spoken by Garrick in the form of an appeal for the Decayed Actors' Fund to which the profits of the evening— the second time that season—were to be devoted. 'Decayed Actors' Fund!' Dr. Johnson is supposed to have remarked rather crudely.

252

'Alas! he will soon be one himself!' And the same melancholy thought inspired Garrick's best-known line:

A fellow feeling makes one wond'rous kind.

When the curtain fell on the play, the claps, it was said, sounded like muffled drums. A deep hush fell and the audience waited motionless and silent as Garrick came forward slowly and stood for a few moments unable to speak. Then in low, unrhetorical tones, he made a simple and moving speech. At one point his emotions overcame him, and he could not continue until relieved by a rush of tears. It is quoted here in full.

'Ladies and Gentlemen,

'It has been customary with persons under my circumstances to address you in a farewell epilogue. I had the same intention, and turned my thoughts that way; but indeed I found myself *then* as incapable of writing such an epilogue, as I should be *now* of speaking it.

'The jingle of rhyme, and the language of fiction, would but ill suit my present feelings. This is to me a very awful moment; it is no less than parting for ever with those from whom I have received the greatest kindness and favours, and upon the spot where that kindness and those favours were enjoyed.

'Whatever may be the changes of my future life, the deepest impression of your kindness will always remain here' (putting his hand on his breast), fixed and unalterable.

'I will very readily agree to my successors having more skill and ability for their station than I have; but I defy them all to take more sincere, and more uninterrupted pains for your favour, or to be more truly sensible of it, than is your humble servant.'

As he made his last bow, he gave the audience a long look which had in it something like agony. The moment held some of the bitterness of death, and in her box Mrs. Garrick cried bitterly.

CHAPTER XIX

IN RETIREMENT

1776 – 1778

Now that Garrick was free, invitations were showered on him, and, in his relief that the ordeal of saying farewell was over and pleasure in being made much of by his friends, he thought he had lost all interest in the stage. Mrs. Garrick and he had always spent part of the summer months in visiting the country houses of the many members of the aristocracy who gratified him with their friendship: Lord and Lady Spencer would expect them at Althorp, Lord Pembroke at Wilton, and Lord Camden at Bayham Abbey. Sir Watkyn Williams Wynn now claimed them for a long-promised visit to Wynnstay, and the Caldwells of Castle Caldwell were particularly anxious for them to come over to Ireland. Garrick would have liked to revisit the kingdom where he had been honoured with every mark of regard and kindness, he wrote in his gracious way, but Mrs. Garrick was so sick and distressed by the sea, he went on, and, as he had not left her one day since they were married near twenty-eight years ago, he could not now leave her.

And so the summer passed pleasantly with sociabilities and holiday-making, but, as soon as Drury Lane reopened, habit was too strong for him, and his thoughts went back to the old life. Sheridan liked and respected him and, generally speaking, took his advice on theatrical affairs. Most of those on the payroll had been re-engaged, with the exception of Mrs. Siddons, who had not favourably impressed anyone, and Loutherbourg, who refused an invitation to remain at half his previous salary. Taking up the 'cleansing' of the stage where Garrick had left off, Sheridan gave revised versions that season of several of the stock Restoration comedies, purging them of their obscenities (and at the same time of their wit) to suit the delicacy and refinement of the new generation. October saw the début of a young actress for whom Garrick foretold a great future, and, having noted with surprise that he chose comedy for Mrs. Siddons, we are equally startled to read that he advised tragedy for the youthful Mrs. Robinson (the future 'Perdita'), saying that her pathos reminded him of his favourite Cibber. A few years earlier he had rehearsed her in the part of Cordelia, intending to act with her, but her sudden and unexpected marriage had wrecked his plans. When seeking re-engagement after the failure of her marriage, she had recited some of Juliet's speeches in the green-room, and Garrick, who was present, urged Sheridan to present her in that rôle. At the rehearsals he coached her in every detail, often going through the whole of Romeo's part himself until he was completely exhausted, and on the night he sat in his old place in the orchestra to give her confidence. She pleased the audience well enough, but the beauty of her face, and, more particularly, her figure, which suited her for 'breeches' parts, soon took her into comedy and thence to the Prince of Wales's[1] protection.

Mrs. Robinson was only one among many to become famous in comedy who made an apparently false start in tragedy; for tragedy, depending largely, it was thought, on good technique in which an absence of true dramatic feeling would pass unnoticed, was the natural choice for a beginner—just as Beethoven's noblest and most intellectual works are considered suitable for youthful and immature soloists. While ranking aesthetically higher, tragedy was paradoxically regarded as easier than comedy, to which an actor had to contribute more of himself, and this point of view is still widely held. 'No, no,' said Garrick to an actor of tragic parts who yearned to play comedy instead. 'You may humbug the town some time longer as a tragedian, but comedy is a serious thing.'

This may suggest that Garrick was himself better in comedy than tragedy, but it is not possible to say in a word at which he excelled. If the final test of acting is its effect on a contemporary audience, Garrick's Lear has never been equalled, and his Richard III and Hamlet were hardly inferior. We can, nevertheless, say

[1] Later George IV.

that could we look back through the centuries we should probably prefer him in comedy. With all its tears and sensibility, the eighteenth century did not find its true expression in tragedy, and Garrick, even in his greatest rôles, depended too much for his effects on ingenious byplay, and sensuous beauty of attitude, movement and voice—or so it would seem to us. 'I cannot say she killed herself well,' was his reasoned verdict on Mlle Clairon's performance, 'but she died well.' Her miming, rather than her interpretation of character and ideas, had absorbed his attention. It was a consciousness of this deficiency in the tragic acting of his time that goaded Dr. Johnson into harsh criticisms and made him appear more unresponsive to the art as a whole than he was in fact. 'Garrick and Henderson excepted,' he recalled at the end of his life, 'I never met with a performer who had studied his art or could give an intelligible reason for what he did.' Kemble was to bring more mind to his acting, as Dr. Johnson might have expressed it, and after Garrick's death took the trouble to consult Dr. Johnson on the interpretation of Hamlet. 'To be sure, sir,' said Dr. Johnson, agreeing with the young man on some point. 'I told Garrick so long since, but Davy never could see it.' Tragedy was to benefit from Kemble's contribution to it, but those who had seen Garrick in their impressionable years were not as deeply moved by the new and more thoughtful style. 'Mr. Kemble is a very fine actor, sir,' said the old prompter at Drury Lane.' 'But Mr. Garrick—*ah, that was quite another thing.*' Each successive great tragedian added subtleties to the interpretations of the famous rôles, and thus it should not be regarded as belittling Garrick, to whose inspiration the stage owes more than to that of any other actor who has ever lived, to say that Irving, bringing a stronger intellectual grasp of his part to an equal perfection of stage technique, would probably seem to a modern audience the better Hamlet. Dr. Johnson, as always, sums up the matter briefly, soberly and well. 'Garrick, madam,' he said to Mrs. Siddons, 'was the only actor I ever saw whom I would call a master in tragedy and comedy; though I liked him best in comedy. A true conception of character and natural expression of it were his distinguishing excellencies.'

John Bannister, Garrick's last protégé, was surely a born comedian, but here again it was in tragic parts that Garrick rehearsed him. Bannister was a student at the Royal Academy at the time he was introduced to Garrick, probably by his father, Charles Bannister, an old-established member of the Drury Lane company. John had shown great promise in painting as a little boy, but, with acting in his blood, found his interest in art giving way to an increasing enthusiasm for the stage; until, at seventeen, his one ambition, he told Garrick, was to become an actor. In later life he used to describe in the course of a lecture one of his interviews with Garrick in the Adelphi, and, although it is not in itself an important episode in the life of the great actor-manager, Bannister's meticulously accurate reporting of the scene brings him to life with a vividness that pages of fine and imaginative writing might fail to accomplish.

'After frequent visits to Garrick,' Bannister began by explaining, 'he was pleased to say that he perceived a—a—a something in me which conveyed a—a promise, a—an indication of theatrical talent; and here I am led into an imitation of his manner in private. He had a sort of a—a—a kind of a—a hesitation in his speech, a habit of indecision which never marked his public exertions.

'One morning I was shown into his dressing-room, where he was before the glass, preparing to shave; a white night-cap covered his forehead; his chin and cheeks were enveloped in soap-suds; a razor-cloth was placed upon his left shoulder; and he turned and smoothed his shining blade upon the strop with as much dexterity as if he had been bred a barber at the Horse-Guards, and shaved for a penny: and I longed for a beard that I might imitate his incomparable method of handling the razor.

' "Eh! well—what! young man—so, eh?" (this was to me) "So you are still for the stage? Well, how—what character do you—should you like to—eh?"

'I should like to attempt Hamlet, sir.'

' "Eh! what? Hamlet the Dane! Zounds! that's bold—have you studied the part? Well, don't mind my shaving—speak the speech—the speech to the ghost—I can hear you—never mind my shaving."

'After a few hums and haws, and a disposing of my hair so that it might stand on end,

'*Like quills upon the fretful porcupine* [*sic*],

I supposed my father's ghost before me, armed cap-a-pie; and off I started.

'*Angels, and ministers of grace, defend us!*
   (he wiped the razor)
Be thou a spirit of health, or goblin damn'd
   (he stropped the razor)
Bring with thee airs from heaven, or blasts from hell
   (he shaved on)
Thou com'st in such a questionable shape
That I will speak to thee.
   (he took himself by the nose)
   I'll call thee Hamlet,
King, father, royal Dane. O, answer me!
Let me not burst in ignorance.

'He lathered on. I concluded, but still continued my attitude, expecting prodigious praise; when, to my eternal mortification, he turned quick upon me, brandishing the razor, and, thrusting his half-shaved face close to mine, he made such horrible mouths at me that I thought he was seized with insanity, and I was more frightened at him than my father's ghost. He exclaimed in a tone of ridicule,

   "*Angels, and ministers of grace, defend us!*

"Yaw, waw, waw, waw!" The abashed Prince Hamlet became sheepish, and looked more like a clown than the gravedigger. He finished shaving, put on his wig, and with a smile of good nature took me by the hand, and said, "Come, young gentleman, eh! let's see now what we can do." He spoke the speech; and how he spoke it, those who have heard him never can forget.'

After this Garrick gave Bannister many lessons, and, when the time came in 1778 for his first appearance at Drury Lane, rehearsed him in Zaphna, a leading part in *Mahomet,* a translation of Voltaire's tragedy—a curious choice, for the play had never been a success even when Garrick had acted Zaphna himself. Moreover, a few weeks earlier, Bannister had played one of Woodward's most famous parts at the Haymarket, and, with the memory of that great comedian's[1] performance still fresh in the minds of his audience, had scored such an outstanding success that it should have been obvious where his real talent lay. It was twenty years since *Mahomet* had last bored London playgoers, and, in spite of all the trouble

[1] Woodward died in 1777.

Garrick took with both Bannister and Zaphna and his other protégé, Mrs. Robinson, as Palmira, it interested them no more now. In the end, Bannister renounced his ambitions and had the good sense to concentrate on comedy, but Garrick's belief in his tragic powers and the time he spent in teaching him remained one of the comedian's proudest memories.

It never occurred to anyone at the time that Garrick was just as much entitled to a knighthood as his friend, Sir Joshua Reynolds, and a weak little rumour in 1777 that he was to be created Sir David soon died away. Whether it was his profession, his association with the Whigs, or merely the King's personal indifference to his acting that went against him, it is impossible to say. All we know is that, while painting, sculpture and architecture met with comparatively generous recognition from the Crown, their sister arts were ignored. A hundred years were to pass before the stage, in the person of Sir Henry Irving, was honoured by a knighthood. The most that King George III did to show his appreciation of Garrick's lifelong services to the theatre was to send for him to read *Lethe* before the Royal Family at Windsor in the spring of 1777, and the coolness of his reception hurt Garrick's feelings very much. He had taken great pains with a prologue, comparing himself to a feeble old blackbird roused into singing better than ever before at the behest of a royal eagle (a phenomenon Dr. Johnson thought unlikely to occur in nature), and had introduced a new character, a Jew, into his farce in honour of the occasion. He read sitting at a table, using different voices but with little of the byplay and movement that might have helped him to forget his surroundings, and the King's 'Very well' was literally all he received for applause. 'It was as though they had thrown a wet blanket over me,' he complained.

'He has been so long accustomed,' said a fellow-guest to Dr. Johnson as they sat drinking tea together in Mrs. Thrale's drawing-room, 'to the thundering approbation of the theatre, that a mere "very well" must naturally disappoint him.'

'Sir,' said Dr. Johnson, whose attitude to the House of Hanover had undergone a marked change for the better since the award of his pension, 'he should not, in a Royal apartment, expect the hallooing and clamour of the One Shilling Gallery. The King, I doubt not, gave him as much applause as was rationally his due;

and, indeed, great and uncommon as is the merit of Mr. Garrick, no man will be bold enough to assert he has not had his just proportion both of fame and profit. He has long reigned the unequalled favourite of the public; and therefore nobody will mourn his hard fate if the King and the Royal Family were not transported into rapture upon hearing him read *Lethe*. Yet Mr. Garrick will complain to his friends, and his friends will lament the King's want of feeling and taste—and then Mr. Garrick will kindly *excuse* the King. He will say that His Majesty might be thinking of something else; that the affairs of America might occur to him; or some subject of more importance than *Lethe;* but, though he will say this himself, he will not forgive his friends if they do not contradict him.'

After this display of malicious humour at Garrick's expense, it is only fair to add that, later that very evening, Dr. Johnson defended Garrick against the same charge on which he had just by implication found him guilty. It used to be thought by their friends that Dr. Johnson made a practice of contradicting whatever was said about Garrick, and his criticisms were regarded as inconsistent in themselves. But the contradictions did not arise only from Dr. Johnson's mixed feelings on the subject and consequent changes of mood; they were the essence of Garrick's complex character, and, with a proper understanding of the facts, everything that Dr. Johnson said of him can be justified. 'Garrick is accused of vanity,' he said in a more serious moment, that evening, 'but few men would have borne such unremitting prosperity with greater, if with equal, moderation. He is accused, too, of avarice,' he went on, 'but, were he not, he would be accused of just the contrary; for he now lives rather as a prince than an actor; but the frugality he practised, when he first appeared in the world, and which even then was perhaps beyond his necessity, has marked his character ever since; and now, though his table, his equipage, and manner of living, are all the most expensive and equal to those of a nobleman, yet the original stain still blots his name. Though, had he not fixed upon himself the charge of avarice, he would long since have been reproached with luxury and with living beyond his station in magnificence and splendour.'

A remarkable tribute paid to Garrick that same spring in the House of Commons soon wiped out the memory of the unfortunate

evening at Windsor. It was the greatest honour paid him outside
the theatre, and shows us the effect his personal prestige was having
on the traditionally low status of a stage player. During the course
of a heated debate, two members seemed to be coming to blows,
and someone moved that the Gallery be cleared. The strangers withdrew, with the exception of Garrick, who lingered behind for a
moment enjoying the piquant scene. Whereupon a country squire
of the old school, in whose eyes an actor had remained a rogue and
a vagabond, rose to his feet, and called the Speaker's attention to
the fact that a stranger was still present and that the stranger
should withdraw. But Burke had seen his friend, and appealed to
the House not to exclude a man to whom they were all indebted—
a master of eloquence from whom everyone present had learnt the
elements of rhetoric. Fox, and after him Townshend, rose to speak
in the same strain, paying warm tributes to their old preceptor, as
they called him, and the House almost unanimously agreed to
exempt Garrick from the general order to withdraw from the Gallery. At the next sitting, the squire complained bitterly of the
impropriety and irregularity of the incident, saying that Garrick
was 'glorying in his situation', as though Garrick's unconcealed
gratification were an insult to the House. But he found no sym-
pathizers: on the contrary, it was suggested, although not in debate,
that Garrick should have the exclusive privilege of occupying a
seat in the Gallery whenever he pleased.

Old Sheridan's arrangement with his son to take charge of the
rehearsals soon broke down; whether they quarrelled over money,
as one story runs, or whether he came into conflict with Garrick,
as another would have it, no one can say. But by the time *The
School for Scandal* was ready for the stage we find Garrick back at
Drury Lane voluntarily helping the author to superintend the
rehearsals, and he must therefore have some of the credit for the
perfect balance and superb acting of the play on its first night, the
8th of May 1777. All the performers had learnt their technique
from Garrick, and, from long experience of acting under his management, blended well together; there was no star actor among
them to attract disproportionate attention, but all were excellent
comedy actors; their parts, moreover, had been written by Sheridan
with their stage personalities well in mind. As a result of this happy
conjunction of circumstances, the performance that evening made

stage history, and set a standard of perfection no subsequent revival of the ever popular play has been able to attain. Garrick's prologue and Colman's epilogue, if not very good, served their purpose, and signified to the audience the approval and goodwill of the two most distinguished comedy writers of the older generation, and only the morbidly envious Cumberland grudged Sheridan his stupendous success. In three seasons the play realized over £21,000 and, without it, the sharp falling off in the profits which followed the loss to Drury Lane of Garrick's managerial gifts would have been disastrous to the new patentees. And Garrick, too, was not unaffected; he held a mortgage on Willoughby Lacy's share for £22,000, and the ten per cent interest he very properly exacted by dint of much pressure and unpleasantness might otherwise have gone unpaid.

For some time now he had been interesting himself in a very different type of play—as dead to us to-day as Sheridan's comedy is sparklingly alive. Hannah More's tragedy, *Percy*, was largely written under Garrick's roof, and he and Mrs. Garrick read and criticized each act as soon as it was completed. Their affection for the young Bristol schoolmistress had grown since their first meeting four years earlier, until their house became her second home, and she meant more to them than any of their own nieces. For Mrs. Garrick, it was the beginning of a forty years' friendship that was to console her in her long widowhood.

An Evangelical Blue Stocking, a fashionable actor and a Roman Catholic ex-ballet dancer made an incongruous trio when so described, but in fact Hannah More and the Garricks shared many interests, and found much happiness in being together. There was nothing at any time in the Garricks' way of living to offend her religious susceptibilities, and they respected, though they did not share, her strict Sabbatarianism. 'Nine,[1] you are a Sunday woman,' Garrick said to her one Sunday afternoon, when preparations began for a little music in a country house at which they were fellow-guests. 'Go to your room, and I will recall you when the music is over.' Lacking perhaps very genuine piety, he had in its place a reverence for tradition and respectability, as symbolized by the Church, which deepened with the years and may explain why so

[1] 'Nine'—suggesting the embodiment of the Nine Muses—was Garrick's nickname for Hannah More.

many doctors of divinity were to be found at his table. Nor were they all high dignitaries of the Church; one of his most endearing traits had been his affection for old Mr. Beighton, by this time in his grave, a clergyman as simple, saintly and impoverished as the Vicar of Wakefield. Garrick had shown him many thoughtful kindnesses at Hampton, and never rested until he had induced Lord Camden to find him a living that would bring him in more than his £30 a year as Vicar of Egham, and so rendered his last years more comfortable.

Hannah was much liked by the distinguished men and women who dined in the Adelphi, and, as she wrote to her family, she found their conversation highly improving, and had seldom heard so much wit under the banner of so much decorum. Garrick's humour, whimsical and sprightly rather than mordantly witty, was in tune with her own. For Hannah, too, was gay and talkative, and had more humour, worldly wisdom and tolerance than her later writings suggest. She had laughed at *Tom Jones*, for instance, until Dr. Johnson sternly rebuked her for having read it, and brought home to her its impropriety and sinfulness. She thought it as natural for Mrs. Garrick to go to the Pantheon attired in the extravagant mode of the day as it was for herself to sit at home in her severely plain dress conscientiously reading herself into a headache. And in her demure way she enjoyed the latest scandal if it had in it elements of drama and fantasy. In the summer of 1776, Garrick gave her his ticket to attend the sensational trial in the House of Lords of the Duchess of Kingston for bigamy (he was too tired with the strain of his farewell performances to use it himself), and she and Mrs. Garrick sat there storing up every detail of the extraordinary scene to retail to him when they got home. 'It is time I retired,' said Garrick, 'now that I am being out-acted by the Duchess of Kingston.'

Hannah, like all the Blue Stockings and the scholarly men in their circle, indulged in flattery to a degree that those outside it found nauseating. She irritated Dr. Johnson into an outburst of savagery uncharacteristic of his usually gentle manner with young ladies, and Mrs. Thrale into surreptitious ridicule. But Garrick liked it, and his pleasure was plain for all to see. She could not lay it on too thickly for him, and, in return, he praised her writing extravagantly. Where Garrick was concerned, however, Hannah said no more than she felt; not only was he the world's greatest actor in her eyes, but he had purified the stage, cleansing it of harmful influences, and, fired with the ambition of using the theatre as a school for morals, she began to write plays with a high didactic purpose. When they first met, she had already written a dramatic dialogue for use in girls' schools, as well as a tragedy which is said to have been acted in the country. Since then her two poems, *Sir Eldred of the Bower* and *The Bleeding Rock*, had found great favour in literary circles, and both Dr. Johnson and Garrick professed boundless admiration for them, reciting whole stanzas by heart to the gratified poetess.

Hannah spent most of the summer of 1777 writing her tragedy, *Percy*, and by November Harris had promised to act it at Covent Garden before Christmas. Garrick was full of it; he read it aloud on every possible occasion, talked about it, wrote about it, worried about it—never had any play absorbed more of his thoughts. The prologue and epilogue he had himself supplied at Hannah's request and to her complete satisfaction. She had never read a sweeter or more beautiful thing than the prologue, she assured him; the first stanza was strikingly descriptive; the second, elegantly pathetic; and the third, highly poetical. She was more than flattered that he should think her not unworthy of so great a treasure. Garrick, delighted with her enthusiasm for what others were to regard as a jingle, asked her what payment she intended to make him. Dryden, he said, used to have five guineas apiece for his prologues, but, as he was a richer man, he would be content with a handsome supper and a bottle of claret. A beef steak and a pot of porter were all she could afford, was her laughing reply, and in the end he sat down to a meal of toast and honey and expressed himself well rewarded.

The reception of the play justified Garrick's belief in it, and Hannah could hardly believe her good fortune when she made over £400 by it. Men, as well as women, in the audience wept bitterly, and it had the longest run of any tragedy produced that winter. Garrick's prologue did well enough, but it gave some offence to the Chevalier D'Eon, or Mlle la Chevalière D'Eon, as that curious being now wished to be called:

15. DRURY LANE IN 1775

from an engraving by B. Pastorini in the Print Room, Victoria and Albert Museum

Did not a Lady Knight, late Chevalier,
A brave, smart soldier to your eyes appear?
Hey! presto! pass! His sword becomes a fan,
A comely woman rising from the man.
The French their Amazonian maid invite—
She goes—alike well skilled to talk or write,
Dance, ride, negotiate, scold, coquet, or fight,
If she should set her heart upon a rover,
And he prove false, she'll kick her faithless lover.

The indeterminate sex of his notorious contemporary seems a singularly inappropriate subject to choose for the prologue to a play by a refined young lady, but at the time the approach to this particular mystery was uncomplicated by suspicions of sexual abnormality. When the stout French exile with the smooth white throat, soft voice and small hands and feet, whose fencing was soon to earn the admiration of all London, put on female clothes that summer and declared himself a woman, there was much astonishment, but he was accepted as such until the surgeon who examined him after his death pronounced him wholly male and exposed a mystery that has never been satisfactorily explained.

Long before his sex had become the subject for large-scale wagering, D'Eon had provided a fascinating topic for after-dinner conversation—ever since, in fact, he had been found guilty of treason by his Government for some reason unknown six months after his arrival in this country as First Secretary to the French Legation at the end of the Seven Years' War. A few details of his early history were known: he had served in the French Army, seen active service, and, before coming to England, spent some time as a secret agent at the Russian Imperial Court, where, it was rumoured, he had learned many secrets by disguising himself as a woman. Many stories circulated of his wearing women's clothes, but never for any other reason than espionage or escape from his enemies. But what crime against his own country had he committed while in England? Why had Louis XV so evidently been afraid of him? What was the nature of the secret documents he was known to possess? Was it true, as Lord Camden believed it to be, that he could prove Lord Bute and the Princess of Wales guilty of taking French money at the time of the Peace of Paris? Why, if he were in disgrace, did

Louis XVI pay him a pension, and why was he now visiting France at the invitation of her Government?

All these questions invited lurid conjectures, and Garrick had too keen a sense of the dramatic not to share the general curiosity. He must often have seen D'Eon at the Angelos', the natural rendezvous of foreigners as well as of expert fencers, and possibly at the house of his friend, John Wilkes, to whom D'Eon, as a victim of persecution by an autocratic government, was an object of pity. Very much the rough soldier in everything but a few aspects of his appearance, he drank and smoked heavily, becoming noisy and coarse in his cups, but if any woman made advances to him he left the house in a panic. For many years Garrick avoided him, for fear of giving offence to his friends in the French Government, but Tom Davies tells us that D'Eon paid one visit to Hampton House. The evening was not a success: to amuse his guest, Garrick impersonated a Frenchman and an Englishman in turn, as each would behave in a similar situation. The contrast, comic and gratifying to an Englishman, was offensive to a Frenchman, and D'Eon did not hide his displeasure.

When Garrick heard in the summer of 1776 that D'Eon had admitted himself to be a woman he did not believe it, until medical certificates, now recognized as false, gave the decision to those who had betted on his female sex. Even then, D'Eon's reluctance to put on petticoats puzzled his acquaintances, and twelve months elapsed before London saw the stout, soldierly figure dressed in the laced cap, old-fashioned stomacher and wide skirts, so familiar to us in caricatures, inspiring the picturesque legend that he was the natural daughter of Louis XV. By the time Garrick came to write his prologue he had accepted D'Eon as a brawny old maid, and humorously instanced her masculine accomplishments as an argument in favour of feminism. D'Eon liked this joke no better than the other, and, although he was in France at the time, the news of his resentment travelled back to the London coffee-houses.

It is now known that D'Eon came to England in the first place as Louis XV's personal secret agent, and in that capacity acquired documentary proof that the French King was planning, unknown to his ministers and on the morrow of the Peace of Paris, an invasion of England. These papers, the publication of which might have led to war, D'Eon was disinclined to hand over without adequate compensation for his dismissal from the diplomatic service. His possession of the dangerous secret is enough to account for nearly all the puzzling features of his story, but does not explain why he declared himself to be a woman, since he appears to be a simple case of arrested sex development, and never felt at ease in petticoats. The only theory that has any probability is that his financial interest in the wagering led him into the declaration and then, caught in a trap of his own setting, he was forced to continue the masquerade by the French Government, who regarded him as less dangerous in woman's attire and made it a condition of his pension.

Hannah told her family that in all the many months she had spent with the Garrick's at Hampton and the Adelphi, she only once met an actor under their roof. Garrick had never cared for the society of stage folk, and now that there was no longer any need to keep up an appearance of good fellowship, he thankfully withdrew from their haunts. Barry's death in January 1777 meant nothing to him—they had never been friends; Woodward passed away four months later unmourned in the Adelphi; while Foote's disappearance from the social scene that same autumn could have been nothing but a relief, although Garrick behaved with great generosity to his old enemy during the misfortunes that shortened his life. Considering the poison Foote habitually insinuated into his conversation, it is surprising to find how sorry everyone felt for him when the last victim of his satirical pen, the Duchess of Kingston, retaliated through her agents with a libel, similar in kind, and equally unfounded, to that of Kenrick on Garrick. During the trial that resulted in an acquittal for Foote, Garrick gave practical help which elicited a letter of passionate gratitude, but, his ordeal over, Foote, who had never been able to stand up against the mildest attack on himself, collapsed like a punctured balloon, and died some months later of cerebral haemorrhage. There must have been something in his manner that softened his cruel witticisms and gave an impression of underlying kindliness, for no one commented on the fittingness of his end, or spoke otherwise than pityingly of him.

Mrs. Clive was one of the few of his old associates whom Garrick cared to meet, and no one seeing them drinking tea together in her Twickenham villa would have believed how she had raged at him in the years gone by. No longer smarting under real or imaginary grievances, she was generous now in her expressions of praise. 'Damn him,' she would say, 'I believe he could act a gridiron.' Garrick basked in the sunshine of her sincere admiration for him, but, looking back over his career, the actress he remembered with the greatest affection was still Mrs. Cibber. 'I once solely conquered Clive myself,' he remarked to her near neighbour, Horace Walpole, 'but as to Mrs. Cibber, she could persuade me out of anything.' The actors now competing for public favour interested him very little. Henderson scored his first London success as Shylock at the Haymarket in the summer of 1777, but Garrick made no comment, professing—rather pointedly, it was thought —to find great merit in the performance of some minor part. 'Oh, sir, I am no judge,' he replied, when a member of the audience pressed him for his opinion of the new star actor in whose abilities he had never believed. And when Henderson, realizing his ambition at last, appeared at Drury Lane that autumn in Cumberland's new tragedy, *The Battle of Hastings,* an impudent patchwork of other men's work, Garrick was equally evasive. 'Sir, what all the world says, must be true,' was his only comment when asked for his judgment on the play and its performance.

The favours shown him by the titled great were a source of never-ending satisfaction to Garrick, and the fame and fortune of his later years had done nothing to lessen the respectful attentiveness to rank that, as a young actor, had won him their affectionate regard. 'Mr. Garrick did the honours of the house *very respectfully,*' Mrs. Delany had written of a visit to Hampton paid by the Duchess of Portland in 1770, 'and, though in high spirits, seemed sensible of the honour done them. As to Mrs. Garrick, the more one sees her the better one must like her; she seems *never* to depart from a perfect propriety of behaviour, accompanied with good taste and gentleness of manner, and I cannot help looking upon her as a *wonderful creature,* considering all circumstances relating to her.' His intimacy with Lord Camden, the ex-Lord Chancellor of England, was particularly gratifying to him because his lordship's manner to men whom he regarded as nobodies was inclined to be haughty. 'Pray, now,' said Garrick to Boswell, who came to breakfast with him one morning in 1778, 'did you—did you meet a little lawyer turning the corner, eh?'—anxious that his friend should know that Lord Camden had taken the trouble to come round to the Adelphi before breakfast. 'Garrick was right,' remarked Dr. Johnson when Boswell reported the saying to him. 'Lord Camden *was* a little law-yer for associating so familiarly with a player.'

Garrick may have been fond of lolling with a lord, as Wilkinson unkindly expressed it, but he did not on this account neglect or slight his old friends in less socially distinguished walks of life. Dr. Johnson had nothing to complain of on this score; Garrick saw him constantly at the Turk's Head, at Streatham, or in the Adelphi on what he and Mrs. Garrick called their *sauerkraut* evenings, when that dish was served to a select company of eminent men from the learned professions. Hannah More told her family that to enjoy their company properly they had to be together, and she never saw Dr. Johnson happier or better-humoured than when Garrick was talking to him and teasing him. Each of them now had much to endure: Johnson's failing health and brooding fear of death brought on sad speechless moods that would last for days, while it was only Garrick's zest for living that enabled him to recover his gaiety after the severe bouts of internal pain to which he was frequently sub-jected. He had but to remind Dr. Johnson of one of their boyish escapades in Lichfield and the Doctor would cheer up and cap his story with another even more fantastic. Our last glimpse of them together is at the Summer Exhibition of the Royal Academy in 1778, where Dr. Johnson is speaking to Garrick about the unhappy Mauritius Lowe, the execrable painter whom the Doctor had char-acteristically chosen for his protégé. Garrick had given Lowe some sittings, but, horrified by his incompetence, had cancelled the order, offering to buy his drawing of Homer in its stead. Lowe was in great distress, Dr. Johnson told his friend, and, on reaching home, Garrick sent Lowe an extra ten pounds as a present.

These touching signs of affection between the Doctor and his Davy do not mean that they ceased for a moment to make fun of each other to their friends. Fanny Burney was paying her very first visit to Streatham that August when Garrick's epilogue to Fletcher's *Bonduca* happened to be mentioned. Dr. Johnson said flatly that it was a miserable performance, and everyone agreed that it was the worst Garrick had ever written. 'I don't know what is the mat-ter with David,' Dr. Johnson went on. 'I am afraid he is grown superannuated, for his prologues and epilogues used to be incomparable.'

'Nothing is so fatiguing,' commented Mrs. Thrale, 'as the life of a wit. He and Wilkes are the two oldest men of their ages I know; for they have both worn themselves out by being eternally on the rack to give entertainment to others.'

'David, madam,' said the Doctor, 'looks much older than he is; for his face has had double the business of any other man's. It is never at rest; when he speaks one minute, he has quite a different countenance to what he assumes the next. I don't believe he ever kept the same look for half an hour together in the whole course of his life, and such an eternal, restless, fatiguing play of the muscles must certainly wear out a man's face before its real time.'

'Oh, yes,' cried Mrs. Thrale, 'we must certainly make some allowance for such wear and tear of a man's face.'

The next to be mentioned, Fanny Burney tells us, was Sir John Hawkins, and Mrs. Thrale said, 'Why now, Dr. Johnson, he is another of those whom you suffer nobody to abuse but yourself. Garrick is one, too, for if any other person speaks against him, you browbeat him in a minute!'

'Why, madam,' was the answer, 'they don't know when to abuse him, and when to praise him. I will allow no man to speak ill of David that he does not deserve.'

Dr. Johnson was as good as his word. No one in his presence accused Garrick of meanness without being promptly and firmly put down, and told that, on the contrary, Garrick had given away more money than any man in England. And, indeed, we know of no instance of anyone in distress, whether deserving or not, who appealed to Garrick in vain. Many of his loans were mere business transactions, for his friends and fellow-actors seemed to have regarded him almost as a professional money-lender. Burke, for instance, had borrowed £1,000 from him to help in paying for his country estate, and this loan could only have been a convenience. It was one of George's duties to see to the legal side of these transactions (his training in a lawyer's office came in useful), and to collect the interest when it fell due. Yet there were many occasions when Garrick lent money on no security at all, and never asked or received a penny of it back. Anyone who could claim an association with Lichfield was doubly sure of help, and the Canon of that diocese dispensed money and comforts to the poor with instructions not to reveal that they came from Hampton House. The poor of Hampton village were no less well looked after, and on the first of every May the children were invited to come into his garden where they received presents of cake and money.

Garrick did more for his friends and relations than sign cheques in their favour—an easy matter for a man with more money than he could spend. He pestered his influential acquaintances for good openings for them, and was never damped by rebuffs. No one had ever wanted to employ either of his brothers (he had offered their services often enough), but that did not deter him from approaching Lord Buckinghamshire on his appointment as Lord Lieutenant of Ireland in 1776 for a place on his staff for George's son, David —an unsatisfactory young man with much of his father's unsteadiness and ineffectiveness. Once again his application met with a courteous but decided refusal. Whenever any of his friends in France or England wrote a book, Garrick procured them subscriptions, and when Hannah lay ill in her London lodgings, he took the trouble to leave a stew-pan of hot minced chicken, a canister of tea and a pot of cream at her door.

His loyalty to Lichfield stopped short at paying it many visits; unlike Dr. Johnson, he found no pleasure in sitting with the genteel, elderly ladies that made up much of its society. Mrs. Garrick and he had little in common with his married sister, Merriall Docksey, or his bachelor brother, Peter, who had spent all these years in the wine trade and lived on in the old family home. Peter, David, Merrial and George were all that were left now of the Garricks. William had died unmarried many years ago at Minorca, after reaching the rank of Captain in the Royal Navy, and the other sisters had long been in their graves. Garrick did not think many of his letters to his family worth preserving, and consequently we do not know for certain how often he went back to Lichfield. Peter had expected him to bring his wife there on their honeymoon, but the young couple did not come. Lord and Lady Burlington had 'only grave faces and cool answers' when it was suggested, so David told his brother, and the visit was postponed. They were certainly there in 1768, for they had come thence when they had the mortifying experience described for us by Cradock. Lord Warwick had asked them to spend a week at Warwick Castle, or so Garrick had interpreted a message, but there must have been some misunderstanding, because when the Garricks and their friend, the Reverend William Arden, alighted at the Castle they were shown round like ordinary tourists by the servants and offered no more than a cup of chocolate before being escorted back to their carriage. And their last visit was in 1777, when they returned to Lichfield for their niece's wedding—presumably Miss Merriall Docksey.

It was his younger brother whom Garrick made his particular responsibility, and without his protection poor George would have fared very badly. He was foolish, extravagant and dissipated, but he worshipped his celebrated brother and listened humbly to the scoldings his imprudence brought down on him. On one of the few occasions he answered back, he claimed to have provided for part of his sons' education. But he could not have sent Carrington and Nathan to Eton on the small salary he received, and their uncle must have paid most of the fees. At any rate, Garrick watched over their welfare from the time they were small boys as though he considered himself their guardian: in term-time, he and Mrs. Garrick would drive down to Eton, take them out for a good feed and send them back with a guinea each in their pockets, and in August they had them at Hampton for the holidays. None of the three sons turned out very well, or repaid his kindness with any show of affection, and it may have been of them that Garrick was thinking when he said, a day or two before he died, that he did not regret being childless; he knew the quickness of his feelings was so great that if it had been his misfortune to have had disobedient children, he could not have supported such an affliction. The eldest, Carrington, Garrick sent to St. John's College, Cambridge, in 1775, and after he was ordained the following year gave him the living of Hendon, which Garrick, as Lord of the Manor, had in his gift.[1]

---

[1] In 1756 Garrick, who liked to invest in land, bought a large estate in Hendon. In 1765 he bought the Lordship of the Manor from James Clutterbuck. There is no evidence known to me that he spent a night at Hendon, much less made any house there his home. Opposite the front entrance of Hendon Hall is an obelisk of stone which bears the following inscription:

DAVID GARRICK
Born, A.D., MDCCXVI.,   Died, MDCCLXXIX
He was owner of this Estate
Vicarial Patron
and Lord of the Manor
of Hendon.

But the life of a country parson gave the young man more leisure than was good for him, and he died at the age of thirty-four, 'a martyr,' says his friend, Cradock, 'to a too free use of the bottle.' His younger brother, David, was extraordinarily like his namesake in appearance, and as short as Carrington was immensely tall. He could not have been in the army very long when he left his regiment in 1776 on the pretext of ill health; then he wrote to his uncle coolly asking him to provide six thousand guineas for a purchase. Garrick sternly refused to do any such thing, and expressed his strong disapproval of the way he was lounging about the town doing nothing. But when the young man married an unusually sweet-natured girl a couple of years later on an income of exactly nothing a year, his uncle forgave everything and made a handsome settlement on the two of them. As for Nathan, little is known of him after he left Eton, but it is significant that, although he survived his uncle, he, alone of George's five children by his first marriage, is not mentioned in Garrick's will.

George's two daughters, Bell and Kate, were sweet, docile girls, and received their uncle's kindness with becoming gratitude. He sent them to Paris in 1773 to finish their education with a Mme Descombes, who had had Lord Camden's daughters under her care. There they learnt French, music, history and drawing, and how to embroider and make ruffles, tippets and sleeve-knots. Their stay was cut short after two years by poor Bell's indiscretion. She was detected by Madame carrying on a flirtation with a young officer of dragoons who had installed himself in the same house, and used to waylay her on the stairs. Madame reported the whole shocking affair to Uncle David, who ordered her to bring both girls back to London immediately. He worked himself up to an unbelievable pitch of horror and indignation, and the nineteen-year-old Bell imagined her life ruined. She did not dare accompany Mme Descombes to Adelphi Terrace, but stayed tremblingly at home expecting her uncle to send for her. Her shame was misinterpreted as disrespect and gave fresh offence. 'I hope I need not assure you of my total obedience and submission to all your commands,' she wrote in the course of a grovelling apology. 'Dear Sir, shut me up for ever rather than abandon me, and cease for Heaven's sake to load me with your curses. I have many more ills than I can bear. Ease me of one which outweighs all the rest—that of your hatred.'

'Your letter is so properly written,' replied Garrick—the same Garrick who twenty-six years earlier is believed to have slipped letters into Mlle Violette's sedan chair under Lady Burlington's disapproving nose, 'with such a feeling for your situation, a true compunction for the cause of it, and a resolution to take warning for the future, that I will forgive you, never upbraid you again with the distress you have brought upon us and yourself, provided that you will show your gratitude by telling every circumstance of this unhappy affair, that I may be the better able to deliver you from the villain; and that hereafter you will let your good sense and delicacy combat with your passions and not involve yourself and family in the greatest affliction by another unwarrantable, indecent and ruinous connection. Indeed, my dear girl, I cannot account for your rash and almost incredible behaviour; you seem'd to have lost your great ornament and safeguard of your sex—delicacy of apprehension. When the great barrier that Nature has cautiously fixed between passion and prudence is so easily overleap'd, even by our sex, we see the daily consequences; but when your sex is possessed with such a madness, the horror that attends it is best described by the number of the most miserable wretches that have fallen a sacrifice to their imprudence.'

After this, who is going to believe that nothing more serious had occurred than the exchange of a few love letters and tender words on the stairs, and that de Molière (that was, oddly enough, his name) was of good family and character, and wanted to marry the pretty young English girl with whom he had fallen in love at first sight? All this Monnet discovered when, at Garrick's request, he called on de Molière's commanding officer. He would get the letters back if possible, he promised Garrick, but my dear friend, added Monnet, put all that under your feet and forget all about it. One feels a little sorry for Bell, but perhaps it was better that way. Garrick forgave her, left her £6,000 in his will, and, married to an English soldier with three little sons growing up round her, she soon forgot her handsome French dragoon.

CHAPTER XX

POETS' CORNER

1779

G ARRICK never really got over the chill he had caught in the beginning of September 1778, by remaining late at Drury Lane to see the effect of some new scenery. For a few days his condition had caused great anxiety, and the sharpness of the attack frightened him into making his will while he was convalescing at Lord Palmerston's[1] country house in Hampshire later that month. But he assured his friends that he had recovered, and, watching the King reviewing his troops at the camp near Winchester, his high spirits deceived those who recognized him into thinking that he looked very well. 'A horse! a horse! my kingdom for a horse!' he cried, striking a stage attitude, and the King, hearing the familiar voice, remarked to those round him that no one but Mr. Garrick could speak the words in that way.

Back in London, he took up his old life with an effort. Hannah More did not pay her friends her usual winter visit; she stayed at home in Bristol to write another tragedy, which she sent up to them act by act for their criticism. Bell was married, Kate was with her family, but Mrs. Garrick's Austrian niece, on a long visit to this country with her mother, brought young life into the Adelphi and Hampton House. Garrick liked the young girl well enough to leave her a thousand pounds as a legacy, but he could not help noticing uneasily how the presence of their guests revived in Mrs. Garrick a longing for her own people and native land, and, when he came to make his will, the wish to keep intact for as long as

[1] Father of 'Pam'.

275

possible his two homes with all their treasures and associations led him to impose severe financial penalties on his widow in the event of her leaving England—a step he dreaded more than her re-marriage.

He had many worries that autumn. The season at Drury Lane opened badly, and the stories that reached him of the empty houses, refractory actors and actresses and slack management made him very sad and anxious for the future of Old Drury. A blackmailer who signed himself 'Curtius' wrote to him in November threatening to write three letters for *The Ledger* which would, he said, blacken the private character of the great Roscius and humble him to the dust, unless the writer received a satisfactory answer which would reach him if left at a certain accommodation address. The pseudonym is supposed to hide the identity of the man who ruined Foote with his libels, and it is curious to reflect that in an age when men and women were hanged or transported for theft, libellers and blackmailers, whose offences inflicted much greater sufferings on their victims, usually went scot-free. Without the slightest notion of what Curtius intended to say, Garrick wrote a long conciliatory reply, urging him to make the fullest inquiries from those who had known Roscius a long time before believing stories spread by dis-appointed men, declaring that he would rather have his praise than his blame, and the letter ended with a most unconvincing assurance that, whatever the outcome, he was not in the least alarmed. The correspondence dragged on, and among the last letters Garrick received was one from his tormentor graciously promising to stay his pen until his victim was in a fit state to defend himself.

The Spencers came to London in November for an important debate in the House of Lords, and tried to persuade the Garricks to go back with them to Althorp for their usual Christmas visit. There was a certain scarlet and white silk material to be had at Mr. King's, the mercer, Lady Spencer told Mrs. Garrick, which was to be a sort of uniform for the ladies of the Althorp party, and she hoped that Mrs. Garrick would be so gracious as to have one. She was full of affectionate solicitude for Garrick's health, and felt a little reassured when he roused himself sufficiently to take her with Mrs. Garrick to the first performance of Fielding's pos-thumous play to which he had contributed a prologue. But he did not feel well enough to join the Christmas house party, and it was the end of December before he reluctantly set off for Althorp.

Once there he revived, and was often in such fine spirits, Mrs. Garrick afterwards told Hannah More, that she could not believe he was ill, until a terrible bout of pain in the region of his kidneys accompanied by a severe attack of shingles disillusioned her. As soon as he felt a little easier he determined to go back to London to be under the care of his own doctor, and, travelling by easy stages, Mrs. Garrick got him home by Friday, January 15th. On Saturday Mr. Lawrence, the apothecary, found him trying to dress, saying that he felt fairly well apart from a certain new and alarming symptom. Lawrence assured him that he need not be uneasy, and ordered him a warm bath and an emetic, but when Sunday brought no improvement Lawrence considered it advisable to call in Dr. Cadogan. The doctor took a grave view of his condition, and told his patient that the disorder was so uncertain in its progress that if he had any worldly affairs to settle it would be prudent to do so as soon as possible. Garrick said quietly that nothing of that sort remained undone, and that he was not afraid to die. On Sunday he was free of pain, but Dr. Cadogan could see that he was losing ground, and he sent for several eminent physicians, many of whom were Garrick's personal friends and came in that capacity. Garrick greeted them one after another as they approached his bedside, and when it came to Dr. Schomberg he smiled, took him by the hand and said affectionately. 'Though last, not least in love.'

It was probably in the afternoon of this day that an old friend of Garrick's called to see him, and was persuaded by Mrs. Garrick to stay on and have dinner with her. She was worn out with nursing and hoped to find some relief from her anxiety in his company. While they were talking, Garrick came into the room. His face was yellow, his eyes were sunken, and he moved slowly and with difficulty. He had become a very old man overnight, and in his rich dressing-gown looked as though he were made up to go on the stage as Lusignan,[1] the aged King of Jerusalem. He sat down, and for the whole of the hour he remained in the room did not utter a word or move a muscle of his face. Then he got up and went slowly back to his room.

On Monday he began to sink into a coma, but every now and then seemed to rally a little. 'Well, Tom,' said the dying man to

[1] From Aaron Hill's *Zara*.

his servant, 'I shall do very well yet, and make you amends for all this trouble.' Fresh doctors were called into consultation, and poor Garrick stared at the figures round his bedside with bewilderment. He asked Lawrence who the strange gentlemen were, and on being told that they were all physicians shook his head, repeating Horatio's lines in Rowe's *Fair Penitent*:

> *Another and another still succeeds,*
> *And the last fool is welcome as the former.*

On Tuesday evening, the surgeon who came to blister and bleed him made light of his patient's illness, assuring Mrs. Garrick that he would be well in a day or two, and urged her to go and lie down. But she tended the sick man as usual during the night, and every time that she gave him a drink he pressed her hand, and spoke to her affectionately. At eight o'clock the next morning, Wednesday, January 20th, he swallowed his last dose of medicine, said softly, 'Oh, dear!' and fell back dead.

As soon as she heard the news, Hannah More hurried up to London to comfort her friend, but when she arrived at the Adelphi she found that Mrs. Garrick was on the point of leaving for Mrs. Angelo's house where she intended to stay until the funeral was over. So Hannah went ahead of her and was there to greet her when she arrived. Mrs. Garrick was expecting to see her and ran into her arms, and the two women remained silent for some minutes. At last she whispered, 'I have this moment embraced his coffin, and you come next.' She soon recovered herself, and in the weeks that followed Hannah marvelled at her composure. 'Groans and complaints are very well for those who are to mourn but a little while,' remarked Mrs. Garrick when Hannah expressed her astonishment, 'but a sorrow that is to last for life will not be violent and romantic.'

Two days after Garrick's funeral, his brother, George, followed him. He had been constantly ailing since his serious illness in the summer of 1775, and Garrick in his letters to Lichfield had given Peter little hope of his ever being well again. While he lay between life and death that summer, Garrick had been distracted with anxiety; the two brothers were devoted to each other, and it was as well that neither had to mourn the other. No one, alas, outside his own family mourned poor George very deeply. At Drury Lane his presence had been resented by the actors, who suspected him, not without reason, of talebearing, and made him the subject of many contemptuous jokes. His habit of standing on guard in the wings while Garrick was acting, saying, 'Hush, hush,' irritated one of them into remarking that his salary might best be described as 'hush-money'. It was now recalled that whenever he had returned to the theatre after being busy elsewhere, his first words had been, 'Has David wanted me?' and this suggested the final, rather touching, joke that his brother must have wanted him.

Garrick was buried in Westminster Abbey on February 1st, and it would be interesting to know who planned his funeral procession. It could not have been George, Peter did not come to London for the occasion, and Mrs. Garrick certainly had no part in it. The executors of his will were, of course, officially responsible, but its splendid pageantry is strongly reminiscent of the Drury Lane stage procession, and as R. B. Sheridan is described in a contemporary newspaper account,[1] as well as by Hannah More, as Chief Mourner, it seems likely that it was he who presented a spectacle which, except for its lack of colour, was the most magnificent and impressive in which Garrick had ever taken part. The line of carriages extended over the whole length of the route from Adelphi Terrace to Westminster Abbey, and the crowds in the street were so dense that a military guard was necessary.

'Four men in mourning,' runs the opening paragraph of Davies's *Order of Mr. Garrick's Funeral,* 'with staffs covered with black silk and scarfs, on horseback, as porters. Six ditto, with mourning cloaks, etc. A man in mourning to bear the pennon, with scarf, etc. Two supporters. Six men in cloaks as before. Surcoat of arms. Helmet, with crest, wreath and mantlet. State lid of black ostrich feathers, surrounded by escutcheons. Hearse full dressed with THE BODY.'

After the hearse came the clergy of Saint Martin's, and the ten pall-bearers, whose names make an imposing list: the fifth Duke of Devonshire, Lord Camden, Earl Spencer, the Earl of Ossory, the second Viscount Palmerston, Sir W. W. Wynn, the Hon. Hans Stanley, J. Patterson, R. Rigby, and Albany Wallis. Next, in an oddly conspicuous place, came R. B. Sheridan as Chief Mourner. In the family coaches were Garrick's three nephews, Carrington, David and Nathan, and Bell's husband, Captain Schaw. The rest

[1] In the Enthoven Collection at the Victoria and Albert Museum.

of the procession took the following order, each section effectively set off by pages and cloaked horse men with rich velvet horsecloths: Drury Lane actors, Covent Garden actors, members of the Club (known by this time as the Literary Club), and intimate friends. Finally came thirty-five empty coaches from Garrick's stables with coachmen and footmen in black.

At the Abbey doors the Bishop of Rochester and Dean of Westminster followed by a full choir singing Handel's anthem, met the coffin, and it was carried in state to the side of its last resting-place under the pavement of Poets' Corner at the foot of Shakespeare's monument. The Bishop read the service in a low voice, every word being audible in the perfect silence. As the coffin was being lowered, Burke could not control his sobbing, and tears rolled down Dr. Johnson's face.

On the evening of the day after the funeral, Hannah More went with Mrs. Garrick back to Adelphi Terrace. Hannah was surprised to see her friend go alone into the room where Garrick had died exactly a fortnight ago. She had a delight in it, wrote Hannah to her sister, beyond expression. The next morning Hannah asked her how she went through it. Mrs. Garrick told her very well; that she first prayed with great composure, then went and kissed the dear bed, and got into it with a sad pleasure. She found her first homecoming to Hampton a week or two later more harrowing. Dragon, Garrick's dog, ran to meet his master, and his disappointment was so heartrending to see that Mrs. Garrick went and shut herself up for half an hour. The quiet beauty of her riverside home brought her peace, but, as the months lengthened into years, her disinclination to see anyone outside her own intimate circle increased, and she never went back to the full social life she had enjoyed when Garrick was there to share it with her.

Two years passed before she emerged from her seclusion, and then, at a party given by Bishop Shipley, she met Dr. Johnson for the first time since her bereavement. They said little to each other that evening, but the next morning he called on her. Mrs. Garrick told him that she was always more at her ease with persons who had suffered the same loss as herself, but Dr. Johnson, recalling the cat and dog existence he had led with his wife during their short married life, was too honest to let this pass, and he told her that that was a comfort she could seldom have, considering the superi-

16. DRURY LANE IN 1776

from an engraving by P. Begbie in the Print Room,
Victoria and Albert Museum

ority of her husband's merit and the cordiality of their union. He went on to pay tribute to Garrick's generosity, and then, with a strange failure of tact, broke off to rebuke Hannah More for reading books written by Catholics.

Dr. Johnson felt the loss of his friend very keenly. While Garrick lay on his deathbed, he steadfastly refused to believe that there was any cause for anxiety. No arguments or recitals of facts which Mrs. Thrale had heard, she tells us, would persuade him of Garrick's danger. A few years later he displayed the same obstinate blindness when Mr. Thrale, whom he loved perhaps more deeply, lay dying. After Garrick's death, Dr. Johnson let it be known that, if Mrs. Garrick wished it, he would edit her husband's works and write his life. But Mrs. Garrick made no sign, and he had to content himself with helping Tom Davies with the book to which all subsequent biographers of Garrick are of necessity deeply indebted. It was just about this time that Dr. Johnson was writing his short life of Edmund Smith, and, in the course of it, he made the well-known reference to Garrick that must take the place of the Latin epitaph Johnson had in mind to compose but never completed. After paying a tribute to their boyhood's friend, Gilbert Walmesley, whose conversation had supplied much of the material for his essay, Dr. Johnson wrote: 'I hoped to have gratified [David Garrick] with this character of our common friend; but what are the hopes of man! I am disappointed by that stroke of death, which has eclipsed the gaiety of nations, and impoverished the public stock of harmless pleasure.' These were the words Mrs. Garrick had engraved on Garrick's monument in Lichfield Cathedral.

It is generally assumed that Mrs. Garrick made no reply to Dr. Johnson's offer because she did not think he would do Garrick justice, and did not wish him to write his life. But Mrs. Garrick seemed incapable of taking active steps about anything, and it is unnecessary to search deeply for her motives in leaving much undone that should have been done by Garrick's widow. The very qualities that had made her a perfect companion for Garrick ill suited her for facing life alone. She had never had the chance to develop a character of her own: from the Burlingtons' protection she had passed into that of Garrick, and, throughout their life together, it was he who had made all the decisions in matters great and small. 'I think and so does Mrs. Garrick think . . .' he had been in the habit of beginning, but she had always followed his lead, and the care of the household linen, the ordering of the food, and the choice of her own clothes had been her only responsibilities. She had never had the handling of more than a few pounds, and her extraordinary attitude towards money after Garrick's death was probably due as much to ignorance of practical affairs as to meanness and avarice.

Under the terms of his will, Garrick left his widow, subject to certain conditions, his houses in the Adelphi and at Hampton with their contents for her life, a legacy of £6,000 and an annuity of £1,500, the payment of which was to be regarded as the first charge on his estate. After the payment of legacies to the value of £40,000, the residue was to be distributed as though he had died intestate. When Dr. Johnson went to Lichfield three years after Garrick's death, he found that Garrick's legatees had not received a penny, and in London the undertaker was ruined while waiting for the £1,500 owed him for the funeral expenses. The chaotic state of the Drury Lane finances at the time may provide some excuse for this delay, and, in any case, the four executors, one of whom was Lord Camden, were primarily responsible. But when, having come into a larger income than she could spend, Mrs. Garrick allowed her legal advisers in 1807 to institute law proceedings in Chancery in order to obtain a share of the comparatively small sum which, by the residuary clause, was to be divided among Garrick's next of kin, it is difficult to defend her. By modern standards, it is true, her estimated income does not spell wealth, but it was more than she needed; by 1815 she had saved £12,000 which she distributed among her German relations.

Mrs. Garrick displayed the same inertia when it came to the erection of a monument to Garrick's memory in Westminster Abbey. Time went by, nothing was done, and, despite the flattery lavished on him during his lifetime, not one of Garrick's rich and distinguished friends concerned himself in the matter. It was left to his solicitor, Albany Wallis, to pay this tribute to the best actor of all time. In the great distress of Wallis's life, when his thirteen-year-old son had been drowned in the Thames, Garrick had been very kind to him, taking him away from the sight of the river, and afterwards putting up a monument in Westminster Abbey to the boy's memory. Wallis now repaid his debt by erecting another to Gar-

rick at his own expense, high up on the farthest corner of the wall
opposite to the stone that marks his grave. But Wallis was no connoisseur of the arts, and his choice of a sculptor was unfortunate
in the extreme. No one is likely now to sympathize with Charles
Lamb who owned himself scandalized by the theatrical airs of
Webber's figures in consecrated ground; the modern eye is accustomed to the baroque. The trouble is that the monument is a poor
example of its kind. By the 1780's the great baroque sculptors were
dead, and Flaxman had hardly begun his career. But with Nollekens, Bacon and Banks doing good, if unequal, work, Garrick, who
in life had shown himself a generous and discriminating patron of
the arts, should have been better served in death.

In the fourth year of her widowhood, Mrs. Garrick made some
attempt to pick up the threads of her old social life, and we find
her with Hannah More back in London among the coterie known
as the Blue Stockings, giving and attending small parties. Mrs.
Montagu, Miss Elizabeth Carter, Mrs. Vesey, Mrs. Boscawen and
Horace Walpole gave her a warm welcome, noticing little change
in her; she looked serene and well, and dressed as elegantly as ever.
She spoke very little, but was followed and addressed by everybody. At one of these gatherings in 1782 she met the Scottish judge,
Lord Monboddo, for what was probably the first time, and at the
age of fifty-eight so much attracted him that he proposed and was
rejected by her twice that summer. He cannot be suspected of for-
tune-hunting. By living in Scotland, she would have forfeited her
bequests under Garrick's will, receiving in their stead an annuity
of £1,000. Moreover, he had his own estates, and was not in need
of money.

Lord Monboddo's theory, elaborated in his two books, that
the orang-outang was a class of the human species,[1] and could,
with care and patience, be taught to speak, earned him the reputation of being half-mad—so unbalanced that the blasphemy was
forgiven him. In fact, by studying man as an animal and observing
his kinship with apes, he laid the foundation of anthropology and
prepared the way for Darwin's theory of evolution. In 1780 he
made the first of his annual visits to London during his vacation
from his judicial duties in Edinburgh, and his books, though ridi-

[1] This suggested to Peacock one of his most amusing characters, the amiable
and chivalrous Sir Oran Haut-ton, the orang-outang hero of *Melincourt*.

culed, gained him the entry into literary circles. Dr. Johnson and he had already met; cordially hating each other, they cannot be described as old friends. In 1773 Johnson had stayed with him on his country estate while touring the Hebrides with Boswell, and only the mutual forbearance customary and necessary between host and guest had prevented them from coming to blows. Mrs. Garrick's decision, never for a moment in doubt, was a wise one: Lord Monboddo had many amiable qualities, but some of his theories, less startling to his contemporaries than evolution, would have made him tiresome to live with. A strong believer in the virtue of the heroic ages and the degeneracy of his own, he despised all inventions and social customs later in origin than the days of Homer, and Mrs. Garrick, had she married him, would, for instance, never have been allowed to enter a wheeled carriage. Some of his personal habits, too, were peculiar: at three o'clock every morning he had to have what he called his 'air bath', which consisted of standing naked by a wide-open window for a specified length of time.

Mrs. Garrick and Hannah More never wavered in their loyal affection for each other, but, as Hannah's religious convictions became more exacting, their intimacy waned. By 1787 Hannah had decided that as a Christian she could not enter a play-house, and refused to see Mrs. Siddons take the leading part in her own tragedy, *Percy*, the copyright of which she had surrendered; whereas Mrs. Garrick's only remaining pleasure in life was to talk of her Davy and his acting. She had her own box at Drury Lane, and every promising actor was presented to her for her approval and blessing. She is unlikely to have admired Kemble's acting, but, as the leading actor of his day, she paid him the compliment of giving him a cane belonging to Garrick, and a manuscript copy of his version of *Hamlet*. Edmund Kean's romantic style was much more to her taste; as Richard III he strongly reminded her of Davy, and she would coach him in those details of his performance she regarded as weak in comparison. When he attempted Abel Drugger, however, she was outspoken in her condemnation. 'Dear Sir,' she wrote, 'You cannot act Abel Drugger, Yours, M. Garrick.' 'Madam, I know it, Yours, E. Kean,' was the reply.

She was happiest at Hampton, seeing few people outside her own family. Horace Walpole called on her uninvited one Sunday in 1795, and was quite surprised to be let in. She had a hundred head of nieces with her, she told him, as she met him at the door, and his first impression on entering the crowded drawing-room was that she had spoken no more than the truth. There were six gentle-women, he reported, and a husband of one of them and two boys. An elderly fat dame, he went on, affected at every word to call her aunt. For the first years of her widowhood she evidently kept the house in repair; for Mrs. Montagu's nephew, calling on her in 1793, found her grumbling in her guttural tones about the workmen in the house. 'She has been pilding [*sic*],' he wrote to his aunt, laughing at her consonants just as Garrick had done, 'her house was to be rebaired [*sic*], and it tumpled [*sic*] down and she has been opliged [*sic*] to eat her dinner first in one corner and then in another, and the pricklayer [*sic*] and his bosse are likely to eat her out of house and home.' From another source we learn that when the mason presented her with a bill which she regarded as excessive, she called him a damned fellow and told him to get out.

As she grew old, she simplified her way of living, assuring her friends that she was poor, until nothing remained of her former splendour. When Queen Charlotte called at Hampton, she found the great actor's widow peeling onions. Asking for a knife, the Queen sat down beside her, and the two German-speaking women peeled onions together like a couple of hausfraus. This illusion of poverty became an obsession, and in extreme old age Mrs. Garrick denied herself the ordinary comforts of life, allowing both houses to deteriorate until their condition was described as ruinous. She lived in one room with a single servant, who was obliged to supplement her wages by surreptitiously showing the house and grounds to inquisitive passers-by. A dish of tea was all Mrs. Garrick felt able to offer her visitors.

At the great age of ninety-eight she came to London to see some alterations that had been made to Drury Lane. She was now a little bowed-down old lady, leaning on a gold-headed stick, and her wrinkled face in its large bonnet looked all nose and chin. She was resting in her chair before setting out for the theatre, when her maid handed her a refreshing cup of tea. 'Put it down, hussy,' she said irritably. 'Do you think I cannot help myself?' The maid put it down, and left her mistress alone. When she came back a few minutes later, Mrs. Garrick was dead.

APPENDICES

I

David Garrick to his brother, Peter Garrick,
written during the winter of 1741.

My dear Brother.   London Tuesday Night.

  As you finish'd yr last Letter with saying
tho you did not approve of the stage yet you would
always be my Affect^e Brother I may now venture
to tell you I am very near quite resolv'd to be
a player; as I have the Judgment of the best
Judges (who to a Man are of Opinion) that
I shall turn out (nay they say I am) not only the
Best Trajedian but Comedian in England. I would
not say so much to anybody else but as this may
somewhat palliate my Folly you must excuse me.
Mr. Lyttleton was with me last Night and took me by the
hand and said he never saw such playing upon the
English Stage before—I have great offers from
        to Gentlemen
Fletewood, but he's going to see ⌃ & I don't doubt
but make (?) for myself very greatly—We have greater

My Dear Brother.   London Tuesday Night;

As You finish'd y.ʳ last Letter with saying tho' you did not approve of y.ᵉ Stage Yet you wᵈ always be my Affect.ᵉ Brother I may now venture to tell You I am very near quite resolv'd to be a player; as I have y.ᵉ Judgment of y.ᵉ best Judges / Who to a Man are of Opinion / that I shall turn out (Nay they say Sir) not only y.ᵉ best Trajedian but Comedian in England. I would not say so much to any body else, but as this my Somewhat palliate My Folly you must Excuse it. M.ʳˢ Heton was w.ᵗʰ Me last Night & took Me by y.ᵉ and & Said he never saw Such playing upon y.ᵉ English Stage before — I have great Offers from Fletewood, but he's going to Sell to Gentlemen & I don't doubt but make for myself very greatly — We have great.

II

SAMUEL JOHNSON

PROLOGUE

SPOKEN BY MR. GARRICK

at the
Opening of the Theatre-Royal, Drury Lane, 1747

When Learning's triumph o'er her barb'rous foes
First rear'd the stage, immortal Shakespeare rose;
Each change of many-colour'd life he drew,
Exhausted worlds, and then imagin'd new:
Existence saw him spurn her bounded reign,
And panting Time toil'd after him in vain.
His pow'rful strokes presiding Truth impress'd,
And unresisted Passion storm'd the breast.

   Then Jonson came, instructed from the school,
To please in method, and invent by rule;
His studious patience and laborious art,
By regular approach assail'd the heart:
Cold approbation gave the ling'ring bays,
For those, who durst not censure, scarce could praise.
A mortal born, he met the gen'ral doom,
But left, like Egypt's kings, a lasting tomb.

   The wits of Charles found easier ways to fame,
Nor wish'd for Jonson's art, or Shakespeare's flame,
Themselves they studied—as they felt they writ;
Intrigue was plot, obscenity was wit.
Vice always found a sympathetic friend;
They pleas'd their age, and did not aim to mend.
Yet bards like these aspir'd to lasting praise,
And proudly hop'd to pimp in future days.
Their cause was gen'ral, their supports were strong,
Their slaves were willing, and their reign was long:

Till Shame regain'd the post that Sense betray'd,
And Virtue call'd Oblivion to her aid.

Then, crush'd by rules, and weaken'd as refin'd,
For years the pow'r of Tragedy declin'd;
From bard to bard the frigid caution crept,
Till Declamation roar'd, while Passion slept;
Yet still did Virtue deign the stage to tread,
Philosophy remain'd, though Nature fled.
But forc'd, at length, her ancient reign to quit,
She saw great Faustus lay the ghost of Wit;
Exulting Folly hail'd the joyful day,
And Pantomime and Song confirm'd her sway.

But who the coming changes can presage,
And mark the future periods of the stage?
Perhaps, if skill could distant times explore,
New Behns, new Durfeys, yet remain in store;
Perhaps, where Lear has rav'd and Hamlet dy'd,
On flying cars new sorcerers may ride:
Perhaps (for who can guess th' effects of chance?)
Here Hunt[1] may box, or Mahomet may dance.

Hard is his lot that, here by Fortune plac'd,
Must watch the wild vicissitudes of taste;
With ev'ry meteor of caprice must play,
And chase the new-blown bubbles of the day.
Ah! let not Censure term our fate our choice,
The stage but echoes back the public voice;
The drama's laws, the drama's patrons give,
For we that live to please, must please, to live.

Then prompt no more the follies you decry,
As tyrants doom their tools of guilt to die;
'Tis Yours, this night, to bid the reign commence
Of rescued Nature and reviving Sense;
To chase the charms of Sound, the pomp of Show,
For useful Mirth, and salutary Woe;
Bid scenic Virtue form the rising age,
And Truth diffuse her radiance from the stage.

---

[1] **Hunt**, a famous boxer on the stage; Mahomet, a rope-dancer, who had exhibited at Covent Garden Theatre the winter before, said to be a Turk.

III

OLIVER GOLDSMITH

RETALIATION

Here lies David Garrick, describe me who can,
An abridgment of all that was pleasant in man;
As an actor, confess'd without rival to shine;
As a wit, if not first, in the very first line;
Yet, with talents like these, and an excellent heart,
The man had his failings, a dupe to his art.
Like an ill-judging beauty, his colours he spread,
And beplaster'd with rouge his own natural red.
On the stage he was natural, simple, affecting;
'Twas only that when he was off he was acting.
With no reason on earth to go out of his way,
He turn'd and he varied full ten times a day:
Though secure of our hearts, yet confoundedly sick
If they were not his own by finessing and trick:
He cast off his friends as a huntsman his pack,
For he knew when he pleased he could whistle them back.
Of praise a mere glutton, he swallowed what came,
And the puff of a dunce he mistook it for fame,
Till, his relish grown callous, almost to disease,
Who pepper'd the highest was surest to please.
But let us be candid, and speak out our mind,
If dunces applauded, he paid them in kind.
Ye Kenricks, ye Kellys, and Woodfalls so grave,
What a commerce was yours, while you got and you gave!
How did Grub-street re-echo the shouts that you raised,
While he was be-Roscius'd, and you were be-praised.
But peace to his spirit, wherever it flies,
To act as an angel and mix with the skies;
Those poets who owe their best fame to his skill,
Shall still be his flatterers, go where he will;
Old Shakespeare receive him with praise and with love,
And Beaumonts and Bens be his Kellys above.

DAVID GARRICK

JUPITER AND MERCURY

The reply

Here Hermes, says Jove, who with nectar was mellow,
Go fetch me some clay,—I will make an odd fellow:
Right and wrong shall be jumbled, much gold and some dross
Without cause be he pleased, without cause be he cross;
Be sure as I work to throw in contradictions,
A great love of truth, yet a mind turned to fictions:
Now mix these ingredients, which warm'd in the baking,
Turn'd to learning and gaming, religion and raking.
With the love of a wench, let his writings be chaste;
Tip his tongue with strange matter, his pen with fine taste;
That the rake and the poet o'er all may prevail,
Set fire to the head and set fire to the tail:
For the joy of each sex on the world I'll bestow it:
This scholar, rake, Christian, dupe, gamester and poet,
Though a mixture so odd he shall merit great fame,
And among brother mortals—be Goldsmith his name!
When on earth this strange meteor no more shall appear,
You, Hermes, shall fetch him—to make us sport here!

IV

DAVID GARRICK

ON JOHNSON'S DICTIONARY

1755

Talk of war with a Briton, he'll boldly advance
That one English soldier will beat ten of France;
Would we alter the boast from the sword to the pen,
Our odds are still greater, still greater our men:
In the deep mines of science tho' Frenchmen may toil,
Can their strength be compar'd to Locke, Newton and Boyle?
Let them rally their heroes, send forth all their pow'rs,

APPENDIX

Their verse-men, and prose-men; then match them with ours!
First Shakespeare and Milton, like gods in the fight,
Have put their whole drama and epic to flight;
In satires, epistles, and odes would they cope,
Their numbers retreat before Dryden and Pope;
And Johnson, well arm'd like a hero of yore,
Has beat forty[1] French, and will beat forty more.

V

DAVID GARRICK

A RIDDLE[2]

Kitty, a fair, but frozen maid,
  Kindled a flame I still deplore;
The hood-wink'd boy I call'd in aid,
Much of his near approach afraid,
  So fatal to my suit before.

At length, propitious to my pray'r,
  The little urchin came;
At once he sought the midway air,
And soon he clear'd, with dextrous care,
  The bitter relics of my flame.

To Kitty, Fanny now succeeds,
  She kindles slow, but lasting fires;
With care my appetite she feeds;
Each day some willing victim bleeds,
  To satisfy my strange desires.

Say, by what title, or what name,
  Must I this youth address?
Cupid and he are not the same,
Tho' both can raise or quench a flame—
  I'll kiss you, if you guess.

1 The number of the French Academy employed in perfecting their language.
2 Answer: a chimney-sweep.

VI

DAVID GARRICK

HEART OF OAK

1759

Come cheer up, my lads, 'tis to glory we steer,
To add something new to this wonderful year,
'Tis to honour we call you, not press you like slaves,
For who are so free as the Sons of the Waves?
 Heart of oak are our ships,
 Jolly tars are our men,
 We always are ready,
 Steady, boys, steady!
 We'll fight and we'll conquer
Again and again.

We ne'er see our foes but we wish them to stay,
They never see us but they wish us away;
If they run, why we follow and drive them ashore,
For if they won't fight us we cannot do more.
 Heart of oak, etc.

Great Britain shall triumph, her ships plough the sea;
Her standard is Justice; her watchword, 'Be free!'
Then cheer up, my lads, with one heart let us sing,
Our soldiers, our sailors, our statesmen, our King.
 Heart of oak, etc.

VII

DAVID GARRICK

SWEET WILLY O

A Song

The pride of all nature was sweet Willy O,[1]
    The first of all swains,
    He gladden'd the plains,
None ever was like to sweet Willy O.

He sung it so rarely the sweet Willy O,
    He melted each maid,
    So skilful he play'd,
No shepherd e'er pip'd like the sweet Willy O.

All nature obey'd him, this sweet Willy O.
    Wherever he came,
    Whate'er had a name,
Whenever he sung follow'd sweet Willy O.

He charm'd 'em when living, the sweet Willy O.
    And when Willy dy'd,
    'Twas Nature that sigh'd,
To part with her all in the sweet Willy O.

VIII

DAVID GARRICK

EPITAPH ON HOGARTH IN CHISWICK CHURCHYARD

Farewell, great painter of mankind,
    Who reach'd the noblest point of art;
Whose pictur'd morals charm the mind,
    And thro' the eye correct the heart!

[1] Shakespeare. Written for the Shakespeare Jubilee at Stratford, 1769.

If genius fire thee, reader stay;
  If nature touch thee, drop a tear:
If neither move thee, turn away,
  For Hogarth's honour'd dust lies here.

IX

DAVID GARRICK

PROLOGUE

SPOKEN BY MR. GARRICK

June 10th, 1776
in aid of the Actors' Fund

A veteran see! whose last act on the stage
Intreats your smiles for sickness and for age;
Their cause I plead—plead it in heart and mind;
A fellow-feeling makes one wond'rous kind;
Might we but hope your zeal would not be less,
When I am gone, to patronise distress,
That hope obtain'd the wish'd-for-end secures,
To soothe their cares, who oft have lighten'd yours,
Shall the great Heroes of celestial line,
Who drank full bowls of Greek and Roman wine,
Caesar and Brutus, Agamemnon, Hector,
Nay, Jove himself, who here has quaff'd his Nectar!
Shall they who govern'd Fortune cringe and court her,
Thirst in their age, and call in vain for porter?
Like Belisarius, tax the pitying street,
With '*Date Obolum*' to all they meet?
Shan't I, who oft have drench'd my hands in gore,
Stabb'd many, poison'd some, beheaded more;
Who numbers slew in battle on this plain;
Shan't I, the slayer, try to feed the slain?
Brother to all, with equal love I view
The men who slew me, and the men I slew:

I must, I will this happy project seize,
That those, too old to die, may live with ease.
Suppose the babes I smother'd in the Tower,
By chance, or sickness, lose their acting pow'r,
Shall they, once Princes, worse than all be serv'd!
In childhood murder'd, and, when murder'd, starv'd?
Matrons half ravish'd, for your recreation,
In age, should never want some consolation:
Can I, Young Hamlet once, to Nature lost,
Behold, O horrible! my father's ghost,
With grisly beard—pale cheek—stalk up and down,
And he, the Royal Dane, want half a crown?
Forbid it, Ladies; Gentlemen, forbid it;
Give joy to age, ye Gods![1] I make my last appeal;
You have a right to judge, as well as feel;
Will your high wisdoms to our scheme incline;
That Kings, Queens, Heroes, Gods, and Ghosts may dine?
Olympus shakes! that omen all secures;
May every joy you give be ten-fold yours.

[1] To the upper gallery.

BIBLIOGRAPHY

ADOLPHUS, JOHN, *Memoirs of John Bannister* (1839).

ANGELO, HENRY, *Reminiscences* (1828).

ANON., *Life of Mr. James Quin* (1766).

D'ARBLAY, MME, *Diary and Letters* (1904—5).
Early Diary of Fanny Burney (1907).
Memoirs of Dr. Burney (1832).

BAKER, DAVID ERSKINE, *Biographia Dramatica* (1812).

BELLAMY, GEORGE ANNE, *Apology for the life of Bellamy by Herself* (1786).

BLUNT, REGINALD, *Mrs. Montagu, Letters and Friendships, from 1762—1800* (1923).

BOADEN, JAMES, *Memoirs of John Philip Kemble* (1825).
Memoirs of Mrs. Siddons (1893).
Private Correspondence of David Garrick (1831—2).

BOSWELL, JAMES, *Life of Dr. Johnson*, ed. by G. B. Hill (1887).

CARLYLE, ALEXANDER, *Autobiography* (1860).

CIBBER, COLLEY, *Apology for the life of Cibber by Himself*, ed. by R. W. Lowe (1889).

CIBBER, THEOPHILUS, *Dissertations on theatrical subjects* (1756).

COOKE, WILLIAM, *Memoirs of Charles Macklin* (1804).
Memoirs of Samuel Foote (1805).

CRADOCK, JOSEPH, *Literary and Miscellaneous Memoirs* (1828).

CUMBERLAND, RICHARD, *Memoirs* (1806).

CUNNINGHAM, ALLAN, *Lives of British Painters, Sculptors and Architects* (1829—33).

DAVIES, THOMAS, *Dramatic Miscellanies* (1784).
A Genuine Narrative of the Life and Theatrical Transactions of Mr. John Henderson (1778).
Life of Garrick (1780).

DELANY, MRS., *Autobiography and Correspondence* (1862).

DIBDIN, CHARLES, *Professional Life of Mr. Dibdin* (1803).

DIDEROT, *Paradox of Acting*, trans. by Pollock (1883).

DISHER, M. WILSON, *Clowns and Pantomimes* (1925).

EVERARD, EDWARD CAPE, *Memoirs of an unfortunate son of Thespis* (1818).

BIBLIOGRAPHY

FITZGERALD, PERCY H., *Life of David Garrick* (1899).

FOOTE, SAMUEL, *Works* (1799).

FORSTER, JOHN, *Life and Times of Oliver Goldsmith* (1890).

GARRICK, DAVID, *Dramatic Works* (1768).

Poetical Works (1785).

The Diary of David Garrick being a record of his memorable trip to Paris, ed. by R. C. Alexander (1928).

Essay on Acting (1744).

GENEST, JOHN, *Some Account of the English Stage* (1832).

GENTLEMAN, FRANCIS, *The Dramatic Censor* (1770).

GILLILAND, T., *The Dramatic Mirror* (1808).

HASLEWOOD, JOSEPH, *The Secret History of the Green-Rooms* (1793 and 1795).

HAWKINS, SIR JOHN, *Life of Johnson* (1787).

HAWKINS, LAETITIA, *Anecdotes* (1822).

HEDGCOCK, FRANK ARTHUR, *David Garrick and his French Friends* (1912).

HILL, GEORGE BIRKBECK, *Johnsonian Miscellanies* (1897).

HILL, JOHN, *The Actor* (1755).

HITCHCOCK, ROBERT, *Historical View of the Irish Stage* (1788—94).

JOHNSON, SAMUEL, *Letters,* ed. by G. B. Hill (1892).

KIRKMAN, JAMES, *Life of Charles Macklin* (1799).

KNIGHT, JOSEPH, *David Garrick* (1894).

LEE, LEWIS, C., *Memoirs* (1805).

LITTLE, DAVID MASON, *Pineapples of Finest Flavour. A Selection of unpublished letters of David Garrick* (1930).

MACMILLAN, DOUGALD. *Drury Lane Calendar* (1938).

MARTIN, SIR THEODORE, *Monographs* (1906).

MEAKIN, ANNETTE M. B., *Hannah More* (1919).

MURPHY, ARTHUR, *Life of David Garrick* (1801).

Preface to Johnson's Works (1792).

NAPIER, ROBINA, *Johnsoniana* (1884).

NICOLL, ALLARDYCE, *Development of the Theatre* (1927).

History of 18th Century Drama (1925 and 1927).

NORTHCOTE, JAMES, *Memoirs of Sir Joshua Reynolds* (1813—15).

NOVERRE, JEAN GEORGE, *Letters on Dancing and Ballets,* trans. by Cyril W. Beaumont (1930).

ODELL, G. C. D., *Shakespeare from Betterton to Irving* (1921).

BIBLIOGRAPHY

O'KEEFE, JOHN, *Recollections* (1826).

PAGE, EUGENE RICHARD, *George Colman the Elder* (1935).

PARSONS, MRS. CLEMENT, *Garrick and his Circle* (1906).

PEAKE, RICHARD BRINSLEY, *Memoirs of the Colman Family* (1841).

PIOZZI, HESTER LYNCH, *Anecdotes of the late Samuel Johnson* (1932).

READE, ALEYN LYELL, *Johnsonian Gleanings* (1933).

REYNOLDS, FREDERICK, *Life and Times* (1826).

RIPLEY, HENRY, *History of Hampton on Thames* (1885).

ROBERTS, WILLIAM, *Memoirs of Mrs. Hannah More* (1885).

ROBINSON, MARY, *Memoirs*, ed. by J. Fitzgerald Molloy (1895).

ROGERS, SAMUEL, *Table Talk* (1887).

SHAKESPEARE, WILLIAM, *Works*, ed. by H. H. Furness (1871).

SMITH, J. T., *A Book for a Rainy Day* (1845).

Nollekens and his Times (1829).

STOCKDALE, PERCIVAL, *Memoirs* (1809).

TAYLOR, JOHN, *Records of my Life* (1832).

VICTOR, BENJAMIN, *History of the Theatres of London from 1760* (1771).

History of the Theatres of London and Dublin from 1730 (1761).

WALPOLE, HORACE, *Letters*, ed. by Mrs. Paget Toynbee (1903).

WELLSTOOD, F. C., *An Inventory of the Civic Insignia belonging to . . . Stratford-upon-Avon* (1940).

WHEATLEY, H. B., *The Adelphi and its Site* (1885).

WILKINSON, TATE, *Memoirs* (1790).

The Wandering Patentee (1795).

Also Garrick's Correspondence in manuscript in the Forster Collection, Victoria and Albert Museum, the manuscripts of Captain James Saunders at Stratford-upon-Avon, *London Magazine* and *Gentleman's Magazine*.

INDEX

Abbreviations

C.G. Covent Garden   G. Garrick
D.L. Drury Lane   G.F. Goodman's Fields

For plays by Shakespeare, *see* Shakespeare, William

Abington, Frances, 183, 213, 219, 228, 233, 248; refuses Kate Hardcastle, 225
'Aboan', G. as, 29
Actors' Fund, *see* D.L. and C.G. theatres
Adam, James, 239, 240, 249
Adam, Robert, 144, 239, 240, 249
Addison, Joseph, 16, 19; *Cato*, 98, 109, 243
Adelphi Arches, 16
Adelphi Terrace, 239, 242, 243, 246, 257, 263, 267-269, 273, 275, 278-280, 282
Alchemist, The, see Jonson, Ben
Alembert, Jean le Rond d', 177
Algarotti, Francesco, 170
'Altamont', Ryan as, 75
Althorp, 254, 277
Angelo, Dominico, 206, 211, 216, 266
Angelo, Mrs. Dominico, 206, 278
Angelo, Henry, 206
'Anne, Lady', 36, 37; Miss Angela Baddeley as, 36; Mrs. Siddons as, 233
'Antonio', Quin as, 28
'Antony', G. as, 132
Apology, An, see Churchill, Charles
Apprentice, The, see Murphy, Arthur
Arden, Rev. William, 272
Argyll, Duke of, 151
Arne, Dr. Thomas Augustine, 51, 52, 94, 167; Stratford Jubilee, 208-210. *Judith*, 209
'Arthur, Prince', 63; Mrs. Bellamy as, 72
Aston, the Misses, 12, 204
Aston, Sir Thomas, 6, 7

Bacon, John, 283
Baddeley, Miss Angela, as Lady Anne, 36
Baker, Thomas, *Tunbridge Walks*, 77
Ballet, 117, 128-132
Banks, Thomas, 283
Bannister, Charles, 257
Bannister, John, 256, 257
Baretti, Giuseppe, 198, 199

Barry, Spranger, 115, 120-123, 125, 136, 219, 227; acts with G. in Dublin, 72; London début, 78; leaves D.L., 107, 108; Dublin theatrical venture, 132, 133, 141, 142; G. re-engages, 187; death, 267; as Mahomet, 98, 99; as Othello, 78; as Romeo, 97, 126, 127, 182; the rival Romeos, 109-111, 215
Barry, Mrs. Spranger, 142, 182, 188, 196, 213, 228
Bath, G. at, 71; Henderson acts at, 230, 231; Quin at, 86, 115; Mrs. Siddons acts at, 233
Bath, Earl of, 95, 149
Battle of Hastings, The, see Cumberland, Richard
'Bayes', C. and T. Cibber as, 42, 43; G. as, 42, 43, 46, 75, 252; Henderson as, 231
Bayham Abbey, 254
Beard, John, 166, 167, 188
'Beatrice', Miss Pope as, 184, 213; Mrs. Pritchard as, 97
Beauclerk, Topham, 105, 198, 199, 240, 242
Beaumont and Fletcher, *Philaster*, 169, 170
Beaux Stratagem, The, see Farquhar, George
Becket, T., 240
Bedford Coffee-house, 17, 23, 26, 95, 125, 154, 164
Bedford, Duke of, 102, 103
Beethoven, 255
Beggar's Opera, The, see Gay, John
Beighton, Rev. Thomas, 263
'Belcour', King as, 219
Bellamy, George Anne, 67, 121, 182, 228; G. flirts with, 72, 73; elopement, 97; as Juliet, 109-111
'Benedick', G. as, 97, 107, 114, 167, 184, 213, 252; Henderson as, 231
Betterton, Thomas, 40
Bickerstaffe, Isaac, 199, 209, 215, 220, 237, 238
Biddy, 146
Birch, Dr. Thomas, 224
'Biron', 140
Bleeding Rock, The, see More, Hannah

301

'Bobadil', Henderson as, 231; Woodward as, 120
Boleyn, Anne, 156
Bonduca, see Fletcher, John
Booth, Barton, 82
Boquet, 129, 131, 184
Boscawen, Mrs., 283
Boswell, James, 10, 55, 184, 190-192, 199-201, 228, 238, 240, 241, 243, 245, 247, 269; at Stratford Jubilee, 210-212
Boucher, Francois, 117 N., 129
Bouverie, Hon. Mrs., 211
Boyce, William, 134 N.
Bracegirdle, Anne, on G., 43
Brent, Charlotte, 167
British Inquisition, The, 126
British Museum, 146 N.
Bronkers, the, 4
Brothers, The, see Cumberland, Richard
Brown, 'Capability', 144, 148
'Brute, Sir John', G. as, 62, 229, 252; Quin as, 75
'Brutus', 82; Quin as, 21
Buckingham, Duke of, The Rehearsal, 42, 43, 134
Buckinghamshire, Lord, 271
Bulkley, Mrs., as Kate Hardcastle, 225
Burbage, Richard, 36
Burke, Edmund, 148, 194, 195, 198, 199, 223, 236-238, 261, 270, 280
Burlington, Lady, 100, 102-104, 118, 173, 271, 274, 281
Burlington, Lord, 100, 102-104, 118, 271, 281
Burney, Dr. Charles, 94, 114, 239, 242, 245-247; History of Music, 246, 247
Burney, Charlotte, 245-247
Burney, Fanny, 123, 239, 245-247, 269, 270
Busybody, The, see Centlivre, Susannah
Bute Lord, 160, 265
Button's Coffee-house, 17
Byron, Lord, 11

Cadogan, Dr., 277
Caesar, Colonel, 139
Calcraft, John, 236
Caldwells, the, 254
'Cali', 99
Camden, Lord, 248, 254, 265, 269, 273, 279, 282
Canaletto 206
Cardigan, Lady, 103
Carlin, C. A. Bertinazzi, as Harlequin, 114

Carlisle, Lord, 208
Carlyle, Alexander, 101, 102, 147
Carmontelle, 179
Carter, Elizabeth, 283
'Castalio', 42; Barry as, 72
Cato, see Addison, Joseph
'Cato', Johnson compared to, 227; Quin as, 21, 75; T. Sheridan as, 142
Cave, Edward, publishes G.'s poem, 23, 24
Centlivre, Susannah, Busybody, The, 134; Wonder, The, 252
'Chalkstone, Lord', 24, 185, 186
'Chamont', G. as, 41, 56; T. Sheridan as, 72
Champmeslé, Mlle, 19
Charles I, King, 36
Charlmont, Lord, 240
Charlotte, Queen, 285
Chatham, first Earl of, see Pitt, William
Chatsworth, 147
Cheere, Sir Henry, 205
Cheere, John, 205
'Cherry', Polly Woffington as, 67
Chesterfield, Lord, 73, 157, 190
Chinese Festival, The, 131, 132, 148, 155
Cholmondeley, Hon, Mrs., 49, 52, 68
Christmas Tale, A, see Garrick, David
Churchill, Charles, 152, 173, 174; Apology, 162-164; Epistle to Hogarth, 174; Rosciad, The, 161, 164, 191
Cibber, Colley, 22, 51, 85, 90, 123, 124, 182, 185, 192, 210; as Bayes, 42, 43; as Richard III, 38; Provok'd Husband, The, 97, 196; Papal Tyranny, 64, 65; version of Richard III, 36-38, 45, 64, 91, 222
Cibber, Susannah, as singer, 51, 94; and Mr. Sloper, 52, 63, 69; retirements from stage, 61, 73, 107, 108; acts with G., 63, 67, 75, 85, 154, 167; friendship with G., 68, 69, 93, 94, 268; at C.G., 75, 108, 109, 115; at D.L., 85, 86, 97, 107, 121; ill-health, 115, 142, 154, 155, 182; successors on stage, 183, 192, 228, 255; as Constance, 63, 142; as Juliet, 97, 110, 111, 165; as Ophelia, 63
Cibber, Theophilus, 52, 53, 114, 160; as Bayes, 42, 43; as Dauphin, 65
Clairon, Mlle, 116, 175, 176, 217, 256
Clandestine Marriage, The, see Colman George
'Clarence', 37
Cleone, see Dodsley, Robert

'Cleopatra', Peg Woffington as, 87; Mrs.
    Yates as, 132
Clive, Kitty, 78, 83, 86, 97, 109, 124,
    141 N., 183, 186; as the Lady in
    Lethe, 24; as mimic, 139; in retire-
    ment, 228, 267, 268; on Peg Woffing-
    ton, 49 N.; quarrel with Cibber, 63;
    tribute to G., 250, 251, 268
Clough, Mrs., 1, 3, 6
Club, The, see Literary Club
Clutterbuck, James, 158, 272 N.
Collier, Jeremy, 90
Colman, George, 158-162, 168, 169, 170,
    173, 174, 179, 180, 193, 195, 196, 208,
    212, 225, 237, 240, 249, 250, 262; and
    Henderson, 231, 232; produces Gold-
    smith's play, 223; Clandestine Mar-
    riage, The, 185-188; Jealous Wife,
    The, 158, 185
Colson, John, 12-15
'Columbine', 113, 114
Comédie Française, 129
Comédie Italienne, 129
Congreve, William, 156; Mourning
    Bride, The, 97, 200
'Constance', Mrs. Cibber as, 63, 142;
    Mrs. Furnival as, 72; Mrs. Pritchard
    as, 65; Mrs. Yates as, 142
'Cordelia', 44, 45; Mrs. Robinson as,
    255; Peg Woffington as, 50
'Coriolanus', 82; Quin as, 21
Corneille, Pierre, 128
Correggio, 220
Costume, 82, 83, 206, 217
Covent Garden Theatre, passim; mo-
    nopoly, 25, 26; Rich as manager, 50;
    rival King Johns, 64; G. acts at, 73-
    77, 85; rival Romeos, 109-111; build-
    ing and alterations, 80, 81, 156; pan-
    tomime at, 111-115, 119; Half-Price
    Riots, 166, 167; Beard and Mrs. Rich
    as co-managers, 166, 167, 188; Col-
    man as manager, 187, 188, 223, 224,
    232; Actors' Fund, 188; Goldsmith's
    first play produced at, 223-225, 228;
    Harris as manager, 250, 264; com-
    pany at G.'s funeral, 280
Covent Garden Piazza, 16, 17; Mac-
    klin's tavern in, 125-127
Coventry, Lady, 123
Coventry, Lord, 103
Cradock, Joseph, 248, 271, 273
Craven, Lord, 208
Crewe, Mrs., 211
Crisp, Samuel, 123
Critical Review, The, 160, 161
'Croaker', Shuter as, 196, 197
Cumberland, Duke of, 100

Cumberland, Richard, 21, 240, 244,
    262; on G.'s acting, 76; G.'s joke on,
    219, 220; introduces G. to Romney,
    220, 221; at Goldsmith's play, 227;
    Battle of Hastings, The, 268; Broth-
    ers, The, 218; Fashionable Lover,
    The, 220; West Indian, The, 218-220
Cumberland, Mrs. Richard, 218
Curioni, Signor, 124
Curtius, 276

Daily Advertiser, The, 111
Dance, George, 172
Dance, James, see Love, James
Dance, Nathaniel, see Dance-Holland,
    Sir Nathaniel
Dance-Holland, Sir Nathaniel, 172
Dancer, Mrs., see Barry, Mrs. Spranger
Darnley, Lord, and Peg Woffington, 52
Darwin, Charles, 283
Dauphine, Marie Josèphe, 116
Davenant, Sir William, Macbeth, ver-
    sion of, 60, 61, 91, 92; Tempest, ver-
    sion of, 91
David Garrick, see Robertson, Thomas
Davies, Thomas, 15 N., 65, 112, 164,
    190-192, 199, 231, 266, 279, 281
Davies, Mrs. Thomas, 191
Delane, Dennis, 86
Delany, Mrs., 268
'Demetrius', G. as, 98
Denmark, King of (Christian VII),
    185
Descombes, Mme, 273
Desnoyer, 102
Dévisse, 118
Devonshire, fourth Duke of, 104, 147,
    173
Devonshire, fifth Duke of, 279
Dexter, 122, 123, 142
Dibdin, Charles, 209, 213, 215
Dictionary, Johnson's, 89, 148, 179,
    190, 192, 198, 291
Diderot, Denis, 177; Paradoxe, 178
Distrest Mother, The, see Philips,
    Ambrose
Diversions of the Morning, The, see
    Foote, Samuel
Docksey, Miss Merriall, 2, 271, 272
Dodsley, Robert, Cleone, 154, 155,
    193
Dorset, Duke of, 208
Dorset Garden Theatre, 80
Douglas, see Home, John
Draper, 26
Dragon, 280
'Drugger, Abel', G. as, 56, 57, 167,
    246, 252; Kean as, 284

303

Drury Lane Theatre, *passim;* Fleetwood as manager, 23; monopoly, 25, 26; G.'s first appearance at, 46; Actors' Strike, 58-60; rival King Johns, 63-65; Lacy buys patent, 69, 70; Lacy and G. as co-managers, 78, 79, 85; building and alterations, 80, 81, 165, 249; rival Romeos, 109-112; Chinese Festival Riots, 131, 132; Half-Price Riots, 166, 167; lighting and scenery, 183, 184, 215-217; Actors' Fund, 188, 252; costume at, 217; R. B. Sheridan as manager, 249, 250, 254, 255; G.'s farewell performances, 252, 253; financial loss, 262; company at G.'s funeral, 280

Dryden, John, 80, 241, 264; satire on, 43; *Tempest* version, 91

Dublin, Aungier Street Theatre, 51, 72, 132; Crow Street Theatre, 141; Smock Alley Theatre, 50, 51, 66, 72, 132, 138, 142

Dumesnil, Mlle, 175, 178

Duenna, The, see Sheridan, R. B.

Duncaid, The, see Pope, Alexander

Dupré, 129

Durham Yard, 16, 239

'Edgar', 45

Edial, Johnson's academy at, 10, 11

Edict of Nantes, 2

Emily, Princess, 100

Enthoven Collection, Victoria and Albert Museum, 279 N.

Eon, Chevalier D', 264-267

Epistle to Hogarth, see Churchill, Charles

Essay on Shakespeare, see Montagu, Elizabeth

Evans, Thomas, 239

Every Man in his Humour, see Johnson, Ben

Exeter, Lord, 170

Fair Penitent, The, see Rowe, Nicholas

Fair Quaker of Deal, The, see Shadwell, Thomas

Fairies, The, 124

'Faulconbridge', G. as, 63, 142; T. Sheridan as, 142

False Concord, see Townley, James

False Delicacy, see Kelly, Hugh

'Falstaff', costume of, 83, Quin as, 21, 22, 76, 115

Falstaff's Wedding, see Kenrick, William

'Fanny', Mrs. Palmer as, 186

Farquhar, George, 84, 156, 158; *Beaux Stratagem, The,* 67; *Constant Couple, The,* 49; *Recruiting Officer, The,* children's performance, 1; Peg Woffington in, 49

Fashionable Lover, The see Cumberland, Richard

Fatal Marriage, The, see Southerne, Thomas

Favart, Simon, 129

'Felix, Don', G. as, 252, 253

Ferdinand I, King, 170

Fêtes Chinoises, Les, 129-131

Fielding, Henry, 96, 276; *Mock Doctor, The,* adaptation, 23; satires, 25; tips a penny, 53; *Tom Jones,* 54, 55, 263

Fielding, Sir John, 198

Fitzgerald, Percy H., 40 N.

Fitzpatrick, Thaddeus, 163-167

'Flash, Captain', Woodward as, 77

Flaxman, John, 283

Fleetwood, Charles, 35, 64; breaks Actors' Strike, 57-59; promises to produce *Irene,* 23; sells patent, 69

Fletcher, John, *Bonduca,* 269

Foote, Samuel, 105, 121, 124, 125, 142, 148, 149, 182, 213, 214, 231, 236, 241, 249, 276; on Dublin beggars, 51; and Rich, 74; mimics G., 96; Woodward mimics, 108; quarrel with Macklin, 127; and Tate Wilkinson, 134-140; at Stratford Jubilee, 208; puppet show, 224, 225; on T. Sheridan, 227; *Diversions of the Morning, The,* 138; *Handsome Housemaid, The,* 224; *Taste,* 124

Ford, Dr. James, 250

Formalism, 18-20, 175, 176

Fountain Tavern, 23

Fox, Charles James, 261

Fox, Henry, 155

Francis, Dr., 236, 237

Francis Lady, 235 N.

Francis, Sir Philip, 235-237

French, 206, 217

'Fribble', G. as, 77

Fribbleriad, The, see Garrick, David

Friendship in Fashion, see Otway, Thomas

Frodsham, Bridge, 229

Furnival, Mrs., 72, 78

Gainsborough, Thomas, 205, 216

Garney, Dr., 140

Garrick, Mrs. Arabella, 1-8, 10, 12, 15, 32; death, 26

Garrick, Arabella (Bell), *see* Schaw, Mrs. Arabella

Garrick, Carrington, 206, 273, 279
Garrick, David, childhood, 1-13; stay
in Lisbon, 3, 17; ride to London, 13;
enters Lincoln's Inn, 14; studies at
Rochester, 14, 15; sets up as vintner, 15-17; first poem printed, 23,
24; first play performed, 24; as
Harlequin, 27, 134; first appearance
in Ipswich, 29; first appearance in
London at G.F., 31, 32, 35; first appearance at D.L., 46; and Peg Woffington, 48-53, 67, 68, 121; acts in
Dublin, 50-52, 69-73; 27 Southampton Street, 53, 104, 121; and Mrs.
Cibber, 52, 63, 67-71, 85, 93, 94, 107,
268; illnesses, 69, 90, 173, 187, 275-
277; and G. A. Bellamy, 72, 73; acts
at C.G., 74, 75, 85; co-manager of
D.L., 78, 79, 85, 86; Lichfield visits,
85, 271; courtship and marriage, 99,
100, 103, 104; first visit to Paris, 115-
118; buys Hampton Houe, 144-147;
travels abroad, 167-180; Actors' Fund,
188; Literary Club, 189, 190, 242;
Freeman of Stratford, 203; attacked
by Junius. 253-237; buys No. 5 Adelphi Terrace, 239, 240; farewell performances, 251-253; death and funeral, 277-280; will, 275, 276, 282,
283; fortune, 122; monument in
Westminster Abbey, 282, 283
Admiration of Shakespeare, 90, 91,
200; advice to young actors, 175,
232; as employer, 121, 122, 140,
141; as manager, 217, 218, 262,
263; character, 93-96, 152, 153;
choice of roles, 41, 42; generosity,
121, 148, 188, 190, 191, 193, 229,
230, 262, 263, 269-272; loved by
children, 244-247; meanness, 53,
68, 190, 191, 260; physical charac-
teristics, 40, 41, 105, 142, 247, 248,
269, 270; politics, 236; practical
jokes 145, 149-151, 176, 177, 219,
220, 242, 243; religion, 146, 262,
263; snobbishness, 95, 123, 156,
157, 268, 269; style of acting, 54-
57, 142, 143, 178, 179, 256; vanity,
122, 153, 179, 180, 184, 185, 194,
195, 228, 229, 241, 260, 263, 264
Parts: Aboan, 29; Antony, 132;
Bayes, 42, 43, 46, 75, 252; Benedick, 97, 107, 114, 167, 184, 213,
252; Brute, Sir John, 62, 63, 229,
252; Chamont, 41, 56; Demetrius,
98; Drugger, Abel, 56, 57, 167, 246,
252; Faulconbridge, 63, 142; Felix,
Don, 252; Fribble, 77; Hamlet, 54-

57, 75, 120, 222, 223, 229, 243, 252,
255, 256; Harlequin, 27, 134; Hastings, 76; Hotspur, 76; Iago, 72;
John, King, 63, 64, 142; Kitely,
120; Lear, King, 43, 44, 46, 50,
75, 150, 151, 167, 176, 204, 229,
252, 255; Lothario, 42, 75, 76, 142;
Lusignan, 252, 277; Macbeth, 60,
61, 91, 92; Marplot, 134, 154;
Mock Doctor, 23; Orestes, 67;
Othello, 29, 30, 65, 66, 72; Ranger,
77, 167, 233, 252; Richard III, 31-
33, 35-40, 46, 56, 77, 167, 172, 233,
248, 252; Romeo, 97, 98, 110, 126,
127, 255
Portraits by Carmontelle, 179;
Dance-Holland, 172; Gainsborough, 205; Liotard, 116; Lowe,
269; Nollekens, 171, 172; Reynolds, 179; Wilson, 179; Zoffany,
179
Works: Christmas Tale, A, 216;
Clandestine Marriage, The, see
Colman, George; Fribbleriad, The,
164, 166, 180; Hamlet, version of,
223, 224, 284; Harlequin's Invasion, 134, 206; Heart of Oak,
134 N., 293; Jubilee, The, 212,
213, 215, 219; Katherine and Petruchio, 132; Lethe, 24, 185, 259,
260; Lying Valet, The, 32; Miss-
in-her-Teens, 77; Ode to Shakespeare, 210, 211; Sick Monkey,
The, 180; Winter's Tale, The,
version of, 132
Garrick, David (of Lisbon), 3, 15
Garrick, David (son of George), 271,
273, 279
Garrick, Mrs. Eva Maria, 99-106, 115-
118, 122, 136, 137, 140, 141, 144,
147, 151, 167, 168, 171, 173, 176, 185,
205, 206, 208, 209, 218, 245, 248, 253,
254, 262, 263, 268, 269, 271-273, 275-
285
Garrick, George, 168, 169, 170, 174,
187, 206, 270-273; childhood in Lichfield, 2, 10; solicitor's office, 35, 270;
assistant to managers, 79; salary,
122; and Henderson, 230; death, 278,
279
Garrick, Jane, see La Condé, Mrs.
Jane
Garrick, Jane (Jenny), 2, 6
Garrick, Kate, 273, 275
Garrick, Magdalen (Lenny), 2, 6
Garrick, Merriall, see Docksey, Mrs.
Merriall
Garrick, Nathan, 206, 272, 273, 279

Garrick, Peter, 2, 11, 15, 16, 23, 26, 31-35, 56, 57, 88, 271, 278, 279
Garrick, Captain Peter, 1-7, 12, 13, 15, 24, 32
Garrick, Wiliam, 2, 271
Garrick Fever, 52
Garrick's Villa, see Hampton House
Garrigues, G.'s family name, 3 N.
Gastrell, Rev. Francis, 204
Gay, John, Beggar's Opera, The, 50, 63, 167
'Gelidus', 14
General Historie of the Turkes, A, see Knolles, Richard
Gentleman's Magazine, The, 10; Johnson writes for, 23, 24; supports G., 60
George II, King, 28, 58, 100, 102, 131, 217, 229 N.
George III, King, 109, 143, 144, 154, 155, 181, 227, 236, 259, 260, 275
George IV, King, 255
'Gertrude, Queen', 223
Gibbons, Grinling, 80
Giffard, Henry, 24-27, 29, 31, 33, 46, 47
Giffard, Mrs. H., 62, 78
Gilliland, T., 97
'Gloster', Quin as, 76
Godolphin, Lord, 149, 151
Goldsmith, Oliver, 218, 240, 242; quarrels with G., 193-196, 198; libelled by Kenrick, 238; burlesque with G., 242, 243; Good Natur'd Man, The, 153, 194-198, 242; Popular Dictionary of Arts and Sciences, 242; Retaliation, 243, 244; She Stoops to Conquer, 153, 193, 223, 226, 227; Traveller, The, 194; Vicar of Wakefield, The, 194, 198
Goodman's Fields Theatre, 25-27, 31, 33-35, 46, 134, 175
Good Natur'd Man, The, see Goldsmith, Oliver
Grafton, Duke of, 58, 78, 117
Gray, Thomas, 46, 154
Greville, Fulke, 94
Grimm, Baron, 177
'Guildenstern', 223
Gwynn, Nell, 49

Halifax, Lord, 34
'Hamlet,' Bannister as, 257, 258; G. as, 54-56, 75, 120, 222, 223, 229, 243, 252, 255, 256; Henderson as, 231, 256; Holland as, 165; Irving as, 256; T. Sheridan as, 67, 142; Wilkinson mimics G. as, 140

Hampton House, 144-149, 159, 169, 170, 181, 185, 189, 190, 208, 246, 248, 266, 267, 268, 272, 275, 280, 282, 284, 285
Handel, George Frederick, 94, 280; Messiah, The, 51, 52
Handsome Housemaid, The, or Piety in Pattens, see Foote, Samuel
'Hardcastle, Kate', Mrs. Bulkley as; 225, 226
'Harlequin', 134, 181; G. as, 27; Rich as, 74, 111-114
Harlequin Sorcerer, see Rich, John
Harlequin's Invasion, see Garrick, David
Harlequinade, see Pantomime
Harlot's Progress, The, see Hogarth, William
Harris, Thomas, 250, 264
'Hastings', G. as, 76
'Haut-ton, Sir Oran', 283 N.
Harvard, William, 86, 161, 183
Hawkins, Sir John, 146, 189, 192, 217, 247, 270
Hayes, Katherine, 115
Haymarket, Little Theatre in, 25, 96, 97, 108, 117, 125, 127, 129, 134, 182, 224, 232, 249, 258
Haymarket, Opera House in, 80, 111, 117, 130; Mrs. G. dances at, 102, 103
Haymarket Theatre, 182 N.
Heart of Oak, see Garrick, David
Hector, Edmund, 9
Hector, Dr. George, 5, 9
Hedgcock, F. A., 130, 178 N., 184 N.
'Heidelberg, Mrs.', 186
Helvetius, Claude Adrien, 177
Henderson, John, 230-233; as Shylock, 268
Hendon Manor, 274
Henrietta Maria, Queen, 36
'Henry VIII', costume of, 83; Quin as, 21
Hereford, G. born in, 1
'Hermia', Signora Passerini as, 124
'Hermione', Polly Woffington as, 67
Hertford, Lord, 208
Hervey, Hon. Henry, 6, 7
Hifferman, Dr. Paul, 160
Hill, Aaron, 20, 85; Zara, 252, 277 N.
Hill, 'Sir' John, 160
Hippisley, John, 75; in Miss-in-her-Teens, 77
Mis Majesty's Theatre, 182 N.
History of England, see Smollett, Tobias
Hoadley, Dr. Benjamin, 85; Suspicious Husband, The, 77, 159

Hoadley, Dr. John, 157
Hogarth, William, 145, 170, 173, 174; on G.'s versatility, 56; G.'s epitaph on, 241, 242; *Harlot's Progress, The,* 65
Holbach, Baron d', 177
Holland, Lord, 236
Holland, Charles, 172, 183, 186, 213, 228; as Hamlet, 165
Home, John, at Hampton, 146, 147; *Douglas,* 154
Homer, 269, 284
Horace, 170
'Horatio', 223; G. as, 278; Quin as, 21, 75, 76; T. Sheridan as, 142
'Horatius', 217
'Hotspur', G. as, 76; Henderson as, 231
House of Commons, 260, 261
Hume, David, 154
Hunter, Mrs. 9
Hunter, Rev. John, 3, 4, 7-9

'Iago', G. as, 72; T. Sheridan as, 72
Ilchester, Lord, 134
Irene, see Johnson, Dr. Samuel
Irving, Sir Henry, 40, 259; as Hamlet, 256; as Shylock, 29
Italian Comedy of Arts, 113

Jackson, John, 113
James I, King, 155
James, Dr., 6, 7
Jane Shore, see Rowe, Nicholas
Jealous Wife, The, see Colman, George
Jew of Venice, The, see Lansdowne, Lord
'John, King', 63, 64; G. as, 63, 142, 143; T. Sheridan as, 142
Johnson, Michael, 2
Johnson, Mrs Michael, 9
Johnson, Nathaniel, 9, 15
Johnson, Dr. Samuel, 15, 68, 94, 107, 224 N., 243, 251 N., 284; youth, 2, 4, 5, 7-13; marriage, 9, 10, 280, 281; arrives in London, 14, 241; introduces G. to Cave 23; shocked by King Lear, 45; on actors, 46, 47, 87, 179, 241, 248; tea with G. and Peg Woffington, 53; on G. as Hamlet, 55, 256; on T. Sheridan, 71, 72, 201; and Lord Chesterfield, 73, 190; talks in wings, 87; Prologue for D.L., 89, 90; on G.'s ignorance of Shakespeare, 91; on Mrs. Pritchard, 92; on Polonius, 120, 121; dislike of G.'s mimicry, 146, 189, 240; poverty, 8, 9, 23, 148; at Hampton, 148;

maltreatment of books, 148, 193, 247; and Foote, 148, 149; on *Cleone,* 154; liking for Murphy, 159, 160; defends G., 184, 185, 241, 242, 260, 269, 270; Literary Club, 189, 190; coldness with G., 189-201; befriends Goldsmith, 194, 223, 225; quoted at Jubilee, 209; on G.'s *Ode,* 211, 232; on Hamlet's madness, 222 N.; on G.'s vanity, 228, 259, 260; on G.'s politics, 236; on Bickerstaffe, 237; attacked by Kenrick, 238; at evening gatherings, 240, 269; mimicked by G., 241, 247; on G.'s retirement, 252, 253; and Hannah More, 263; Lichfield visits, 271, 282; at G.'s funeral, 280; epitaph on G., 281; *Dictionary, see* that heading; *Irene* written in Lichfield, 11, 12; read to Peter G., 23; produced at D.L., 98, 99; *Rambler, The,* 14, 196 N.; *Shakespeare,* edition of, 192, 193, 238
Johnson, Mrs. Samuel (Tetty), 9-11, 13, 241, 280
Johnsonian Gleanings, see Reade, A. L.
Jones, Inigo, 16
Jones, William, 240
Jonson, Ben, 161; *Alchemist, The,* G. in, 56, 57; Every Man in his Humour, 120
Jubilee, The, see Garrick David
Jubilee, at Stratford, *see* Shakespeare, William
Judith, see Arne, Dr. Thomas Augustine
'Juliet', Mrs. Bellamy as, 110, 111; Mrs. Cibber as, 97, 98, 110-112; Mrs. Robinson as, 255
Junius, 152, 235-237

Katherine and Petruchio, see Garrick, David
Kauffman, Angelica, 239
Kean, Edmund, as Abel Drugger, 284; as Othello, 29; as Richard III, 284; as Shylock, 29
Kelly, Hugh, *False Delicacy,* 196, 197; *School for Wives, The,* 242
Kemble, John, 40, 256, 284
Kenrick, William, 193, 211, 238, 239, 267; *Falstaff's Wedding,* 193
Kent, William, 103
King Thomas, 181, 183, 186-188, 196, 206, 213, 219, 228, 232; in *Jubilee,* 213; as Lord Ogleby, 211
King's Theatre, *see* Haymarket, Opera House in
Kingston, Duchess of 263, 267

'Kitely', G. as, 120
Knolles, Richard, *General Historie of the Turkes, A*, 11

La Condé, Mrs. Jane, 31
La Condé, Louis, 31, 34
Lacy, James, 73, 84, 85, 122, 131-133, 136, 138, 165, 168, 174, 175, 187, 205, 206, 209, 212, 248; buys patent of D.L., 69; takes G. as partner, 78, 79
Lacy Willoughby, 248, 249, 262
'Laertes', 223
La Fontaine, Jean de, 180
Lamb, Charles, on *King Lear*, 45; on Webber's monument, 283
Langton, Bennet, 105, 240
Lansdowne, George Granville, Lord, *Jew of Venice, The*, 27
Lawrence, Mr., 277, 278
'Lear, King', 67, 83, 90; G. as, 43-46 50, 75, 150, 151, 167, 176, 204, 229, 252, 255; Henderson as, 231; Reddish as, 213; Rich burlesques G. as, 78; Wilkinson mimics G. as, 140
Le Blanc, Abbé, 178
Ledger, The, 276
Lee, Nathaniel, *Rival Queens, The*, 19
Leicester House, Mrs. G. refuses invitation to, 102; *Cato* rehearsed at, 109
Le Kain, Henri Louis, 116, 176, 217
Lethe, see Garrick, David
Levié, 117
Lewes, Lee, as Young Marlow, 225
Licensing Act, 25, 96
Lichfield, 31, 32, 187, 269-272, 282; G.'s youth in, 1-13; meets Peter G. in, 15; popularity in, 17; ale, 19; grocer despises G., 56, 57; G. revisits, 85; Mrs. Gastrell at, 204; ride from recalled, 241
Lichfield Cathedral, 281
Lichtenberg, George, 55
Lighting, 81, 183, 184, 215, 216
Lincoln's Inn, G. and, 14
Linley, Thomas, 250
Liotard, Jean Etienne, 116
Literary Club, the, 189, 190, 193, 197, 240, 280; G.'s election to, 242
Little Theatre, *see* Haymarket, Little Theatre in
Lisbon, G.'s stay in, 3; recalled, 17
Lloyd, Robert, 160-163
Lobo, Father Jerome, *Voyage to Abyssinia*, 9
'Lofty', 242; Woodward as, 196, 197
London Magazine, The 205, 212, 213

'Lothario', G. as, 42, 75, 76, 142
Louis XV, King, 116, 265, 266
Louis XVI, King, 265
Loutherbourg, P. J. de, 215-217, 254
Love, James, 173
Lowe, Mauritius, 269
Lowndes, Mrs., 6
'Lumpkin, Tony', Quick as, 225
Lun, *see* Rich, John
Lun, junior, *see* Woodward, Henry
'Lusignan', G. as, 252, 277
Lyddal, G.'s stage name, 29
'Lysander', Curioni as, 124
Lyttelton, Lord, 34, 37, 95
Lyttelton, George, *see* Lyttelton, Lord

'Macbeth', 90; Barry as, 136; G. as, 60, 61, 91; Henderson as, 231
'Macbeth, Lady', 61; Mrs. Pritchard as, 91, 92; Peg Woffington as, 136
'Macheath, Capt.', Peg Woffington as, 49, 50
Macklin, Charles, 20, 35, 52, 53, 78, 86, 96, 108, 109, 121, 142, 182, 202; views on acting, 17; trial for murder, 18; hatred of Quin, 22; on G.'s Lear, 43-45; on G.'s meanness, 53, 60; and Fleetwood, 57-60; C.G. Tavern, 125-127; as Macbeth, 217; as Mercutio, 110; as Papal Legate, 65; as Shylock, 27-29, 88
Macklin, Miss, 125, 183
Macklin, Mrs., 59
Macready, W. C., 45
Mahomet, see Voltaire
'Mahomet', 11, 12; Barry as, 98, 99
Mahomet and Irene, see Johnson, Dr. Samuel
'Malaprop, Mrs.', 186
Malcolm, Sarah, 115
Manchester, Duke of, 208
Mansfield, Lord, 135, 166, 167
'Margaret, Queen', 37
Maria Theresa, Empress, 102
'Marlow, Young', Lee Lewes as, 225, 226
Marlowe, Christopher, 36
'Marmozet, Mr.', 157
'Marplot', G. as, 134, 154; Woodward as, 134
Marr, 'Dagger', 150, 151
Melincourt, see Peacock, T. L.
'Mercutio', Woodward as, 110
Messiah, The, see Handel, G. F.
Middlesex, Lord, 102
Miss-in-her-Teens, see Garrick, David
Mock Doctor, The, see Molière
Modena, Duke of, 99, 100

INDEX

Molé, François René, 176
Molière, *Mock Doctor, The,* G. acts in, 23
Molière, de, 273, 274
Monboddo, Lord, 283, 284
'Monimia', 41, 42
Monnet, Jean, 117, 118, 129, 183, 184, 274
Monsey, Dr. Messenger, 149-151, 159
Montagu Elizabeth, 95, 149, 283, 285; *Essay on Shakespeare,* 200, 201
Moody, John, 166; as Major O'Flaherty, 219; in *The Jubilee,* 213
More, Hannah, 262-264, 267, 271, 275; *Bleeding Rock, The,* 264; *Percy,* 262, 264, 265, 284; *Sir Eldred of the Bower,* 264
Morellet, André, 177, 178
Mossop, Henry, 122, 123, 133, 139, 142
Mourning Bride, The, see Congreve, William
Murphy, Arthur, 123, 148, 160, 199, 208; *Apprentice, The,* 159; *Orphan of China, The,* 154, 155, 158, 159, 193

Nepos, 11
New Place, Stratford, 202 N., 204
Nollekens, Joseph, 171, 172, 283
North, Lord, 208
Nouveau Calendrier des spectacles de Paris, 130
Noverre, Jean George, 114, 117 N., 128-133

O'Brien, William, 133
Ode to Shakespeare, see Garrick, David
Offleys, the, 7, 10
'O'Flaherty, Major', Moody as, 219
'Ogleby, Lord', King as, 186-188, 211
Old Bailey, 149
Onslow, Speaker, 94, 95
Opera House, see Haymarket, Opera House in
Opéra Comique, 129
'Ophelia', 222, 223; Mrs. Cibber and Peg Woffington as, 62, 63; G. addresses Mrs. Bellamy as, 73
'Orestes', G. as, 67
Orford, Lady, 170
Orleans, Duke of, 179
Oroonoko, see Southerne, Thomas
Orphan of China, The, see Murphy, Arthur
Orrery, Lord, 40
Ossory, Earl of, 279
'Othello', 21; Barry as, 72, 78; Foote as, 125; G. as, 29, 30, 65, 66, 72; Kean as, 29

Otway, Thomas, 156; *Friendship in Fashion,* 108; *Orphan, The,* 41, 42, 72
Ovid, 112
Oxford University, Johnson at, 8

Palmer, Mrs., 186
Palmer, John (the elder), 230
Palmerston, second Viscount, 170, 236, 275, 279
'Palmira', Mrs. Robinson as, 259
'Pantaloon', 112
Pantomime, 19, 111-115, 119-121, 134, 217; Rich in, 74
Paoli, General, 199, 212
Papal Tyranny, see Cibber, Colley
Paradoxe, see Diderot, Denis
Parma, Duke of, 172
'Partridge', on G., 54
Passerini, Signora, 124
Patterson, John, 279
'Peachum, Polly', quarrels over, 63; Miss Brant as, 167
Peacock, T. L., *Melincourt,* 283 N.
Pembroke, Lady, 211
Pembroke, Lord, 205, 254
Pepys, Samuel, 91
Percy, see More, Hannah
'Perdita', see Robinson, Mrs.
Peregrine Pickle, see Smollet, Tobias
Petrarca, 247
Philaster, see Beaumont and Fletcher
'Philaster', Powell as, 169, 170
Philips, Ambrose, *Distrest Mother, The,* 67
Phill, 245, 247
'Pierrot', 112
Pilgrim's Progress, The, 218
Pitt, William (first Earl of Chatham), 34, 95, 123, 236
'Polonius', Woodward as, 120
'Polydore', 42
Pope, the, 171, 172
Pope, Alexander, on Macklin's Shylock, 29; on G.'s Richard III, 40; *Dunciad, The,* 161
Pope, Jane, 183, 186; as Beatrice, 184, 213
Popular Dictionary of Arts and Sciences, A, see Goldsmith, Oliver
Porter, Mr., 9, 10
Porter, Mrs., see Johnson, Mrs. Samuel
Porter, Lucy, 9
Portland, Duchess of, 268
Pot, Mr., 99
Powell, William, 167-169, 174, 175, 183, 184, 186-188, 196, 197, 228, 232

309

Préville, 129, 176, 177
Price, Betty, 105
Pritchard, Mr., 85, 86
Pritchard, Hannah, 75, 83-86, 96, 109, 124, 182, 192, 228; as Beatrice, 97; as Constance, 65; as Irene, 98, 99; as Lady Macbeth, 61, 91, 92; in *Miss-in-her-Teens*, 77
Provok'd Husband, The, see Cibber, Colley
Provok'd Wife, The, see Vanbrugh, Sir John
Public Advertiser, The, 221, 235
'Punch', 87, 112, 163, 179, 225
Puppets, 224, 225

Queen Mab, see Woodward, Henry
Queensberry, Duchess of, 87
Quick, John, as Tony Lumpkin, 225, 226
Quin, James, 69, 73, 76, 83, 84, 115, 165, 176, 182, 185; on Macklin, 21, 28, 43; on G. as Richard III, 38-40; rivalry with G., 43, 75-77; on Peg Woffington, 49; in Dublin, 51, 52; on Macbeth, 60, 61; on G. as Brute, 62; on G. as Othello, 65; at C.G., 67, 96, 97; stage costume, 82, 83, 217; at Bath, 86; on G. as Macbeth, 91; teaches George III, 109, 143; at Hampton, 147

Racine, Jean, 19, 128, 175
Ralph, James, 160, 194
Rambler, The see Johnson, Dr. Samuel
Rameau, 117 N., 129
Ranelagh Gardens, 205
'Ranger', G. as, 77, 167, 233, 252
Raynal, G. I. F., 177
Reade, A. L., 15 N.
Reade, Charles, *Peg Woffington,* 48
Realism, 54, 55
Recruiting Officer, The, see Farquhar, George
Reddish, Samuel, 232; as King Lear, 213
Rehearsal The, see Buckingham, Duke of
Reprisal, The, see Smollet, Tobias
Reynolds, Sir Joshua, 179, 189, 194, 195, 198, 199, 201, 207, 220, 221, 223, 238, 243, 244, 259
Rich, Christopher, 74
Rich, John, 25, 59, 64, 69, 84-86, 96, 108, 109, 115, 119, 122, 130, 135, 155, 157, 188; interviews Peg Woffington, 50; engages G., 74; jealousy of actors, 77, 78; as Harlequin, 111-114;

Harlequin Sorcerer, 119
Rich, Mrs, John, 188
'Richard III', 21, 90, 91, 181; bailiffs and, 57, 58; costume of, 83; G. as, 31-33, 35-40, 46, 47, 56, 75, 167, 172, 233, 248, 255; Gloster based on, 76; Henderson as, 231; Holland as, 213; Kean as, 284; Mossop as, 123; Quin as, 75; Rich as, 75; T. Sheridan as, 67, 142; Wilkinson as, 135
Richardson, Samuel, 148, 190
Richmond, Duke of, 99
Rigby, Richard, 279
Riots: *Chinese Festival,* 132; Half-Price, 166, 167
Rival Queens, The, see Lee, Nathaniel
Rivals, The, see Sheridan, R. B.
Robertson, Thomas, *David Garrick,* 56
Robinson, Mrs. ('Perdita'), 255; as Palmira, 259
Rochford, Lady, 95
Rochford, Lord, 68 N.
Roderick Random, see Smollett, Tobias
'Romeo', Barry as, 108-111, 122, 182; G. as, 97, 98, 110 111, 126, 127, 255; the rival Romeos, 109-111
Romney, George, 220, 221
'Rosalind', Peg Woffington as, 139
'Rosaline', 99
Rosciad, The, see Churchill, Charles
Roscius (G), 52, 276
Roscius, the Bath, 231
'Rosencrantz', 223
Ross, David, 122, 182, 183
Roubiliac, Louis François, 145, 146
Rousseau, Jean Jacques, 185
Rowe, Nicholas, 85, 156; *Fair Penitent, The,* 42, 75, 76, 142, 278; Jane Shore, 76
Royal Academy of Arts, 198, 221, 257, 269
'Rusport, Charlotte', Mrs. Abington as, 219
Ryan, Lacy, 21, 75, 76, 96, 109, 165, 182

Sabbatini, 100
Sadlers Wells, 111
St. James's Chronicle, The, 161, 179
Saint James's Coffee-house, 240, 243
Saint Paul's Church, C.G., 16
Sallust, 11
Sandford, Samuel, 38
Sandwich, Lord, 34, 246
'Scaramouche', 112
Scenery, 81, 82, 206, 207, 216, 217

Schaw, Captain, 279
Schaw, Mrs. Arabella, 273-275, 279
Scheemakers, Peter, 171, 205
Schomberg, Dr., 277
School for Scandal, The, see Sheridan, R. B.
School for Wives, The, see Kelly, Hugh
Sentimentalism, 196, 223, 224
Shadwell, Thomas, Fair Quaker of Deal, The, 131
Shakesparelli, Signor, 124
Shakespeare, William, 19, 20, 34, 156, 161, 172, 175, 177, 178, 182, 200, 213, 280; G.'s appreciation, 89-91; Johnson's edition, see Johnson, Dr. Samuel; Jubilee, 202-214; statues, 145, 146, 205; Voltaire on, 169, 174, 222; Antony and Cleopatra, 132; Hamlet, 120, 121; G. in, 54-56, 176, 252; G.'s version, 222, 223; in modern dress, 217; Peg Woffington and Mrs. Cibber in, 61-63; Henry IV, G. and Quin in, 76; Henry V, 215; Henry VIII, 156, 215; King John, 63-65, 142, 143; King Lear, 43-45, 50, 91, 132, 217, 252; Macbeth, 60, 61, 83, 94, 116, 176, 192; Merchant of Venice The, 27-29, 88; Midsummer's Night's Dream, A, musical version, 124; Much Ado about Nothing, 97, 184; Othello, 11, 12, 65, 66, 72; Richard III, 35-40, 64, 135, 222, 252; Romeo and Juliet, 97, 98, 110, 111, 122, 126, 127, 215; Taming of the Shrew, The, G.'s version, 132; Tempest, The, 91, 124; Two Gentlemen of Verona, The, 166; Winter's Tale, A, G.'s version, 132
Shakespeare's mulberry tree, 203, 204, 209, 214
Sharp, Thomas, 204
Sheridan, Frances, 250
Sheridan, Richard Brinsley, 249, 250, 254, 255, 279; Duenna, The, 249; Rivals, The, 249; School for Scandal, The, 261, 262
Sheridan, Thomas, 66, 67, 71-73, 132, 137, 142, 182, 201, 227, 249, 261
She Stoops to Conquer, see Goldsmith, Oliver
Shipley, Bishop, 280
'Shore, Jame', Mrs. Siddons as, 233
Shuter, Edward, 86, 109, 133, 183; as Croaker, 195-197
'Shylock', Henderson as, 231, 268; Irving as, 29; Macklin as, 27-29, 88
Sick Monkey, The, see Garrick, David

Siddons, Mrs., 82, 83, 92, 143, 183, 230, 233, 234, 254-256; debut at D.L., 233; in Percy, 284
Sir Eldred of the Bower, see More, Hannah
Sloper, Mr., 52, 63, 69, 94
Smith, Edmund, 281
Smith, 'Gentleman', 206, 225, 228
Smollet, Tobias, 160; History of England, 158; Peregrine Pickle, 157; Reprisal, The, 157, 158; Roderick Random, 157
Society of Arts, 171, 194
Southampton Street, No. 27, 51, 104, 121, 132, 135, 144, 148, 150, 151, 218, 239
Southerne, Thomas, Fatal Marriage, The, 140 N.; Oroonoko, 29
Sparks, 86
Spectator, The, 16
Spencer, Lady, 170, 171, 254, 276
Spencer, Lord, 171, 208, 254, 279
Stafford, Lord, 214
Stanley, Hon. Hans, 279
Steele, Sir Richard, 17, 84
Steevens, George, 202, 203, 213
Stratford-upon-Avon, 202-214
Strawberry Hill, 146
'Strickland, Mrs.', Mrs. Siddons as, 233
Suard, 178
Suspicious Husband, The, see Hoadley, Dr. Benjamin
'Suspirius', 196 N.
Swinfen, Dr., 8, 32, 33
Swinfen, John, 31-33
'Sylvia', Peg Woffington as, 49

Taste, see Foote, Samuel
Tate, Nahum, King Lear, version of, 45, 91, 132
Taylor, Dr., 98
Temple, R. T. Grenville, Lord, 236
Templeman, Dr., 194
Terence, 11
Thornton, Bonnell, 160, 161
Thrale, Henry, 159, 189, 209, 237, 281
Thrale, Mrs., 159, 197, 199, 209, 241, 259, 263, 270, 281
Tom Jones, see Fielding, Henry
Torre, Signor, 248
'Touchstone', King as, 213
Townley, James, False Concord, 186 N.
Townshend, Charles, 261
Traveller, The, see Goldsmith, Oliver
Troublesome Reign, The, 64, 65
Tully, 11
Tunbridge Walks, see Baker, Thomas

311

Turk's Head Tavern, 189, 197, 198, 240, 269

Vanbrugh, Sir John, 80, 85; *Provok'd Wife, The,* G. in, 62
Veigel, Charles, 102
Veigel, Eva Maria, *see* Garrick, Mrs. Eva Maria
Vertue, George, 103
Vesey, Agmondesham, 240
Vesey, Mrs., 283
Victoria Embankment, 240
Vicar of Wakefield, The, see Goldsmith, Oliver
Violante, Mme., 49
'Violetta', 218
Violette, Mlle, *see* Garrick, Mrs. Eva Maria
Violetti, Mlle, *see* Garrick, Mrs. Eva Maria
Voltaire, 85, 169, 174, 175, 177, 178, 200; on *Hamlet,* 222; *Mahomet,* 258; *Zara,* Hill's adaptation, 252
Voyage to Abyssinia, see Lobo, Father Jerome

Wales, Frederick, Prince of, 34, 102, 109
Wales, Augusta, Princess of, 265
Wallis, Albany, 279, 282, 283
Walmesley, Gilbert, 1, 2, 7, 8, 10, 12, 13, 73, 204, 281
Walpole, Horace, disparages G., 46; nephew marries Polly Woffington, 68; at Duke of Richmond's party, 99, 100; on Mrs. G., 104, 283, 285; at Hampton, 146; on *Orphan of China,* 154, 155; at Beauclerk's, 240, 243; at Twickenham, 268
Walpole, Sir Robert, Licensing Act, 25; on Macklin's Shylock, 29
Warburton, William, 210, 213
Ward, Mrs., 108, 183; as Cordelia, 97
Warwick, Lord, 271
Webber, Henry, 283
West, Benjamin, 217
West Indian, The, see Cumberland, Richard
Westminster, Dean of, 280
Westminster Abbey, 205, 213, 279, 280, 282, 283
Wheeler, Francis, 202
Whitefield, George, 40, 183
Whitehead, William, 155, 195, 213
White's Chocolate-house, 57
Wilcox, Mr., 14

'Wildair, Sir Harry', Peg Woffington as, 49, 115
'Wilful, Jack', 49
Wilkes, John, 236, 266, 270
Wilkinson, Dr. John, 135, 237
Wilkinson, Tate, 134-141, 229, 269
Williams, 'Mrs.', 160, 190, 191
Williams, Mr. Emlyn, 36
Wilson, Benjamin, 179; *Shakespeare in his Study,* 205
Woffington, Peg, as actress, 48; childhood, 49; interview with Rich, 50; at D.L., 50, 62, 78, 86, 89; acts in Dublin, 50-52; lives with G., 52, 53; parts from G., 67, 68, 93, 121, 122; at C.G., 87, 109, 115, 122; Foote mimics, 96; Wilkinson mimics, 136-140; death, 140, 228; as Cleopatra, 87; as Cordelia, 50; as Macheath, 49, 50; as Sir Harry Wildair, 49, 109; as Sylvia, 49
Woffington, Polly, *see* Cholmondeley, Mrs.
Wonder, The, see Centlivre, Susannah
Woodfall, H. S., 236, 237
Woodward, Henry, at C.G., 75, 183; Foote mimics, 96; mimics Foote, 108; at D.L., 109, 119-122, 132-134, 154; in Dublin, 141; and Fitzpatrick, 164; refuses Tony Lumpkin, 225; speaks prologue for Goldsmith's play, 227; and Mrs. Bellamy, 228; advice to Mrs. Siddons, 233; succeeded by Bannister, 258; death, 267; as Beau in Lethe, 24; as Bobadil, 228; as Captain Flash, 77; as Harlequin, 114, 115; as Lofty, 196, 197; as Mercutio, 110; as Polonius, 120, 121; *Queen Mab,* 111, 119
World, The, 190
Wren, Sir Christopher, 80
Wyndham, Colonel, 71
Wynn, Sir Watkyn Williams, 254, 279

Yates, Mary Ann, 155, 183, 227, 228, 233, 248; as Cleopatra, 132; as Constance, 142
Yates, Richard, 78, 86, 183, 227; as Harlequin, 27, 134
York, Duke of, 172, 182
Younge, Elizabeth, 228, 233, 248

'Zaphna', Bannister as, 258, 259
Zara, see Hill, Aaron
Zoffany, John, 179
Zucchi, A. P., 239